An Introduction
to Literature in Brazil

INSTITUTE OF LATIN AMERICAN STUDIES
COLUMBIA UNIVERSITY

An Introduction to Literature in Brazil

by AFRÂNIO COUTINHO

Translated from the Portuguese

by GREGORY RABASSA

COLUMBIA UNIVERSITY PRESS

NEW YORK & LONDON

1969

Gregory Rabassa is Professor of Romance Languages at Queens College, CUNY.

The Institute of Latin American Studies of Columbia University was established in 1961 in response to a national, public, and educational need for a better understanding of the nations of Latin America and a more knowledgeable basis for inter-American relations. The major objectives of the Institute are to prepare a limited number of North Americans for scholarly and professorial careers in the field of Latin American studies, to advance our knowledge of Latin America through an active program of research by faculty, by graduate students, and by visiting scholars, and to improve public knowledge through publication of a series of books on Latin America. Some of these studies are the result of research by the faculty and by graduate students. It was also decided to include in this series translations from Portuguese and Spanish of important contemporary books in the social sciences and humanities.

An Introduction to Literature in Brazil, by Professor Afrânio Coutinho, is the first of these translations to appear in this series. Professor Coutinho is a well-known Brazilian scholar and literary critic. He is a member of the Brazilian National Academy of Literature and Professor of Brazilian Literature at the University of Brazil in Rio de Janeiro. In 1967 Professor Coutinho was Visiting Professor of Brazilian Literature in the Institute of Latin American Studies at Columbia University. It was during his residence at Columbia University that this translation was prepared by Professor Gregory Rabassa with Professor Coutinho's constant advice. The faculty of the Institute believes that this book fills an important need, the need for an introduction to and a survey of the rich literature of Brazil for the English reader. We are grateful to Professor Coutinho for his book and to Professor Gregory Rabassa for his skillful translation.

The publication program of the Institute of Latin American Studies is made possible by the financial assistance of the Ford Foundation. The translation of this book by Professor Coutinho was financed by a grant to the Columbia University Press from the Committee on Latin American Translations of the Association of American University Presses. The Rockefeller Foundation supported the Committee's work financially.

Preface

❧

The title of this study might lead one to believe that it is a history of Brazilian literature. This is not the case. It is, rather, what could be called a "history of the history of Brazilian literature," for it is a cogent attempt to reorganize the structure of the body of writing in Brazil to bring it more in line with the realities of its inception. It is also an attempt to put the study of Brazilian literature more in line with recent insights that have been universal, doing away with a persistent myopia that has long been present. Those who have no knowledge of Brazilian literature will learn much from this book, but they will have to go elsewhere in many cases for certain details of biography and plot description. People who already know something about writing in Brazil will find their knowledge enhanced as the facts are placed in a more realistic perspective than has been the wont in the past. It is, therefore, a study that can be of great value on different levels of approach.

The book is made up of the introductions that Professor Coutinho has supplied to the various divisions of the four-volume work, *A Literatura no Brasil*, which contains the contributions of various specialists and is under his general editorship. What Coutinho and his colleagues have attempted to do is to apply to Brazilian literature in a definitive way the new directions in literary criticism that have been laid out by such movements as the Anglo-American "new criticism," the Slavic school, the German-Swiss stylistic approach, and other similar groups in the world-wide renovation of literary study that has sought to replace the standard nineteenth-century methods. The book is therefore an introduction both to literature in Brazil and to the methods best employed for its study. What Coutinho tries to do essentially is bring about the divorce of literary study from the study of general history and the shackles it has applied. The reader will note that the influences of history, ideas, and social movements are not negated or ignored, but that these must take a place of importance subsidiary to the essence of literature itself. The divisions are according to stylistic movements rather than historical or ideological ones. Instead of attempting to explain literature through history, Coutinho shows them to be coeval phenomena that interact but maintain their essential independence of direction.

In this way the panorama of Brazilian literature takes on more meaning, with the result that the analyses here are of great value to the student of literature as he sees Brazilian works both in their native context and in the light of universal movements. The historian and the social scientist will find that the influences and effects of literature can quite often come from sources which are not so evident in the political and social history of a nation, particularly a developing one. Underlying this aim is the struggle to find what is truly "Brazilian" in the culture, a struggle which has plagued critics and polemicists for years and one which permeates the efforts of the younger critics writing in Brazil today, largely through the pioneering of Afrânio Coutinho. Thus Brazilian criticism today is not out of touch with the national reality—quite the contrary; it has the advantage of being able to apply universal yardsticks to the local problem. In a sense, and as will be seen in the work itself, this drive towards a definition of the Brazilian within the universal is an outgrowth of the cultural revolution called Modernism, which is arbitrarily dated from 1922 but has earlier roots, and whose "Pope," Mário de Andrade, is in so many ways the forerunner of the critical renovation in Brazil. Spanish literature experienced a similar phenomenon with the vague yearnings of the generation of 1898 which have finally been given a more accurate direction by the criticism which has emerged in more recent years. Although its literature has come into the mainstream, first with poetry and more recently with the novel, Spanish America has yet to produce any school of criticism to deal with its literature and critical writing there remains essentially inchoate and sporadic. This could be due to the lack of national unity.

This translation of the book differs somewhat from the Brazilian original, principally in the bibliographical section. The original edition has a bibliography rich in non-Brazilian works on literary theory which have no direct bearing on Brazilian literature as such. Many works familiar to American and European students of literature have been eliminated, and only those works directly concerned with Brazilian or Portuguese literature have been kept. The footnotes are quite thorough in noting books that have bearing on what the author is saying, so that additional listing in the appendix would be wasteful. No attempt has been made to translate book titles into English unless an English translation of the work exists. Too often such cases make for artificiality as no such title exists in reality.

GREGORY RABASSA

Afrânio Coutinho

❦

Afrânio Coutinho was born in Salvador, Bahia, in 1911. He received his education there and in 1931 he was graduated as a Doctor of Medicine. He left this profession for secondary-school teaching, giving courses in literature, history, and philosophy. In 1934 he began to publish articles in reviews and journals in Salvador and Rio de Janeiro. His first book, *A Filosofia de Machado de Assis,* was published in 1940.

From 1942 to 1947 he lived in New York, where he was editorial secretary of *Seleções do Reader's Digest.* During this time he studied at Columbia University and elsewhere, mainly in the field of literary criticism. He had the opportunity to become acquainted with the new directions of the Anglo-American New Criticism, which he was later to introduce into Brazil, as well as the work of the Slavic school of Jakobsen and Wellek and the stylistic studies of the German-Swiss school as propounded by Spitzer and Hatzfeld.

Upon his return to Brazil in 1948, he settled in Rio de Janeiro and wrote a column for the literary supplement of the *Diário de Notícias* of that city. In it he conducted a campaign for the renovation of Brazilian criticism, one which was ultimately successful and has resulted in a large number of younger critics generally following his path. In 1952 he was awarded the chair in literature at the Colégio Dom Pedro II, and in 1964 he was named to the chair of Brazilian literature at the National Faculty of Philosophy of the University of Brazil in Rio de Janeiro. In 1967 he was Visiting Professor of Brazilian Literature at Columbia University, and upon his return to Brazil that year was named dean of the newly organized Faculty of Letters of the University of Brazil. He is editor of the review *Cadernos Brasileiros,* published in Rio de Janeiro. In 1962 he was elected to the Brazilian Academy of Letters.

Works by Afrânio Coutinho

Daniel-Rops e a Ánsia do Sentido Novo da Existência, Bahia, 1935.
"L'Exemple du métissage," *L'Homme de couleur* (Coll. Présences), Paris, Plon, 1939.
A Filosofia de Machado de Assis, Rio de Janeiro, Vecchi, 1940; 2nd edition, Rio de Janeiro, São José, 1959.
Aspectos da Literatura Barroca, Rio de Janeiro, 1951.
Bibliografia para o Estudo da Literatura Barroca, Rio de Janeiro, 1951.
O Ensino da Literatura, Rio de Janeiro, M. E. S., 1952.
Por uma Crítica Estética, Rio de Janeiro, M. E. S., 1953.
Correntes Cruzadas, Rio de Janeiro, A Noite, 1953.
Da Crítica e da Nova Crítica, Rio de Janeiro, Civilização Brasileira, 1957.
Euclides, Capistrano e Araripe, Rio de Janeiro, M. E. S., 1959.
Tradição e Futuro do Colégio Pedro II, Rio de Janeiro, 1961.
Introdução à Literatura no Brasil, Rio de Janeiro, São José, 1959.
A Crítica, Bahia, Livraria Progresso, 1959.
Machado de Assis na Literatura Brasileira, Rio de Janeiro, São José, 1960.
Conceito de Literatura Brasileira, Rio de Janeiro, Livraria Acadêmica, 1960.
Recepção de Afrânio Coutinho na Academia Brasileira de Letras, Rio de Janeiro, 1962.
No Hospital das Letras, Rio de Janeiro, Tempo Brasileiro, 1963.

Works edited by Afrânio Coutinho

A Literatura no Brasil, 4 volumes, Rio de Janeiro, Editorial Sul Americana, 1955–1959.
Obra Crítica de Araripe Júnior, 3 volumes, Rio de Janeiro, Casa de Rui Barbosa, 1958, 1960–1962.
Obra Completa de Jorge de Lima, Rio de Janeiro, José Aguilar, 1959.
Obra Completa de Machado de Assis, 3 volumes, Rio de Janeiro, José Aguilar, 1959.
Brasil e Brasileiros de Hoje, 2 volumes, Rio de Janeiro, Foto Service, Ltd., 1961.
Romances Completos de Afrânio Peixoto, Rio de Janeiro, José Aguilar, 1962.
Biblioteca Luso-Brasileira, Rio de Janeiro, José Aguilar.

Contents

❦

An Introduction
to Literature in Brazil

General Introduction

ﯼ

The work *A Literatura no Brasil* (Literature in Brazil) aims at a survey of the history of Brazilian literature. Its plan presupposes a concept and a method.

THE QUESTION OF LITERARY HISTORY

The problem of literary history is among the most complex. The matter has aroused debate among specialists over the last few decades. It is certain that there can be no solution. We have left behind the kind of mentality that refuses to face up to the methodological and conceptual problem[1] in matters of literary historiography and limits itself to taking inventory of facts out of the literary past. What characterizes the present state of the problem is not a flight into method, but rather a crisis of methods.

This crisis was well defined at the First International Congress of Literary History in Budapest, in 1931, where the theme was, no less, "methods of literary history." However, since 1895 in Germany, on the heels of a great anti-historicist reaction that had its start in the ideas of Dilthey, since 1902 in Italy, based on the ideas of Benedetto Croce, and since 1910 in France, coming out of the works of Gustave Lanson, the crisis of methodology in the study of literature had been evident in one form or another. It has survived down to the present in various other countries such as England, the United States, the Soviet Union, and those of Central Europe.

A large part of the controversy revolves around the idea of going back to the historical method in order to penetrate in a more organic way the realities of the literary phenomenon and the process of its development. As Paul Van Tieghem reports on the work of the Congress, the crisis bespeaks "a reaction against the precise and historical study of literature that considers that links of causality can be demonstrated among authors and works." It reflects, furthermore, a reaction against certain abuses of scholarship that

left aside the intimate worth of the art and the thought contained in the work for the accumulation of biographical data and sources. . . . On the other hand, the historical explanation of facts, abused by certain schools in the name of moral determinism, became enormously discredited in any number of fields; the notion of time was discussed; therefore, when faced from this angle, the methodological crisis in literary history is but one aspect of the general crisis of historicism.[2]

The conflict is well balanced, therefore. On the one side, *historical* literary history; on the other, attempts at a methodological renovation of an esthetic or philosophical nature. On the one side, nineteenth-century historical and documentary methods, scholarly and positivistic, for which the study of literature should be the examination of conditions or circumstances that surround the creation of literary works. It is thereby an historical discipline[3] based on historical method, on the notion of the historicity of the literary fact, and on the possibility of establishing causal relationships and conditioning among facts. On the other side is an anti-historicist reaction that rejects the nineteenth-century identification of spirit with nature and attacks the abuses of the historical method. The reaction in certain more extreme forms denies its aim of explaining the work of art totally, beginning with the knowledge and explanation of its origins in the historical, social, or economic milieu, or going even deeper into the denial by refusing the very principle of the method, that is, the historicity of the literary phenomenon and the possibility of establishing links of cause and conditions. Opposed to the historical school and the historical, philological, or scholarly method, whose peak was between 1860 and 1890 (L. Sorrento), are the esthetic school and the esthetic or critical method.

Starting with the old biographical repositories of writers, literary history began in the sixteenth century, with partial efforts, compilations, and bio-bibliographical surveys. Of course, one must recall along the way the names of Vico, Tiraboschi, the Benedictines of Saint-Maur. Finally in the nineteenth century, literary history gained the full investiture of a system. And yet, this concept and this system had been conditioned to the general spirit of the times and had been shaped by the vogue of science that presided over the study of forms of life and culture, shaped especially by the methods of the natural sciences and by certain notions such as that of environmentalism, conceiving as it did of literature as the product of outside determinants (the milieu, race, and moment of Taine) and as the result of the material and natural causality of things that underlie the spirit. In addition, the very technique of the work, the research, and the presentation of results obeyed a particular orientation, concentrated on the inventory of facts, the minutiae of lives, sources, and influences. This "factualism" was joined with an "antiquarianism," or false acceptance and idolatry of the past because it was past. It was what has been labeled "positivism" in the methodology of literary work.

Positivism developed along two parallel lines: the German historical or romantic school—Herder, the brothers Schlegel, and the brothers Grimm—which considered products of the spirit as having their origins in the "genius of the people," accentuating thereby an interest in popular poetry and things "historical" and the mystical or divine origins of such products. The other, the positivist school was French in origin, sponsored by Auguste Comte. It sought support in the natural sciences to establish a method of historical and literary research and to explain spiritual facts through the general laws of historical evolution, sociological genesis, and psychological characteristics, stressing the role of biological heredity and social and geographical frames in the conditioning of spiritual facts.

Along the lines of this general orientation, the studies of literary history after the nineteenth century went in various directions, all within the limitations of the historical method. The following among them should be noted, as defined by Van Tieghem:[4] (a) *comparative literature*. This is the study of the relationship among the various modern literatures, and it attempts an explanation of a literary work by means of its sources, imitations, and influences (J. Texte, L. P. Betz, A. Farinelli, F. Baldensperger, et al.); (b) *general literature*. Going beyond comparative literature, it puts a work into its international milieu, studies it in its relationship to works that have been produced in the same period or in parallel periods in different countries and that are analogous in form and spirit (Van Tieghem); (c) *sociological literary history*. This is the study of the public to whom the works are directed, the various elements, their characteristics and reactions, the successive or parallel variations in taste, the influence of this on writers (Hennequin, Lacomde, Lanson, Mornet, Schücking, et al.); (*d*) *geographical literary history*. This groups writers and works together by province or region (Pierce, Nadler, Dupouy); (*e*) *generational and periodic literary history*. This divides the evolution of literature into periods (*Periodisierung*) or, more specifically, into "generations," with the aim of better explaining the successions and alternations of which literary history is composed (Georges Renard, Cysarz, Petersen, Thibaudet, Peyre, Pindes, Marías, Carilla, Portuondo, et al.).

The historical approach to the literary phenomenon, the analytic method that was developed with the spirit of a naturalist, was an attempt to apply to the study of literature nineteenth-century scientific technique. It was inspired by the cult of the isolated and concrete fact and submission to the object. The value of the approach was placed in doubt when the twentieth century began to take note of the esthetic content of a work of art and consequently sought a method for the capture and appraisal of the formative elements of that content. It was beginning to be understood that artistic or esthetic criticism had a proper function in the interpretation of art. Under the influence of Hegelian idealism, parallel currents developed in Germany and Italy, in Germany under the aegis of Dilthey as it took the form of *Geistesgeschichte* or "history of the spirit," and in Italy both Croce and De Sanctis reacted against mechanical practices in the names of an esthetic sense of literature.

This revolt against positivism and historicism in the methodology of literary study[5] is based on the serious objections to the historical method that Van Tiegham outlines in the work cited above: (*a*) It gives too much importance to the historical and social milieu considering the scanty influence they bring to bear on many of the most interesting works. (*b*) It clings to minor biographical details, as if the life of the man was an essential conditioning influence on the soul of the writer, where the work has its origin. (*c*) It is tolerant of mediocre authors under the pretext that they can clarify and explain their contemporaries while, quite the contrary, there should be no place for them in literature as they do not know how to create beauty. Additionally, in matters such as this the difference between the great and the small is not one of degree, but of nature. (d) It makes excessive use, untenable even in principle, of statistics, catalogues, and other numerical means of approaching a work of art. (e) It goes on to broader and broader analyses, as if the question of quantity, as far as influences are concerned, for example, were not completely disreputable in relation to quality. (f) It gives great emphasis to influences and imitations, as if the only thing that is to count in art were not the personal element of the spirit and the work. (g) It accumulates, by means of labor that is as patient as it is fruitless, small facts and fragments of texts (index cards) which lose their real meaning and value when removed from the living organism of which they are a part as it tries to build up artificial structures. (h) It pretends to explain a literary work, or the details of that work, through known facts and texts, as if in that way we were to learn about its total reality, forgetting that the spirit of the writer was directed or fed during its creation by an infinite multitude of encounters that have disappeared without a trace.

Such a reaction was not an isolated phenomenon. Its effect was felt in all centers of humanistic studies in both the New World and the Old. Let us begin with France, where the historical method had its deepest roots, thanks to Sainte-Beuve, Taine, Gaston Paris, and, above all, the powerful influence of Gustave Lanson, who had built up the Sorbonne into a citadel of historicism. The ideas and methodological guideposts he used in his lectures and in his famous and influential manual, *Histoire de la littérature française* (1894), became the "Lansonian Method," a local label for the historical method. The phases of this movement have been described by Van Tieghem,[6] making it necessary here to refer only to their salient features. From 1910 on, partisans and adversaries of the historical method made themselves heard in sharp polemics; in France around Lanson; in significant books, such as those by Rudler, Morize, Audiat, Nadler, Schücking, Dragomirescou, Cysarz, Van Tieghem, Cazamian, Eckhoff, Richards; in the collective work edited by Ermatinger; in the work of the Slavic Formalists; in the noisy polemic in the *Romanic Review* (of Columbia University) among J. E. Spingarn, Daniel Mornet, Bernard Fay, Paul Van Tieghem; in the important article by René Bray in the *Revue d'Histoire Littéraire*; in numerous studies published in England

and the United States that followed different lines but all with an anti-historicist bent, the "new criticism" that was esthetic in origin; in France itself, the books by Jean Hytier and S. Étienne showed a dissatisfaction with the historical method that had begun to be even more evident in the Sorbonne meeting of 1948, when the defenders of the traditional method, as Pommier reports, recognized the signs of a ferment for renovation.

This is not the place to expound the various approaches proposed as substitutes for the historical method and positivistic materialism. Let mention only be made of those oriented towards the contents of the work: the psycho-historical method or the biography of a literary work (Audiat) that studies the work in its intimate life, the development of its thought, its emotion, its style; the esthetic-critical method (Dragomirescou), which studies the work in itself, the originality that makes it a first-rate work, its psychological and esthetic elements; the philosophical, biological, and moral method (Dilthey, Cysarz), which sees in the work an expression of the life of the spirit or the culture (*Kulturgeschichte*); the German school of *Geisteswissenschaftler*, which searches out the typical philosophy in a work of art, the eternal law, the creative center, mythology, and so forth. (Klukhohn, Ermatinger, Gundolf, Cysarz, Bertram, et al.); other German schools (in Germany the anti-positivist revolt had been broad and vigorous), which, even though still restrained by a kind of positivism, would interpret a work of art as the product of a race, a nation, a people, a tribe (Nadler et al.).

There are other currents especially preoccupied with problems of form and style: poetic expression, techniques, composition, style, genres, temperaments, currents, and periods. Such is the case of the Russian formalist or, rather, structuralist school (Veseloski, Jirmunski, Jakobsen, et al.). The same can be said of the many representatives of the Anglo-American "new criticism" (Richards, Empson, Blackmur, Brooks, Burke, Ransom, Warren, et al.), as well as of the new school of stylistic research (Spitzer, Hatzfeld, Vossler, Dámaso Alonso, et al.).

Thus there has been opened to literary history or rather to the science of literature, as has been the tendency to describe this body of studies (*Literaturwissenschaft*), a broad perspective and an inexhaustible field of study.

Today we seem to have gone beyond the polemic between the two opposite directions. The reaction against historicism and positivism brought about a correction of the exaggerations that had caused a hypertrophy in the role of historical, social, economic, and biographical investigations in explaining a literary work. It has made it quite easy to see that historicist exclusivism will of necessity deform the vision of reality. The extreme position of the reaction is not without its dangers too, however, because we run the risk of forgetting some elements the registry of which prevents us from falling into a false esthetic isolationism. There is room for synthesis: the close analysis of a work of art as such in its totality and unity does not exclude the knowledge of certain relevant facts that locate it within the history of civilization. Historical methods are therefore necessary: biographical research, the study of the historical milieu (economic, social, diplomatic facts, and so forth), the investigation of sources, influences, and relationships, the study of editions and the reading public are all needed. In short, everything is relevant that can bear witness to the relationship of the work to history, period, and generation, such as customs, language, currents of thought and spirituality. One must be aware, however, that as far as an understanding, explanation, and judgment of literature is concerned, history must not be a primary factor but a secondary one. It is a known fact that history is always incomplete, abusive, and disorienting at times in its effect upon the critical spirit that must judge the true value of works. It would be wise for the critic to mistrust the excesses and exaggerated pretensions of the historical method. History's place here is merely to prepare the way for criticism, never to do away with it, replace it, or condense it. What is most essential is a study of the work itself, and this has to be the overwhelming finality of literary criticism. Historical methods do have a special role, the establishment of concrete facts. What is forbidden to them is providing concept, orientation, norm, and plan.

Although basically of an esthetic nature, a literary fact is nonetheless historical, that is, it occurs within a determined time and in a determined space. There are historical elements which cloak it and also join it to civilization—the author's personality, language, race, geographical and social milieu, moment. There are esthetic elements which constitute its nucleus and also stamp it with those peculiar characteristics that make it distinct from every other fact of life (economic, political, moral, religious): type of narrative, plot, motivations, point of view, characters, melodic line, movement, theme, prosody, style, rhythm, meter, and so forth, all differing according to the literary genre. In the organization of a work of art, the latter group of elements make up what is "intrinsic," while the first group is "extrinsic." The analysis of a work by its intrinsic elements, its interior, is the practice of intrinsic, ergocentric, or esthetic criticism; extrinsic criticism is one that views the work by its exterior, extrinsic, or historical elements.

Historical criticism has long been dominent due to the greater ease with which one can grasp the exterior or historical understanding of a literary fact. The problems of esthetic or intrinsic analysis, however, are always pending. If they have not yet been completely solved, and if there does not even exist any technique adequate to the solution of all the difficulties surrounding them we do know, nonetheless, where and how they are located, a challenge to the acumen of critics and esthetes.

Because of this fact and the prestige of the historical sciences, because of the concept introduced by romanticism, which led to a confusion of the history of art forms with that of national institutions and made of literature a mere "document" for the study of the development of a "national spirit," literary history became confused with the history of civilization. Later on, under the impact of positivism and the natural sciences, it became a study of the circumstances or causes that produce or condition the production of art, "the external circumstances—political, social, economic—in which literature is produced" (Sidney Lee). There was a complete domination by the external, that which is neither literary nor esthetic, in the study of literature. Literary history was more *history* than *literary*. It was but a branch of the historical sciences, of the history of culture, which viewed literary works as representative "documents" of a race, a period, a nationality, a personality, the most qualified testimony, it would seem, for the understanding of a culture. What was especially interesting was the extrinsic and not the intrinsic. Literature, according to this concept, included everything that was in print, standing as evidence for the interpretation of an individual, of the psychology of a race or a nation, of social evolution, of philosophy, of religion, of human behavior. For biography and the history of ideas and institutions, literary works were nothing more than storehouses of documents and proofs.

Against this historical concept of literary history (literary history as a part of the history of culture), there were drawn up other ways of understanding the nature and finality of literary history.[7] The monograph of the Committee on Research Activities of the Modern Language Association of America shows that literary history can also be conceived of as the history of an art, with literature being approached as this art, that is as works produced by the imagination (poetry, novel, drama, epic).[8] Seen in this way, works of art are not "documents" but "monuments."

As an understanding of literature in this way literary history can assume two shapes: on the one side, it can study literary art in terms of historical causality, accentuating the analysis of the external or historical circumstances (political, social, economic) that condition its birth. This is the method of Taine and the Marxists. It is the historical, social, economic method, and to it are joined studies of biographical, psychological, and psychiatric interpretation and those of ideological analysis. All of them exaggerate the dependence of literature upon environment and author, with the presupposition that there is an absolute causal connection between these factors and the work in question.

The other type of literary history is one that examines works in terms of literary tradition, as part of the process of the development of literature itself as art, relatively independent of the locale, the environment, or the author, relating the work to others of the same genre or style. It identifies periods by the similarity of stylistic characteristics and esthetic conventions, analyzing literary craft, themes, genres, conventions, techniques, structural elements, linguistic resources and so forth. It is towards this second type that the attention of those who aspire to a *literary* history of literature, close to esthetics and linguistics, is turned.

Following René Wellek, it is possible to reduce to six the types of literary history that have existed since the Renaissance: (*a*) literary history as a catalogue of books; (*b*) intellectual history; (*c*) the history of civilizations or national spirits; (*d*) the sociological or genetic method; (*e*) the concept of historical relativism (the work of art as a mere reflection of the times); (*f*) literary history as the history of the internal development of the art: while literature is in constant contact with other human activities, it has its own specific characteristics and functions and a development of its own that cannot be reduced to any other activity; otherwise, it would cease to be literature and it would lose its *raison d'être:* it would become second-rate philosophy, religion, or ethical system, or even propaganda.[9]

This last concept of literary history is the ideal to be reached by those who conceive of literature as having a specific nature and finality with its own value and demanding a scale of its own for its proper judgment. In this concept literature has value of its own and is not simply the vehicle of other values. It is the view of those who aspire to turn literary studies into an autotelic discipline not subject to the use of methods borrowed from other disciplines or sciences. Clearly, a literary method for the study of literature, past or present, by means of history or criticism, does not imply in any way a lack of recognition of the contributions that can be made to the interpretation of a literary work by extra-literary studies, no matter what the discipline or whether it concerns an extrinsic or historical element. What is essential is for one to be aware that these studies and contributions do not comprise *literary* criticism or history. They are legitimate external contributions with roots in sociology, history, economics, psychology, anthropology, and psychoanalysis. They are not criticism, even though they may be of help to criticism. Criticism and literary history in unison, as they should be, examine a literary work by its intrinsic or artistic elements. The other disciplines that deal with nature or the spirit can uncover data that will help these in their task, but they cannot provide them with their method or replace them as a *modus operandi.*

Seen from this perspective, literary history, by being *literary,* need not lose its scientific character. Or rather, this is precisely how it will be scientific, for as Lanson observes in his masterful chapter in the collective work, *De la méthode dans les sciences,* "literary history, if it wishes to have a bit of the science about it, must begin by outlawing any imitation of other sciences, no matter which they may be." It must not adopt the methods of other sciences but must assume a scientific attitude, "an attitude of the spirit as it faces reality," and share with the scientist "disinterested curiosity, severe probity, painful patience, submission to fact, a reluctance to believe, to believe ourselves as well as to believe others, the incessant need for criticism, control, and verification." [10]

This concept does not isolate the literary phenomenon like a meteor in space. It recognizes its relationship and bonds with all of human life. It does require, however, that the literary work be faced in its turn as a whole, as a specific unity, with its own peculiar elements and characteristics, with its own nature and finality, "an organic system of signs" (Wellek) for the study and interpretation of which a special method is imposed, the critical or "poetic" method.

Conceiving of the nature and the task of literary history in this way, it becomes evident that the finality, the object of its study, is the literary work itself, its structure and development. This does not imply the withdrawal or isolation of other knowledge necessary to placing the work and to understanding its relationships in time and space. They may be secondary, subsidiary, and auxiliary bits of knowledge, but they cannot be left out. It is not a question of preaching eclecticism, or compromise, or a conciliation of methods, as some of the participants at the Budapest congress seemed to want. One must only recognize a function for the historical method that it alone can fulfill, marginal to the critical task, in the preparation of material upon which the critic's eye will fall. It is the specialized system of chores, techniques that are auxiliary and preparatory for the work of criticism. If one adopts these techniques one can accept the advice of Lanson referred to above concerning the necessity of the literary historian's beginning his apprenticeship with the work of Langlois and Seignobos. In the same spirit the manuals of Morize, Rudler, and Amiet are necessary, even indispensable. One must not lose sight, however, of the fact that all of these tasks are collateral or auxiliary, as is a knowledge of economic, social, and political history, the history of ideas, the history of the other arts, ethnology, anthropology, philosophy. Literature is not in a position of dependence or submission in relation to other phenomena of life. It is not an epiphenomenon of economics or social life. It is on a par in its relationship with them, carrying the same value as any other expression of human activity.

PERIODIZATION

Closely related to the problem of the concept of literary history is that of periodization. "There is no methodological problem of greater importance in the field of history than that of periodization . . . a basic and not an external problem," Henri Berr and Lucien Febvre say in a chapter in the *Encyclopedia of the Social Sciences*. The periodic divisions of human evolution are criticized as arbitrary, as lacking in objectivity (the result in most cases of conventions or fortuitous circumstances), never corresponding to the internal realities of the periods or to the immanent forces that have generated or guided them.

As one of the most difficult themes of historical science, periodology demands a good formulation if we do not wish to see history as a continuous and directionless flux, a heap of chaotic and indistinct events. It is a fact, as René Wellek stresses, that it is impossible to separate the concept of the period from the basic concept of the historical process and the theory of the evolution and development of history. Transferred to the field of literary history, the problem grows in difficulties, given the still uncertain character of the discipline as concerns its nature and finality. Literary history, as has been stressed in the preceding pages, has not yet drawn the boundaries of its activities, has not yet created a methodology of its own for investigation and exposition, has not yet distinguished as its object, the work or the circumstances of its formation. It is still thought of as an encyclopedia with room for everything—social and intellectual history, biographical information, the geographical, social, political milieu sandwiched in between critical essays and bibliographical notes. It is still in short "a discipline indiscriminately involved with everything," as Manfred Kridl says, having a variety of ways for its conception and practice. Literary history is dominated by the belief that it is but a mere division of general history, so that literary phenomena are seen and interpreted as epiphenomena of political, social, and economic facts, or as superstructures dependent upon and products of the socioeconomic structure.

Therefore the periodological divisions in literary history up to now have generally been conditioned to political divisions. Periods correspond to reigns (for example, Louis XIV), or receive labels based on the names of important monarchs (Elizabethan, Victorian). Periods may also be based on dates that are more or less arbitrarily chosen from the calendar, and which only show the necessity of a scheme for the presentation of the work and no normative principle. Centuries, decades, or isolated dates can offer no sense, nor can they reach beyond conventional choices, one thing being as good as the next. In this way, a political or simply numerical criterion based on political divisions or initiated by some great historical or literary event cannot offer any orientation whatsoever to the literary characterization of the period because they imply a recognition of the dependence and determination of literature by political or social events.

The same is true in relation to the literatures in the Portuguese language. The divisions proposed for Portuguese literature mix labels taken from general history (Middle Ages, modern times) with others that come from the history of art (Renaissance), or with simple numerical terms sixteenth, seventeenth, eighteenth centuries, *Quinhentismo*, for example), with terms of literary content (romanticism, classicism), adopting as dividing lines, sometimes the division of the centuries, sometimes the deaths of important figures or the publication of famous and influential works (the death of Camões, the publication of *Camões* by Garrett). In the same way, in Brazilian literature, the traditional divisions make reference with only slight differences to political and historical criteria (colonial period, national period) with more or less arbitrary subdivisions by centuries or decades or by literary schools.

The confusion and inadequacy becomes even more obvious in the light of the variety of designations for the divisions: era, epoch, period, phase, age. Here we have a great confusion among authors as to the use of these terms. They are used indiscriminately, sometimes with distinct meanings, sometimes synonymously. It would seem that "era" is the most general term, followed by "epoch," and then by "period." Fidelino de Figueiredo in his periodization of Portuguese literature adopts "era" as the broadest division (medieval era, classical era, modern era), and "epoch" for his subdivisions, divided chronologically. In any case, literary terminology varies in the use of these terms, just as it does with those based on movements and schools.

The lack of scientific criteria in the establishment of periods makes many people skeptical and the lack of rigor suggests to them that a period is nothing but a name, neutral and without meaning, a label no different from any other and without the slightest connection to its contents. In this way, they arbitrarily reduce the period to a piece of time, a purely mechanical and didactic convenience, denoted by dates that have political or social significance. This extreme nominalism is matched, as Wellek stresses, by the opposite metaphysical system of Cysarz and others who approach the periods as true metaphysical entities, superior, previous, and independent of the individuals who represent them. The notion of period, Wellek says categorically, cannot be left to nominalism or skepticism. Its use is necessary, and periodological terms do have a scientific function. We must conceive of them not as arbitrary linguistic labels, nor as metaphysical entities, but as names that designate the system of norms that dominate literature in a given moment during the historical process (Wellek).[11]

The periodological principle, just as the principle of literary history itself, must have its origins in a general concept of literature. We must conceive of the literary phenomenon not merely as a passive reflection or copy of the politico-social or even the intellectual development of mankind, not forgetting however the interrelationships that exist among them or even the reciprocal influences. We must consider that literature has its own and autonomous development, one that cannot be reduced to that of other activities or even to that of the body of all those activities. And so we will have to recognize that the ideal literary periodization will follow a purely literary criterion developing from the notion that literature develops as literature.

A period is therefore a section of time (within universal development) dominated by a system of literary norms, standards, and conventions, the introduction, diffusion, diversification, integration, and disappearance of which can be traced (Wellek). Every work of art must be understood as an approximation to this system. On the other hand, Wellek emphasizes, the system of norms, the "regulatory ideas" of the system must be derived from literary art, so that the general development of literature can be divided into literary categories.

The history of a period will show the rise and fall of the system of norms, the changes from one system to another, with the result that its unity will never be complete, but relative. During the period, a certain scheme of norms is more completely realized, coinciding with or superimposing itself upon other concordant forms that have other norms. The new periodology described in this way contains another important notion: instead of a succession of periods like airtight blocks, what we have is an overlapping series. The systems of norms that are replaced during two periods never begin and end at precise moments, but they continue in some aspects and are rejected in others. The new norms replace the old ones, overlapping, interpenetrating, crossing, and superimposing, creating "frontier zones" of transition on the fringes of the periods. Thus, instead of temporal unities, they are rather typological unities, with the articulation brought about in depth or by layers. In this way, the "myth of dates and limits" is dispelled (Berr and Febvre). Ended too is the "chronological tyranny" mentioned by Oto Maria Carpeaux, for whom this reaction against chronology is the visible finality of modern tendencies of literary historiography.

According to this definition of a period, its description is a matter of diverse chapters: the study of the characteristics of the literary style that dominates it and its stylistic evolution; the esthetic and critical principles that constitute its system of norms; the definition and history of the term that designates it; the relationship of literary activity to other forms of activity, by which the unity of the period as a general manifestation of human life is brought out; the relationships among diverse national literatures within one same period; the causes that give birth and death to the period's body of norms, causes of an internal or literary order and of an extra-literary, that is social, or cultural order (this is where the thesis of generational periodicity comes in, according to which changes are due to the appearance of new generations); the analysis of individual works in relation to the system of norms, discovering to what point they are representative or typical of the system (an analysis which must focus on the esthetic-stylistic characteristics of the work itself, and not on the circumstances that conditioned its genesis: author, milieu, race, moment, and so forth); an analysis of literary forms or genres within the periodological framework, stressing the acquisitions made under the new system of norms or the discordances that made it, therefore, improper for the development of those genres. The description of realizations and failures of periods will give us a picture of continuous development in the process of literature as literature.

The period is, therefore, a system of literary norms expressed in a style. The old concepts of "Renaissance," "Baroque," "Romanticism" have lost, as Oto Maria Carpeaux emphasizes,

all flavor of school, revealing their infinite wealth of nuances and immanent contradictions, revealing themselves as states of the spirit and universal styles of feeling and living; it is now possible to outline the centuries-old history of these "stylistic blocs," their contradictory transformations, their most subtle underground relationships, their symbolic and stylistic expressions. These styles create [Carpeaux goes on] new universal possibilities of expression and realization in all sectors of spiritual activity; there are medieval, renaissance, baroque, classical, and romantic literature, art, music, religion, philosophy, state, and economy; there is, above all, in all periods, an ideal type of man for that period: medieval man, renaissance man, baroque man, classical man, romantic man; and these men would have been silent and therefore forgotten had certain among them not possessed the individual gift of artistic expression, perpetuating themselves in works that endure.[12]

Occupying the center of epochs or periods is the body of concepts that man holds of his destiny, of himself, of future life and God, of the best way to give symbolic representation to those concepts, and of translating his esthetic vision of reality into a style.

To describe an epoch in literary terms according to the principles of that "critical genre that is the historical narrative of literature" (Getto) is to proceed to the definition and characterization of the style that gives it its own unmistakable physiognomy. Therein resides the liveliest and most organic literary historiography, completely adequate to the very nature of the literary phenomenon because it goes towards what is most intimate and intrinsic. On the other hand, it also fulfills the idea of parallelism and the confrontation of literature with the other arts in search of mutual elucidation. By means of comparative criticism, establishing parallelisms, synchronisms, and influences among the diverse national literatures within the same period that thus denotes its unity, literary works may be interpreted in the light of a universal perspective, as was proposed by the advocates of "general literature" (Van Tieghem), thus clarifying the role of international themes, types, modes, and currents.

The historiography of stylistic periodization provides a more flexible concept of literary development and one closer to reality because it is at the very core of the esthetic phenomenon. It has as its points of reference concepts of both individual style and the style of the period as defined according to Hatzfeld:

Individual style is the particular aspect of a verbal artifact which reveals the attitude of its writer in the choice of synonyms, vocabulary, stress on abstract or concrete word-material, verbal or nominal preferences, metaphoric or metonymic propensities but all of this not only from the viewpoint of the *écart* from the dictionary and syntax but also from the viewpoint of the fictional whole the organization of which these choices serve in all the artistic details and ramifications.

Epoch style is the attitude of a culture or civilization which comes to the fore in analogous tendencies in art, literature, music, architecture, religion, psychology, sociology, forms of politeness, customs, dress, gestures, etc. As far a literature is concerned epoch style can only be assessed by the conveyances of style feature, ambiguous in themselves, to a constellation which appears in different works and authors of the same era and seems informed by the same principle as perceptible in the neighboring arts.[13]

Stylistic periodization provides the historian with a liberation from "chronological tyranny." There is no shoal more dangerous for literary historiography than that of chronology. It is quite true, as Carpeaux makes clear, that "destroying the chronological tyranny does not mean violating chronology," but to base a periodic division on mere dates or numerical divisions is an inexplicable empiricism at this time when people are seeking to establish the limits and the methods of the science of literature. Such periodology can only be chosen as a simplistic process, a flight from the difficulties of the problem or an attempt to ignore them.

In the light of simplistic chronology, there is no explanation of countless facts of literary history, such as coincidence or concomitance in time among different or opposing forms, even of style. The precursors, Lanson's *"attardés et égarés,"* the discordant appearance of the same style at different points, and other cases are easily interpreted through the application of the concept of the individual's style and that of epoch to the definition of periods. What happens with the problem of frontiers between periods, happens also between neighboring civilizations and cultures. As vital unities endowed with reality, they cannot have clear borders or precise margins between them, nor fixed beginnings and ends. On the contrary, what really exist are "frontier zones" (Fidelino de Figueiredo) in which individualized happenings, expressed by means of dates, cannot become anything more than signals or terms of reference, indicators of the passage from one period to another. This is what Van Tieghem means when he states:

But in literature, as in the other arts, as in politics and religion, as in all ways of human activity, successive movements do not replace each other purely and simply: each one is joined to its successor, even when the latter disavows it and turns against it, by that most durable part of the novelties that it had brought forth in its time; therefore they become richer and richer through these successive acquisitions. History, and literary history in particular, is the picture of these destructions and these acquisitions, of these breaks and this continuity. [And he states elsewhere:] In literature, as in other domains of the spirit, the new does not take the place of the old except by partially adopting previous conquests by joining them to others, and it only drops completely what has definitively lapsed.[14]

What is certain, thanks to a stylistic perspective, is that we are prepared to understand the concomitance in time of diverse or opposing stylistic phenomena. This is what the example of the seventeenth century shows us: predominantly baroque stylistic blemishes appeared, but in France, the classical style created a vogue that obscured the baroque features still there; the baroque was unforeseeably mixed with classical elements in many works and authors, in Racine and Bossuet, for example, or in others, like Pascal, who had been formerly considered completely classical and who today through stylistic analysis have been incorporated into the baroque. A similar situation occurred in the nineteenth century, with the mixture, crossing, overlapping, and superimposing of diverse and opposing stylistic manifestations such as symbolism and Parnassianism, realism and romanticism, none of which ever followed one another chronologically in an exact way, but rather came together and became intertwined to produce the literary forms of the twentieth century. How could this be explained according to pure chronology? How could one define these manifestations in their evolution except by a theory of the internal development of styles? Wölfflin illustrated this theory for the passage from Renaissance style to the baroque, aided in his concept of formalism by the distinction of stylistic traces and the two systems of norms that regulated those periods.

Therefore, one admits the unity of the period and concedes that that unity is produced not by stylistic homogeneity but by the predominance of a certain style that determines the general tone, thanks to a constellation of signals. This does not exclude the possibility of a concurrence of other styles during the time and of geographical differences and variations among the diverse arts, as well as the prevalence of the dominant style of the period. One can however deduce the value of stylistic categories for the definition of periods in the history of literature and of the other arts. Concepts of style in the analysis of works of art can be used as a much more exact critical touchstone, as much in the study of masterpieces as in that of lesser works. The relationship between individual style and the style of the period is a ready instrument for analysis and interpretation. Even considering the concomitances of the style, and further the relativity with which individual styles should be established—because, as Paul Frank says, only with great difficulty can a work be defined as belonging in its totality to a certain style—the definition of the work is most facilitated as it is closer to a characterized style.

Styles are the dynamic force of periods. To reveal them in their intimate essence is to penetrate the very nature of the period. Stylistic forms develop and transform by the way in which the artist's concept of the world and the proposal, conscious or unconscious, change and evolve. As he interprets or reinterprets the world, the artist demands that stylistic forms change and adapt themselves to his necessities. The transformation of style, as Wölfflin shows, obeys internal laws of evolution. Nevertheless, corresponding to the intentions of the artist to express and provide a vehicle for his vision of reality, his beliefs and experiences, this expression could not be effected through any other form, since there is an intrinsic adjustment between the vision of the world to be transmitted and the stylistic form that was developed to give it expression. The baroque, for example, was a stylistic form that was developed in order to express a new conception of the world, and only by means of it could be found the optimum way of doing that.

In the history of modern arts and letters, thanks to an application of the comparative method, the principle styles that prevail as periodological unities have been the following: Renaissance, baroque, neoclassical, rococo, romantic, realist, impressionist, and modernist. From the influence of the history of the arts, according to the new orientation, these stylistic concepts and definitions continue with a generalized application to the history of modern letters. Given the analogous nature of artistic phenomena, the arts differing most basically in the means they employ, it is much more natural for the defining criteria to pass from one art form to another than between political and literary history. Therefore, the use of concepts such as romantic, classical, or realist is general and unrestricted in all of the arts. The use of the term baroque is already being generalized in literary criticism since Wölfflin's studies as the definition of the whole period, not just the literary aspect, but all of the post-Renaissance period. The same is true of the terms rococo ("a fundamental work on the rococo in literature floats in the air," Cysarz affirms), and impressionism.

THE BRAZILIAN SOLUTIONS

The problem of literary history and the correlative periodology have received in Brazil solutions that have fallen entirely within the empirical formula, either being simply chronological or of a sociological and historicist bent. It is significant that ever since Varnhagen the problem has aroused the interest of historians and the Viscount might be considered as the founder of both general and literary historiography in Brazil. The literary discipline was seen as a dependency of general, political, social, and economic history, and its method was nothing but a transfer of the historical method. The idea was that literature did not reach beyond being a reflection of human activities in general. This historical approach was definitely inherited from Portugal since, as Fidelino de Figueiredo reminds us,[15] Portugal had always been dominated by the "historicist obsession," which both in Portugal and Brazil "never dampened the hope for an immediate acceptance of the new philosophical orientation of this branch of studies." This very orientation is advocated and initiated among us with the planning and elaboration of this work.[16]

From the simplistic concept that literature is a historical phenomenon, one can see that literary history must of needs be part of general history. Literary historiography in Brazil in its primitive phase, before Sílvio Romero, consisted of merely descriptive expositions, when not limited to bibliographical catalogues and collections or anthologies of didactic intent.[17] The criticism of these books has already been done so thoroughly that there is no need to discuss it here.[18]

It is with Sílvio Romero that literary historiography in Brazil reaches a confrontation with scientific bases and a preoccupation with concepts and methodology. This fact places him among us as the systematizer of the discipline, no matter how restricted his attempts may have been. His work is a monument that, although refutable in many aspects, must be studied because of the honesty of his conception and his

methodological zeal. Romero began, according to his own words in
the first chapter of *História da Literatura Brasileira*, with a concept of
the historical evolution and formation of peoples, taking into account
ethnographic contributions to that formation; his vision of history was
"philosophical and naturalist"; his target was to find the "laws that
have governed and will continue to determine the formation of the
genius, spirit, and character of the Brazilian people." For this it was
necessary "to show the relationship of our intellectual life with the
political, social, and economic history of the nation." His work is "a
naturalist study of the history of Brazilian literature." Influenced by
positive determinism, he investigated material and environmental factors, "the elements of a natural history of our letters," searching for
them in ethnology, geology, and biology, in social and economic factors. For him, literature

has the breadth given it by German critics and historians. It includes all
the manifestations of a people's intelligence: politics, economics, art, popular creations, sciences . . . and not, as was the custom to suppose in Brazil, only the so-called *belles lettres,* a term that ultimately was almost exclusively applied to poetry.

It can be seen that Romero's concept of literature and literary history comes from German romantic sources. These identify it with
national genius and interpret its evolution in accord with the growth
of national feeling. This concept, furthermore, had dominated the
majority if not all of our literary historians. It also had roots in positivist and naturalist philosophical thought, the Spencerian and Dar-
winian evolutionism that made up the naturalist climate of the later
part of the nineteenth century.

In any case, Sílvio Romero consolidated the historicist and sociological concept of literature by adopting historical methods for literary history. He had a powerful influence on his successors. The study
of literature should begin with a knowledge of its static part, the
base on which nationality, race, territory, social and economic milieu
are built; in short, with sociological introductions. Even José Veríssimo,
who opposed Romero by defending a concept of literature as "literary
art" or *belles lettres,* did not run away from the view of literature as
an expressive form of national feeling. Veríssimo felt that the progress
of one coincided with that of the other, and in addition adopted an
expositive criterion that was purely chronological and a periodological

criterion that was entirely politico-historical in make-up (colonial and national periods).

The periodological problem, however, is the crux of the matter, and it is there that our literary historians stumble, unable to stamp literary history with an autonomous meaning in relation to general history. Without exception, beginning with Wolf, they use political criteria mixing it with pure chronology, even when they admit to subdivisions based on schools or genres. Let us examine these divisions:

Ferdinand Wolf: from the discovery to the end of the seventeenth century; first half of the eighteenth century; second half; 1800 to 1840; 1840 to 1863.

Fernandes Pinheiro: phase of formation (sixteenth and seventeenth centuries); phase of development (eighteenth century); reform (nineteenth century).

Sílvio Romero: period of formation (1500–1750); period of autonomous development (1750–1830); period of romantic transformation (1830–1870); period of critical reaction (1870 on). This scheme was later modified to: period of formation (1592–1768); period of autonomous development (1768–1836); period of romantic reaction (1836–1875); period of critico-naturalist reaction (1875–1893 or 1900). Romero did not stop there, and in the preface to the second edition, he suggests another division: classical period (1549–1836); romantic period (1836–1870); anti-romantic period (1870–1900). Still a fourth classification seemed feasible to Romero: classical period (1592–1792); period of ulterior transformations (1792–   ).

José Veríssimo: colonial period and national period with a stage of transition (1769–1795). He rejects any division for the colonial period, which would "only be didactic or chronological at best," with the presupposition that any systematic division would be arbitrary. For the second phase, he orders the phenomena chronologically by schools and genres.

Ronald de Carvalho: after the inevitable sociological introduction (in imitation of Sílvio Romero), periods of formation (1500–1756), transformation (1756–1830), autonomy (1830–1925).

Artur Mota: (sociological introduction), epoch of formation (four periods: embryonic, elaboration, initiation, differentiation), up to Gregório de Matos; epoch of transformation (four periods: *mineiro*, patriotic, religious, transition); epoch of autonomous expansion: Romanticism (literary emancipation, 1836; religious phase, Indianism, skepticism, concrete nationalism, patriotic poetry, condor poets); epoch of autonomous expansion: Realism (anti-romantic reaction of scientific and social poetry, naturalism, interest in psychology, Parnassianism, symbolism, futurism). He states that with this division the chronological method and the logical classification demanded by Taine and others are reconciled.

Afrânio Peixoto: colonial literature (imitation of the mother country, three phases: classicism, cultism, Arcadism); reactive literature (reaction against the mother country: political and literary nativism, idealization of the savage); emancipated literature (national problems: abolition, war, republic, settlement of the backlands, regionalism); foreign influences: European (naturalism, Parnassianism, symbolism), United States, and others.

This outline of the principal periodological systems of Brazilian literary historiography aims to show the complete absence of any correspondence between them and literary reality. Sílvio Romero, in the first edition of his study, defends his division, considering it "the natural division of Brazilian literary history," and he proposes three others in the second edition, saying "what matters is to affirm that the author not take great stock in what he proposed in the text of the book and in the systems that are there." He states later on that those of Wolf and Fernandes Pinheiro "still seem inferior to those that I suggested." On the other hand, Afrânio Peixoto confesses

not to understand too well the phases of "formation," "development," "reform," and "literary transformation in Brazil." [And he asks:] Was there perhaps a sociological or political final touch in Brazilian "formation?" And if we are already definitively "formed," how can one speak immediately thereafter of "development?" Reform? It has a religious or moral touch. Transformation? Into what? Brazilian literature has advanced and will continue to advance.

These observations have pertinence, but they do not convince one of the merits of the divisions proposed by the multifaceted Bahian writer.

In the case of Sílvio Romero, we can synthesize the spiritual state of all of our literary historiography as far as periodization is concerned. His attitude of skepticism and hesitation arises because he has no conception of the process of literary evolution. His skepticism is reflected in the variety of divisions, here based on political facts, there

on purely chronological facts, with no meaning whatsoever in relation
to the reality of the development. In this way, we can vary the divisions and classifications *ad infinitum* depending on the convenience in
a purely mechanical way or with didactic intent. This results from
seeking interpretive criteria that are foreign to the literary phenomenon, which is not considered according to its own nature as an
autonomous manifestation, but as the simple reflection of socio-politi-
cal activity.

From Wolf to Sílvio Romero, and from José Veríssimo to Ronald
de Carvalho, the problem of periodization is joined to the nationalistic
content of literature, and literary history becomes the verification of
growing nationalism. It is disguised at first as nativism, and becomes
increasingly conscious until it bursts forth into a truly national feeling.
The succession of periods in these divisions obedient to the progressive
idea reveals the preoccupation with discovering the growth of the
national component in literature, the intent to have "literary progress
related to our national evolution, . . . the generation and the march
of national feeling through literature" (Veríssimo). Literature, in this
way, is restricted to the position of a document or testimony of
political facts; its autonomy corresponds to the affirmation of the
national personality of the country recently liberated from the yoke
of the mother country. Literary history is subordinated to the political
process, with our historians looking towards the dates of political
events to delimit the literary periods. Or, at best, they use political
and administrative denominations (origin, initiation, formation, autonomy, modernity, differentiation, elaboration, emancipation, nationalism,
and so forth), with literary or cultural names (realism, naturalism,
classicism, that is, reference to literary genres), and with others of
generational meaning. The periods may take their stamp from great
personalities, the appearance of important books, or from simple
chronological denomination, or even from vague and meaningless
designations (for example, Romero's "ulterior reactions").

This lack of orientation, so evident in the skepticism of Sílvio Romero, has its origins as a problem of major importance in the philosophy of history, in the absence of a concept of literature as an
autonomous phenomenon that is in constant reciprocal action with
other forms of human endeavor. It comes from the tendency to sub-

ordinate literary phenomenon to the historical, from the lack of a periodological philosophy of an esthetic nature.

The solution lies in a literary historiography that would describe the evolutionary process as the integration of artistic styles. The hesitations and the mistakes of periodology would be corrected by the adoption of such a systematization.

This is the solution that has inspired the conception and the planning of *A Literatura no Brasil.* Its divisions correspond to the great artistic styles that have been represented in Brazil from the very first moments in which men here had thoughts and feelings and gave them an esthetic shape.

Understood in this way, the evolution of esthetic forms in Brazil took shape in the following styles: baroque, neoclassicism, Arcadism, Romanticism, realism, naturalism, Parnassianism, symbolism, impressionism, and modernism. The description of this evolution is the task proposed here.

Thanks to stylistic periodology, the history of literature can be freed of:

1. The tyranny of chronology. It escapes this implicit problem which all literary historians have run up against in their intention of finding "divisions that are perfectly exact, or laying them out in quite distinct categories" (Veríssimo). Free of chronological mechanics, the periods can erase precise frontiers and exact delimitations, and appear as they really are, groupings that overlap, interpenetrate, and superimpose themselves, all of which can explain concomitances, precursors, and laggards as simple phenomena of literary history.

2. The tyranny of sociology. It rejects the notion of causality of static elements—physical, social, biological, and economic milieu. These factors are conceded priority in the genesis of artistic phenomenon by Taine, by Marxism, and by other concepts of literature as an expression of society, making it in that way a mere superstructure in relation to those elements.

3. The tyranny of politics. A system of styles removes from the historian's mind the preoccupation with investigating national feeling in literary evolution, a preoccupation that was generalized by the romantic influence. Soares Amora correctly brings up the problem of the determination of literary nationality, of the conquest of literary

autonomy, and of the definition of national character.[19] He sees it as one of the constants of Brazilian criticism and American criticism in general. Sílvio Romero arrives at a criterion for gauging literary values through national character. ("The more . . . it works towards the determination of our national character, the greater are its merits.") Artur Mota, José Veríssimo, and others identify literature and its progress with the forward march of the national spirit. Instead of defining and characterizing the literature by its subordination to political criteria (under the influence of the romantic exaggeration of national feelings) what is important for a truly poetic criticism is the quality of artistic expression according to its own characteristics and not its value as any testimony of nationalism. The esthetic-stylistic periodological concept will correct this tendency to apply principles of nationalism to the interpretation of the literary phenomenon and to see in literature an expression of national conscience. The stylistic phenomenon has eluded the comprehension of our historians, who have been confused by political preoccupations. José Veríssimo among others, for example, points out that "only by the end of the eighteenth century do we begin to feel something in Brazilian poets that has begun to set them apart," and makes thereafter absolutely erroneous affirmations about the collision of styles in that period.

Stylistic periodology is, therefore, one of the most important chapters in the progress of the history of science of literature towards its emancipation from general history.

DEFINITION & CHARACTERISTICS OF BRAZILIAN LITERATURE

If we take an interpretive look at the literature produced in Brazil, the structure of its formation will be seen at once. Among us, the rhythm of literary activity followed a double movement: on one side, the disintegration and abandonment of the old consciousness, on the other, the foundation of a new one. Given the fact that we were a nation colonized by Europeans (Portuguese), without a native tradition that could serve as a useful past, the evolution of our literature became the struggle between an imported tradition and the search for a new tradition of local or native coinage. This conflict in the relationship between Europe and America, this effort at the creation of a local tradition to replace that brought from Europe marks the dynamic force of literature from the very beginning of colonial settlement and its first expressions. It is a theme that appeared faintly beginning with the first colonial century when the Jesuits study the languages, ethnography, and social life of the Indians, making use of literature (poetry and drama) to penetrate and to influence the minds of the natives and of the colonists. Anchieta stands above all, with his epic of spiritual conquest and religious imperialism.

This didactic intent was trying to adapt itself to the local situation, even by polylinguism to appeal to the variety of tongues that characterized the various audiences. There also grew up from an early date a theme of exaltation of the land, the "*diálogos das grandezas*," a kind of nativist boasting called *ufanismo*, which created a whole cycle of literature that ranged about the myth of El Dorado. Ideas of the noble savage and the promised land and its riches were the bases of the myths that from the very beginning brought out "prosopopoeias," "*diálogos das grandezas*," "tidal islands," the birth songs in praise of a nascent civilization and the deeds of travelers, warriors, and missionaries. Throughout the seventeenth and eighteenth centuries, with the lyric poets and the orators, outstanding among whom are Antônio Vieira and Gregório de Matos, a new voice was making itself heard, differing with that of the mother country in a struggle to rid itself of the Portuguese appearance that had characterized it. The struggle would reach its culmination with romanticism.

This struggle between two traditions, the Luso-European and the nascent native one, found expression in another theme: the conflict between the concept of literature as a spontaneous and earth-born product and the concept of literature as the flower of a complex culture and an individually conscious elaboration. This theme, remote in origin, had penetrated deep into our literary theories, bringing face to face throughout our evolution two types of writers: the inspired ones, telluric, virginal, instinctive, who sought inspiration in the land, in the unconscious; and the refined ones, cultured and rootless, who turned towards European literary sources. Afrânio Peixoto so well described this group when he stated that the Brazilian, instead of *going* to Europe, *returned* to Europe.

A further result of this conflict was the problem of the relationship of the writer to nature. Efforts at fixing a tradition inclined towards nature, whence literary consciousness would now take on an attitude of exalted contemplation, now a shadowy, tragic pessimism, with successive waves of enthusiastic lyricism and boasting with a pessimistic realism. Indianism, ruralism, and regionalism are the high points of this feeling, a constant in our lyric poetry, pointing out the role played by nature in our mental life, and the persistence of nativist aspirations. This presence or prestige has tended to dissolve as the process of urbanization has become more extensive and deeply rooted since the nineteenth century.

The conflict between these two tendencies—the one dragging us towards Europe and the one trying to establish a new local tradition—gave rise to the poles of our literary consciousness, producing the drama which the country is still experiencing. It is a drama reflected not only in the creative imagination, but also in the criticism and understanding of literature, for it involves the very concept of the nature and function of literature in Brazil. This is our great tradition and the one that still governs literary life: culturally and literarily, we have been a nation in formation. The long road towards this self-dominion had two high points: the romantic-realist phase of the nineteenth century and the contemporary modernist period.

It was during the decade between 1920 and 1930 that Brazilian literary consciousness reached its maturity. At that point Brazilians lost their feeling of cultural exile, and one can mark that time of "the birth of Brazil and the consequent diminishment of Europe among us," [20] as Gilberto Amado so rightly says, adding in 1926:

. . . Brazil increased its power of assimilation. Europe for us today is a trip, study, or recreation, the pleasure of the climate, the artistic enchantment, the variety of active days far from daily obligations, intellectual attraction, simple curiosity. It does not live inside us, however. Basically, it does not interest us except as a theater, a spectacle, a book. Those of us in this generation having broken with it completely. . . . European matters do not impress us except as events and her men as figures in the human drama. There have not been established between them and us any of the deep ties that join us here to all matters and all men in our own milieu. The work of social culture, the consequence of the formation within the country of a unanimous life is reflected in the depths of our souls, which it fills completely with its sound, leaving no room for other echoes. What is certain is that these new generations are free of the nightmare that afflicted Nabuco, and there is no other cause to which to attribute this fact than the Republic, to its capacity to create a Brazil within Brazil.

This grasping of an awareness of Brazil by Brazilians, corresponding to a return from intellectual exile, was nonetheless a slow-moving progress, the consequence of romanticism. During that period, when cultural ties to the mother country were still strong, we had already gained an awareness of our new physical and social mold, and the notion that literature could be produced with new forms, could express new aspects of sensibility and a new experience. It was the moment in which the old colonial psyche yielded to spiritual forces that were taking shape in the soul of the people, producing a new literary mentality. At this juncture, waves of energy gave impetus to the movements that brought on an extraordinary intellectual richness for Brazil then and now.

The "shock of recognition" in this change can be found in the polemic that grew up around the *Confederação dos Tamoios* (1856), in which José de Alencar, Araújo Pôrto Alegre, Monte Alverne, Alexandre Herculano, Castilho, Pinheiro Guimarães, and Dom Pedro II himself all participated. It is the moment in which literary awareness took shape, in which literary problems were faced in a technical way, in which the feeling arose that literature was being formed in a new shape.

It was Alencar who saw this transformation and the post of patriarch of Brazilian literature must therefore be reserved for him. A study of his letters concerning the *Confederação dos Tamoios* (1856) and his literary autobiography, *Como e Porque Sou Romancista* (1873), as well as his polemic with José Feliciano de Castilho (1872), will verify his ideas of literary problems, how he studied them in depth in classic and modern works, through treatises on poetics and rhetoric, and in the great representative works of different genres, reporting in his argument the proofs offered by the great writers. Alencar was well aware of the problem of creating a "Brazilian" realization in literature; it was the absorbing preoccupation of men of letters of the time, according to that "instinct of nationality" which characterized the period, as Machado de Assis was to point out later (1873).

In Alencar the two lines that were to give substance to our literary awareness converge: the technical line, the formation and evolution of genres and forms; and the "Brazilian" line, the process of differentiation of literature in Brazil. Alencar followed the first line with that shapeless and characterless genre that is romantic fiction, only occasion-

ally showing a more accomplished result. It was he who elevated that
genre to a high degree of development, not only in its structural but
also in the thematic aspect. He offered solutions that paved the way
for Machado de Assis, who received, in a manner of speaking, a tradition that was already outlined and alive and which he had only to
develop.

On the other hand, it must be noted, Alencar continued in an error
that had arisen from the overlap and fusion of cultures. The problem
has found various solutions, such as the polylinguism of the Jesuits.
He continued the error of confusing the elements of the cultures in
contact with the result that themes from one would be imposed upon
the other, or that local backdrops would be used for heroes who
spoke and felt like Europeans. Authors desired to "create a more
independent literature," as Machado de Assis points out in his essay
Instituto de Nacionalidade, and there was the tendency in the literature
of the period to "dress itself in the colors of the country." Machado
rightly considered erroneous the opinion that would "only recognize
national spirit in works that dealt with local matters," and even though
he admitted that "a nascent literature should feed itself principally
upon matters offered by its region," he concluded that "what should
be demanded of the writer before anything else is a certain intimate
feeling that will make him a man of his time and his country, even
when he deals with matters that are remote in time and space."

This was the proper doctrine. Alencar's position, however, made
possible the clearer vision of the problem for those who took their inspiration from him, like Machado de Assis. Facing the attempt at
exaltation of the land, following the old tradition that had begun with
Pero Vaz de Caminha's *Carta* and had shown up again in Gonçalves
de Magalhães's national epic poem, Alencar reacted by pointing out
the artificiality with which Magalhães had formulated the problem of
nationality in literature. Provoked by romanticism, the question was
very much alive in those times in the minds of men of letters. Where
could literature find nationality? Where could it find its national
qualities? Where were the new elements in a literature that had been
built upon the transplant of an old literature?

The problem of literary nationality, in the romantic atmosphere,
was presented in essentially political terms. Our literary historians

studied literary autonomy according to that orientation, with Sílvio Romero having established the capacity for national expression as a valuable criterion of literary excellence. With literature and politics mixed together in romanticism, political autonomy was transferred to literature, and political and literary issues became confused. Literature was used by political campaigns favoring national independence and the abolition of slavery, or as a means of arousing martial spirit (for the Paraguayan War, the Canudos campaign), and as republican propaganda. The most widespread types of intellectual activity were oratory, journalism, political essays, and polemics. The typical literary man of the period was a fighter, one who combined letters and politics or public activity. Literature exercised, in that way, a civic function as a force for nationalistic expression.

It is easy to see, therefore, how difficult it was to face the problems of literature, beginning with that of its autonomy, according to a strictly literary perspective. There was no attempt to show that literature and politics constitute forms of life endowed each with its own development, and that the autonomy of one does not necessarily imply that of the other. This has, in fact, occurred in Brazil, where politics tended to reach maturity before literature, a process still going on today.

In reality, the question of the autonomy of colonial literatures should not be described in political terms. It should not have any political content or meaning, or be identified with political independence. They may be parallel, but one phenomenon does not depend upon the other, both coming to fruition out of the consolidation of the awareness of the people as a people. Nationality becomes objective in the same way, whether in the shape of politics, whether in language, in poetry, or in popular tradition and other forms of life. It was the nineteenth century that stamped on nationalism, on the idea of nation and nationality, a political sense and a sense of statehood. Nationalization thereafter became the process of the integration of masses of people into a common political form, into a centralized form of government over a unified territory, to which there are also corresponding literary, folkloric, and linguistic manifestations. This is the origin of modern emphasis on the nation-state that has become an absolute, the source of the whole life of a community and its art and literature. The aim of national life was to attain the supreme form of organized activity, the sovereign state, to which aim should be sub-ordinated all mental and sentimental activities of individual and social life, all moved by a common conscience.

Such a doctrine inspired Brazilian critics and historians to interpret the autonomy of our literature as defined in conformity with political autonomy. Such an interpretation was also the result of an urge to give greater expression to the national conscience.

Literary autonomy however escapes an explanation in political terms. Its nature is, rather, esthetic. It is the march or the conquest of national expression. As defined by Pedro Henríquez Ureña it is the current of efforts "in search of our expression," [21] and

within that vital continuum that does not admit parcels or fractions, it is possible to point out periods, attitudes, moments that succeed and pene-trate one another, through which a consciousness is formed or, if one pre-fers, a vision of that peculiar world . . . that is expressed with gradual fulfillment in our literature.[22]

José Antonio Portuondo thus describes the phenomenon of Spanish American literatures in a way quite applicable to Brazilian literature.

This esthetic character, this search for literary self-expression, this development of the self-awareness of the Brazilian literary genius will each have to be followed in their literary elements and forms whose evolution bears witness to that path. For example, the evolution of fiction from its romantic beginnings to Machado de Assis shows it to be a genre in search of expression and, with it grows a literary aware-ness that will take possession of it and its technical resources.

The same can be seen in lyric poetry. If we trace its evolution from Arcadism, passing through Gonçalves Dias to Castro Alves, we can see how in the author of the *Espumas Flutuantes* it attained the full status of an esthetic, formal, stylistic, and thematic physiognomy that is purely Brazilian. This definition that, within romanticism, only Alves reached (although he reached it completely and well) was described by Eça de Queiroz (in an episode reported by Afrânio Peixoto in his introduction to the collected works of Castro Alves (1921)). As he was listening to a reading of "Aves de Arribação," Eça interrupted at a certain point to exclaim: "There you have all the poetry of the tropics in just two lines." It was the formulation of a Brazilian esthetic in lyric poetry, of a Brazilian poetical language.

Therefore, establishing literary autonomy was discovering the moments in which forms and literary devices became literary forms and devices and lent themselves, at the same time, to the fixing of new aspects and a new esthetic perspective, or an esthetic vision of the new reality. These moments were given body by esthetic styles, the succession of which made up the increasing number of moments that were searching for literary self-expression. It was unimportant whether or not they were imported, because these forms had gone through a peculiar process of adaptation here.

The problem of literary autonomy is badly placed when it is subordinated to that of political independence. They are two different activities, of different make-up and with different content, meaning, and finality, and they cannot be identified. This occurs however with the division of Brazilian literary history along the lines of nationality into colonial period and national period, the latter being characterized by the "process of divergence from Portuguese literature" (Soares Amora).

In fact, the formation of national literary consciousness began long before the period of political independence. Literature took on a different physiognomy the instant a new man was formed in America. In a lecture in Buenos Aires in 1939, Ortega y Gasset[23] stated that the colonizer became a new man as soon as he became established in the New World, and that the change did not require centuries but was immediate, merely consolidated and reinforced with the passage of time. New experiences, a new life remolded him, adapting him to the different environment and creating a new type of society and economy, where native and foreign cultures were fused and mutually influential.

Placed in a new "situation," for whose formation a physical milieu and a peculiar social and economic organization would come together, man had to create a different spirit, new attitudes, desires, ideals, hopes, sensibility, and psychology, in short, a new conception of life and human relations, based on a new reality. Corresponding to the new situation there would be, of course, a vision different from that of the European, or from that of the colonist when he was still living in Europe. The impact of the new milieu made a new man of him, and the transformation was so complete that it lasted three centuries. From a new man, a half-breed in race and culture, of necessity there would arise a new literature, just as a new way of speaking the language of the mother country, a different "speech," would arise. The differentiation of "speech" is worthy of mention because there is a close relationship between the way Portuguese is spoken in Brazil and the literature that emerged here.

The attempt by Alencar at nationalization of the language side by side with the nationalization of literature through Indianism, was consolidated by Castro Alves with the formation of a Brazilian style in poetry. It was followed by the polemic between Rui Barbosa and Carneiro Ribeiro over the language of the Civil Code (1902). There was a retreat into Portuguese canons which increased the gap between the spoken language and the literary one, and a reaction in favor of the artificial restoration of peninsular modes of expression, both traditional and classical. The deep currents of "nationalism," however, were operating in the collective unconscious, and from them came the outbreak of ruralism and regionalism. These reemerged in a noisy way in the back-country style of Euclides da Cunha and, in certain aspects, in Coelho Neto, just as they would later in Monteiro Lobato (1918). Obviously impressed, most likely, perhaps, after the appearance of Araripe Júnior's masterful study *Dois Grandes Estilos* (1907), Rui Barbosa took a different tack in his esthetic-stylistic concepts. He incorporated into his prose in late years certain Brazilian touches, as can be seen in his speeches during the presidential campaign of 1919, where his allusion to Lobato's Jeca Tatu, for example, was evidence that his imagination was being attracted towards local motifs. Modernism was to consolidate this evolution as it struggled to reduce the distance between the written and the spoken language, and integrated the latter into the former.

A literature, therefore, will always arise where there is a people who live and feel. It is a function of their peculiar spirit.

In fact, although at times many writers have insisted on considering themselves Portuguese, there is no way to disguise the "newness" of what was being produced in Brazil from the very beginning, when the imagination of the new man began to construct his images in terms of his new reality.

Therefore, the four centuries of literature in Brazil accompany the march of the Brazilian spirit in its mutations and its struggle for self-expression. Literature lives this struggle. The process of differentiation did not result from a conscious attitude or one of compulsion, but simply from the acceptance of the new life. There has been a constant presence down to our own times of foreign nutrients, especially Portuguese and French, that dynamized our creative energy, putting its mark on all literary movements and bearing witness to our intellectual immaturity. However there has also existed since early times a rugged and harsh Americanism or Brazilianness, a genuine nativist quality, that appears in the literature, conditioning the form and the material, the structure, the themes and the selection of material. It is much like that "intimate feeling" to which Machado de Assis referred and which indicated the advent of a new man.

In short, the autonomy of Brazilian literature, defined as a corollary of the political independence of 1922, is a problem that is falsely located. What can be described is the development of literary forms in search of a Brazilian expression as differentiated from a tradition of genres.

Instead of searching literature for the reflections of political autonomy and the formation of a national consciousness, criticism and literary history should investigate the autonomy of the forms, following their evolution in order to verify the moment in which fiction, poetry, drama, and essay obtained a typically Brazilian cast in their structure and themes, something peculiar and distinctive that could be considered a new contribution to the genre, a new tradition.

Yet, simply recognizing that native quality does not imply a value judgment. There is no motive of boasting in this, nor any praise of nationalistic spirit, by which national superiority would be seen in the possession of these autonomous expressions of culture. It is simply the registration of a fact observed in our literary past. Furthermore, this native character did not always find superior esthetic expression. The poverty of our literary history led Tristão de Ataíde to state that "Brazilian literature exists, but it is not alive," and José Veríssimo to define it as composed of dead books and insignificant names.

The description of the development of this native quality, of these literary waves in search of self-expression, this self-awareness of the Brazilian literary genius, does not show the full maturity and autonomy of the literature, a fact that is far from realization. The struggle is still going on in our times. We are still not free of certain complexes and embarrassments of adolescent immaturity which upset and disorient creative impulses. There can be noted a singular impotence in our creative spirit that does not fully realize itself, does not ripen. From that lack of depth in our literature, from the feeling of failure, frustration, and incompleteness there emerges a literature of adolescents, as José Veríssimo so well observed, a literature "made for young people, usually secondary school pupils and preparatory students, with no knowledge of books and even less of life."

There is no literary life that is organized on a professional basis and which could offer the writer social and economic independence, as there are no active professional societies (which, when they do exist, become perverted into political organizations instead of looking after professional and technical interests). The exercise of literature is done under parasitic or ancillary circumstances. The absence of university education and the resultant self-instruction, and also the lack of professional organization in the exercise of intellectual activities (that is, the lack of a literary "clergy"), makes the exercise of letters among us still a side-line. Intellectual production, therefore, will never go beyond the episodic and, consequently, superficial and deficient, or the sporadic. It will be dependent upon personal circumstances of genius and wealth. One might even say that it often shows a kind of heroism; Euclides da Cunha, for example, worked on his books during his free time from the tiring field work and nomadic life of an engineer. What time did he have to spare for proper research and exact documentation? This is a natural consequence of the lack of organization of the intellectual profession.

Improvement will never be possible so long as the intellectual is dependent upon professions foreign to his calling that rob him of his time and energy. When an intellectual's living off his work is mentioned, one thinks habitually that this means his drawing subsistence from his writings. But such a state of affairs is true for only a small number of people anywhere. What is desirable is that intellectual work, the product of the spirit, find a guaranteed and organized market, and that the intellectual fulfill functions that fit his nature. In countries where the profession is remunerative, intellectuals fulfill their calling in universities, publishing houses, magazines and newspapers, all congenial environments for their work. Brazilian literary people are scattered among heterogeneous activities or are prisoners of public administration, where everything conspires against the spirit.

We in literature will always be a pack of part-timers and dilettantes. Literary life is therefore a luxury, and an excrescence.

These conditions are totally inadequate for pure literary activity. Men of letters either condemn themselves to financial defeat or let themselves be attracted by other activities—political journalism, law, medicine, bureaucracy, non-specialized teaching, active politics, and so forth. As a rule, however, they are professionals in those activities and cultivate letters in their rare moments of leisure, with no specialization, no appropriate terminology, no literary spirit. They often find in literature a ticket for their admission into politics, administration, or society, and are held to literature only by sentimental ties, never by reason of constant faithfulness of study and production. Without leaders, without guides, without masters, without critics, without study, without technical formation, what literary production can they bring forth that will not be a bastard fiction in which gold and dross are mixed, or a poetry languishing in imitation, or journalistic criticism? It is clear that there are many exceptions, some isolated talents, some conscious artesans and original artists. A literature as such however is built up not by adolescents but by mature people. It is not the sum of isolated and exceptional cases. It is the result of a linked and continuous effort, of careers maintained against all hazards and with all sacrifices, in the stubborn day by day conquest of instrument and forms, of patterns and normative traditions, certain in the awareness that, as José Veríssimo has stressed elsewhere, "if the lack of a systematic education were required as a motive for spontaneity and originality, few literatures could show those qualities better than ours."

It will not be done by reserving for literature those who are not any good for anything else; it will not be done by tolerating marginalism and social alienation of the man of letters who can only fulfill his role when completely adjusted; it will not be done by limiting its exercise to the well-off, under the pretext that it brings no material rewards; it will not be done by cloaking the man of letters only in the sympathetic tolerance shown actors, soccer players, and singers. Such circumstances cannot create literature. A specific function in the community is reserved for literature, that of creating beauty as the supreme form of entertainment for the spirit.

In this way, literature that is superficial, imitative, and discontinuous will erroneously seem to raise the problem of its characterization. It lacks the elements for the development of distinctive traces and defining characteristics, and it has not yet possessed a personality with an unmistakable physiognomy.

Nevertheless, it becomes possible to mention certain distinctive characteristics of social reality that are reflected in the life and exercise of literature and even in literary forms (novel, short story, drama, poetry, essay) whether by communicating a particular theme to them, whether by forcing them into accommodations. If it does not seem possible to speak about a distinctive overall make-up, from which the constitution of a literary personality could be derived, there are, however, certain marked tendencies that in the future may imprint the defining traits on our literary physiognomy, if by chance we accept the thesis of the existence of a collective and permanent character of a community or literature.

At the beginning, it will be necessary to consider two possible ways of characterization: general or national, and regional. The latter has already been adopted among us by Viana Moog in his essay *Uma Interpretação da Literatura Brasileira* (1943), an attempt to define Brazilian literature in the light of the regional criterion. To the questions: What does Brazilian literature consist of? What are its fundamental characteristics? What are its tendencies? Will it have stable and permanent values capable of surviving the transformations through which the world is passing? Will it constitute a homogeneous unity susceptible to definition, or is it still in the confused, vague, and complex phase of indetermination? These are the questions to which Moog cannot give a categorical and definitive answer. "Even with a most rigorous approach, it is impossible to gather from the body of Brazilian literature any large truth, any large synthesis adjustable to the rigors of a definition." Starting with the premise that "we are not in the presence of a homogeneous and defined unity, as European literatures are," he concludes that "it is necessary to renounce the idea of taking it in as a whole in one general sweep," and he leans towards a regional characterization, with an "analysis of the cultural nuclei whose sum is the heterogeneous complex of so-called Brazilian literature." [24]

The ideas of Viana Moog for the sociological interpretation of Brazilian cultural reality coincide with those that Gilberto Freyre has expressed in various studies since 1926, in which the emphasis is placed on the study of regional bases of culture.[25]

Others, quite the contrary, try to describe the qualities of literature as an interpretation of the national character. The thesis of Paulo Prado in his essay on Brazilian sadness, *Retrato do Brasil* (1931) ("a sad race, the product of the fusion of three sad races") has been used in interpretations of Brazilian literature as impregnated with melancholy and sadness, whether dressed in lyrical clothing, or incorporated into the pessimistic and tragic vision of regionalist fiction.

The study by Sérgio Buarque de Holanda, *Raízes do Brasil* (1936), offers broad and clarifying ideas concerning the Brazilian character, in accord with the principle of giving it a unitarian interpretation. His analysis of the "cordial Brazilian," characterized by "an extremely rich and overflowing emotional base," probably reflects a singular trait of our temperament, whose reflection should be noted in literature. In any case, this branch of the study of social psychology, which is the investigation of the character of a people, could shed light on the understanding of certain thematic components and certain tendencies in our literary psyche.

Without pretensions of a definitive work, nor with complete confidence in the enduring qualities of the defining traits, it is admissible to suggest some characteristics in the evolution of our literature and our literary activity.

The predominance of lyricism. This is a trait inherited from Portuguese literature. There as here, lyricism "absorbs the attentions of those who have felt literary inclinations," and is dependent "on the same feeling of love, the same personal confession, the same spread of melancholy, of nostalgia, of the contradictory pain of loving and hating life." In lyricism, as Fidelino de Figueiredo who studied it as a characteristic of Portuguese literature points out, not only is the poetic genre understood, but also is found "a determined way of personal being, subjectivism, the preferential curiosity of looking into and exposing moral life itself, the pleasure of making the whole soul patent, of affirming the individuality itself at its most basic level." [26] This lyricism, while it expresses itself in one genre, impregnates all others, novel, theater, oratory, and essay.

If some of the highest moments in our literature are due to lyricism, from it at the same time come certain fundamental vices or defects in our production and in our work habits. It would not be far from the mark to blame the propensity for lyricism for the superficiality, the versatility, the sentimentality, and for the scarcity of substantive values in our literature; for verbalism, for the excessive coloristic tendency; for the absence of doctrinaire content and critical and philosophical spirit. (This last characteristic Figueiredo found also in Portuguese literature.) Lyricism is also responsible for subjectivism and the opinionated spirit, and for the lack of a notion of value that dominates our literary criticism. Only with difficulty can criticism be oriented by objective analysis, by judgment based on concrete patterns, by a criteriology, an epistemology, a philosophy of values, a method, a philosophical and analytical instrumentology, a rigorous terminology.

The exaltation of nature. It is the most common means of expression for lyricism. It originated in the period of colonization, when the myth of El Dorado began, and with romanticism especially. There grew up a line of boasting (*ufanismo*) in prose and verse, in which the land and nature appear as divine in the most diverse forms. Related to this is the tendency towards the exaltation of local life and man, which explains the movements of Indianism, ruralism, rusticism, forms of *ufanismo* in relation to the country, that have marked the evolution of our literature in waves of enthusiasm that alternate at times with counter-waves of pessimism and defeatism.

The absence of tradition. The struggle between imported tradition and a possible new tradition, which was the basis of the drama of our intellectual evolution, did not permit the attainment of a tradition that could be a "useful past" for the inspiration of writers. Each writer, each generation has felt itself obliged to begin from the beginning in a disastrous negation of that principle of harmony in artistic production, the balance between tradition and individual talent to which T. S. Eliot has referred. That rejection of continuity renders us not only incapable of receiving old conventions, but also scarcely able to create new ones. Brazilian literature lives in a dilemma between an antitraditional element that is struggling to take shape, to open a path, and to consolidate itself, and a reactionary element that defends a dead past, a past that has no meaning for us. Owing to that negation of continuity, however, there is a periodic disintegration of the tendencies towards the creation of traditions. The disintegration is offered no resistance and degenerates into frustrated movements. Instead of the balanced pendulum of the law of permanence and change, what has been proven among us is a cannibalism of generations: each new generation, marked by a skepticism and iconoclasm, instead of trying to shape itself, has but one aim, the destruction of the one that went before, in accord with the myth of the sovereignty of the current generation. There is a corresponding ecstasy of artistic realization and of critical acuteness, something actually possible only in a climate of continuity.

As a matter of fact, Portuguese literature has been prejudged as a tradition in relation to the Brazilian. The former has not been distinguished by any high esthetic model, attained in only a few cases; in its best phase, it is dominated by a moral and didcatic preoccupation. To this must be added the circumstance of its having been philological fodder, scrutinized by grammarians and philologists of the standard school in search of "examples" of "good writing." Reading Portuguese authors becomes impractical without this thought in mind and the thought impedes appreciation of its possible literary qualities. More is needed than grammars and dictionaries to make a literature.

The alienation of the writer. Divorced from a tradition, the man of letters feels himself separated from his predecessors whom he in any case ignores, from the society that does not recognize him, and from his peers to whom he pays no attention. He is an exile in his own land. An indelible mark on our intellectual life is the complete lack of attention of the writer for other writers, past or present. What results is a marginalism, isolation, and a soon-to-be-forgotten aspect, as if all had been built on sand. The resulting impression is that literary works are made from froth and disappear with time.

Divorce from the people. What is dramatic about this isolation is that it contains an error. In spite of the disdain among writers for one another literature is produced for themselves. It is a polished literature, made by one class for the pleasure of that same class, keeping in mind the enormous abyss that separates elite and people in Brazil, an elite that is both cultivated and the master of life's circumstances and the people, a distant, illiterate, and disinherited mass. The people were never touched by literature which was destined for a small public, a class. There are signs of change however with the access of the masses to political, economic, and social power and to the possession of cul-

ture. The risk endures because no one is allowed to state that the
change will not be accomplished to the detriment of esthetic values,
with a leveling off of esthetic patterns as they adapt themselves to the
masses. The conflict between "highbrow" and "lowbrow" tendencies
could be resolved in favor of the lower one. The divorce from the
public has resulted in a literature that has not served the public.

The absence of a technical conscience. Artistic and intellectual life
has grown in spite of education and divorced from the educational
system for better or for worse. Intellectual life went its own way and
self-education has been the rule. There was never any specialized education in letters that would furnish technical information. Literary
education is a mockery that has held a place subordinate to the teaching of language and has not been freed from history or biography. It
is a teaching lacking in esthetic sense, incapable of inspiring a truly
comprehensive sense of the literary phenomenon as such and not as a
linguistic, historical, or biographical document. This absence of real
literary education means an absence of technical awareness, with
creativity rarely attaining that degree of perfection that comes from
the merger of artistic vocation with the skill of an artesan.

The cult of improvisation. A people of romantic sensibility intensified by romanticism, the Brazilians believe in the miraculous force of
improvisation, the cause and effect of the lack of a technical consciousness. Their faith in spontaneity, in natural art, in inspiration from
the soil, makes them despise study and technical formation. There is
an overweening pride or godliness and a gauging of values with little
or no study. The virginity of the soul and the writer's lack of culture
are reflected in the facile abandon and in the rapidity and abundance
of production, in the lack of care and of interest for perfection, in the
artistic untidiness and lack of fulfillment, which, with rare exceptions,
make up the norm and the characteristics of our literary production.
To this cult of improvisation is also owed the subjectivist and per-
sonalist tendency in criticism which is not based on a criterion of
evaluation or is inspired in a table of values for its judgments. There is
no criticism based on a code of norms and values, on stable terminology, on stable epistemology and criteriology. It must be noted that
this cult of improvisation is a consequence of that "spirit of adventure" pointed out by Sérgio Buarque de Holanda, which, as opposed

to the "spirit of work," is characteristic of the conditions of our life and the heritage of colonization.

Literature & politics. They are mixed together, and it is difficult for us to conceive of a pure man of letters who is not at the same time, a fighter, a "thinker," a guide of public opinion, and it is an almost absurd effort to try to understand literature without the ties that bind it to politics and turn it into an instrument of propaganda and civic action. This was the situation especially in the nineteenth century—independence, abolition, wars, republic—and it has continued to be the case in our century without any liberation of literature from politics. What is worse is that such a situation has repercussions even in literary and critical theories, as we have seen in the concept of literature, literary history, and periodization. Art is not understood in its specific function, but as a means of action, as pragmatic art. The pure man of letters is a rare specimen. The profession of letters is not a scholarly profession, it has not yet found an organization. It is the prisoner of the liberal professions and administrative and bureaucratic careers. By making themselves social or political leaders, writers have not become intellectual and literary leaders. Their absence gives rise to a dissipation of young intellectuals, who are lost, or who deviate or die out from a lack of guides and masters within literature itself.

Imitation & originality. In a transplanted literature, the dilemma of imitation and originality polarizes the awareness of writers. On one side, a symptom of immaturity, the deliberate search for originality in an effort to find a tone of Americanism; on the other, the tendency towards imitation of and submission to the European tradition. In spite of the search for a native tradition, the provincial and colonial sensibility that dreams of civilized Europe, exalts it, and sees it as the permanent resort of culture, still has not been lost. It is the feeling of expatriatism referred to above that is still alive in cultural life.

Mother country & province. Brazilian life can be compared to a scale in which the two balances are the mother country and the provinces, tipping now one way, now the other, with the first acting as a factor of imbalance and sterility, the second as a means of enrichment and "rebarbarization" or revival as the roots sink into the springs nearest the people. Regionalism, therefore, is a constant in our literature, with movements of literary renovation always coming from the peripheral layers. The diverse focal points of culture and civilization also have an esthetic personality, and Brazilian regionalism is a search for representative symbols of the national experience.

Contemplating the history of Brazilian literature, we have not fled into any pessimistic impression. It *is* a poor literature. We have not yet come into full possession of a literature, obviously, because we have not yet succeeded in completely constructing or consolidating the formation of the country, and without that a vigorous and original literature cannot come to fullness. Whatever period is placed under observation, there will always be something lacking in it, a certain density, a certain gauge, a certain richness that would give it personality. Furthermore, the Brazilian intellectual has a removed mental state that places him out of harmony with the period and lends a distant cast to the literature produced by him. It is still impossible to speak of the personality of Brazilian literature.

The answer to these problems must lie in the mystery of creative sources. But literature is neither a mystery nor a miracle: it is a means for the communication of a vision or experience of reality, or, in the worlds of the poet, something that can *Donner un sens plus pur aux mots de la tribu.* (Mallarmé)

FOREIGN INFLUENCES

A theme that must be considered for any philosophy of Brazilian literary history is that of foreign influences. "We have listened too long to the courtly muse of Europe," Emerson said in his declaration of American literary independence, "The American Scholar." What can we Brazilians say, we whose literature "has not had a movement of its own in its evolution," has never reached beyond "a chronological juxtaposition of imitations," to borrow what Fidelino de Figueiredo has said concerning Portuguese literature?

The product of the great migratory movement of men, ideas, and institutions that took place beginning in the sixteenth century, Brazilian civilization, like the others that had emerged elsewhere in America, had developed new forms of life, new social institutions, attitudes, behavior, and ways of thinking that resulted in the deep modification of the patterns of human existence relating to Europe. It is difficult to judge however which was the heavier weight, the new element or the inherited one. The intercourse of ideas and feelings produced here by European culture is a constant of our spiritual life, and it places in relief the importance of the foreign element as a seed for cultural fertilization. In fact, foreign influence has affected Brazilian life in all of its phases, acting through various channels: through the colonist and later through the immigrant, through the importation of ideas, through imitation. A neglected chapter in the intellectual history of Brazil is that of the importance of foreign influences and debts. It would be a Herculean task to analyse and investigate, and track these ideas down to their sources.

Starting with an original stock of notions that had been transplanted with the first impulses of colonization, Brazilian cultural life went its way in relation to European culture, sometimes repeating its forms, sometimes reinterpreting them and adapting them to individual and social native conditions, sometimes trying to turn its back on them in its anxiety to create a peculiarly Brazilian tradition. But the persistence and the strength of European intellectual influences, the habit of looking to Europe in search of inspiration and guidance became the fulcrum of Brazilian mental life, which was marked by an extraordinary capacity for the assimilation of foreign values. The very idea of Europe was the center of our concentric waves of culture.

Brazilian literary evolution never went beyond a reflex of European movements. Tristão de Ataíde has called this phenomenon the "law of repercussion," which describes a country materially and spiritually dependent, on which the cultural waves of Europe break with a certain regularity. The most eastern of American countries, with stronger bonds to Europe than to the American continent itself, European events echoed here before they did on the rest of the continent and were closer to us than the original things that have come out of that American soil. This makes a cultural life with universal meaning, or one intensely attracted towards universality.

José Veríssimo has pointed out the existence of a lapse of about twenty years between European movements and their repercussions here. With the progress of the country and the shortening of world distances, thanks to modern means of communication, there is a tend-

ency for that lapse to lessen. Tristão de Ataíde has already pointed this
out with respect to Brazilian modernism, which grew up at practically
the same time as its European sources.

In this way, literature in Brazil has always shown itself sensitive to
foreign influences. This is a chapter that currently shows great challenge to Brazilian literary scholars. It should not be said that all has not
been prepared. Here and there, the comparativists have produced evidence or suggested tracks. This matter of foreign influence, however,
has been far from totally treated, and much is yet to be done to
deepen its study by bringing into discussion the analyses, without
which any attempt at synthesis and generalization would be foolhardy.

It is not sufficient to prove this influence, a more than obvious fact.
Important are surveys of sources and influences, with incontrovertible
data and proofs in the light of the modern comparativist technique. It
is a difficult and complex task, but without further effort it is not
permitted to formulate any conclusion except in very general terms.

The first great influx to consider is, of course, the Portuguese. During the first centuries, it was more than influence; the two literatures
were juxtaposed. It was the literature of Portugal that incubated the
nascent Brazilian literary spirit. It served as a vehicle for the inheritance
of European, Western, and Christian ideas that laid the foundations of
our consciousness. It gave us classical values, literary techniques, and
artistic models that could be adapted to the new environment, yielding
to the birth of something endowed with a Brazilian sense. In relation
to this foundation the first antagonism developed, an urge to give a
local stamp to the European heritage.

Portuguese literature brought to Brazil the medieval and Renaissance
heritage, principally the former since Brazil did not really have a
Renaissance.[27] From the Middle Ages came our old poetic yardstick,
in the form of popular lyrics and courtly versions of troubador ballads, traditional dramatic forms that had grown up in the plays of Gil
Vicente and the Brazilian Jesuit theater. The importance of the
medieval legacy is broad, because sixteenth-century Brazil, through
the voice of Anchieta and his colleagues, is a continuation of the Middle Ages. There was little contact with the Renaissance that could
justify any attitude except indifference and reaction, although the
literature that grew up with this nascent Brazil would not remain completely untouched by Renaissance influence. Europe was being shaken

at the very foundations of its civilization and culture, and this could not fail to have repercussions in Brazil.

Actually, the Brazilian mentality grew up under the spirit of the European through the impact of the discoveries and his contact with new lands. This had caused a real ideological revolution for the European, on the level of the technico-formal revolution brought on by the diffusion of the new metrical yardsticks of Italian origin. The new art did not attain anything but a tardy infiltration unless perhaps that "stumbling and underdeveloped pastiche" (Sérgio Buarque de Holanda) which is the *Prosopopéia* of Bento Teixeira. The ideological revolution would be translated from its beginnings into successive waves of enchantment with the new land, which gave birth to the boastful lyricism of exaltation of local things and countryside. This was one of the lines of Brazilian lyricism and, more than that, of Brazilian literature itself, to which we owe, without doubt, our currents of Indianism, ruralism, and even regionalism. In fact, all this movement must be interpreted as a broad and uninterrupted attempt at the creation of a local tradition, by means of the search for regional types, themes, and motivations for prose and and poetry. In regionalist fiction, this effort to absorb local color gave Brazilian prose one of its most characteristic aspects.

Still, one must link to Renaissance atmosphere, the cycle of the literature of expansion, this family of the first poets and prose writers, to whom we owe the *"diálogos das grandezas,"* the accounts of travelers, the tales of shipwrecked sailors, the description of the land and its inhabitants, the chronicles of missionaries and soldiers. In the same way, it is to this type of literature of expansion, riding the impulse of the Renaissance, that there is also joined the more recent forms of Indianism, ruralism, and regionalism.

As for the other part of this Renaissance revolution, the technico-formal part, there was only a slow penetration and introduction of new criteria and, perhaps, the first example of that law of repercussion. The *ottava rima* or decasyllable, and the sonnet had varying fates in Brazil: the former never willingly became acclimated, and imitators of Camões did not manage until the eighteenth century to elevate it beyond mediocre pastiches. The sonnet in Brazil, beginning with Gregório de Matos in the seventeenth century and passing through Cláudio Manuel da Costa in the eighteenth (a high expression of delayed Renaissance influence), had to wait until Parnassianism for a favorable environment.

Therefore, if Brazil, as Sérgio Buarque de Holanda rightfully points out, did not have a Renaissance, having passed directly from the Middle Ages into the baroque, it is certain that Renaissance elements had penetrated its literature. On another side, in spite of the weak Renaissance resonance, Greco-Roman culture, due to the humanistic education supplied by the Jesuits, had been an active factor in the first three centuries, when the concept of imitation was the main esthetic norm that governed literary creation.[28] The classical languages, particularly Latin, enjoyed a prestige until the eighteenth century that was never challenged as an instrument of culture and a source of education. From the exaggerations of this cult there grew the vast senate of clerics and lettered men, scholars and chroniclers, artificial poets of cloister and salon, drenched in Latin and mythology. One cannot, however, dismiss the merit as a stimulant and a discipline that classical education had, even during the nineteenth century. It was even then not rare for men of culture to dominate the ancient languages in the original, and the beneficial effects could be felt.

In short, the first great influence exercised on the nascent literature of Brazil was that of the Portuguese, whose great authors, Camões, Gil Vicente, Sá de Miranda, the chroniclers, the poets of the *cancioneiros*, and the prose writers of the seventeenth century, just as the romantic poets and the realists later on, constituted a constant presence in our psyche, interrupted only when we enter the twentieth century. Together with them the ancient classics, particularly the Romans, Virgil, Horace, Cicero, Ovid, and Seneca, form a most important source of inspiration. This scheme was only modified with the advent of French influence, beginning with the end of the eighteenth century.

The baroque period opened up a new and important source of influence, the Spanish, marked especially by Quevedo and Góngora. To this source, furthermore, we owe another rather significant influence, that of the picaresque novel, which is suggested in certain prerealistic forms of the nineteenth-century Brazilian novel.

In the eighteenth century, Italian influence is obvious; neo-classical and Arcadian rococo goes to the Italy of Metastasio in search of its esthetic norms and models of literary life. Dante and Petrarch, however, are influences beyond schools, and among the moderns one must point out this or that isolated figure, for example Leopardi.

The periods of the Enlightenment and romanticism had a greater role than that of the Renaissance, as they enthroned the massive French influence that marks the whole nineteenth century and the twentieth. Romanticism, realism-naturalism, Parnassianism, symbolism, and other currents of the present century were felt, not just in contemporary writers, but also in previous periods in the moralists and other classics. In addition to these influences of a literary character, one must not forget currents of thought originating in France that for all time exercised a decisive role in our mentality, such as the positivist-naturalist complex, even though they were associated with certain Germanic philosophical currents.

As for the English, except for Shakespeare, the romantic poets, and the realists in the novel, their contribution has not been ponderable, dispersed here and there among isolated writers. Even less can be said of other literatures—German, Russian, or Scandinavian, for example.

In any case, we have little concrete knowledge as concerns foreign influences in our literature, beyond conjecture of intuition or even casual approximations, which characterize the majority of particular affirmations. Something scientific has already been done in relation to isolated figures such as Gregório de Matos and Machado de Assis. The terrain, however, remains vacant, waiting for exploration by a comparatist methodology. Yet it is incontrovertible that from the results of these investigations, much will be gained for the understanding of our literature; such is the force with which the winds from the east blow upon our clime.

CONCEPT & PLAN OF THE WORK

This work of literary history, *A Literatura no Brasil*, follows a scheme of order and doctrinaire organization:

* * *

1. Its guiding principle is esthetic, the esthetic or poetic concept of literature.

Brazilian criticism has been dominated by the study of extrinsic or outside factors that condition the genesis of the literary phenomenon. Deeply and broadly influenced by nineteenth-century theories, especially those of Taine and Sainte-Beuve, it has allowed itself to be impregnated by the historical method in its examination of literature. To this orientation we owe the naturalist phase of 1870 to 1915. This was the most compact, the most voluminous phase, the one which contributed most and, therefore, the one that exercised the most influence (and still does) with people like Sílvio Romero, Araripe Júnior, Capistrano de Abreu, and a few dozen other critics who followed the same doctrine. We can see from this that criticism among us has always been, generally, an effort towards the analysis of the literary work from without, from its periphery, in its historical, social, and biographical mold, in its environment, in its external causes, in the outside elements that presumably differentiate it. The circumstances of the life of the author, his psychic states, the complex of the cultural life of the group in which he appeared, everything that made up the social, political, moral, historical atmosphere from which the work emerged, is what has made up the critical study according to the naturalist orientation. Even after the golden phase, this orientation has persisted in many of its fundamental postulates.

There have been reactions against the naturalist and historicist tendency in criticism in Brazil. Among the most serious was the one, inspired in the esthetic theories of symbolism, that Nestor Vítor (1868–1932) undertook. The work of this critic, notable in many aspects, has yet to receive its due consideration or a study adequate to its definitive evaluation. From within the same spiritual climate there came a small book that has not had the attention it deserves either: *Crítica Pura* (1938), by Henrique Abílio (1893–1932). To this type of reaction we also owe the criticism of Tristão de Ataíde (1893) that follows the lines mentioned here, and we must also mention Mário de Andrade (1893–1945), whose main preoccupation was with the intrinsic and esthetic elements of the literary work.

All in all, the great body of our criticism, even when freed from the postulates of the naturalist school, is one of historical and biographical origin. The literary work is seen as a social institution. In order to interpret it, it will be necessary to bring out the components of the social structure in which it has appeared. Critical study, therefore, would be reduced to a simple kind of social study and the work would be made out to be a simple document. In their turn, biographical critics see literature as the manifestation of a personality, and for them the ransacking of the biography of the artist is task enough to clarify the nature of the work, even in its most obscure aspects. With either of the two orientations, the literary work loses its central position in the critical process, with the truly literary value becoming secondary and criticism itself ceasing to be criticism as it becomes history or social enquiry.

A directed and conscious reaction against this state of affairs becomes necessary. This does not mean that one should abandon the other type of literary study. It would be neither possible nor desirable. What is essential is to put it in its proper place. Since in the study of literature all clarifying contributions must be taken into account, the usefulness of internal and external perspectives in literary study is relative. The reaction in our case, however, is imposed since there is an absolute monopoly of extrinsic and historical criticism. It is necessary to break the exclusivism in the understanding that other approaches to the literary phenomenon would be licit and useful.

And other approaches would be more legitimate. The historical method must take a secondary place in view of the very esthetic nature of the literary phenomenon. For an esthetic-literary fact, an esthetic-literary method is more adequate, one inspired in esthetic-literary theory. What is needed is simply a delimitation of fields of study, a specialization of methods, a specification of doctrines. What is rejected is the application in the literary field of methods from other disciplines. One must try to find an esthetic-literary method for the study of an esthetic-literary phenomenon. Ever since Aristotle, there has been a distinction between poetic truth and historical truth, that is, between fiction and history. Therefore, the method for the study of fiction must be distinct from that for studying history. Literary works are organic unities in which all constituent elements fulfill specific functions, as Manfred Kridl has affirmed, adding that the essential character of literary study is the description of the works in their constituent elements. This was what Van Tieghem meant when he stated that literary works "are not signs of anything but themselves, they are signs of themselves which in theory do not express anything but themselves."

This book, *A Literatura no Brasil,* represents one more reaction against sociology, naturalism, and positivism, against historicism in the name of esthetic values, in the name of intrinsic criticism, or esthetic-literary criticism, or poetic criticism. This was an ideal that was already held by Flaubert in the past century: in a letter to George Sand, he asked when criticism, after having been historical and philological, would become artistic. This reaction is also the repercussion or the expression among us of the international movement that characterizes such a sense.

By an esthetic or a poetic concept of literature, it is understood that:

2. Literature is an art, the art of the word, a product of the creative imagination, the specific means of which is the word, and the finality of which is the awakening in the reader or listener of an esthetic pleasure. It has therefore a value in itself and an objective, which it would seem is not that of communicating or serving as an instrument for other values—political, religious, moral, or philosophical. Endowed with a specific composition that is afforded by intrinsic elements, it has an autonomous development. Criticism is, above all, the analysis of these intrinsic components, of this esthetic substance, and is to study the work as an art and not as a social or cultural document, with a minimum of reference to the socio-historical environment.

3. Literary history (more *literary* than *history*) is the history of this art in its autonomous development, in its various forms. In other words, it is the study of literature in time. Understood by study is the use of all methods of analysis and critical interpretation of literary works, which means the recognition that criticism is the basis of the history of literature. In this way, the question of literary history is based on the fact that works are examined not as documents (of personalities, periods, social, geographical, or biological milieu), but as artistic monuments to be understood and evaluated and classified on their own terms. From this perspective, literary history will progress to become the science of literature (*Literaturwissenschaft*).

4. This concept does not imply a lack of knowledge of the relationships of the literary phenomenon, which does not exist in a vacuum. It recognizes the ties in time and space, and it tries to establish these connections, but it does not recognize in other forms of life any precedence that is causal or conditioning for the genesis of the artistic phenomenon, one that might make of it an epiphenomenon based on

social, economic, juridical, and political structures or those that grow out of them. It places the literary phenomenon on a plane of equality with other facts of life with which it has a relationship of reciprocal influence, explaining themselves mutually. This does away with the preoccupation with environmentalism, typical of nineteenth-century determinism, that demanded as an introduction to history long chapters about the physical milieu, race, and the social moment. The approach was according to Taine's formula, which was long a universal scientific dogma, but has been left behind completely by present-day social and biological sciences.

5. The external factors, the object of the genetic explanation of literature, are not conditioners of the characteristics and qualities of a literature. Literature is understood and is explained from within, in its own nature, according to its own laws, in the peculiar and intrinsic elements of its structuralization. Its history is seen through the evolution of these elements, of its types, of its forms, of its genres. The evolution is internal and not conditioned by extra-literary social or political influences. It has its immanent development, without recourse to any crutches, and does not turn to an explanation of historical-social manufacture.

In this way, problems such as the conditioning influences of milieu, race, and moment do not belong to literature. They belong legitimately to sociology, to history, to the social sciences in general. It is not for literary history to investigate the historico-social environment from which works emerge, much less to reduce itself to this investigation. This was the rule until quite recently, when it was thought possible to prepare the interpretation and even completely explain literature by the environmental conditions in which it was produced, by the influences of political, social, and economic factors. The mysterious act of creation flees from or is independent of external conditioning, which is incapable of dominating or guiding such forces. The nineteenth-century scientific abuse that reduced criticism to a mere verification of the production conditions of a work reflected the thinking of a race in a determined moment and in a physical and social milieu. The abuse begun from a lack of faith in literature, conditioned it to external factors, and made criticism and history the same thing. It did away with criticism in favor of history, and literary studies became

nothing more than historical studies of literature. Literature must receive, however, a legitimate critical perspective, an intention and a
technique that are esthetic first of all.

The historico-sociological mold, therefore, must play a secondary
role here, one in which it is put in the background, without any explaining or conditioning. It is only to articulate the literary phenomenon with other activities of the spirit. The dominant idea is
that of the equidistance and the parallelism of literature in relation to
the other arts.

6. By freeing literature from the historical, criticism does not abandon the historical method, which has its place everywhere that is
necessary, in the manipulation of all material that readies the terrain
for criticism. That is, it aids the establishment of the text, chronology,
biography, the study of sources and influences, the analysis of documents, bibliography, and so forth.

7. But chronology and biography do not constitute fundamental disciplines of literary history as it is put forth here. On the contrary, they
are secondary and subsidiary elements, chronology not even forming
the basis for periodization, biography furnishing only data useful to
the understanding of the work. As branches of history, their use in
the *literary* history of literature is relegated to clarification for criticism. Biography almost monopolized literary studies in Brazil completely, criticism included, to a point where it became a serious devia-
tion that was in need of correction.[29] Under the influence of Sainte-
Beuve, it absorbed critical interpretation itself, and it inverted the
natural order of literary studies: instead of approaching the work
through the author, as might be the legitimate objective of literary
biography, it went on to use the work as a bridge to reach the author,
who was romantically idealized in his individuality. Biographical hypertrophy reached the point of eliminating a reading of the works in
favor of gaining knowledge about the life of the author.

8. The primacy of the work is the basis of the norm of poetic
criticism defended and put forth in this book. Instead of authors, their
works will be the object of literary study. For this the diverse resources of critical analysis have been developed today, among which
the most widespread are the processes of exact analysis (the "close
reading") of the Anglo-Americans, the processes of formalist or structuralist criticism of the Slavs, the modern methods of stylology of the

Swiss, Germans, Italians, and Spaniards (*Stilforschung*), the processes of *explication de texte* of the French. We do not forget, however, techniques that have their origins in psychoanalysis, anthropology, symbolic logic, symbology, and mythology, either alone or in combination. This is how contemporary literary criticism will reach the most advanced stage of its evolution, rapidly heading towards the phase of the complete autonomy of the methods of analysis of the literary work, which is its ultimate aim. True criticism is intrinsic or ergocentric, in which the work is the center of interest, and of the work, the interior or intrinsic elements give it its specifically esthetic character. These methods of analysis start, furthermore, with a concept of the literary work of art as "a system of signals with a specific esthetic proposition" (Wellek), or "a dynamic and stratified system of norms" (Ingarden).

9. The study of a work becomes objective in terms of literary tradition, with the analysis of its internal literary structure and genres or literary forms, with themes, stratification, articulation, emotional tonality, form-content, technical devices (metric, rhythmic, and prosodic scheme, strophic structure, rhythmic pattern, order of construction, technique of narrative, characterization, typology, dramatic conventions, style, vocabulary, poetic language, figures, symbols, signals, imagery, metaphors, etc.), its description and history, in an attempt to identify what is new in it and what is a continuation, according to the scheme of convention and revolt, or tradition and renovation, that has generally marked its evolution.

10. As *literary* history, a concept of genres is implied which derives from the very concept of literature on which it is based. Literature is an art, the product of the creative imagination, and has as its end the awakening of esthetic pleasure as defined by Aristotle in his *Poetics*; genres have to be understood according to this perspective. The problem of genres has aroused a sharp polemic in recent times.

A reformulation of certain principles of categorizing has become necessary. An ancient problem, studied since Aristotle, Horace, and other Greco-Roman literary theoreticians, it has aroused among moderns a system of neoclassical poetics on one side, which sees the genres as absolute entities and external to the work itself. On the other side has been the post-romantic reaction, even negation, especially of Benedetto Croce, for whom the genres do not go beyond being names or labels that have no reality. Contemporary poetics has restudied the matter, and tends to face it according to a more just and balanced concept which recognizes the legitimacy of the notion and the essential reality enclosed in it as far as literary technique is concerned.

A genre represents a system of devices or esthetic conventions that are manipulated by the writer and intelligible to the reader, and which, for exterior form (for example, structure, metric pattern) as well as interior form (attitude, theme, narrative type, and so forth), lend to certain works a common physiognomy that puts them into a natural grouping. Natural phenomena and not arbitrary inventions, they are formations, from inside outward, that are imposed on the author who, in turn, can reshape them. They correspond to the aptitudes of the author and also to those of the public. Thus, a novel is a novel, both in Balzac and in Joyce, in Flaubert and in Virginia Woolf, despite the differences that the genre may offer between one author and another. The same might be said of the epics of Homer and Camões, Virgil and Milton.

As for enumeration and classification, contemporary poetics, as René Wellek points out, has a tendency, according to the poetic concept of literature, to reduce genres to those that truly have a poetic nature (*Dichtung*), having their origins in the imagination and aiming at esthetic pleasure. According to this esthetic concept, literary genres are limited to four groups, built around certain primordial tendencies: essayistic literature, narrative literature (fiction and epic), dramatic literature (tragedy and comedy), and lyric literature.

Each one of these groups, and the sub-varieties it contains, is the result of the way in which the author has addressed the reader or listener in order to transmit his interpretation or imitation of reality. If he does it directly, in his own name, explaining his own points of view, we have the essayistic genres, the essay, to which certain secondary types belong, such as the maxim, the letter, the speech; if he does it indirectly, that is, by using devices to mask or cover up his interpretation of reality, three groups result, according to whether the device is: (*a*) a story that gives body to his interpretation in narrative literature (fiction, epic); (*b*) a mimetic representation in dramatic literature (tragedy, comedy . . .); (*c*) symbols, images, music in lyric literature.

In this way, it is easy to distinguish what is not literature. Many activities of the spirit are excluded which formerly, according to neo-classical poetics, were considered literary genres: journalism, history, conversation, the didactic genres, and mixed genres, even philosophy, which informs, teaches, and constructs systems to explain the world, do not come under the specifically literary objective, which is to communicate pleasure.

The immediate consequence of this principle is a reduction of scope and an exclusion of works and genres that have been habitually treated in our literary histories, such as the prolific production in the sixteenth and seventeenth centuries of *"diálogos das grandezas,"* historical relations and logs, travelers' tales, etc., and journalism, which belong more to historiography, sociology, or the history of culture, and not to literary history. By placing all these materials, social, political, and cultural history within literary history, we transform it thereby into a national encyclopedia, into a panorama of the life of the people. According to the criterion of Germanic inspiration that was adopted among us by Sílvio Romero, literary fact tends to be welded to historical fact; instead of defining as literature all written manifestations of a people (Sílvio Romero, Artur Mota), literary history is transformed into the history of culture. This book restricts itself to works of an esthetic nature, to those belonging to properly literary genres, works of the imagination, essayism, narrative, drama, lyrics.

Beyond this, there is still room for works of "applied literature," those which denote esthetic content or communicate esthetic value by means of literary expression, or which, in one way or another, may have exercised an influence in literature. In Brazilian intellectual life there is a complex relationship between literature and other activities of the spirit, the same themes being manipulated by literature and by journalism, sociology, philosophy, political and juridical thought. It is necessary, however, to study these relationships without losing sight of the fact that the interest is predominantly literary and without forgetting that, using the terminology of De Quincey, "literature of knowledge" is different from "literature of power."

11. The periodological concept is another esthetic characteristic of this work. Based on the notions of individual style and the style of the period, it constructs its periodization according to a stylistic scheme, describing periods as the rise and fall of a system of norms or conventions, trying to identify the point of exhaustion of the devices and

the beginning of aspiration for new ones. Everything that discriminates and on which literary periods are based is relevant—inspiration, feeling, literary forms—including generational groups, which in a neater way sometimes mark the change of systems of values (for example, the generation of 1870). Periods are, therefore, strata or layers, analyzed and defined—without forgetting however the cultural aspects—by their specifically stylistic aspects, in accordance with that ideal that literary history should be the history of a verbal art, and should have in style and in stylistic analysis its *raison d'être* (Wellek, Vietor, Auerbach, Hatzfeld, Alonso, Spitzer, et al.).

Stylistic periodology breaking with strict chronology, offers an organic understanding of literary movements. It does not isolate the phenomena of time and space. On the contrary, by associating itself with genological analysis, that is, with the study of literary genres in their evolution and characteristics, following the progress of forms within styles, stylistic historiography will violate chronological frames, because it does not take phenomena according to generational limits or those of schools.

Such is the case, for example, with realism. This phenomenon is not studied as a "school" according to the French concept, delimited by the years of the nineteenth century, and to which one or more generations are joined. Thanks to modern critical tendencies of stylogical origin, we are getting farther away from the traditional conception. Realism, therefore, is seen as a stylistic phenomenon—on the individual level and on the level of the period—passing beyond the narrow limits of the French realist school to become a broad phenomenon of universal scope, which unfolds forward, in new and different forms, into the twentieth century.

Consequently, in accordance with the principle of order that oriented the symposium of the journal *Comparative Literature* (Summer, 1951) that was specially dedicated to it, realism is understood first as the artistic style that characterizes the principal tendency of modern literature, starting in the nineteenth century, involving Slavic, Scandinavian, Romance, and Anglo-Saxon literatures. Instead of being the static antithesis of romanticism, realism was rather a continuous and unfolding style in the long process of adaptation to reality, to society, to nature, by literature since remote times (Auerbach).

The movement does not stop in the nineteenth century. Various

esthetic manifestations of the twentieth century are nothing but pro-
longations of realism or were generated by it in contact with other
tendencies. An example is impressionist fiction, which reflects the
coming together of realism and symbolism; socialist neonaturalism,
populist, regionalist, expressionist, existentialist fiction, the psychological novel of the "stream of consciousness" type. In one way or another, they share a realist spirit and style and cannot escape a realist
frame if we take a stylistic perspective of the periodic division, backed,
especially, by the comparativist technique.

In Brazil, realism was not restricted to the nineteenth century or to
the realist-naturalist school, but penetrated the twentieth century in
different nuances and produced manifestations that any other classification could not have.

This criterion is also of help for the understanding of regionalist
fiction, which has great importance in our literature. Brazilian fiction,
as it became dissociated from romanticism, sought to include the
regional picture as a consequence of the exhaustion of other motivations and ambiences. This incorporation was produced by realism as an
artistic style and as a strategy of realization. One of the strengths of
realism in Brazil was the exploration of the regional element, and it
sought out the regional magma that was most adaptable, creating a
tradition that has come down to the present time. For that reason, it is
licit to study regionalist fiction within the framework of realism,
giving it the emphasis that is found in this study. It is also licit to study,
as has been done here, the realist phenomenon with greater extension
in time and space, following the progress of genres such as the short
story, the novel, and theater, in which realism reached its best form,
coming down to present times.

The stylistic conception, therefore, broadens and violates the frontiers of periods, favoring the interpretation of genres, the evolution of
which comes about within styles.

What happened with realism also took place with the baroque. The
traditional classification and hierarchy of modern literary history is
therefore upset. In order to understand the new ordering of literary
phenomena that comes out of it, one must abandon current prejudices
and notions concerning periods and the succession of movements. It
becomes absolutely necessary to renounce ideas of chronological succession and precise frontiers between movements.

12. Taking its inspiration from an esthetic concept and taking its shape along the lines of stylistic periodization, this view of Brazilian literature cannot help but note the parallelism that exists between literature and the other arts. The evidence is too eloquent not to merit special attention, especially since it backs up the argument in favor of stylistic periodization and literary history as a history of styles.

13. Since literature is an expression of the spirit, it is natural that the most influential factors for its development would be the instruments for acqusition and propagation of culture and systems of education. "The quality of a population probably is related more closely to its educational status than to any other determinant," T. Lynn Smith states in *Brazil: People and Institutions*.

Interesting to point out in the development of literature is the influence that humanistic education has had upon it. Even without technical literary education, the type of classical instruction that held forth in Brazil did furnish a solid base of humanistic education that promoted an intellectual elite and a special group of men of letters especially during the nineteenth century. This type of instruction gave the man of intellectual vocation a solid instrument for labors of the spirit. It was but a base, however superior its quality, to facilitate the subsequent task of specialization that was accomplished personally. Self-teaching was the rule for a real literary formation, as it still is today. Secondary education in literature is simply a mistake, and at the higher level, in the Faculties of Philosophy, Science, and Letters, it is still too new to provide the yield expected. In earlier days, however, self-teaching found an extraordinarily fertile terrain thanks to classical studies.

Related to this theme is that of literary education by foreign influence, a powerful factor that has intervened in our intellectual formation and in our literary movements since their beginnings until the present time. Instead of seeking supposed genetic explanations in the physical or social milieu, it is probably more legitimate to establish bridges of approximation. We must investigate sources that have served the formation of styles, elements coming from outside, instruments that have served as vehicles for the idea-forces of foreign origin, the Christian concept of life and styles of art, language, code of morality and laws, traditions, usages, and attitudes, a whole humanistic behavior towards life. No one could rightly conceive of the baroque or romantic movement as phenomena coming from local causes of land or race, because they embody international currents of mental and artistic life. At best, we shall have to look for the differences that have existed among us and the motives that have determined them. Many variations are of a teachnical nature, introduced into baroque art by artists in Minas Gerais, men like Aleijadinho, who out of necessity adapted the material at hand, soapstone.

14. When this study was conceived, it was recognized that popular forms of literature play an outstanding role. The study of the themes and forms of oral literature, its penetration and transformation as raw material in written artistic literature, and the interaction among the forms are important branches of literary studies, and the most advanced currents of contemporary criticism show the importance of the contributions of folkloric science. Folklore, obviously, is not a literary discipline in the strict sense, but a branch of the social sciences and anthropology. The material that forms the common basis of traditions, however, can be changed into the "raw material of literature." Constance Rourke describes, "the theater that is behind the drama, the primitive religious ceremonies that were previous to both, the narration or story that anticipates both the drama and the novel, the monologue that was the rudimentary source of many forms." Literary criticism with a folkloric base is today one of the developments of anthropological studies in which the English school of Taylor, Frazer, Lang, and Hartland stands out. It attempts to analyze literary art in terms of its roots in folkloric tradition, in the relations of art with primitive rituals, in archetypal heroes, in myths and symbols, all with a common layer of traditions (legends, proverbs, festivals, myths, ceremonies, forms of the lyric, tales, fables, etc.). This is the root that most strongly holds the artists of a country to their native soil and which distinguishes the artists from those of other countries.

One must investigate, therefore, the manifestations of the popular soul, as can be seen in the work of contemporary critics like the English Gilbert Murray, F. M. Cornford, Jane Harrison, Jessie Weston, Colin Still, G. Wilson Knight, George Thomson, for ancient comedy and tragedy or Shakespearean drama; the Americans William Troy, Francis Fergusson, Kenneth Burke, Parker Tyler, Stanley Edgar Hyman, Joseph Campbell, Constance Rourke, and others for the novel and drama, as they start with myths, rites, and archetypal heroes; or yet, with Maud Bodkin, as she develops the Jungian concept of archetypal patterns and that of the collective unconscious in the analysis of poetry; or yet, in studies of myth and its relationship to literature, thanks to the mythological criticism that enjoys an enormous vogue at the present time.

In Brazilian literature, investigations of folklore and its relation to literature are still in an initial phase. Practically speaking, folkloric studies have not emerged from the period of the collection and classification of the material. This work is necessary and preliminary to their study, when they can be used by criticism as an instrument of analysis and interpretation of the more elevated forms of literary art. Criticism then will have at its disposal a vast analytical instrument, by means of which it will study questions of style, genre (origins, influences, transformations, preferences, and so forth), types, themes, motives, etc. The myth of hidden treasure, for example, so old in Western literature was reborn in Alencar, possibly through the influence of ideas from the mining Brazil of the eighteenth century.[29]

Brazilian lyricism sinks its roots into the popular ballads sung by untutored troubadors in the cities and the backlands. The simple men arriving in the colony tried to expand their joy or show their sorrows and fears as they faced new facts, at times hostile, that nature had placed before them. These men sought inspiration in their imaginations. On the other side, from the primitive cosmogony of Indians and Negroes there came a whole world of notations, myths, legends, tales, anecdotes, types all tied to men, animals, forces of nature, and agricultural activities. It was a whole collection of mythological fables that was incorporated into the psychology of the people, and came to symbolize ways of reacting, attitudes, forms of behavior. The study of this folkloric material which made up the unconscious underlayer of the Brazilian people, of Portuguese, Negro, Indian, and half-breed origin, blended together over four centuries, will certainly serve to clarify many novelistic or lyrical derivatives. During romanticism, for example, the function of popular poetry was rather significant, and the turn to popular legends and traditions that took place at that time was an essential factor in the development of lyricism.

Other investigations will bring clarifications for the problem of ruralism and the myth of the inhabitant of the *sertão*, as well as that of the *gaúcho*, and, later on, that of the *cangaceiro* (Lampião et al.), a central figure in the "drought cycle" of regionalist literature. As a last case, if we keep in mind the role of folklore in a book as important in contemporary literature as *Macunaíma* (1928), by Mário de Andrade, we shall understand how useful to criticism and literary history are folkloric studies in the eulcidation of types, themes, motives, and so forth.

15. Special attention is given to bibliography as an indispensable instrument for literary studies, as was shown by Fidelino de Figueiredo, among others, in his work *Aristarcos* (1941). It is a branch of intellectual technique that has been given increasing attention in Brazil, in analysis as well as the systematization of presentation. There is much yet to be done in this field: the first steps, however, show that a bibliographical awareness is growing among us.

A collective work, the whole is inspired in the idea that literary history is no longer possible except as a cooperative effort. In the first place, the historian is faced with a mountain of material in print to be read and evaluated. Is this possible at the present stage? Veríssimo states that he had read all of the works about which he had to speak. In relation to what had been published, he had to read much less than would be true fifty years later. And we must not forget that the knowledge of that past has grown enormously since then, thanks to the unprecedented research, from his time on. And we still have the great number of works published in that past that cannot pass unperceived by the conscientious historian, because culture is a great continuation. So a single individual must admit that the task is insuperable. Cooperation becomes necessary, in spite of new difficulties, as a result of the very nature of our method: the demand for conciliation between the unity of planning and conception and the execution by diverse authors. The necessity for submission to the whole does not imply any renunciation on the part of the authors of their technical skills or critical depths. On the contrary, without individual skills, it would be impossible to attain the efficiency aimed for in the plan.

An effort has been made here to bring forth as much as possible a work of conciliation between history and criticism, with the first subordinated to the second, the supreme arbiter of literary study. The prevailing norm for its conception and elaboration is, therefore, of a critical nature. Foremost is the idea that literary history must make use of critical categories and base itself upon a clear epistemology. No longer adequate to the task is the theory of knowledge for which, as Waggoner pointed out, facts are objective and critical judgment is subjective. Therein lies the conflict in the nineteenth century between literary history and criticism. By applying itself exclusively to a collection of facts, literary history eschewed the acquisition of a critical and philosophical instrument.

There was an attempt to impose objectivity or the dispassionate observation of the phenomenon without prejudgment and with an exhaustive investigation of bibliographical sources and, above all, by an examination of the works. With this as a guideline, there was an attempt to escape that fearful science referred to by João Ribeiro, and which has been so harmful to Brazilian culture, criticism, especially "the lazy science of mere personal opinion about the things criticized." It was an opinion, ultimately, whether obtained from predecessors or formed during simple conversations. An opinionated and infallible tone is one of the most harmful vices our criticism has suffered.

Therefore, by admitting the historical contribution, we do not lose sight of the general norm that is literary and critical, and we emphasize literary analysis by means of the study of works as such, interpreting them in the light of literary tradition and by the contribution they have brought to it. By adapting the genological method to the stylistic —the two most adequate approaches to the study of literature—the literary phenomenon can be examined, one must insist, as an autonomous phenomenon, not a subordinate one, but rather the equivalent of other forms of life to which it is related. In short, the guiding principle of the book is esthetic and not historical.

This work is an attempt to offer, by means of some of its most notable representatives, a cross-section of Brazilian criticism, from north to south, in the century of the Brazilian literary past.

Literary history is a task that is always on the move, and it is the chore of each generation to remake and complete it. From the state in which these bits of knowledge have been left by their predecessors, each generation has been made to feel the necessity of an updating and a consequent critical revision and renovation.

A Literatura no Brasil sets out, therefore, to establish a new order and hierarchy of values, a revaluation and reinterpretation of Brazilian literature based on a proper gathering of facts. These have been established and suggested by research and current critical thought. Following the patterns recommended by Wellek, it attempts to avoid an "excessive determinism that reduces literature to the mere passive mirror of other human activities," concentrating, although without extremes, on the study of the work itself, in the light of an esthetic theory of literature and literary history.

The plan of *A Literatura no Brasil* obeys the scheme outlined below.

It consists of three parts. The first includes the study of generic or propedeutic problems of a cultural nature, in their relationship to the literary phenomenon: the cultural panorama of the European Renaissance; literary language; folklore; education; the relation between the writer and his public; the relation of literature to a knowledge of the land.

In the second part, an attempt is made to study the various literary styles that have developed in Brazil with their respective criticism and literary ideas: baroque, neoclassicism, Arcadianism, romanticism, realism, naturalism, Parnassianism, symbolism, impressionism and modernism.

In the third part, themes and isolated forms are faced: essayism, oratory, the relations of literature to philosophy, journalism, the arts, and so forth.

From Baroque to Rococo

ᢻ᠍᠊ᢻᡗ᠍ᠪᡐ᠍ᠪ

FROM EXPANSION TO UFANISMO

It is to the *cycle of discoveries* of sixteenth-century Portuguese literature, defined by Fidelino de Figueiredo as "that body of works dealing with the maritime discoveries and their moral and political consequences," that the first literary manifestations of the Brazilian colony belong.[1]

According to historians, the Portuguese sixteenth century is made up of the combination of medieval, classical, and national elements. Medieval elements are: the old metrics, the origins and structure of the Vicentian theater, the royal chronicles, and the novel of chivalry. Classical elements (imported from Italy) are: the classical theater, comedy and tragedy, the pastoral novel and eclogue, the new metrics with its varieties of form, and the epic. National elements are: the internal development of the Vicentian theater, or the world in which it took place, historiography, or the narration of great colonial deeds and the chronicles of expansion, the epic as transformed by Camões from a classical genre into an instrument of the national idea, and the new genres, linked to the narratives of discovery, such as tales of shipwrecks and the logs of travelers.

A study of the literature produced during the first three centuries of colonial life shows that some of these items are included or that the literature obeys the inspiration of the motives that dominated the cycle of discoveries. These were the most original contribution of the Portuguese to universal literature, based, furthermore, in large part on solid economic motives: the slave trade, the conquest of new lands, markets, and sources of wealth, the expansion of commerce. Out of it came the first tendencies expressed here in literary dress; from it came the "first letters" in Brazil. Accompanying this literature of expansion and discovery are the first books written by Portuguese or Brazilians in Brazil, dealing with people, places, and things in the colony. The work of the Jesuits, both the more typically literary lyric and drama parts, and the mountain of letters and reports on conditions in the colony, forms a chapter of the Portuguese spiritual expansion. The literature of travelers and discoverers, nautical logs, tales of shipwreck, geographical and social descriptions, descriptions of nature and of the Indian (which Sílvio Romero defined as the two principal tendencies of Brazilian literature in the sixteenth century), the attempts at epic poems with a local subject are so many other episodes in this Brazilian branch of the literature of sixteenth-century Portuguese overseas expansion that has been studied so well by Hernâni Cidade.[2]

The first great manifestation of these forces is the development of the myth of *ufanismo*, a lyrical exaltation of the land and countryside, a belief in an El Dorado or an "earthly paradise," as Rocha Pita first called it, a tendency that was to be a permanent line in Brazilian literature, both in prose and in verse. Pero Vaz de Caminha, Anchieta, Nóbrega, Cardim, Bento Teixeira, Gandavo, Gabriel Soares de Sousa, Fernandes Brandão, Rocha Pita, Vicente do Salvador, Botelho de Oliveira, Itaparica, and Nuno Marques Pereira are examples from the long list of those who sang of "culture and opulence," or were the authors of *"diálogos das grandezas,"* all of which make up this singular literature of catalogues and exaltation of the resources of the promised land. This literature, it might be said in passing, is not far removed from its origins in the economic reasons behind the evaluation of the land in European eyes.

The majority of these works do not belong to literature in the strictest sense, and their importance comes from their being part of that cycle of the literature of discovery and their inclination towards the land of Brazil, with the anxiety that dominates the conscience of the seventeenth-century Brazilian to know it, reveal it, and expand it. If we try an evaluation of it by exclusively esthetic criteria, except for rare moments, the inferior quality is immediately evident. Therefore, the position that is reserved for these works in literary history must be limited to the mere annotation of the style of life and art characteristic of the time. An easily observed phenomenon in the history of literature is that the most obvious testimony of a period appears in mediocre works and not in the great ones. Rightfully, the attention they merit is in the province of the history of culture and historiography, or that of social ideas, because they are signposts along the road. They express an awareness of a common land, the insurgent spirit, the historical sense, and the feeling of nationality, in a word, Brazilianness, right from those very first formative years. The knowledge of the geographical, economical, and social factors on which Brazilian civilization was built comes from them. The repercussions of that literature of the land are of obvious importance in all literature of the imagination, but the analysis of it cannot be done with literary instruments which can only make note of it.

With their expression of the myth of *ufanismo*, however, these works cannot escape the impregnation of the artistic style in vogue during the period. Brazilian literature really comes out of Western baroque literature. It was under the aegis of the baroque, defined not only as an artistic style, but also as a cultural complex, that Brazilian literature was born. All one has to do is study the example of Jesuit literature, works of *ufanismo* but with literary meaning. Represented were Botelho de Oliveira and Nuno Marques Pereira as well as Vieira and Gregório de Matos; Vieira's influence was on sacred oratory, and on the whole family of poets and prosists of the academies. If Brazilian intelligence began to express itself in the form of "literature of knowledge" (De Quincey), "literature of power" can be seen here and there even though it acquired an esthetic category only later.

Thus the study of the main authors with an esthetic feeling can be justified during this phase of Brazilian literature. They are expressions, some of them rather representative, of the literary baroque, and as such they should be analyzed and evaluated. They are valuable as evidence of an artistic style, the characteristic marks of which are faithfully reflected as has been proven by recent studies. The baroque impregnation, however, was so imbedded in the writers of the period that even the historians and thinkers could not escape it. Typical examples are the cases of Rocha Pita and Frei Vicente do Salvador, whose prose reflects the baroque contamination, especially in its aspects of lesser quality.

The literary genres most cultivated at the time were the dialogue, lyric poetry, and the epic, along with historiography and pedagogical meditation, from which the baroque draws its greatest part, mixing the mythological with the descriptive, the allegorical with the realistic, the narrative with the psychological, the martial with the pastoral, the solemn with the burlesque, the pathetic with the satirical, the idyllic with the dramatic. This does not mention the mixture of language, already initiated as an imposition of the work of evangelization itself, and the new linguistic sensibility out of which the differentiation of a Brazilian style will emerge.

The recognition of the baroque character in the definition of the literature produced in Brazil from the middle of the sixteenth century to the end of the eighteenth upsets the traditional classification of that literature, and imposes a new periodization of stylistic origin upon it. Furthermore, as F. Simone has said in relation to universal literature, the concept of the baroque brought about the dissolution of the traditional historiographical scheme.

With the dependence upon the criteria in force in Portuguese literary historiography, by which writers of the sixteenth, seventeenth, and eighteenth centuries are habitually defined as classical, it is the custom to describe as classical the Brazilian authors of the same period, in spite of the variety of types of poetry that cross various borders of influence such as palace, classical, baroque, and Arcadian.

Nothing could be less proper. The word *classicism*, so difficult to define, becomes absurd when used to label disparate literary manifestations such as the Renaissance and the seventeenth and eighteenth centuries, including such figures as Camões, Vieira, and the Arcadians. Until now, this label prevented us from seeing clearly the stylistic differences among the diverse manifestations of that long period that lasted from the end of the Middle Ages up to romanticism. To call this period of Brazilian literature classical is to give the epithet a vague meaning, basing it only on the fact that the writers of the time were imitators of the ancient classics, the most imprecise meaning that could be given to the expression; even the use of the term as praise for model writers is inadequate, because, with rare exceptions, these early Brazilian authors cannot be seen in such a light.

If we wish to give literary terms a precise critical value, and if, as in the case of periodic definitions, we wish them to possess an objective validity not only as a model for judgment but also as a historico-esthetic concept for the characterization of the artistic specimens of a period, we must restrict their sense, making them equivalent to the works or the concrete facts that they attempt to define. Without such definition, as Whitmore shows,[3] the term will only cloud our ideas concerning the phenomenon in question. They should be based, as Whitmore insists, on an inspection and knowledge of the facts at the expense of theory and critical activities.

In a general way, the term classicism is used to designate the movement which began in the Renaissance for the restoration of the forms and values of the ancient world, especially those from the ages of Pericles and Augustus, who were considered the models of artistic and philosophical perfection. The movement varied according to country, however, which from the critical point of view makes it imprecise. Various European literatures adopted it with divergent meanings, so that in some of them the term could not even be applied, as was the case with Spain. Italian classicism means form during the fifteenth and sixteenth centuries; French classicism during the reign of Louis XIV, the high point of the classical attitude, is rationalist, regulative, controlled; the English is neoclassicism; the so-called Portuguese classicism, from the sixteenth through the eighteenth centuries, is a mixture of Renaissance and baroque elements, and, in the end, Arcadianism. What is classicism, then, judging from these experiences? What value for definition can the concept have? Even in French literature, where the term is current usage in the critical vocabulary, it is more licit, perhaps, to speak, as Lebègue stresses,[4] about classicisms in the plural rather than about classicism, keeping in mind the diverse waves of so-called classicism, from Malherbe to Chapelain, to Boileau, to Perrault, to Fénelon (a phenomenon pointed out by Adam[5]). In any case, from Goethe to Sainte-Beuve, to André Gide, to T. S. Eliot, the concept is still cloaked in fog.

It is important, therefore, without abandoning the term classicism, to limit it to a determined use. As he attempts to define the notion, Henri Peyre[6] places himself within the French critical tradition, for which genuine classicism is French.[7] He sees it as the literary and artistic production of France between 1600 and 1690, but he does examine the diverse meanings of the term, noting the following: (*a*) Authors destined for use in "class"; (*b*) Model authors, the "best," the great authors of all literatures and therefore used in class; (*c*) The classical authors, or the writers of antiquity. To these meanings must be added: (*d*) Authors who imitate the classics, who are their adepts, or follow their lessons (neoclassics); (e) Certain cultural periods that have attained superior perfection, more or less inspired by classical antiquity; (f) A body of esthetic characteristics defining the cultural, artistic, and literary style of a period.

This last meaning is the only one that gives critical validity to the concept, restricting it to the definition and characterization of the system of artistic and cultural norms of a determined moment in the historical process. According to this doctrine, in the history of arts and literature, classical style, baroque style, and romantic style are different forms of artistic realization, embodied in precise historical moments. It is the task of criticism to distinguish among them and delimit the respective areas of action, using for identification their systems of norms.[8]

It is easy to infer from the definition of classical art and literature, in the light of Wölfflin's conceptualization, that Brazilian literature of the colonial phase cannot be interpreted as classical, nor the period as one of classicism, unless the terms are employed only to indicate the general norm of the period, the imitation of models from antiquity, which defines nothing.[9]

The first three centuries of literature in Brazil, since there was really no Renaissance, show the merging of artistic styles, the baroque, the neoclassic, and the Arcadian. These were forms of esthetic physiognomy well-characterized by dominant signs and principles, characteristics in space and time, meshing, mixing, and penetrating one another, sometimes adding to each other, not always succeeding each other or being limited by an exact chronology. The baroque movement was born with the first Jesuit writers. It penetrated the seventeenth and eighteenth centuries, appearing in the prose and poetry of *ufanismo*, in the native poetry of Gregório de Matos, in the exhortations of Vieira and his successors, in the poetry and prose of the academies, and even reaching romanticism under a protective coloring of decadence. During this process, in the eighteenth century, neoclassicism and Arcadianism share rococo taste, and only with difficulty can we separate their manifestations blended during that century with elements of the baroque movement. The eighteenth century especially reflects this mixing, crossing, and interacting of styles.

Concerning this definition of artistic and literary styles in colonial Brazil, one must point out the fact that there are superior and inferior

forms and that the Brazilian literary baroque, for example, except in a
few isolated cases, is an expression of minor art. It is quite the opposite
of the baroque in the plastic arts, where it reached a very pure and
high level.

An understanding of Brazilian literature produced during the baroque, neoclassical, and Arcadian periods demands the prior establishment of an esthetic concept that regulated literary creation during
the whole period between the Renaissance and romanticism (a concept
that only the latter movement was able to dethrone), the concept of
imitation. Under the influence of romantic theories, the modern critic
was despoiled of the proper perspective for an evaluation of Renaissance and baroque literature. By means of an overevaluation of the
individual, the originality of the creation was canonized, and a belief
was reached in the exclusively subjective origins of poetry, where
inner inspiration was the only source of creativity. The doctrine that
inspired the poets of the Renaissance and the baroque period was
different. In the sixteenth, seventeenth, and eighteenth centuries, the
general norm of literary creation was imitation. Even as they reacted
against the Renaissance, the baroque writers did not fail to respect that
rule. In contrast to the romantics, inspiration was not enough for
poetical success and perfection. It was necessary to join originality to
tradition in order to attain the intention of the poet.

Perhaps no literary period owed more to esthetic doctrines and rules,
and for its study and interpretation it became necessary to examine
the cloth of the literary theory from which it had been cut.[10] This
norm had its origins in the educational system in vogue, based on the
famous *Literae Humaniores*. Rhetoric played an important role in it
through the work of the classical rhetoricians, Aristotle, Isocrates,
Cicero, Horace, and Quintilian. The rhetorical tradition dominated the
period as a solid current of interpretation and criticism, as well as one
of intellectual and literary formation, whose essential objective was to
teach one how to speak and write with persuasion. There was even an
identification or confusion among rhetoric, logic, and poetics, of which
Ramus was the symbol. Under the influence of this tradition, the rule
of imitation constituted the common denominator of the literature
produced at the time. Imitation was a prime rhetorical and pedagogical
rule and it was never confused with plagiarism. The normative principle
of the imitation of models was easily accepted by masters of Greco-

Roman rhetoric, not as an inferior process, but as a formative discipline through which the virtues of the great authors could be emulated. This particularly Roman tradition was reaffirmed during the Middle Ages and it came down to modern times through the work of the humanists, and became a fundamental principle of Renaissance and baroque literary theory.

From the imitation of nature, conceived as the generating force of all things, the normative spirit of the Romans transformed the concept into a rhetorical discipline of imitation of model authors. These, in modern times, became confused with the ancient classics; that is, instead of going to nature, the ones imitated were those who had already imitated nature in an excellent way. Thus, as Ian Jack stresses, it was, in the light of the classical credo, a worthy activity, in which art did not mean an effort at self-expression or the manifestation of a personality, and imitation did not imply a motive of inferiority or plagiarism, as the modern critic habitually thinks.[11] To transfer present-day patterns of judgment that were created in the shadow of a different esthetic doctrine to the study and gauging of the literature of a period formed on the norm of imitation as the basis of orthodox literary pedagogy is to show a lack of perspective. No literary genius of the Renaissance, the baroque period, or neoclassicism escapes the tribute: Shakespeare, Montaigne, Cervantes, Góngora, Quevedo. There are whole pages of Seneca in Montaigne, and it would be a waste of time to try to track down the footprints of Seneca and Plutarch in Shakespeare.

By not placing themselves within the doctrine that held sway during the period and by not relating it to the critical theory of the times, which differs particularly from that which flourished after romanticism, certain interpreters of Brazilian literature of the seventeenth and eighteenth centuries have fallen into an error of judgment. The same thing has happened to critics of English literature of the Augustan phase (1660–1750), as Jack has pointed out. At that time it was a sign of artistic superiority and not inferiority (as is thought today, after the overevaluation of originality and individual genius that romanticism imposed on the Western literary mentality) for a writer to show that he was imitating a model from antiquity. In that imitation there was a whole gamut of tones, from simple inspiration to a gloss, even reaching translation. If there was not a writer, great as his prestige might have been, who avoided the rule, why must we struggle to apply the same criterion to the understanding of Brazilian literature during that phase? Do immunities only prevail for foreigners, perchance, while our few figures of the period are called plagiarists? The mistake is all the more serious as we forget the relevant role that rhetoric played in education in all of Latin America, even well into the nineteenth century.

A victim of this error of perspective is Gregório de Matos, accused by a line of Brazilian critics as a mere copier of Góngora and Quevedo, forgetting what those two geniuses themselves owe, through imitation, to ancient models.

The Matos question deserves more careful attention, beginning with the recognition of imitation as an esthetic norm of the period, a typical example of how the knowledge of the literary theory that shapes a period helps in the interpretation of it. In addition, it is necessary to bear in mind the problem of the authenticity of the texts attributed to him. As is well known, his poems were collected in handwritten codices done by copyists who may have attributed to him the work of some other writer. One must not impute, therefore, the total responsibility for these appropriations without paying attention to the conditions of the intellectual life of the time. There were no presses in the colony, and the transcription of texts was not rigorous. There was also the question of originality and the rights of the author, especially if one ignores the pervasive role of the doctrine of imitation. Thus, there are more than enough reasons to respect the positive and elevated part of his contribution. In a period in which everything was stunted, Brazilian letters were already speaking for themselves with the half-breed originality to which the baroque movement gave all manner of devices and means of efficient realization. If it imitated, and it doubtless did, it was within good rhetorical doctrine of the time; nor could it avoid, at the same time, the mirror quality that letters in the new continent had then and still have.[12]

The investigation of the origins of Brazilian literature raises the problem, which might seem to be superfluous, of when and with whom it began, whether in the sixteenth or the seventeenth century, whether with Anchieta, Bento Teixeira, Matos, or Botelho. In reality, it is not easy to establish the first plaints of nativism, of the anti-Portuguese insurrectional instinct, of the feeling of Brazilianness, or of the formation of a national awareness. It is believed that this feeling became concrete and took shape from the moment in which, in contact with a new reality, a new man was rising within the colonist.

Even if it is impossible to pinpoint the beginnings of nativist feeling in a written document, it is the task of literary history to decide which are the texts that bear witness to the dawn of an esthetic preoccupation that those who have dealt with the problem have insisted upon (Sílvio Romero, José Veríssimo, Afrânio Peixoto, and Érico Veríssimo).

From the evaluation of Jesuit literature, now widely known, rises the meaning of the work of Anchieta, the gentle evangelist of the heathen, and his designation as the father of Brazilian literature. This is also the opinion of Afrânio Peixoto, for whom the writings of Anchieta were the first written *for* Brazilians or *in* Brazil.[13] (He wrote in the sixteenth century when most of what was being written was informative literature *about* Brazil for Europeans.) Discounting the literature of knowledge of the land, written by travelers and interested people within the scheme referred to above, it is natural that the work of Anchieta should stand out, and even if it does not have esthetic value of the highest level, placed in its historical situation it is the high point of the baroque spirit in America.

Literary effort began with the settlement of São Vicente, where Martim Afonso de Sousa founded a flourishing sugar plantation in 1532 to which Anchieta was sent. The latter worked in the school that he helped Nóbrega to set up on the Piratininga plateau, the germ of the city of São Paulo. The fragile intellectual life of the colony followed the development of various social centers, Bahia, Pernambuco, Rio de Janeiro, Vila Rica, and São Paulo, whose importance in turn was related to the cycles of sugar, brazilwood, tobacco, gold, diamonds, and coffee that characterize the Brazilian economic evolution.

THE LITERARY BAROQUE

The etymology of the word *baroque* has been the cause of much controversy. Some believe it to be Iberian in origin, from the Spanish *barrueco* or the Portuguese *barroco*, denoting a pearl with an irregular surface. Others, such as Agostinho de Campos, feel that the form *barroco* is the original and legitimately Portuguese form instead of the gallicized *baroco*. In 1888, Wölfflin proposed another theory, related to scholasticism, that it is a mnemonic term used to evoke one of the two forms of the second figure of the syllogism (b A r O c O), in which the minor is particular and negative. In this sense, the first use of the word appears in Montaigne (*Essays*, I, chapter 25), who uses it alongside *baralipton* to mock scholasticism. In the sixteenth and seventeenth centuries, the word denoted a form of reasoning that mixed the false and the true, an argumentation that was strange and erroneous, evasive and fleeting, which subverted the rules of thought. Originally it is negative and pejorative, a synonym for bizarre, extravagant, artificial, high-flown, and monstrous; an attempt at belittling seventeenth-century art, which was interpreted as a decadent form of Renaissance or classical art. This is how the concept was used by neoclassical and Arcadian criticism, which reached into the nineteenth century. As Calcaterra points out, the word came into current usage with the original pejorative meaning. In philosophy: baroque idea, baroque argumentation, baroque thought; in art: baroque image, baroque figure, baroque apostrophe. The concept in its pejorative sense, therefore, followed its course mostly in the plastic and visual arts. It described the art and the esthetics of the period that followed the Renaissance, interpreting these as degenerate, one that showed a lack of clarity, purity, or elegance of line, and which used all manner of ornamentation and distortion, resulting in a style that was impure, distilled, and obscure. A recent author, Gilbert Highet, however, seems to prefer the old explanation of the irregular pearl, since it has, to his mind, an esthetic rather than an intellectual meaning. He stresses, however, that in both explanations the dominant idea is a feeling of the irregularity, tension, effort, and difficulty that are characteristics of the baroque.

The famous cultural historian, Burckhardt, began a revision of the baroque question (in the *Cicerone*, 1855), but it is to Wölfflin (1864–1945) that we owe a definitive reformulation made in the light of new principles he introduced for interpretation of the history of art. From 1879, when the question was first raised, to 1929, the date when the concept can be considered incorporated into the critical vocabulary thanks to Wölfflin's studies, baroque art was revaluated and was no longer thought of as a degenerate expression, but rather as a form peculiar to a period in the history of modern culture, with its own esthetic value and meaning. That was when the term received a precise definition and became current in the criticism of art and literature. It has recently appeared in manuals of culture and literature.

Wölfflin's theory of the formal analysis of the arts, the basis of the transformation that took place in the study of the baroque, consists of the establishment of certain fundamental principles that show a switch from a kind of tactile representation to a visual one, or from Renaissance art to the baroque.[14] In this way, the baroque represents not a decline, but the natural development of Renaissance classicism towards a later style. This style, as distinct from the classical, is no longer tactile, but visual; that is, it does not admit non-visual perspectives and it does not reveal its art, but conceals it. The change takes place according to an inner law, and the stages of its development in any work can be demonstrated by means of five categories.

Renaissance	*Baroque*
1. linear—felt by the hand.	1. pictorial—followed by the sight.
2. composed on the flat, with an aim to be felt.	2. composed in depth, with an aim to be followed.
3. coordinate parts of equal value.	3. parts subordinate to a whole.
4. closed, leaving the observer outside.	4. open, placing the observer inside.
5. absolute clarity.	5. relative clarity.

This theory of the definition of artistic styles can be applied to literature, and Wölfflin himself has already suggested such a consequence as he contrasts Ariosto's *Orlando Furioso* to Tasso's *Gerusalemme Liberata* as works that on the literary plane expressed the opposition between Renaissance and baroque. As René Wellek points out, however, only after 1914 did the term have widespread use in literary criticism as a definition of works of the seventeenth century.[15] From Germany, where the Swiss Wölfflin was teaching (Munich), the theory spread out, attracting scholars and literary historians who were already concerned about new directions for literary historiography. They wanted to be free from the positivism and socio-historical determinism of the nineteenth century, and felt themselves attracted by the emphasis that Wölfflin gave in his basic book (1915) to the characterization of form and to the criteria for the differentiation of styles. Wellek shows, therefore, that after 1921–1922 the term was broadly adopted among critics and literary historians, first by the Germans, soon after by Swiss, Scandinavian, Italian, Spanish, English, American, and French (these last most reluctantly until recently).

In this way, the literary period that follows the Renaissance, the equivalent of the seventeenth century, is defined as baroque; however the sense of time is not strict since the limits can well be the dates 1580 and 1680, with variants according to country. Renaissance, baroque, and neoclassic were three successive periods, according to Friederich, just like thesis, antithesis, and synthesis. "For it was only the classicism of France after 1660 that could join together in an harmonious masterpiece (for example, Racine's *Andromaque*) the pagan mythology of antiquity and the Christian fervor of the Middle Ages, the two opposite visions of life that writers of the Renaissance and the baroque period respectively had tried in vain to reconcile in their art." [16]

Therefore, the periodization of the stylistic origins of modern literature includes the Renaissance (fifteenth to sixteenth centuries), the baroque (sixteenth to seventeenth centuries), the neoclassic, with the Enlightenment and rational (seventeenth to eighteenth centuries), romanticism (eighteenth to nineteenth centuries), realism-naturalism (nineteenth to twentieth centuries), and symbolism and modernism (nineteenth to twentieth centuries).

Actually, the humanistic, rationalist, and anthropocentric line initiated by the Renaissance as it revived the cult of antiquity, continues with neoclassicism and the Enlightenment of the seventeenth and eighteenth centuries and with the realism-naturalism of the nineteenth century. During the first three modern centuries, we have the formative process of the neoclassical credo in literature; from the Renaissance, passing through the baroque, which loses its impetus as it reacts in the name of freedom, irregularity, and emotion, and invades neoclassicism at the end of the seventeenth century.

The application of the concept of the baroque to modern periodization clarifies, precisely, the position of that intermediate stage between the Renaissance (until 1580, more or less) and the neoclassical phase (after 1680). It was a period that had not been identified, and it was Wölfflin's studies that gave a term to the confusion, emphasizing, which is most important, the artistic and literary production of that phase.[17] The styles of Renaissance and seventeenth-century life were unmistakable, and it would not be proper to qualify the literary and artistic style of the seventeenth century as classical. Wölfflin's critical categories clearly delimited the forms of sixteenth- and seventeenth-century life: the linear and the pictorial, the closed and the open, the multiple and the unitarian, the flat and the deep, the clear and the obscure. His formalism was the new criterion that dissociated the two systems of norms that had regulated men's ways of being and doing during those divisions of time. Thanks to Wölfflin, it is possible for us to identify the Renaissance period by its forms of life and artistic manifestations. These separate it from the baroque period, which is characterized in turn by peculiar forms of existence and culture, by its own style of life and art, thought, action, religiosity, government, amusement, war, prose, and verse. It has been verified that the period offers a perfect unity, expressed not only in the parallelism between literature and the various arts, but also in diverse other forms of life. The unity led cultural historians to adopt the term baroque to designate "the most varied manifestations of civilization in the seventeenth century" (R. Wellek).[18]

The Renaissance was characterized by the predominance of the straight and pure line, by the clarity and neatness of contours. The baroque attempts the conciliation, the incorporation, and the fusion (fusionism is its dominant tendency) of the medieval ideal, spiritual and superterrestrial, with new values that the Renaissance brought into vogue: humanism, the pleasure of earthly things, worldly and carnal satisfactions. The strategy belongs to the Counter-Reformation, with the urge, conscious or unconscious, of fighting the modern spirit by absorbing from it what was most acceptable. Out of that the baroque was born, a new style of life whose contradictions and distortions translated the dilemma of the period into art, philosophy, religion, and literature.

Understood in this way, the baroque period is a stage between the Renaissance, from whose bosom and in reaction to which it emerged, and neoclassicism, through which it was prolonged and into which it dissolved. Inasmuch as the period can be delimited *grosso modo*, one must insist again that historical periods are not separated from each other according to neat contours, but that they interpenetrate and mingle, like patches of oil, for the systems of norms that regulate their lives do not begin and end in any abrupt way. In the case of the baroque, there is one great patch whose nucleus is in the seventeenth century, but whose contours are made up of indentations, and whose interior is spotted with vacuoles and blanks. In the same way, in neighboring periods, one can discover baroque metastases, not to

mention local variants of initiation and termination, with baroque
forms appearing earlier in one place than in another. In short, neighboring styles, expressions of diverse states of the spirit, often coexist and
are mixed. Their forms and shadows can be identified in this or that
writer, who are therefore classical and baroque at the same time. In
the case of the French baroque, for example, classicism only became
possible because of the struggle against the baroque, as happened with
Racine. Leo Spitzer has defined classicism as baroque that has been
tamed.[19]

The concept of the baroque affords, therefore, a new perspective,
by which it is possible to understand seventeenth-century literature,
since for the interpretation of this period, the concepts of the Renaissance and of classicism had been insufficient and inaccurate. Many
literary manifestations of the time defied classification and interpretation because they did not fit the traditional formulas and were therefore
relegated to the background as inferior or intermediary forms of art.
The baroque fills the vacuum that existed between the Renaissance and
classicism[20] by defining diverse works that reflect a common state of
spirit in all modern national literatures.[21]

Consequently, the term baroque, originating in the history and
criticism of the arts, supplies literary criticism and historiography with
one more esthetic concept. By definitively resolving the problem of
classification and evaluation of seventeenth-century literature, which
had defied Renaissance and neoclassical conceptualization, the baroque
has the advantage of being a term with esthetic meaning, encouraging
therefore present efforts to give autonomy to literary history in relation
to political and social history. The concept of the baroque favors the
methodological and conceptual renovation that characterizes the present
state of literary historiography, and that has struggled to give it an
esthetic-literary orientation, contrary to nineteenth-century currents of
historicist, positivist, and naturalist origin. The renovating tendencies
attempted to give primacy to criticism, abolishing the divorce between
it and literary history and scholarship. They are used in the explanation
of a work of art on its own terms, with an analysis of its intrinsic
characteristics. In the hands of critics armed with the methods of
modern stylology and structural or textual analysis and in search of
intrinsic literary values, the concept of the baroque can be extremely
useful to clarify stylistic phenomena that had been obscure and had

resisted interpretation until now. In this vein are the studies of Leo Spitzer, Karl Vossler, Dámaso Alonso, Morris Croll, Helmut Hatzfeld, and others who shed light on the meanderings of seventeenth-century style.

The adoption of the term is gaining ground, therefore, simultaneously as its conceptual clarification spreads. René Wellek, at the end of his study of the baroque in literature, makes clear his preference for the concept:

In spite of the many ambiguities and uncertainties as to the extension, valuation, and precise content of the term, baroque has fulfilled and is still fulfilling an important function. It has put the problem of periodisation and of a pervasive style very squarely; it has pointed to the analogies between the literatures of the different countries and between the several arts. It is still the one convenient term which refers to the style which came after the Renaissance but preceded actual neoclassicism. . . . Baroque has provided an aesthetic term which has helped us to understand the literature of the time and which will help us to break the dependence of most literary history from periodisations derived from political and social history. Whatever the defects of the term baroque . . . it is a term which prepares for synthesis, draws our minds away from the mere accumulation of observations and facts, and paves the way for a future history of literature as a fine art.

From a mere pejorative adjective, the word has evolved, thus, into an evaluative concept, based not on a subjective criterion, but on the analysis and description of specific traits, intrinsic and stylistic in nature, that are found in artistic and literary manifestations of a determined period. From there it becomes a historical concept, the label of a period or stage of Western culture that is equivalent to the seventeenth century and designates the arts, sciences, and social life within its limits.

It should be noted, however, that to have critical and doctrinal validity, the concept must not be used, as it is by some defenders of a "pan-baroque" (Eugenio d'Ors), to designate a type of expression that may occur in any culture and in diverse moments as a universal and permanent tendency, a historical constant. It would destroy the concept completely to apply it to manifestations far-removed from the seventeenth century. There, and only there, did the spiritual conditions convenient for its development lie, as the formal aspect embodies a state of spirit marvellously adjusted to it. This is a relevant point, that of the limitation of the meaning of the expression.[22] The baroque is the adaptation of a style to the spiritual climate and to the ideological content of a determined period, the seventeenth century. This historical baroque, a concrete and esthetic style, a historico-cultural style, also demands a limitation in the use of the expression in order for it to have precision and universal meaning and usefulness in the critical vocabulary, as against an attempt to define a universal phenomenon.

The diverse types of formal organization correspond, as T. M. Greene shows in *The Arts and the Art of Criticism*, to a distinct interest and vision of the world. And he adds: "It was because the baroque artist saw the world and interpreted life in his way what he gradually developed those stylistic forms that most effectively let him express what he wanted to express; the forms were dictated by the intentions of the artist." [23]

In this way, implicit in the concept of the baroque are the definition of a historico-esthetic period and the identification of the style that characterizes it. It is an esthetic criterion for the analysis and under-standing of seventeenth-century works. By designating them as ba-roque, we are formulating thereby a perspective for an understanding and a model for judgment, including, in a proper and total way, the whole literary-artistic phenomenon of the period. We are showing what characterizes them esthetically, what the literary constants of the period are, the components of its style, clearly differentiating them from Renaissance and neoclassical works. To speak of the baroque and the literary baroque is to suggest a complex of unmistakable esthetic-literary values as regards the characterization of the literary work in its intrinsic qualities, its style, its motivations, as well as its ideological content.[24]

The baroque is, therefore, an artistic and literary style and, beyond that, the style of life that dominated the period contained between the end of the sixteenth and the start of the eighteenth centuries, and in which all Western peoples joined. There is a common cultural at-mosphere in that period which is expressed in a style, and which can be felt more intensely at certain particular points, due to the circum-stances of history or national temperament. Whatever these national or individual differences in the expression of the baroque phenomenon may be, there is among the diverse manifestations a common tendency and there are common attributes that make a universal phenomenon of it during the seventeenth century.

For modern theory, the baroque is a broad concept, with a scope that includes varied and different manifestations according to the country involved. It is also known by the local terms of *conceptism* and *culteranism* (Spain and Portugal), *Marinism* (Italy), *euphuism* (England), *préciosité* (France), *Silesianism* (Germany); many of these are imperfect or underdeveloped forms. *Baroque* has the advantage of being a single term, as well as denoting by itself the esthetic and stylistic characteristics contained in the period.

Among critics and scholars there is a continuing conceptual clarification of the baroque as the word becomes more and more established in the international critical vocabulary. What is beyond doubt is the internal unity of the movement, the identity of its esthetic ideals, its homogeneity, the characteristics common to all of its artistic manifestations: painting, sculpture, architecture, music, poetry, and prose.

In a general way, the baroque is a style identified with an ideology, and its unity results from morphological attributes as they translate a spiritual content, an ideology.[25]

The baroque ideology was furnished by the Counter Reformation and by the Council of Trent, to which is owed the peculiar coloration of the period, in art, thought, religion, social and political concepts. We can look at the Renaissance as a movement of rebellion in art, philosophy, science, and literature against the ideals of medieval civilization with a revaluation of classical antiquity, not only in its art forms, but also as concerns its rationalist philosophy and its pagan and humanistic concept of the world, which established modern anthropocentrism. We can understand the baroque then as a counter-reaction to those tendencies, under the aegis of the Catholic Counter Reformation, an attempt to rediscover the lost thread of Christian tradition, an attempt to express it within new artistic and intellectual molds.

This duel between the Christian element inherited from the Middle Ages and the rationalist and pagan element established by the Renaissance under the influence of antiquity, dominated the modern age down to the end of the eighteenth century, when, with the Philosophes, the Enlightenment, and the French Revolution, the rationalist current gained ascendancy. The line of medieval Christian tradition kept itself

alive with a latent and underground form, and it found its tone in the
baroque which raised a dike against the rationalist wave; it was not
completely contained, however and finally overwhelmed the baroque.
What characterized the essence of the baroque spirit was, therefore,
the dualism, the oppositions, contrasts and contradictions, the state of
conflict and tension that arose out of the duel between the Christian
spirit, anti-worldly, theocentric, and the secular spirit, rationalist and
worldly.[26] There existed a series of antitheses—asceticism and worldli-
ness, flesh and spirit, sensualism and mysticism, religiosity and eroticism, realism and idealism, naturalism and illusionism, heaven and earth,
all of which were true dichotomies or "conflicts of antithetical tendencies" (Meissner), "violent disharmonies" (Wellek). These were
translations of the tension between classical forms and the Christian
ethos, between medieval tradition and the growing secular spirit that
started with the Renaissance. The baroque soul is formed by this
dualism, by this state of tension and conflict, and it is the expression
of a gigantic attempt at the conciliation of two poles considered until
then irreconcilable and opposed: reason and faith. The movement was
religious at its core, seeking the restoration of medieval values of life
as against the Renaissance current.

At the same time, however, Western man no longer wished to let
go of the potentialities of earthly life that Renaissance humanism and
the special broadening of the world had revealed to him, thence the
conflict between the ideal of flight from and renunciation of the world
and earthly attractions and solicitations. As he faced the dilemma, instead of an impossible destruction, he sought conciliation, incorporation, absorption. This was a tendency which the Catholic Church understood well, seized, and attempted to lead with wisdom by means of
the Counter-Reformation, and of which the Jesuit spirit is the incarnation.

The Counter-Reformation used the concept of the "open man"
turned towards Heaven, in opposition to the Renaissance idea of the
"closed man" limited to the earth. To this Wölfflin's theory of the
open and closed forms in arts and letters corresponds. Renaissance
rationalism had cut down the Jacob's Ladder that united man to God.
The Counter-Reformation returned to the "vertical line of medieval-
ism," as Stephen Gilman says, reaffirming the ties of man with the
divine, ties that had been broken by the Renaissance. Baroque man

yearns for medieval religiosity, which the Church was able to re-inspire in him by artistic devices and by the dynamic reaction of the Counter-Reformation, reviving the terrors of Hell and the anxiety for eternity. But he was, at the same time, seduced by earthly solicitations and by values of the world (love, money, luxury, position, adventure) which the Renaissance, humanism, and maritime discoveries and modern inventions had placed sharply in relief. Baroque art is im-pregnated with this conflict, with this dualism.

The baroque movement is, then, a result of the spiritual counter-reaction against the humanistic and rationalist Renaissance. The theory of the Counter-Reformation origins of the baroque and its connection with the ideology of the Tridentine movement and with the action of the Society of Jesus, to the point of calling baroque style Jesuit style, is sustained by various students of the phenomenon such as Weisbach, Weibel, McComb, and Hatzfeld. According to Hatzfeld Spain is the mother country of the baroque, and from there it spread out over the rest of Europe. This explains Spain's having been the most im-portant point of irradiation for the Counter-Reformation, in which baroque art is most typically presented. There exists in the Spanish soul, furthermore, a permanent and unconscious baroque spirit that goes back to Roman Spain, as can be seen in Hispano-Roman writers like Lucan, Seneca, and Martial. The baroque spirit, a natural tendency of hers according to Hatzfeld, is exaggerated by Spain into a historical and conscious baroque spirit during the seventeenth century, which used baroque paint to color Italy and other countries through the Jesuit militia and, thanks to the aims of the Counter-Reformation, to rekindle the spirit of true religiosity in the West. As Sommerfeld states, this wave of religiosity was broad and enveloping with great dynamism and exaltation, which pulled clergy and laity along, at-tracted the papacy, and united mysticism and scholasticism in the *Spiritual Exercises* of Loyola. The reaction had been at work and was gaining adepts since 1520 in Spain, even though it is in the Council assembled in Trent from 1545 to 1563 that the laws were codified. The idea of a struggle characterized it, exemplified by the very basis of the Society of Jesus (1540) as a combat militia, the true shock troops of the Counter-Reformation. The fact that it was in Italy, during Michelangelo's final phase (his *Last Judgment* is from 1541), that the first baroque manifestations arose is easily explained by the

intense Hispanic influence that Italy experienced under Iberian domination. Leo Spitzer, in this respect, stated that the baroque arose historically in Italy, but that it was preconceived in Spain. Hatzfeld
asserts that if the Italian Michelangelo was the father of the formal
baroque, the Spaniard Loyola was the one who inspired the spirit of
the Counter-Reformation. The problem of baroque origins can be
summed up, relative to the history of ideas, in Spanish influence in
Italy between the years 1530 and 1540, when Pope Paul III was under
the influence of Saint Ignatius Loyola. From the meeting of Italy
and Spain, from this Mediterranean-Catholic complex, the forms and
ideas that made up the baroque expanded, producing a common climate
for the period that followed, passing gradually from country to country, dominating some before others; not even the adversaries of the
Counter-Reformation could resist its dynamism as they became acquainted with its ideals and methods and became contaminated by
its exaltation.[27]

It cannot be stated that the Counter-Reformation created baroque
style. According to the teachings of Wölfflin, baroque style followed
its own evolution, according to laws that are immanent in artistic
forms, and emerged out of Renaissance style. But as Sommerfeld points
out, the Counter-Reformation outlined baroque style, adapting it to
proposals and necessities, making the style victorious. In the same
way that it set itself up to lead the message of the movement, it
showed itself in the form of church buildings, sculpture, painting, and
literature. If the Counter-Reformation was rather fortunate, it was
no less wise in finding comfort in the baroque, the only style to which
it could adapt itself with all of its rigor. An identical alliance could
not have been made with Renaissance style, whose traits were clarity,
symmetry, finiteness, a sense of the world. On the contrary, baroque
art was well-equipped to speak an emotive language, one of transcendentalism or ambiguity. In this way baroque pomp became the
ideal instrument for the dynamic and exalted Counter-Reformation.

The baroque possessed, therefore, an eminently religious feeling and
it constituted "the molding expression or language of the institutions"
that grew out of the religious energy of the Counter-Reformation,
and it realized "the fusion of formal expression and spiritual expression," as Weisbach says.[28] The ideology current in the baroque resulted from the spiritual movement that had been unleashed by the

Counter-Revolution in its desire to bring together man and God, the heavenly and the earthly, the religious and the profane, reconciling the medieval and Renaissance heritages. Thus, dualism and contrast form the spiritual or ideological axis of the baroque. A period attracted by polar forces, it cannot offer a uniform and placid aspect, cut as it is by antagonistic and contrasting movements. The internal structure of the baroque is fed by this dualism, by this contradictory character. Weisbach pointed out the principal peculiar notions of baroque art, those which give it its "unity of style": heroism, asceticism, mysticism, eroticism, cruelty. These elements are mingled in all of the manifestations of the period, whether in habits and manners of living and acting, whether in the very texture of social life. The poetry of Marino, Donne, Góngora, or Gregório de Matos mixes religiosity and sensualism, eroticism and mysticism in erotico-spiritual outpourings (Weisbach), to form a typical sensual naturalism.

In lyricism as in mysticism, this sensualization of religious matter exists, even though often hidden under all manner of disguises or rhetorical and stylistic devices, distortions, and obscurities so much to the taste of the period.

Along with the erotico-religious factor and the heroic factor, the other constant of the baroque spirit is the preference for the cruel, painful, frightening, terrifying, bloody, and repugnant aspects that signify the intention of drawing out the greatest suggestive effect by sensory means, that is, reaching a convincing impression by means of what the senses grasp. Baroque poetry receives its inspiration from sensory impressions, as Calcaterra has pointed out: "The poetry of the world savored deeply with the sight, the ear, the palate, the nose, the touch." In the Counter-Reformation, heroism assumed a pathetic configuration, while these last aspects gave a melancholy and pessimistic tone to the baroque soul. It was the source of the esthetic of the ugly (the "uglyism" that Lafuente Ferrari speaks of), a common theme in baroque poetry, particularly feminine ugliness; this is also the source of "blood dramas" of good Senecan tradition as well, which had a great vogue in the period as can be seen in Shakespeare's baroque phase. Although this recourse to hair-raising scenes and descriptions, both horrifying and cruel, was a characteristic of the theater, it appeared also in oratory, of Father Antônio Vieira, for example.

Baroque naturalism does not even stop in the face of death, of the tomb, of physical corruption and decay in its intent to obtain figurative and dramatic effects. Aldous Huxley showed how the baroque is an art of death and tombs, in which the figure of death, skeleton and skull, is a common illustrative theme, along with physical disintegration and the act of dying. These "reminders of mortality" (Huxley) try to show man the misery and the inanity of terrestrial life by means of images that give him a sensitive impression of these notions. It is seventeenth-century pessimism about life on earth made pleasant only by belief in the celestial good fortune to which all should aspire by renouncing natural goods, with the typical example of Pascal's thoughts. Next to death, the supreme theme of the baroque, the representation and description of martyrdom and penitence also figure by which the martyr and his moments of pain and pleasure are accentuated. Tranquility and ecstasy, repentance and joy, shame and home, fear and beatitude as they reflect the state of interior tension and violence in the soul can be seen in seventeenth-century iconography.

As he studies the baroque ideology, Stephen Gilman assigns it a tendency towards pessimism, to the conflict between man and the world, and cosmic discontent, with only three exits: disdain, flight, combat. Themes of escape and discontent (the "joy of discontent" that Ortega y Gasset speaks of), the neostoic disdain of the people that developed into *cultismo*, a feeling of frustrated superiority, disenchantment, an atmosphere of despair and melancholy, these are found in baroque art.

Pfandl and Sáinz de Robles emphasize what they call baroque feeling as an important element of the baroque spirit, composed as it is of naturalism, illusionism, the exaggeration of individuality, and the humanization of the supernatural. According to Pfandl, baroque naturalism is expressed in an avid, vital impulse, in brutality, immorality, cruelty, a cynical spirit of mockery, criminality, along with disillusion, truculence, melancholy, hypochondria. Illusion was a part of the spirituality that persisted and was a contradiction of the period which explained the double-faced position of men who were at once saints and libertines, the mixed festivals, religious and profane, sacramental dances in cathedrals and processions, the delights of meditation on death and hell, the mixture and blasphemy and acts of contrition and religious exaltation, and so forth. As for the exaggeration of individuality, what interested the baroque in the individual was ingenuity, wit. The baroque man was endowed with *furor ingenii,* through which he reached egocentrism, a liking for polemics, pamphleteering, intrigues. Lastly, baroque man humanizes the supernatural, he links Heaven and earth, he mixes the two levels in his daily life and does not have to cease being a rogue in order to participate in the celestial vision of things.

To these traits one must add still others that are pointed out by Díaz-Plaja: thematic nihilism, abounding in the melancholy and solitude so alive among those "rare" isolated poets, cultivators of the art of "being alone." To the cult of contrast in art we owe the shock of colors, the exaggeration of reliefs, expressionism; the violent confrontation of opposing ideas, love-pain, life-death, youth-age, for example. These were highly refined themes placed alongside others rooted in baseness and obscenity, the idealized sublime alongside the exaggerated repulsive reality.

All of this ideology finds expression in art and literature through a theme of its own that is destined to infuse an aversion for earthly existence and lead to religion as the only possible antidote for that life which is nothing but a dream, a stage, a comedy, a lie.

Baroque literature, in its drive to translate the ideology of seventeenth-century man into a special form, polarized by contradictory forces and inspired by the exaltation of religious mystery, presents identifiable attributes. It is a literature, to use the words of Lafuente Ferrari, that expresses a deep feeling of the drama of man and the world, the tragic sense of existence, the anguish of man as he faces the Cosmos, the idea of the salvation of the single human through art.

There is a characteristic common to all of it that is expressed in specific qualities and has been studied very well in the general identity of forms and ideas by Helmut Hatzfeld, whose description follows in an abbreviated form.[29]

Baroque literature is a consequence of Aristotelian humanism which dominated the period along with Horatian rhetoric which communicated to the writers certain moralizing preoccupations, reflected in the attention paid the problem of polishing one's self and of language that was decorous and refined.[30] The baroque sensibility reinterpreted Aristotle, giving him an ethico-literary sense through his fusion with Horace. Literature was to be a purge, a stimulus to virtue and the struggle against evil inclinations, joining the search for moral perfection with artistic enchantment, which means that it aimed to instruct by giving pleasure. Out of that sprang an "immanent inquisition" (Bataillon), a preoccupation with "decency and decorum" (Cervantes), *bienséance*, scruples, hypocrisy, the tactic of circumlocution, periphrasis, metonymy to cover indecorous situations.

Another important characteristic according to Hatzfeld's analysis is *fusionism*. Baroque literature applied the Aristotelian rule of the unification of details or isolated elements in a living organism, in an indestructible unity, in an organic whole, so that the loss or change of any of them would bring about the destruction of them all. "A complete body of fable with all of its members," Cervantes defined with precision the structure of this unity. The unification of the details in a whole resulted in a *beau désordre*, "a disordered order," while the fusion of details among themselves produced a "confusedly clear form," that is, the relative and hazy clarity of Wölfflin. Things, people, actions are not described, only evoked; their indistinct and vague outlines come together, reflected as if in a mirror by the vision of the characters: perspectivism, expressionism, and telescoping are the most common forms of expression, along with a prismatic element.

Related to fusionism is the technique of the nullifying passages between parts and chapters. Border lines are erased so that they interpenetrate, the end of one containing something that lays the ground for what follows. Other aspects of fusionism are *chiaroscuro* and echo. The first comes from the fusion of light and darkness, which baroque paintings used to such great advantage but which was also amply explored by literature. It corresponds acoustically to the echo, or the fusion of sounds or well-sounding elements, words or syllables, that was attained by the use of certain traditional figures such as anaphora, paronomasia, the anonym, the parecheme, and the paronym.

Next to material fusion, Hatzfeld shows further that there is fusion between the rational and the irrational, whose form of expression is the paradox by oxymoron. The Counter-Reformation proclaimed the superiority of the divine paradox of mystery and faith over rational clarity, of the tragic sense of existence and the restlessness of struggle over the Apollonian ideal of the Renaissance, of the metaphysical "open man" over the rational "closed man." Paradox was the basis of divided characters that were attracted by opposite poles, by contradictory feelings. These were types "coherently incoherent" who aroused pity and fear, like that "sane madman" Don Quixote, who spoke a language full of combinations of incongruous or contradictory words like cruel kindness and magnanimous lie, that favored a deliberate ambiguity.

Baroque art also expressed the pathos that dominated a whole society, translated into a feeling of splendor and grandiosity, of magnificence and pomp, of majesty and heroic greatness, expressed by the superlative and hyperbole, by the exaggerated epithet. This tendency found its reverse, however, in a penchant for reunification and the nobility of the soul that is responsible for the unstable balance of many Baroque characters as they live between virtue and weakness, between purity and sin, between moral rectitude or arduous struggle, and fall and repentance. There is no mediocrity in this soul because God is there, in the heart and spirit even when confused by sin.

In addition to these characteristics that Hatzfeld has mentioned, Raymond Lebègue has studied certain psychological and thematic elements of the baroque that deserve attention: the intensity, or the desire to give intense expression to the feeling of existence, which was seen in an abuse of hyperbole, in an exacerbation of passions and feelings, in an intensity of amorous pain, of jealousy or repentance (even leading to madness), of sexual desire (translated into fiery words, leading even to murder, rape, incest), in the excesses of despair, in extreme pride, in the joy of strong emotions, of terrifying spectacles, of death, of the macabre, of hallucinations, of the fantastic.

The Jesuits conceived of literature along Horatian lines (*docere cum delectare*) as a means of action on souls, more for proselytizing and instruction than for its pure esthetic value. For pedagogical and moralizing reasons (a concept widespread in the baroque period) the Jesuits found in the theater a vehicle of extraordinary effect which they used extensively both in Europe and in their missions. Drama was the baroque genre best suited to Ignatian intuitions. As in practice it broke with the rules that had dominated Renaissance poetics, even though it respected them in theory, the baroque theater introduced novelties as typical as the dislocation of the center of interest or gravity, the multiplication of points of view and protagonists, disproportion, and ornamental pomp. Also introduced were such operational elements as the division of the stage from the audience, the darkening of the theater (adopted by the Jesuits), the devil as a character, thunder, lightning, fire and smoke, and other devices to suggest the supernatural and the miraculous, or funereal pomp and ceremonies to give an impression of death or hell. It was not only the actors who took part in the play, but the audience too, which had no will of its own and was pulled into the dramatic event and involved in it. In all of Europe, especially Germany, Loyola's disciples gave the genre a great efficacy.

To the general qualities described above, which reflect the metaphysical interests, the melancholy temperament, and the contradictory taste of the baroque soul, the profound sense of the tragic drama of man and the world in the seventeenth century, one must add an analysis of the style. There is produced in the baroque a superimposition of style and ideology, of form and spirit, so that the critical method with which to study it must combine the stylistic point of view with psychologico-historical, stylistic, and ideological criteria. In addition to the ideological content that expresses the religious belief and concept of the world dominant at the time, the baroque can be distinguished by morphological and stylistic attributes to which much of the internal unity of the period is due. These appeared in all of the arts—painting, sculpture, architecture, music, and literature.

The notion at the basis of the study of baroque style is that what distinguishes baroque art in any of its manifestations is a constellation of signs and devices. In isolation, they do not characterize the baroque. Nor do they all appear at the same time, but are scattered here and there, sometimes a distinctive element predominating, sometimes some formal or spiritual factor. This sum of formal and ideological elements is what gives a typical physiognomy to the baroque. Furthermore, what gives a style its peculiar stamp is, first off, the predominance of certain devices and not its exclusiveness.[31]

The baroque style attempts to portray the state of conflict or spiritual tension in man by means of appropriate elements, devices, and figures such as antithesis, paradox, contorsion, *préciosité*, asyndeton, metaphor, emblematic images, sensual symbolism, synesthesia, hyperbole, catachresis. They are the expressions of a state of inner tension between form and content, of a state of turbulence, of aggression, of the "conflict between the individual and an insecure world."

The study of the baroque in its formal aspect derives from the application of Wölfflin's categories to literature, which, in isolation or combined, characterize baroque literature: openness, pictorialness, *chiaroscuro*, asymmetry, as opposed to the clarity, harmony, and proportionality of literature of Renaissance or neoclassical inspiration.

Other interpretations include a sense of the decorative, which results in a deliberate use of ornaments and figures to obtain specific effects. Thus, as Wellek stresses, what denotes the literary baroque as far as style is concerned is an abundance of ornaments, formal elaboration, an abuse of *concetti*, overworked style, richly woven with figures such as antithesis and asyndeton, antimetabole, oxymoron, paradox, and hyperbole.

The baroque offered an excellent field for research and study to the new science of style or stylology, one of the branches into which modern literary criticism of intrinsic tendency is divided. The great masters of modern stylolgy were the ones who best scrutinized the stylistic typology of the baroque. Leo Spitzer, Karl Vossler, H. Hatzfeld, Dámaso Alonso, Morris Croll, among others, combined to untangle the meanderings of baroque expression, extended the map of the baroque to cover writers never before suspected of that contamination, and removed the pejorative prejudices from an understanding of the phenomenon.

As a general element of the baroque style, one notes the preference for wit, witticism, *concetti*, for metaphysical obscurity, and for the *discordia concors* ("a combination of dissimilar images or the revelation of hidden similarities in apparently unlike things"). There is also emphasis on "perspectivism," an impressionistic style in which writers presuppose that truth is known only to God and that we can grasp only its various appearances or perspectives, even when they are contradictory. The baroque is therefore a prismatic style, in which impressions are communicated through diverse facets, the various aspects of an action, which are united in the mind of God. There is a preference for prismatic verbs, by means of which, according to Hatzfeld, an action is deprived of its immediate analysis and seems to be broken up into a myriad of disconnected or unrelated impressions; just as a ray of light is divided by a prism, there exists between author and description, an eye, an ear, or some other sensorial receptacle which influences the impression.

To the pioneer studies of Morris Croll and of Williamson, Merchant, and Hendrickson, we owe a knowledge of the development of baroque prose, developed to replace Ciceronian style, "great style," *genus nobile*, round, periodical, oratorical, peculiar to the Renaissance, when the influence of Cicero was dominant. Baroque prose was epigrammatic, sententious, minor key, terse, asymmetrical, of a *genus humile* which corresponded to the Latin writers of the Silver Age, Tacitus and, most especially, Seneca. This transition is the history of the anti-Ciceronian movement which developed in prose starting with the middle of the sixteenth century; the dialogue *Ciceronanus* (1563) by Erasmus was its most important landmark, even though to Muret (1526–1585) must go the credit for the decisive action in creating a new style and introducing new models from antiquity. Montaigne, Bacon, and Lipsius were the disseminators of this new ideal of taste which installed Seneca and Tacitus in the place of Cicero as the inspiration for seventeenth-century prose.

The anti-Ciceronian revolt that shook literary ideas in the second half of the sixteenth century had as a consequence the creation of a new style which prevailed during the seventeenth century. The characteristics were: brevity or concision allied to obscurity, a manner that was spicy, spasmodic, abrupt, disconnected, witty, sententious, antithetical, metaphorical, a *style coupé*. This *genus humile, submissum, demissum,* philosophical and essayistic style, more to be read than heard, preferred the figures of thought to those of words, *figurae sententiae,* means of persuasion that are aimed at the mind (anaphora, aphorism, antithesis, paradox).

The two styles, *genus nobile* and *genus humile,* served the different aims and temperaments of the two periods. The Renaissance found in the oratorical manner the ideal for spoken literature at public and private gatherings, court ceremonies and festivals; and the baroque, which was a period of withdrawal and meditation, of interiorization and moral reflection preferred a style that was essayistic, philosophical, subtle, familiar, drawn from Roman writers of the Silver Age, Tacitus and Seneca, and dedicated to the practice of stoic philosophy. It is, therefore, the *genus humile,* the Senecan "amble," the style today known as baroque, employed to express not a thought but a spirit in the act of thinking. Its principal characteristics, according to the studies of Croll, are: brevity in its members, imaginative order, asymmetry, the omission of ordinary syntactical connections. These traits gave baroque prose a constant novelty and unpredictability, a spiraling movement, an imaginative progression, and they were obtained by the use of certain syntactical types and figures such as the absolute participial construction, the parenthetical construction (a chain-like order), the anacoluthon, the independence of members, the free progression of sentences which constantly open forward and upward, towards infinity, without consideration for or relationship to the beginning of the discourse.

In her study of the baroque style in Góngora, Evelyn E. Uhrhan established six patterns that she called principles regulating baroque style: transposition (anteposition and postposition); separation (interpolation in an expression of an element that is not part of that expression); duplication (joining of parts of sentences—words, phrases, or expressions of action—by certain linguistic means: parallelism, repetition, a common element); asymmetry (one element in an expression being considerably longer than the others); modification (horizontal, vertical, total); and substitution (various constructions of phrase or clause being used in the place of a single element which would be grammatically sufficient).

In a general way, the state of interior tension, a base of the baroque which is produced by the conflict between contrary convictions or opposing tendencies, seeks the most apt forms with which to express itself. Therefore, as interpreters of the baroque style, among whom is Maggioni with his study of Pascal, point out, its essential principle is a search for a union of the disunited, "unifying disunity," whose manifestations are quite diverse: antinomy, asymmetry, paradox, antithesis, irregular expression, constant movement, alternation, absence of repose, syncopated form, *chiaroscuro*, plurimembration (so well-studied by Dámaso Alonso), punctuation by semi-colon and colon to give flexibility and movement to the prose and to remove any idea of limit from it.

These morphological attributes shape the baroque, unite it to the Tridentine ideology so as to stamp the period with a peculiar physiognomy, ornamental and tragic, dilacerated and melancholy. All of its spiritual products show an essential identity, as if the spirit of a period, as Dvorak says, were a unique spring from whose waters the creations of art, literature, and thought flow.

The modern concept of the baroque is not limited to the traditional acceptance of conceptism, culteranism, Marinism, *préciosité*, Gongorism, and so forth, which carry a pejorative sense. The baroque is not an inferior form but a style with its own qualities and esthetic elements, peculiar to a determined period, the seventeenth century, involving the majority of writers and artists of the time. As Roy Daniels says, the baroque is a comprehensive form of art based on a specific artistic sensibility that, in turn, emerges from a general sensibility.

In accordance with the reclassification that resulted from the application of the concept to seventeenth-century literature, the baroque map includes writers from all Western literatures, some in a complete way, others in this or that aspect. Thus, beginning with Italian literature: Tasso, Marino, Della Porta, Guarini, Bruno; Spanish: Herrera, Góngora, Quevedo, Cervantes, Lope de Vega, Calderón, Tirso de Molina, Gracián, Paravicino, Alemán; German: Gryphius, Opitz, Silesius; English: Lily, Donne, Herbert, Carew, Crashaw, Vaughan, Cowley, Marvell (the metaphysical poets), Shakespeare, Ben Jonson, Webster, Ford, Tourneur, Middleton, Kyd, Marston, Bacon, Browne, Bunyan, and so forth; French: Montaigne, Charron, Sponde, Saint-Evremond, Pascal, Boileau, Corneille, Racine, Desportes, Garnier, D'Aubigné, D'Urfé, Mlle. Scudéry (*préciosité*), and so forth; Portuguese: the collaborators of the *Fênix Renascida*, Francisco Manuel de Melo, Rodrigues Lobo, Frei Antônio das Chagas, Jerônimo Bahia, Violante do Céu (recent studies include Camões in the baroque orbit); Spanish American literature: Balbuena, Hojeda, Caviedes, Sor Juana Inés de la Cruz.

Outside of literature are the names of Michelangelo, Tintoretto, Bernini, Borromini, Monteverdi, El Greco, Velázquez, Ribera, Zurbarán, Rembrandt, Poussin, Bach, and Händel, for example.

The baroque is, therefore, an esthetic movement of universal scope, a form of high artistic value. The revaluation of seventeenth-century literature was followed, naturally, in Portuguese literatures by a reaction against the traditionally pejorative judgment as regards literary production in Portugal and Brazil during the same period. The pejorative concept that dominated criticism held it in disdain, labeling it as conceptism, culteranism, and Gongorism, defining it as a degenerate and decadent form, characterized by an exaggerated preoccupation with form, by the abuse of figured, ornamental, and high-flown style, by the search for obscurity. It was an attitude that completely misunderstood the seventeenth-century phenomenon, showing especially a lack of critical perspective and a terminological imprecision in labeling as classical Portuguese and Brazilian production that appeared in the seventeenth century. It was baroque in origin, spirit, and style, as can be seen when it is studied in the light of the new critical and stylological criteriology to which the revalidation and reinterpretation of the literary baroque is due.[32]

The literature of colonial Brazil is baroque literature and not classical as was the rule to call it until recently. Literature was born in Brazil under the sign of the baroque, from the baroque hand of the Jesuits. It was to the plastic genius of the baroque that was owed the implantation of the long process of interbreeding which was the principal characteristic of Brazilian culture, as European forms were adapted to the new environment through the "transculturation" mentioned by Fernando Ortiz, reconciling two worlds, the European and the autochthonous.

What should be said about Brazilian literature of the seventeenth century is not that it is inferior because it is baroque (or Gongoristic, to use the epithet that came into current usage as a designation of the tendency even outside the seventeenth century), but that it was a baroque literature of inferior quality with rare exceptions. It is generally, in poetry especially, an imitative baroque, lacking in vitality and superior esthetic content.[33] The explanation possibly lies less in the general conditions of life in the colony than in the fact that, for reasons still not clear, literary genres had not developed completely in the Portuguese literature of the period, of which Brazilian literature is but a page.[34] This is in contrast to what had occurred in Spanish, French, and English literatures, and furthermore is a criticism that can be extended to all of Portuguese literature down to present times.

The study of the colonial period offers very great interest for an understanding of Brazilian culture. One can see the initial impact of cultures in the new environment, and the mixture that began immediately is the base of our culture, fundamental to the development of customs and forms of social organization, the fixing of values of life and ethical and legal systems, traits of individual and collective psychology, esthetic experiences. The problems of Brazilian origins are mingled with those of the culture that dominated the period, the baroque, out of which there even arose permanent characteristics:

oratory, a taste for rhetoric and the "word," that contaminated even lyric poetry and fiction.

The importance of the period, however, still stems from the fact that it produced a local expression of a universal style. The period showed rather differentiated qualities, especially in the plastic arts, where the "Jesuit style" produced the best of our colonial architecture.[35] Its high point was reached by Aleijadinho and the art of Minas Gerais, as well as in the baroque art of Bahia, the dazzling art of its churches that is dominated by the "tragic world of the black cut" in which the sky seems to have descended, as Godofredo Filho has said.

In letters, however, one must especially emphasize the contributions of the Jesuits, Anchieta in the fore, of Antônio Viera in oratory followed by a long line of descendants, the poetry of Gregório de Matos and Botelho de Oliveira. Narrative fiction is scarce in the period, but the representative example belongs to the baroque: the *Peregrino da América*. Brazilian baroque literature was not limited to the seventeenth century, and its elements will be found during the eighteenth century in literary academies and in oratory and poetry. It was to have a slow death, through a long process of degeneration, of mummification, in which the esthetic became a virtuosity of inflated style, of exaggerated figures, of plays on words, of twisted construction. If baroque literary manifestations have not always had an esthetic value in Brazil, they are most important as local expressions of the stylistic phenomenon.

Judged as a bloc, the Brazilian Jesuit literature of the sixteenth century is a typically baroque manifestation, from the evidence of its themes, ideology, structure, and intent. A missionary literature, it tried to serve the religious and pedagogical ideal of conversion and catechism. It tried to infuse into people's spirits a gloomy and pessimistic concept of earthly life, the mere transition towards eternity; the feeling of the vanity and inanity of life, of the contrast between light (celestial) and darkness (earthly), between grandeur and humility, spirit and flesh, salvation and damnation. Widespread was the notion of death and hell, of disillusionment (undeception) and horror of earthly things, of the destructive power of sin expressed in physical corruption, of the impermanence of time flowing on implacably to the surprise of man who draws from it the feeling of his own incapacity to stop the march towards decadence and dissolution. Fear dominates this literature, fear of death, of decadence, of hell, of the passage of time. It is the opposite of the joy and pleasure of living, the pleasure of action and of the world, of clarity that one finds in the Renaissance. An art more for the senses than the intelligence, it was through the senses and through the imagination and not through reason that the baroque conquered man. The use the Jesuits made in the theater and in architecture of grandiloquence and sumptuousness, of luxury and pomp, of the complicated and spectacular, of the gigantic and the terrifying, of devices that intimidated and impressed the senses, penetrating through them to the brain, is the result of this.

With Antônio Vieira's prose the baroque esthetic reached its high point in Brazil. Allying the essence of Senecan style, *coupé* and sententiousness, to emphasis, subtlety, paradox, contrast, repetition, asymmetry, parallelism, simile, metaphor, the great religious orator produced pages that are treasures of pulpit eloquence in the Portuguese language. He is a typical example of what Alfonso Reyes meant when he said: "The Gongoristic lyric, which some see as the offspring of the pulpit, [returned] its inheritance and [became] religious oratory [. . . and] some religious orators began to bring the devices of that poetical style into the pulpit."

Gregório de Matos, among his companions of the "Bahian School," made the strongest individual expression of baroque poetry in the colony. In spite of the large debt he owed to the great Spanish poets of the period, especially to Quevedo and Góngora (the influence of the latter was widespread and deep-seated in Latin America, as shown by Emilio Carilla and Sílvio Júlio) Matos's poetry is certainly the first eloquent manifestation of the cultural message that was being implanted in Brazil.

Through theme and stylistic technique, the work of Matos fits into the baroque. His soul was dominated by baroque dualism: a mixture of religiosity and sensualism, mysticism and eroticism, earthly and carnal values and spiritual aspirations. He is a good example of the baroque soul, in his polar situation, his state of conflict and spiritual contradiction. In his poetry, as in all baroque poetry, are joined together the sensual and the religious, the mystical and the licentious, the jovial and the ridiculous, the serious and the satirical, the profane and the holy, Heaven and earth, flesh and spirit, the fire of mystic love, the feeling of sin, the notion of penance, all of this expressed in imagery of sentimental origin and a constellation of figures and devices (echoes, assonances, antitheses, paradoxes, oxymorons) typical of the baroque.

The baroque impregnation was so strong in colonial Brazilian culture that even books foreign to literature did not escape it. In addition to the vast literature of panegyrics that fills the production of eighteenth-century academies, the baroque is the stylistic instrument of literary moralizing and religious intent, of devotion and asceticism, especially of that vast exhoratory literature so important in the colonial period and so popular, even after independence. Political and juridical literature, or administrative documents did not escape it; nor did historiographical prose and that which described the land. From earliest times with Frei Vicente do Salvador and Rocha Pita, this writing was already accustomed to the worst kind of baroque rhetoric.

It is necessary to stress in this respect a point that is always present in relation to the baroque: its distinction from "mannerism." [36] Wylie Sypher and Arnold Hauser consider the latter a style by itself, intermediate between the classical and the baroque. However, as Maggioni likes to see it, mannerism seems not to be a style, but a "manner," which "is to style what a caricature is to a portrait. It implies exaggeration, the emphasis of one or more traits to the detriment of others. In literature, most particularly, it is an absorbing preoccupation with the mechanics of form . . . in a manner that is inorganic [and] luxuriant. . . . Every style can have its mannerism." It is necessary, therefore, not to confuse the high point of the baroque with forms of baroque mannerism, often completely devoid of spiritual content. E. R. Curtius showed the medieval roots of many traits that circulated in baroque literature, "characteristics of medieval style," as Leo Spitzer says, many from the literature of the troubadors and from Petrarch. The baroque transformed these traits, however, giving to them its peculiar concept of life to which they were obliged to adapt themselves. It did the same with the Biblical heritage, which it mingled with classical elements, as in the Jesuit theater, in which two currents, as Weisbach stresses, one Biblical and the other mythological, live intertwined. But in those writers and artists who could not attain stylistic superiority, the elements of baroque mannerism stand out. The same occurs in the minor moments of great baroque writers and in phases of transition or preparation.[37]

In Iberian literatures—and one cannot isolate in the first three centuries of the modern age the Portuguese literatures from the Spanish—a problem stands out in the consideration of the baroque: the distinction between conceptism and culteranism. It is a debate that has come down to the present time, with critics and authors carefully making a distinction, according to which conceptism, favoring the conceit, would deal with the idea, while *cultismo* or *culteranismo* was tied to form, consciously trying to be "cultured," and, consequently, obscure. This polemic in the light of the present doctrine of the baroque no longer has any meaning, because it is practically impossible to isolate two types that are aspects of the same stylistic phenomenon, expressed sometimes under a sententious and conceptist form, and other times by various formal devices. There are writers in whom the two types are mixed, while in others one of them predominates. It occurs very frequently that an author reacts against *cultismo*, and in the very reaction falls into the vices that he is condemning, as was the case with Vieira.

Actually, the culteranist and conceptist faces formed an integral and inseparable part of the baroque esthetic. They were the base of the baroque, whose poetic credo leaned towards difficulty, obscurity through wit and ingenuity on the one side, and towards erudition, stylistic difficulty, neologism, and syntactical over-refinement on the other. The cult of the difficult and hermetic were deliberately obtained by means of conceptual confusion and an elevated and cultured language, an obscurity and sharpness of conceits, a use of high-sounding words, and a twisting of the sentence structure. Mario Praz showed that the liking for wit, with poetry often reduced to just that, is at the core of the baroque phenomenon.

Precepts stand out in the formation of the esthetic ideas of the baroque. The treatises on poetics and rhetoric, which exercised a great role in Renaissance and post-Renaissance literary pedagogy, were the code of norms that pointed the way for writers. Beginning with Aristotelian poetics and rhetoric, there developed a precept directed away from the Renaissance, separating, as Zonta stressed, reason and fantasy. Many of these rules existed in practice before they were incorporated into treatises. They had a broad influence on the Spanish treatises of Carrillo y Sotomayor, Gracián, Jáuregui, and Patón. In Portugal, along with the poetics of traditional Aristotelian-Horatian type, and rhetorical manuals, one must mention as a typical work of the baroque, *Nova*

Arte de Conceitos (Lisbon, 1718), by Francisco Leitão Ferreira (1667–1735), which consisted of thirty lessons that had been presented as lectures at the Academy of the Anonymous. Well-grounded in baroque thought, the generous and anonymous academician studies the various ways of "making conceits on any subject," and the book, although refuting him at times, is within the tradition laid down by Gracián, author of the *Agudeza y arte de ingenio* (1642), the bible of conceptism. Conceptism was part of the atmosphere of the time, and the material that came to make up Ferreira's book was part of the true body of doctrine followed throughout the seventeenth and eighteenth centuries.

Ferreira studies the art of conceits and all of the means of obtaining them in literature: conceptual signals, symbols, hieroglyphics, emblems, designs, metaphors, the ingenious verbal conceit, the ingenious argument, the sentence or moral maxim, the pathetic locution, paradoxical and hyperbolic conceits, amplification, the simile, comparison, and so forth. It is interesting to look at the role given to the emblematic and the enigmatic, the hieroglyphic and the design. These had a great vogue in the conceptualists symbology of the baroque, according to the exhaustive analyses by Mario Praz and Austin Warren of the use made of them by seventeenth-century poets, for example the Englishman Richard Crashaw.

There exists in the baroque an esthetic element that links it to Plotinian Neoplatonism, thanks to which baroque art and literature reveal esotericism, mystery, obscurity, cultivation of the difficult. Literature of cultistic intent draws away from the people and the popular by means of a poetic language that tends to be uncommon, by refined figures, by imagery, and by a symbolism that tends towards obscurity. It is an art of surprise, conquering through surprise and suggestion. It is an art that reflects a period of crisis and struggle, uncertainty and instability, restlessness and torment, imbalance and tension, in which man ceases to be the center of the earth, and the earth the center of the universe. The stylistic complex of this period does not reflect a state of degeneration, but, in its metaphorism, it reflects, as Getto accentuates, the instability of the reality at the center of the baroque vision of the world. In the baroque, the metaphor, as Getto points out further, is not merely an extrinsic rhetorical factor, but responds to the expressive necessity of a way of feeling and manifesting things as an element in a complex collection of allusions and illusions; it is a vision of reality according to which things seem to lose their static and well-defined nature and appear in a universal transfer that changes shapes and meanings. The baroque is a style that translates the religious and philosophical interpretation of a tormented period.

NEOCLASSICISM & ARCADIANISM. THE ROCOCO PERIOD

The classicizing current inaugurated by the Renaissance found an ideal climate in sixteenth-century Italy; held back by the baroque during the seventeenth century, however, only in the last decades of that century would it reach its high point in a movement that was, in fact, the only modern classicism ever realized in literature. It penetrated the eighteenth century, spotted with neoclassical tendencies and schools (rather than classicism and neoclassicism) the various Western literatures, and gave special colorings to the rationalist and "enlightened" currents that were triumphant in anticipation of and preparation for the French Revolution.

The eighteenth century is the meeting-place of spiritual and esthetic currents. Coming from afar, they arrive at a great estuary where they converge and mingle, some disappearing, others changing. The cultural atmosphere of the century shows this interpenetration of visible tendencies in figures and works that represent it. There is no absolute purity of style or ideology. The currents that cross the period impregnate each other, as if, by different paths, they are all heading towards the same objective, having departed from a single source and bearing identifical spiritual elements.

It is a period of crisis, the "crisis of the European conscience," that began around 1680 and was studied so well by Paul Hazard, within which a profound historical transformation took place. During the century, leadership passed from one class to another, from the aristocracy to the middle class. That transfer had its cultural, artistic, and literary manifestations. Seen at the outset was a conflict between ancients and moderns, clearly evident in France and England with the quarrel between ancients and moderns (1687–1716) and the Battle of the Books, and shown in a constant opposition between tradition and progress, classicism and modernism, rationalism and emotionalism, an antithesis found in Voltaire and Rousseau. The century was to be a

French century—*L'Europe des Lumières*—a hegemony that can be described as consolidating the revolution begun in the Renaissance. There was the spread of rationalism, experimentalism, of the spirit of investigation, the scientific concept of the world, and the broad mental renovation based on the progress of science and scientific activity. This spirit found a home in the *Encyclopedia* (1751–1765) of Diderot, d'Alembert, Helvetius, et al., the sum of the whole encyclopedist movement that had begun in 1675. The spirit included Rousseau, Voltaire, Montesquieu, and others, and had a part in the Declaration of the Rights of Man (1789). Encyclopedism and the Enlightenment[38] or the philosophy of illustration became mingled in a movement that was especially intense between 1715 and 1789, for which the *Encyclopedia* was the bible. The bourgeoisie was the social class that gave it application in life, in economics, in art, creating a society dominated by technology, by machines, and by industry. The Enlightenment had its political repercussions even before the French Revolution (1789), which, along with the American Revolution (1776), was its natural consequence. Enlightened despotism came about among some monarchs and heads of state, politician-philosophers who believed that they could conciliate the structure of the old regime with the reformist spirit of encyclopedism.

In literature, during its first half especially, the century is in transition, passing through contradictory tendencies, polarized between liberty and tradition, spontaneity and formalism, expressivity and ornamentalism. Bourgeois subjectivism advances firmly in the place of courtly formalism, not without attempting transitional forms along the way that still show a classical restoration, but in a different sense. Against seventeenth-century baroque taste, which still endures in the eighteenth century in degenerate and decadent forms, the spiritual movement for the conquest of a new artistic form attempts to open a path by means of successive experiences that in their mingling have the effect of making it confused and impure. The baroque taste for the splendid and the grandiose, for ostentation and the out-sized, was followed, without a complete liberation from the earlier period, by a search for the classical qualities of measure, convenience, discipline, purity, simplicity, and delicacy. This constituted the rococo and Arcadian. At the same time, however, as the absolute primacy of reason was sought, sentiment, sensibility, and irrationality were being cultivated. The break with the baroque, which finds strength in the law of imitation, is based on the imitation of the ancients, the only justification for giving the name of classicism to all of these currents. A general movement against authority characterizes the Enlightenment, however, especially during the second half of the eighteenth century.

Out of this comes a tangle of currents that join together to give the eighteenth century its contradictory physiognomy, where diverse social forces, different constellations of ideas and esthetic tendencies collide.

In Brazil too the eighteenth century was a moment of great importance, a phase of transition and preparation for independence. Staked out, populated, defended, with a widespread area, in that century it achieved economic prosperity, a betterment of the material conditions of life, political and administrative organization, an environment for cultural life, fertile soil for the seeds of liberty. It differs from the colony, as Oliveira Lima points out, by the creation of a historical consciousness. From the discovery and possession of the land, from the deeds of the *bandeirantes* as they pushed back the western frontiers, from the defense against the invader, there came naturally the formation of a common consciousness, a national feeling, which replaced the nativist description of nature and the aborigine. Instead of lyrical sentiment, there was a "national" pride in the acts of heroes and in political and military deeds. There emerged the figure of the "Brazilian," half-breed in blood and soul, the local type that miscegenation and acculturation had been developing, firmly grounded, with a sense of ownership of the land he had defended, preserved, and enlarged. He spoke a language that differed increasingly from that of the peninsula in accent and vocabulary, and sang in his own voice songs with local themes and rhythmical modulations that were in tune with the new sensibility the national soul was developing.

The colony went through a period of general economic, administrative, and social progress, to which the spirit and feelings corresponded in their clear orientation towards the acquisition of a national awareness. Exploitation of the mines was followed by a growth of economic and financial resources; the population was growing; the cities were becoming civilized; an aristocratic, class, based on slave labor, had spare time for cultural life, public and religious celebrations, social life; its members went to study at Coimbra in Europe, but later on, when instruction at that university weakened, to Bordeaux, Montpellier, and Paris, returning with the "light" of knowledge and the pleasure of culture, which they communicated to those who had not had the same good fortune. A movement of lettered men, of academies, of salons comes from all of this. On the other hand, between the local man and the peninsula, between the native and the immigrant, the animosity was growing, placing in opposition the developing mixed-blood conscience and Portuguese despotism. It was a nationalist movement that preceded autonomy directed against the absolutism maintained by the Portuguese, both in the mother country and in the colony. A series of uprisings for freedom, forerunners of independence, followed with periodic regularity from the beginning of the eighteenth century.

Along with material progress, spiritual factors joined in the transformation. Against the Coimbran and Jesuit monopoly of education that was shackled by decadent and traditionalist formalism, there were attacks. Luís António Verney's book, *Verdadeiro Método de Estudar* (1746), published in Portugal; and the educational reforms (1759) undertaken by the Marquis of Pombal, the "enlightened" prime minister of Joseph I, were the bases of a struggle against traditional Jesuit methods established in the kingdom and in the colony. With the expulsion of the Jesuits (1759), with Pombal's reforms in Brazil, and the breaking of the commercial monopoly, there was a broad eruption of curiosity about the country from foreign and native scientists. The vogue of science, typical of the century, penetrated the life of the colony. Expeditions ransacked Brazil in search of information about flora, fauna, and geography. Learned societies were established. Typical intellectuals of the period cultivated letters, philosophy, politics, and science at the same time. They were philosophers, economists, and men of letters. They were preoccupied with agricultural and mercantile problems, historical and genealogical problems, with the happiness of mankind and the rights of the citizen. Those were the norms that oriented those "Francophilic" men, intoxicated with France, steeped in French ideas that were considered seditious and subversive. In spite of their cultivators' being closely watched and punished by censorship and inquisition, these ideas continued to spread. They were smuggled into the colony in shipments of forbidden books that would come to be true libraries, such as those of Father Agostinho Gomes in Bahia and Canon Luís Vieira da Silva in Mariana during the time of the *Inconfidência Mineira.*

In this way, the mental revolution moved along against decadent and conventional scholasticism and in the name of scientific culture. The period was dominated by a polemical, irreligious, anticlerical, and rationalist tone, as it tried to incorporate natural science and technology and emphasized the scientific method and rationalist clarity. It opposed twisted baroque expressions in favor of direct and simple language.

Factors of a material order, expressions of the progress of the colony; political factors: on the one side despotism and decadence of life at the Portuguese court, and, on the other, the growing independent and nationalist spirit, related, furthermore, to identical moods in other parts of the American continent; cultural factors: the original modern ideas of the Encyclopedist movement, which had infiltrated the colony with Brazilians returning from study trips to Europe, and with the clandestine importation of books; psychological factors: the greater awareness and maturity of the mixed population, "the physical base of the revolution," that is, the new man who was the differentiating element in the civilization and who by that time had acquired his full historical consciousness; all combined for the consolidation of colonial life, giving the eighteenth century that complex physiognomy and making of it a decisive moment in Brazilian history.

The beginning of the eighteenth century gives a hint of the decadence of the baroque. There is a feeling that new forms will be prepared and new canons will arise. In the shadow of the literary academies an anemic and insipid literature is practiced, a pompous literature of praise and encomium filled with exaggerated metaphors and twisted conceits. It is a time of panegyrics for saints and noblemen, of the historiography of genealogies, of memoirs, of historical stories and descriptions of the land, of military chronicles. It is poetry by versifiers, dominated by artifice and shallowness, and by an encomiastic aim in which the norms of the baroque esthetic are distorted into such forms as the silva, echo, acrostic, *centões,* emblem, cross, pyramid. The distortions reveal a state of decadence and perversion in letters, an exaggeration of conventionalism and imitative intent, with a taste for poems composed in complicated forms that, though they call for great mechanical ability, are devoid of any poetic spontaneity and vitality.

Such a situation also reflected the backward cultural state that existed in Portugal during that phase and which lasted to the middle of the century, when the reforms of Pombal begin, inspired by Verney's book that fought against intellectual obscurantism, decadent scholasticism, and mummified rhetoric.

The typical phenomenon of the period was the establishment of academies, bringing together "people of major literature." The idea of academies, of Platonic inspiration, goes back to sixteenth-century Italy. In Brazil, however, the vogue came from Portugal, where in the seventeenth century, several academies had been established with the good intention of doing service to letters, even though in the end they became centers of the worst kind of Gongorism.[39] At first literary and baroque in nature, during the eighteenth century they came to have a scientific character, like the Royal Academy of History and the Royal Academy of Sciences, or Arcadian, like the Arcádia Lusitana.

In Brazil, at the start of the eighteenth century, certain intellectual activity was already noted. Nuno Marques Pereira mentions in his *Peregrino da América* being amazed at the number of poets there were in Bahia: ". . . one could only find ten people who are not poets among one hundred sons of Brazil who have been students or who are studying, for all of the others write verse in Latin or in the vernacular."[40] It was natural that they would tend to congregate, establishing the academies, the first centers of literary communion and corporative intellectual activity. It was in their shadow that Brazilian literary life was formed, in spite of the low state of their literary production, although in accordance with the taste of the period. For an atmosphere that was quite rarefied for such activity, a strong debt was owed them. More than that, they were the main centers of a sense of Brazilianness, which was now appearing collectively, no longer related only to the splendors of the land, as a pride in patriotic deeds, in the works that inspired their members or were produced by them, works of men such as Rocha Pita, Mirales, Jaboatão, Itaparica, et al. It was a feeling patent in the multiflorous *Júbilos da América* (1754), for example. It would not be going too far, therefore, to stress the importance of this academistic movement in Brazil, as has been done before by Romero,

Veríssimo, Carvalho, Mota, and Figueiredo. It is an index of a nascent associative intellectual spirit, and of a nationalism that was becoming conscious. It was preparation for emancipation, as can be deduced from the very names, which already included the qualification of *brasileiro* or *brasílico*, in frank reaction against the academies of the mother country, by whom Brazilian intellectuals considered themselves "forgotten."

Baroque literature, in spite of its decadence, was still able to infiltrate with a strong instinct for survival the most varied literary manifestations all through the eighteenth century; accompanying the aristocratic decline and the bourgeois rise, however, was an evident change in literary taste to new directions. Instead of attempting to express the power and greatness of life, it looked for grace and beauty, that which enchanted or pleased the sentiment, that which sought an artistic tradition. Although it did not reach preromanticism, the courtly literature of the baroque gave way to a transitional form. This passage was not intense, however. On the contrary, there is a conscious reaction against seventeenth-century baroque expressed in a broad movement of absolute classicism. From the example of the great French generation of Louis XIV, it developed a form of neoclassicism. As Toffanin affirms, classicism had died and the "classical spirit" was born.

Although forming part of that restoration of the forms and traditions of the ancient world which began with the Renaissance, the neoclassical movement of the eighteenth century differed from the classicism of the Italian *Quattrocento* or the Age of Louis XIV. Having appeared as a general European tendency in arts and literatures all through the century, neoclassicism had as its aim recapturing the spirit of the ancients, which it did without spontaneity, rather as a result of erudition and intellectual enthusiasm that came from a liking for archeological classical antiquity. Neoclassicism resulted from the application of formulas and abstract principles, of the preceptivist yoke, of rigid codes of critical values and literary forms, of critical and didactic preponderance, of the preference for intellectual and logical satisfaction in the place of emotion, for exterior elegance in the place of internal unity. Hence there was the coldness, the decorative refinement, the absence of human feelings, passion, and fantasy in this art of constrained creative freedom. It was poor in creative ferment as it cultivated an idealized beauty.

Neoclassicism inspired a code of critical rules that had their origins in the Renaissance, frozen and mechanized by rigid Cartesianism into the neoclassical credo, in which Aristotelian and Horatian principles were blended in accord with the central precept of neoclassicism, imitation of the ancients. Hence came the rule of the three unities for the theater, absolutism as a criterion of taste, the preponderance of form, the respect for decorum, "propriety," clarity, restraint, polish, *bienséance*. This was the spirit that dominated the critical theories of Boileau, Luzán, Pope, Dryden, Rymer, Gottsched, and Dr. Johnson.[41]

In neoclassical literature the forms of expositive prose predominated. Lyric and imaginative forms were completely unfavorable to it, while the epic, drama, heroicosatirical poetry, social satire, and tragicomedy lent themselves marvelously to its expression.

Neoclassicism fanned out through Europe in the postclassical France of Voltaire, Rapin, and Bouhours; in the England of the Augustan Age and Pope, Dryden, Dr. Johnson, Addison, Steele, Swift, Defoe, et al.; in the Germany of Winckelmann, Morhof and Gottsched; in the Italy of Goldoni and Alfieri; in the Spain of Huerta, López de Ayala, Feijóo, Luzán, et al.

The neoclassical manner also infiltrated the Luso-Brazilian spirit of the period as it attempted to combat baroque foliation in the name of the ideal of precision and logic, in spite of the fact that, in the majority of cases, this neoclassicism did not go beyond pseudoclassicism by submission first to the letter rather than the spirit of the classics, and by not always freeing itself from baroque constants. It appeared in some writers as a coloration with "enlightened" paints and in some of ideological liberalism, it contaminated Arcadianism, and it incorporated preromantic elements such as sentimentalism and nationalism. However, as Sílvio Romero stressed, one owed to neoclassical paranetics along with the lyric poetry of the Arcadians some real advances in the language, not to mention the influence that it exercised on philosophical thought and the spirit of autonomy so easily seen in preromantic writers.

The neoclassical form which proved to be the most attractive to eighteenth-century Portuguese literature was the Italian current known as Arcadianism.

Towards the end of the seventeenth century, the young former queen of Sweden, Christina, daughter of King Gustav Adolph, who had shortly before given up her throne and her Lutheranism to become a Catholic, took up residence in Rome. After having wandered through European courts, scandalizing the nobility and the masses with her knowledge and extravagances, with an enormous following and a rich library, she found a refuge in the Vatican. Intelligent, cultured, given to philosophical and literary studies, she had formed the habit during her days in Sweden of gathering together in the royal palace savants, artists, poets, and scientists, with whom she would form real academies for discussion of problems or reading of studies of a literary or scientific nature. In Rome, the queen attracted to her gatherings the fine flower of the Italian intelligentsia, forming an intellectual group that on her death in 1689 would be transformed into the Arcadia (1690). This was organized by friends of the queen who were desirous of keeping whole and growing the seed that she had sown.

With regulations and a program, the new academy, composed of sixteen members and presided over by Crescimbeni, was born.

The name Arcadia came from the legendary region of ancient Greece ruled over by the god Pan and inhabited by shepherds who entertained themselves with songs of love and poetical jousts, characterized by simplicity and spontaneity. It was the homeland of ancient pastoral poetry (Toffanin). Members of the Arcadia called themselves "shepherds," each one of them adopting a Greek or Latin pastoral name, with the president being the "Guardian General." The patron of the institution was the Infant Jesus, the symbol of simplicity (an indication of the absence in the Arcadian movement of contamination by anticlericalism of enlightened irreligiosity). As a sign of the pastoral spirit, the meetings took place in parks or the gardens of the great Roman villas until, in 1725, the opulent King John V of Portugal offered the academy the idyllic Parrasio woods, near the Janiculum.

The express purpose of the Arcadia was to combat *il cattivo gusto*, the bad taste that was the heritage of the seventeenth century. It was, therefore, a movement of reaction against the decadent baroque, with its pompous style, its conceptist subtleties, and its artificial rhetoric. Its program was precise, and it anticipated linguistic and literary reforms with an antiseventeenth-century bias. Proclaimed by the Arcadia to attain this renovation of worn-out canons was a return to the balance and simplicity of classical art, to the naturalness and clarity of primitive Greco-Roman models, in short, to a pure and genuine classicism.

This could be done by establishing true ancient esthetics and poetics, with classical form, with the *buon stile*, with the *naturalezza del dire*, with the good humanistic tradition, and with the Christian content, according to the example of Petrarch or, rather, of sixteenth-century Petrarchism. In this "antiseventeenth-century and classicizing premise" lies the principal inspiration of Arcadianism. It is the last wave of the movement for classical and rational restoration begun in the Renaissance. In opposition to baroque irrationalism, Arcadism reconciles, as Croce, Fubini, and Moncallero point out, rationalism and classicism: the sovereignty of reason and literary authority, the law of imitation, esthetic regularism, rational literary discipline, the seeking of truth in image and feeling, precision and reality of expression, measured tone, discipline, convenience. Reason is thus counterposed to the baroque, aided by simplicity, naturalness of expression, all as paths towards good poetical realization.

The myth of Arcadia is part of the complex of dream regions, products of Renaissance idealism, lands of utopia and cities of the sun. Arcadia is an ideal and fictitious region, one of extreme beauty whence disturbing passions were expelled, a marvelous and happy refuge for ideas and spiritual delights. This ideal region was located in the country, in the midst of pure nature, so that the theme of Arcadia would always be linked to pastoral and bucolic literature. By calling themselves shepherds, the Arcadians showed quite clearly their fantastic desire for escape to a rural paradise, translating their feelings into an ingenuous and idyllic poetry, pastoral in inspiration and motivation, and placing themselves outside of their real conditions. Sannazaro, in the pastoral novel *Arcadia* (1504), introduced the theme and the name into modern Western literature, influencing the development of the Italian Arcadian vogue, from which the movement in other countries began.

What was implicit in the Arcadian dream was a desire for

a free and pure lyrical expression of feelings, [as it is defined by Calcaterra] in contrast to reality and reason, with the supposition that real poetry is inspired by natural enthusiasm and is expressed naturally, in the name of a simplicity that is almost pastoral, by a fictitious primitive innocence, and by a bucolic ingenuousness, considering the feelings as the very source of poetry. [The Italian critic goes on to say:] Its artistic secret, its poetical *quiddità*, will be to grasp lyrically, by an inner route, the contrast between feeling and reason, which had become the two spiritual poles of eighteenth-century life.[42]

Two characteristics made a movement of Arcadia—more a style than a school, José Veríssimo rightly said—that is typically eighteenth-century: its supernational or international tendency and its democratic spirit. Along with its renovating finality, which made the institution join in a war of destruction against the reigning literary aberrations, bringing together not only the most famous men of the time (as is the case of the French Academy), but all of those who pondered a struggle for literary and linguistic reforms, the Arcadia assumed an international stamp, spreading out in branches throughout the various kingdoms of Italy, as well as attracting the association of individuals and cultural groups in foreign countries, which were called "colonies."

In addition, the Arcadia, by its egalitarian organization, was part of the democratic spirit, proclaiming itself a "literary republic," with an elected president and shepherds with fictitious names to show their renunciation of their social condition, all being equal without preference or privilege.

The basic concept of the Arcadian utopia is the identity between civilization and nature, with all beauty, purity, and spirituality residing in the latter. Thence the overevaluation of nature, the seat of pastoral life, exotic and strange, peopled by shepherds and shepherdesses, in contrast to city life, uncomfortable and anguished, from which those who desired the peace of the spirit and the pleasures of pure love had fled. The notion of nature, as shown by Willey[43] had no rival as the universally dominant idea in the eighteenth century: nature and its laws had indisputable authority, playing a significant role in all spheres, containing what would introduce order, unity, and proportion into art and literature. During the whole century, the concept of nature was the model, in spite of the changes that took place during its span. The idea of nature is at the center of the eighteenth-century concept of the world: cosmic nature and landscape nature, the nature of the heart (sentiment), and the nature of the brain (*esprit*).

In the various figures of the period and its diverse esthetic currents, the notion of nature is present as the strongest constant. The very myth of the eighteenth century is that of the union of man and nature, in the countryside. This can be grasped in the painting of the period, Watteau especially, with the creation of *fêtes galantes* and *fêtes champêtres*, groups of young people enjoying themselves, without worries, in peaceful, bucolic, and pastoral environments, with music, dancing, and poetry, or in episodes of the hunt. All of this reflects the concept of the state of nature as a golden and happy situation in an age of purity and goodness. It would be translated into Rousseau's concept of a naturally good man, which became the beginning of a real romantic religion. The feeling of nature, therefore, permeates all of the literature of the eighteenth century, even elements that are classical and mythological, baroque and enlightened.

Of the Italian writers of the period, those who had the greatest influence upon Portuguese literature were Metastasio (1698–1782), Rolli (1687–1765), Maffei (1675–1755), and Goldoni (1707–1793).

From Italy, the Arcadian movement passed to Portugal and to Brazil. Finding in the eighteenth century that Portugal had reacted strongly against Castilianism, with the restoration of political independence from Spain, the Arcadian antiseventeenth-century movement of Italian origin could only find fertile ground. In addition, the ground had been prepared by the vogue of academies, which, after having been centers of culteranism, in the second half of the eighteenth century became bodies of an Arcadian or a scientific and practical nature. This anti-baroque reaction encouraged the return to good classical tradition and also to French norms, from the influences of which the Italians had not yet fled. The academic current, therefore, reacted against its own excesses and continued on in other forms and with other objectives. It was a return to the simplicity and purity of classical models, to the tranquility of ancient life, that inspired this renovation of ancient canons.

In Portugal, Arcadianism was established with the Arcádia Lusitana (1756–1774), which brought together writers of renown and importance in Portuguese literary history such as António Dinis da Cruz e Silva, Gomes de Carvalho, Manuel de Figueiredo, Cândido Lusitano, Domingos dos Reis Quita, Corréia Garção, and José Caetano de Mesquita. There was also the New Arcadia, at the end of the eighteenth century, whose members included Bocage and José Agostinho de Macedo.

In Brazil, the Arcadian movement flourished among the poets of the so-called Minas School:[44] Cláudio Manuel da Costa, Basílio da Gama, Santa Rita Durão, Alvarenga Peixoto, Tomás Antônio Gonzaga, and Silva Alvarenga. Its beginning was marked by the publication of the *Obras Poéticas* (1768) of Cláudio Manuel da Costa. Of all the Arcadians, the only one who really belonged to any Arcadian organization was Basílio da Gama, who had been affiliated with the Roman Arcadia with the name Termindo Sipílio. The Brazilians were, in the words of Alberto Faria, "Arcadians without Arcadias," [45] because it seems beyond doubt that there never existed a Brazilian Arcadia. The terms Arcadians and *Arcádia Ultramarina*, which so occupied our historians, present a problem that has been solved definitively, since no competent document has appeared so far that can prove the latter's existence. This leads one to believe that it was a question of generic, ideal, geographical, or national designation with reference to Arcadian poets who lived in Brazil, or one of the many "academic meetings" or academies that were so common in the eighteenth century.[46]

The importance of Brazilian Arcadians has been brought out by a group of scholars and critics including Januário da Cunha Barbosa, Varnhagen, Pereira da Silva, Joaquim Norberto, Fernandes Pinheiro, Oliveira Lima, José Veríssimo, Ramiz Galvão, Sílvio Romero, João Ribeiro, Alberto Faria, et al.

By offering conditions for the appearance of a group of intellectuals, Vila Rica was able to shelter men of the highest literary culture of the time, who were most receptive of the seeds of renovation replacing decadent Gongorism. In addition, the country was showing signal evidence of intellectual progress, of associative literary life, of more interested public reading, and of a great spread of culture and books.

Therefore, by incorporating the new qualities—individualism and the feeling of nature—the Arcadism of Minas is the real begginning of personal Brazilian lyricism. The old nativism was transformed and developed, preparing a stamp that became, especially after romanticism, the distinctive one of Brazilian literature. It is a new step, a contribution. By means of Arcadian form and sensibility, and by adaptation of the thematic of classical origin to local environment and man, with specific feelings and emotions, Brazilian literature is led into artistic autonomy. It is the "transition from the purely Portuguese phase of our literature to its Brazilian phase," José Veríssimo affirms;

it was also, as Teófilo Braga and Fidelino de Figueiredo point out, a moment in which Portuguese poetry receives an impulse of renovation from the Brazilians. It is important to point out that this new artistic vibration found, for the first time in Brazilian history, a large group of artists who were highly conscious of their office and were endowed with superior poetic gifts.

Essential to the understanding of the eighteenth century, as far as artistic forms are concerned, is the removal of any preoccupation with isolating the currents.[47] The fact is that the currents of the century —the laggard baroque, the neoclassical, the Arcadian, and the Enlightenment—are a mixture, even when they are opposed, making up a network of complex intertwining, as they disappear into romanticism, passing through a preromantic phase in which the confusion of tendencies reaches its high point.

It is certainly difficult, if not impossible, to establish precise limits between the baroque and neoclassic, or among Arcadianism, Enlightenment, and preromanticism. In fact, as Fabini points out, preromanticism is the tendency implicit in all eighteenth-century literature.[47] There can be found in the century a continuation of the classical Renaissance, an impetuous rationalist and enlightened movement, an aristocratic reaction that is expressed in ideal beauty and grace instead of power and grandiosity, a new outbreak of the emotional, or sensibility, and of irrationality, translated into the German *Sturm und Drang* movement and, finally, into romanticism.

Ages or periods offer an internal unity. Ideas, points of view, attitudes, views of the world, values, beliefs, and norms of thought are transformed into life as they flow along their course and create the current ideology, the "spirit of the age." In this process Dvorak shows, as has been mentioned, an identity of impulse in the spiritual products of the period which brings forth an understanding of its spirit as a unique spring from whose waters the creations of arts, literature, and the forms of life would flow. Internal changes in society, therefore, are reflected in the appearance of new styles in the arts, as Wylie Sypher stresses when he studies the problem of the analogy of styles according to formal organization. And he adds:

A style is only an aspect of the course of a large history, and the critic must try to relate the emergence of different styles with the emergence of the human attitudes which represent themselves, in one direction, by the arts

. . . .There are relations between styles themselves and relations between styles and history.[48]

One must not, Sypher points out further, consider styles as absolutes, nor presuppose that every work of art or literature reveals in a thorough way the style of the period to which it is thought to belong. In any case, in the words of W. J. Bate, in *From Classic to Romantic*, "the conceptions of nature and the aims of art run strictly parallel to the concepts of man and his destiny, for art, in one of its prime functions, is the interpreter of values."

In this way, the unity of periods is a fact that has been revealed stylistically, with a close correspondence between the individual style and the style of the period. According to the teachings of T. M. Greene, the characteristic style of an author is usually common to his school and his period, unable to serve in any absolute way as a distinctive element when taken in isolation from an author; this is the case with the baroque and Arcadianism, for example, where characteristics are found in various authors of the period and in different countries.[49]

This notion leads certain historians to attempt a definition of the eighteenth-century period as a bloc, labeling it with a term that comes from the history of the arts—"rococo." [50] The word comes from *rocaille*, in the shape of a shell, which was a common form of decoration in the period and its use lasts to 1830 as applied to artistic manifestations of the postbaroque phase. It is among the Germans especially that the tendency is strong as seen in the works of Ermatinger and Cysarz.[51] In the hope, however, that there will take shape among historians, as did with the baroque period, an integral definition and characterization of the rococo period, it is licit, no doubt, to use the term in comparativist studies of arts and letters, where there is more useful evidence of the unity of the esthetic period. The slowness with which these periodological terms become established is natural, and if, as Cysarz notes, only in the past fifty years has the baroque gained a literary history, the doors are open on all sides to receive a concept of the rococo and a fundamental work on the rococo is in the air.

Along these lines, Hatzfeld has studied the French eighteenth century as an expression of the rococo in art and literature in terms that can be applied to other artistic manifestations outside of France.[52] According to his analysis, the rococo spirit is embodied in particular aspects of the spirit, of the soul, and of French eighteenth-century life, in Marivaux, Gresset, Crébillon, Voltaire, Watteau, Fragonard, Boucher, and Lancret. Hatzfeld shows what this rococo spirit is made up of: (*a*) a gamut of love, from infatuation to idyll, to lasciviousness, to eroticism; (*b*) nature as the ideal place for voluptuous pleasure (*fêtes campêtres,* erotic landscapes, and so forth); (*c*) intimacy in life and in social institutions (interiors, chamber music, *bijous,* intimate scenes, for example); (*d*) masks and disguises as an intimate recourse to veil and to reveal; (*e*) *esprit* (perhaps the major preachment of the rococo spirit), the irony of Montesquieu and Voltaire. These qualities show the inseparability in the rococo spirit of *esprit* and wit and the "rationalist passion." It is to this spirit that certain epithets and qualifying words, such as *mignardise, marivaudage, galanterie, goût voltigeant, jolies bagatelles,* and *gamineries folles* are applied, designating, as Hatzfeld states, a polish art, veiled indecency, correction covered by intelligence and polish, repressed dreams, melancholy irony, evil desires inflamed by reason and transformed into something enchanting, light, idyllic, insolent, insinuating, and contagious. It is the period of the minuet, the mannered dance, of sophisticated elegance, of small and precise movements.

By examining Arcadian literature, one will find the typical elements of the rococo scattered about: the sensual cultivation of beauty, affectation, refinement, frivolity, elegance, melodious and graceful language, sentimentalism, intimism, lasciviousness, love of nature. The art of transition in a period of transition, it expresses the passing of the courtly period leaving a society where the middle class will furnish the models of taste and sensibility as it heads towards subjectivism.

In Brazil, the literature produced towards the end of the eighteenth century generally reflects this rococo spirit and style, with the work of Tomás Antônio Gonzaga as its highest expression.

The Romantic Movement

৵ঃ৻ৄৢ৽

ORIGINS & DEFINITION

In the eyes of the comparativist and the stylistic historian—"stylistician *qua* historian," Hatzfeld calls him[1]—romanticism appears as a broad international movement that finds unity among the stylistic characteristics common to the writers of the period. It is a stylistic period according to the new concept and terminology, and to synthetic perspective, which are all used today in literary historiography.[2] It is also a set of attitudes towards life and literary method.

The use of the word romanticism and its derivatives in literary criticism has already been thoroughly studied.[3] It dates back to the seventeenth century in France and England, with reference to certain poetic creations linked to the medieval tradition of "romances," narratives of heroism, adventure, and love, in verse or in prose, whose composition, themes, and style (particularly evident in Ariosto, Tasso, and Spenser) were felt to be opposed to the models and rules of classical poetics. Thus, romantic and romanesque are terms one meets in the seventeenth century. According to Wellek, Warton (1781) was the first to make use of the classical-romantic opposition, which was to become so widespread, even though the antithesis might not have had for him the full significance that it would attain later on. From the French word *roman* (*romanz* or *romant*), the modern languages derived the current meaning during the eighteenth century, and the word was used during romanticism to designate the literature produced in the image of medieval "romances," fanciful in characters and atmosphere. As for the noun "romanticism," its use is more recent, varying in different European countries during the first decades of the nineteenth century. It was used first between 1822 and 1824 in France.[4]

In Portugal, the word "romantic" was introduced by Almeida Garrett in 1825 in his *Camões*, and in Brazil it still had not appeared in the studies (1826) by Gonçalves de Magalhães and Tôrres Homem, but it is used for the first time in the preface to the tragedy *Antônio José* (1839) as the opposite of classicism.

Whatever the period of introduction of the term "romantic" and its derivatives may be, the phenomenon known today as romanticism in literary and artistic history consisted of an esthetic and poetical transformation that arose in opposition to the neoclassical tradition of the eighteenth century and was inspired by medieval models. The change was conscious and generalized, European in scope; this we can say although there is no agreement concerning the introduction of the word that would come to designate the movement. The new literary period, the new style, was born in opposition to the previous neoclassical style. What it had come to designate was generally understood at an early date: the esthetic movement, translated into a style of life and art, which dominated Western civilization during the second half of the eighteenth century and the first half of the nineteenth. In accord with the concept of synthetic literary history, it is a conjoined and unified movement, with general characteristics common to the various Western nations, positive and negative elements on the level of ideas, feelings, and artistic forms, and, as Wellek says, the same concept of literature and poetical imagination, the same concept of nature and its relationship to man, the same poetical style, formed from a peculiar set of images, symbols, and myths.

The history of the transformations that took place in the Western mind in the eighteenth century and which were echoed in the romantic revolution, has been studied thoroughly in the light of comparativist and synthesizing perspectives by Paul Van Tieghem.[5] To his work especially is owed the emphasis given the preromantic phase, a recent notion in literary history, the fixation of which is necessary for an understanding of the way in which the romantic elements were penetrating, layer by layer, the Western soul, dominating art and literature. During the preromantic period came the struggle against neoclassicism, against the regular rules and genres that it had established and which romanticism would revoke, realizing the ideal already announced in the quarrel of ancients and moderns.

One cannot fix the place in which it first arose, for literary movements are formed gradually, simultaneously in diverse places, without any connection among the parts, the result of the internal evolution of forms and sensibility, and according to laws that are a part of the nature of styles.

The new tendencies that in the middle of the eighteenth century opposed neoclassical ideals as they foreshadowed romanticism, reflected a nonconformist state of mind in relation to classical intellectualism, to absolutism, to conventionalism, to the exhaustion of forms and themes then dominant. Imagination and sentiment, emotion and sensibility were to conquer in a short time the place that reason had occupied. The notion of nature and its corollaries, natural goodness, the purity of life in nature, the superiority of natural, primitive, and popular inspiration, were more and more attractive to man's interest and thought.

A series of relevant facts makes up the framework of this "long preromantic incubation," by which the disintegration of neoclassicism came about: the change of focus of irradiation from France to England, from which the sources of popular and natural poetry emerged to produce an intense European movement (Ossianism) begun with Macpherson's memorable fraud (1760–1763). The rediscovery or revaluation of Shakespeare made up another English contribution to the renovation that was taking place. From Germany, the *Sturm und Drang* (the 1770s), the revival of medieval tales and Germanic legends, along with Scandinavian and Nordic mythology, all concur to orient spirits in the new direction. Herder and Goethe, the brothers Schlegel, and Klopstock head the renovation in the direction of irrationalism, turning the period into the most important one in German literary history. Another great European is Rousseau, whose presence in the century served as a point of irradiation and convergence of the principal tendencies that would define the romantic physiognomy, so much so that some called him the "father of romanticism." Chateaubriand with *Le Génie du Christianisme* (1802) and Madame de Staël with *De la Littérature* (1800) and *De l'Allemagne* (1810) offered content for romantic poetics and literary doctrine.

As Van Tieghem affirms, the facts show that the beginnings of romanticism as such should be placed in the thirteen years between 1797 and 1810: the appearance of the German school, the English Lake

Poets, Sir Walter Scott, Chateaubriand, Madame de Staël. These main frontiers, along with others in different countries, make up the wavy line that configures the period. Therefore, still according to Van Tieghem: 1795 for Germany; 1798 for England (Bowra advances the date for England to 1789, the publication of Blake's *Songs of Innocence*); the beginning of the nineteenth century for France and the Scandinavian countries; 1816 for Italy and somewhat later for Spain; 1822 for Poland. By 1825 all countries had more or less been conquered by the movement, which came to complete exhaustion towards the middle of the century.

Without losing sight of comparativist and synthesizing criteria and the idea of unity in the movement, we can see its characteristics in a partial or overall analysis. These qualities all together constitute the best definition of the phenomenon, revealing that unity has its origins, in the words of Wellek, in a common vision of poetry, a common concept of imagination, nature, and the spirit, or in other words, in a vision of poetry as knowledge of deepest reality by the intervention of imagination; a concept of nature as a living whole and as an interpretation of the world and a poetical style constructed at the base out of myths and symbols.

If we wish to bring the romantic spirit together in one quality, that quality would be imagination. In *The Romantic Imagination*, C. M. Bowra showed the importance that the romantics gave to the imagination and the special conception they had of it. An integral part of the contemporary belief in the individual ego, belief in imagination gave the poets an extraordinary capacity for creation of imaginary worlds, and for believing at the same time in their reality. The exercise of this quality was what made poets of them. On the other hand, the emphasis on imagination had a religious and metaphysical meaning. Thanks to creative imagination, the poet was endowed with a peculiar capacity for penetrating an invisible world that was situated beyond the visible. This turned him into a visionary as he nostalgically aspired to a different world in the past or in the future, another world that was more satisfactory than the one familiar to him. This vision of the other world illuminated and gave eternal satisfaction to sensible things, the perception of which became vivid through interpretation of the familiar and the transcendental.

In a study of romanticism, one must establish first of all a distinction between the romantic state of the soul and the movement or school of universal scope that experienced it from the middle of the eighteenth century to the middle of the nineteenth. The romantic state of soul, or temperament, is a universal constant, as opposed to the classical state, by which humanity expresses its artistic grasp of the real. While the classical temperament is characterized by the primacy of reason, decorum, containment, the romantic is exalted, enthusiastic, colorful, emotional, and passionate. The opposite of the classical, which is absolutist, the romantic is relativist, seeking its satisfaction in nature, in the regional, the picturesque, the savage, and attempting, by means of the imagination, to escape from the real world into a remote past or to distant or fantasied places. The basic impulse is faith, the norm is freedom, the sources of inspiration are in the soul, the unconscious, emotion, and passions. The romantic is temperamental; exalted and melancholy. His attempt is to realize reality and not reproduce it.

These basic qualities of the romantic temperament are merged in artists of diverse times and countries, in Ovid as in Dante, in medieval lyrics, in different manifestations of the Renaissance, until in the eighteenth century it found the supreme instant of realization in a universal and unified movement. One must mention here a certain kinship between the romantic and the baroque spirits.

Unleashed as a reaction against rationalistic classicism, which had been the reigning literary dogma since the Renaissance, the romantic movement was characterized by a body of new ideas, literary themes, and a sensibility that resulted from the currents which had converged from Germany and England during the course of the eighteenth century in the period defined today as preromanticism.

These new elements in England became a reaction against Cartesian rationalism in the name of a theory of knowledge by means of the senses. This realist reaction invaded the sensualism of Condillac, joining it to a mystical sentimentalism. Realism and sentimentalism, therefore, enthrone the idea of nature as the place in which to find the source of all things and the origin of lyricism. Intuition, empiricism, a sense of the concrete, individualism, have as a counterpart the flight from reality, looking beyond reason, evading the world by imagination for some past epoch or supernatural universe. Thus came the sense of mystery, the attitude of dream and melancholy, of anguish and pessimism, which bring to romanticism themes of death, desolation, ruins, tombs, a taste for orgies and *mal du siècle*. Thence, also, a return to the past, to the Middle Ages, to the world of sorcerers, ghosts, and witches, and a rediscovery of the themes of childhood. From the sentimental novel of Richardson, one passed to the dreamy and melancholy lyrics of Young, to Gray's return to the past, to Ossian's fantastic world, to the Gothic novel and the black novel. The feeling of nature, the cult of the ego, religiosity, melancholy, a taste for the past and ruins, the supernatural; these are the traits that the romantic spirit owes to England.

In Germany, from early in the eighteenth century, the lyricism of nature, sentimentalism, the cult of imagination, a taste for the Germanic medieval past, popular ballads, all found support from Klopstock and Herder, finally emerging with the *Sturm und Drang* movement (1770), a literary revolution that aimed at an "assault" upon classical tradition. Goethe and Schiller, and later on Tieck, Novalis, and the brothers Schlegel led literature along the same road that it followed in England, bringing together sensibility and mysticism, melancholy and mystery, particularism and the unknown, passionate exaltation and amorous suffering.

Under the impact of the converging influence of English and German currents, the French fortress of classical rationalism crumbled during the eighteenth century and gave up its bastions of defense to the victory of individualism, the feeling of nature, sensibility, passion, melancholy, a desire for evasion, largely through the powerful influence of Rousseau. From France, romanticism spread out through all of Europe and America, particularly after the liberal and revolutionary impetus that the movement acquired from the French Revolution (1789).

For an understanding and definition of romanticism as a historical movement which gave concrete form in a determined time and place to a state of the spirit, or temperament, it becomes necessary, first of all, to avoid reducing the romantic spirit to a formula, as too many critics and historians have tried. One must attempt to characterize it essentially as a body of traits, a constellation of qualities whose presence in sufficient numbers renders the form distinct from classicism or realism. This combination of qualities, varying in composition, of course, is what serves to identify the romantic spirit.

In conformity with a study by Hibbard,[6] one can point out the following qualities that characterize the romantic spirit:

Individualism and subjectivism. The romantic attitude is personal and intimate. It is the world as seen through the personality of the artist. What it reveals is a personal attitude, an interior world, the state of the soul provoked by external reality. Romanticism is subjectivism, it is the liberation of the inner world, of the unconscious; it is the exuberant primacy of emotion, imagination, passion, intuition, personal and interior freedom. Romanticism is the freedom of the individual.

Illogic. There is no logic in the romantic attitude, and the rule is one of wavering between opposite poles of happiness and melancholy, enthusiasm and sadness.

Sense of mystery. The romantic spirit is attracted by the mystery of existence, which it pictures wrapped in terror and the supernatural. Individualist and personal, the romantic faces the world with a permanent fright, since everything—beauty, melancholy, life itself— always appears new to him and is always awakening original reactions in every person, independent of convention and tradition.

Escapism. The romantic's desire is to flee reality for a world that is idealized, created anew in his image, in the image of his emotions and desires, and by means of imagination. Neither facts nor traditions can awaken the respect of the romantic, as can happen with the realist or the classicist. Freedom means revolt, faith, and nature in communion with the past or in aspiration for the future. Romantic escapism built a new world on the base of dreams.

Reformism. This search for a new world is responsible for the revolutionary feeling of the romantic, tied to democratic and libertarian movements which filled the period and to the devotion to great military and political personalities.

Faith. Instead of reason, it is faith which rules the romantic spirit. It is not bread alone which satisfies the romantic; an idealist aspiring to another world, he believes in the spirit and its capacity to reform the world. It gives value to the mythical faculty and intuition.

The cult of nature. Overevaluated by romanticism, nature is a place of refuge, pure, uncontaminated by society, a place for physical and spiritual cure. Nature is the source of inspiration, a guide, friendly protection. Related to this cult, which held a dominating position in all romanticism, is the idea of the "noble savage," the simple and good man in a state of nature, as expressed by Rousseau; additionally, the vogue of the desert island and of "landscapes" in painting and literature, exotic and uncommon landscapes (exoticism).

Return to the past. Romantic escapism is translated into a flight to nature and the past, idealizing a civilization different from the present one. Ancient ages wrapped in mystery, the Middle Ages, the national past, furnish the environment, the types, and plots for romantic literature. History is evaluated and studied (historicism).

The picturesque. Remoteness not only in time, but also in space attracts the romantic. It is the pleasure of forests, of distant lands, savage, oriental, rich in the picturesque, or simply in different faces and customs. It is melancholy communicated by strange places, the seeds of nostalgia and the grief of absence that are characteristic of romanticism. The picturesque and local color become means of lyric and sentimental expression, and, lastly, of the excitation of feeling. This is the path towards realism.

Exaggeration. In his search for perfection, the romantic flees to a world in which he can find everything he thinks is good, brave, beautiful, loving, and pure, located in the past, in the future, or in some distant place, a world of perfection and dreams.

Having these characteristics as summed up by Hibbard, romanticism can also be distinguished by formal and structural traits.

As a consequence of freedom, spontaneity, and individualism, in the romantic there is an absence of prescribed rules and forms. The supreme rule is individual inspiration, which dictates the proper form of elocution. Hence the domination of content over form. Style is formed by the individuality of the author. What characterizes it, therefore, is spontaneity, enthusiasm, and rapture. While the classicist is a prisoner of rules and the realist one of facts, the romantic is moved by his own will and by his emotions and reflexes.

While the classicist tends to simplify characters, the romantic faces human nature in all of its complexity, constructing multifaceted types, more natural and more human.

From the stylistic point of view, romanticism offers quite a distinct physiognomy, capable of being considered a stylistic period and an individual style, as well as a well-characterized period. Helmut Hatzfeld sums up the qualities that stylistically define romanticism in this way:

Romanticism is the preference given to metaphor in contradistinction to Classicism which is mainly relying on metonymy.

The consequence of this linguistic behavior is a propensity to imagery in general, be it in epic (novelistic) description, be it in lyrical symbolism or allegory.

The intoxication of the eye and the stressing of sensation versus catharsis furthermore recurs to showy substantives and colorful epithets which in the long run shift the stress from the necessarily paler verbal style to a painterly nominal style in which even psychological shades are only expressed by physiognomical traits and gestures.

Romanticism was also distinguished in the problems of genres. Furthermore, it was then that the revisionist notion of genre began, genre as it was put forth by neoclassical poetics, especially by Boileau, in the image of Aristotle and Horace. It was a reaction that would culminate with Croce.

Against the notion of a fixed, immutable genre, pure and isolated, corresponding to a social hierarchy, romanticism began to put forth the possibility of mixture, evolution, transmigration, even the disappearance of genres, their enrichment or sclerosis, the birth of new ones, the existence of diverse forms in a single work; romanticism abolished in this way the systematic and absolutist spirit that dominated the understanding of the problem. We are faced today with a vision that is first descriptive and analytical, without any tendency towards a fixation of rules.

In this way the romantic polemic put in check the classifications and separations, the rules, the subjects, that had been in force concerning the genres according to neoclassical postulates. Since neoclassical literature appeared completely exhausted and sclerotic from submission to a system of rules for each genre, romanticism surged up in the name of freedom from the distinction of genres, as it considered the separation to be arbitrary, and defended the contrary point of view of their mixture. Social subversion itself, the result of the French Revolution, as it broke with ancient hierarchy, was reflected in the abolition of the frontiers between literary forms; because, in the words of Hugo, "the only real distinction in works of the spirit is one between good and bad." Guizot emphasized the impossibility of maintaining classifications and separations according to a stable and ordered society, after it had been subverted by contrasting feelings and necessities. On the other side, the classical spirit would not admit the plurality of emotions and feelings in the same genre, a prerogative of the romantic who delights in a mixed and intimate presentation and opposite states of the soul. For the romantic, seduced more by the complexity of life, the mixture of genres is ordained by obedience to this complexity and to apparent disorder, with prose and poetry appearing side by side, and also the sublime and the grotesque, the serious and the comic, the divine and the worldly, life and death.

The consequences of this formulation of the problem of genres, which did not come about abruptly, but on the contrary after long debates and experimentation, continued to make itself felt in poetry, theater, and novel.

Starting with the concept that poetry originates in the heart where its supreme source resides, and that art has only the duty of making verses, romanticism reduces all poetry to lyricism as the natural and primitive form that has its origins in the individual sensibility and imagination, in passion and love. Poetry became synonymous with self-expression. Consequently, the generic denominations of poetry, lyric poetry, lyricism, poem, were taking the place of the ancient specific terms of ode, elegy, song, which, furthermore, according to Van Tieghem, had lost their precise meaning or had gone out of use along with the decline or the replacement of the genres which they had designated. Romantic poetry, therefore, was personal, intimate, and amorous, still exploring philosophical and religious themes. One must also remember its social (and reformist) aspect, in addition to its narrative that was epic in tone.

As far as the theater is concerned, the revolution was even more drastic, with the resulting destruction, as Van Tieghem stresses, of tragedy as a fixed genre consecrated by immutable laws, and of its replacement by drama of free and varied structure and form, more in keeping with the tendencies of the spirit of the century.

The revolution in the theater, the first genre to attract the romantic spirit, and in which it was largely realized, was developed in opposition to the rules or unities of time and place, from neoclassical poetics, leaving the unity of action or interest to be created by the character at its center. It was the very demand of romantic drama—historical in basis, bringing together social, political, moral, psychological, and religious problems, broad questions, the numerous characters—that brought on the break in unities out of necessity for a greater margin of time and space in which to move. In renouncing these unities, the romantic drama turned towards the national past and modern history instead of Greco-Latin antiquity in search of a new form. "Local color," and customs, formed the basis of reality and an essential characteristic of society. The romantic drama is distinguished further by the union of the noble and the grotesque, the grave and the burlesque, the beautiful and the ugly, in a presupposition that contrast is what attracts attention, showing in this way that it is more faithful to reality. Finally, romantic drama mingled verse and prose.

As for the novel, the importance given to it by romanticism was equally great and, it might be said, the genre offered romanticism the best opportunities for realization of its ideals of freedom and realism —whether psychological, historical, or social—and produced a better atmosphere for sentimentalism, idealism, a sense of the picturesque, and historical and social preoccupation.

With romanticism began the pleasure of precise analysis and realism in the depiction of characters and customs, with the highest examples in Stendhal and Balzac. Simple reality, however, did not hold the romantic novelists, who also were looking for truth through the construction of ideal syntheses and generic types, bringing together varied traits and ones with diverse origins in the make-up of a character. The novel, in this way, blended reality and fantasy, analysis and invention. Therefore, in the novel, as in the theater, a liking for history, for motives and characters, was disseminated in such a way that it stamped the genre with one of its principal forms in the period: the historical novel. Another variety which enjoyed extreme popularity was the Gothic novel, the "black novel" of fantastic or terrifying content, historical or sentimental, reinforced by mysterious incidents, full of ghosts, apparitions, and supernatural voices, taking place in castles, cloisters, or gloomy mansions, and deliberately seeking an impression of horror. The adventure novel too, with plenty of action, danger, extraordinary (and emotional) exploits, was used, and both forms were often found together.

In short, romanticism cultivated lyric poetry, drama, and the novel

which was social and dealt with customs, psychological and sentimental, Gothic and dealing with adventures, and historical, with a
medieval or national theme.

To the innovations introduced in the structure of genres, in inspiration, in theme, one must add reforms in language, style, and the
technique of versification. They generally followed the dominant
tendency towards freedom.

Without renouncing syntax and poetic discipline, romanticism reacted generally against the tyranny of grammar and fought the noble
and pompous style that it considered incompatible with the natural
and the real, and it defended the use of a liberated language that was
simple, without emphasis, colloquial, richer.

On another side, versification had to pass through a softening process, with a greater variety of metric forms, new and more harmonious
rhythms (Van Tieghem), greater mobility and variety of caesuras and
richness of rhymes, so that it could be free of the monotony of classical forms.

The Western romantic movement, the concretization of the romantic spirit as a style of life and art, spread out through Europe and
America in concentric waves formed by successive generations of individuals. These waves have a special physiognomy, the result of a
differentiation of romantic qualities, with some dominating, and of
ideological and artistic preferences revealed by the generations that
constituted them.

Romanticism was preceded by a generation that made up the movement now known as preromantic which developed particularly in
England and Germany during the eighteenth century.

The group is formed by: Macpherson, Young, Gray, Collins, Gold-
smith, Chatterton, Cowper, Burns, Klopstock, Herder, Goethe, Schiller,
Bernardin de Saint Pierre, Foscolo, et al.

Afterward there comes the first romantic generation, made up of
figures born about 1770: Blake, Wordsworth, Coleridge, Southey,
Sir Walter Scott, Wilhelm and Friedrich Schlegel, Tieck, Novalis,
Chamisso, Madame de Staël, Chateaubriand, Lamb, De Quincey, Irving,
Fichte, De Maistre, Courier, Hazlitt, Eichendorff, Uhland, Kleist,
Grillparzer, Beethoven, Bello, Senancour, Hoffmann, et al. Romanticism
in them is not completely formed and in many cases one can see
certain classical elements in their struggle to impose a new sensibility.

The second romantic generation is more numerous, and while the first reaches fulfillment at a more mature age, the representatives of the second, born between 1788 and 1802, show complete possession of the novelty and from their youth they live it in a revolutionary and conscious way. The new generation is composed of: Byron, Atterbom, Brentano, Lamartine, Schopenhauer, Shelley, Keats, Vigny, Leopardi, Mickiewicz, Pushkin, Lenau, Hugo, Manzoni, Espronceda, Garrett, Dumas *père*, Carlyle, Emerson, Macaulay, Michelet, Villemain, Nisard, George Sand, Cooper, Andersen, Stendhal, Merimée, Balzac, Sue, Ranke, Heine, Schubert, et al.

The third generation includes figures born between 1810 and 1820: Musset, Petoeff, Gautier, Nerval, Avellaneda, Herculano, Poe, and Belinski.

Of the romantic writers, those who most influenced the spread and development of the movement in Brazil were: Chateaubriand, Sir Walter Scott, Byron, Lamartine, Hugo, Leopardi, Espronceda, Dumas *père*, Musset, Cooper, Heine, Hoffmann, Sue, Garrett, and Herculano. The great romantic novelists Merimée, Stendhal, and Balzac had a lasting influence that endured into the realist phase of Brazilian literature.

CHRONOLOGY & CHARACTERISTICS OF BRAZILIAN ROMANTICISM

It was because of the very sense of relativism of the movement that romanticism was able to adapt to the local situation, evaluating it in accordance with the romantic rule of exaltation of the past and of national traits. Romanticism in Brazil, therefore, assumed a particular make-up, with special characteristics and traits of its own, along with the broad elements that linked it to the European movement. It is of extraordinary importance, for it was to romanticism that the country owes its literary independence, a freedom of thought and expression without precedent, and acceleration of the evolution of the literary process in an unforeseen way. The period between 1800 and 1850 shows a great leap forward in Brazilian literature as it passed from the shadows of an undefined situation, a mixture of decadent neoclassicism, revolutionary enlightenment, and nativist exaltation, into an artistic manifestation by which a whole group of lofty poets and prose writers

was brought together, consolidating in Brazilian literature the autonomy of its national tonality and of its forms and themes, and the
technical and critical self-awareness of that autonomy.

The study of the evolution and characteristics of the different genres, and the analysis of literary theories and criticism which form the
movement, gave evidence of the genesis of awareness of a literature
attaining independence. The figure of José de Alencar, the patriarch
of Brazilian literature, stands out at that moment, the symbol of the
literary revolution that was taking place. His work was linked to the
implantation of that revolutionary process which placed Brazilian
literature into its definitive frame. By inciting the movement of renovation; by accentuating the necessity of the adaptation of foreign
molds to the Brazilian environment instead of simple servile imitation;
by defending Brazilian motifs and themes, especially those dealing with
the Indian, for a literature that should be the expression of nationality;
by defending the rights of Brazilian linguistic expression; by placing
nature and the Brazilian physical and social landscape in an obligatory
position in romantic descriptivism; by demanding the inclusion of
regions and regionalism in literature; by showing the necessity for a
break with neoclassical genres in the name of a renovation that had as
an immediate consequence the creation of Brazilian fiction, relegating
to the limbo of hackneyed forms the epic, which Gonçalves de Magalhães had tried to rehabilitate in mid-century; by these actions
Alencar gave a strong thrust to Brazilian literature in its march towards
emancipation.

The same revolutionary process is followed in poetry, transferred
to the intimate level, even though forms of an epic and narrative nature
were cultivated with worthwhile expressions alongside lyricism, especially in Gonçalves Dias and Castro Alves. The types that had characterized the neoclassics and even preromantics, however, were left
completely behind.

The romantic movement had, therefore, all of the qualities of a
revolution, giving freedom to manifestations of a national poetic and
literary temperament. To accentuate better this revolutionary note,
there is the parallel with social and political circumstances, also completely revolutionary in nature, that accompanied the gaining of Independence in 1822. The rise of the bourgeoisie through commercial
activity, and the liberal, intellectual, and political professions, and also

the social acceptance of the person of mixed blood through certificates of whiteness, which were the rewards of marriage, wealth, and literary and political talent, as Gilberto Freyre has pointed out, the rise of the bourgeoisie made it an ally or powerful concurrent force of the rural aristocracy, when it did not replace or become its representative in parliaments, in public administration, in government. The bourgeoisie achieved, thus, a position equally influential and rights just as strong for the enjoyment of the benefits of civilization. The moment, under the canopy of a stable and respected throne, was one of general prosperity and progress in all directions. After the presence of the Portuguese court and independence, the process was rising and constant, even though attacked by momentary crises such as that of the Regency (1831–1840). Cultural progress particularly was such that it is difficult to point out a period of greater significance in the history of Brazilian civilization.

Even though Alencar undeniably deserves a position without equal as the figure who represents and symbolizes this revolution on the literary level, the revolution was not, however, the work of a single man as this might suggest. It is only necessary to list the poets of romanticism to prove this assertion. All of this, therefore, places in relief the importance and significance of romanticism in Brazilian literature and culture, an importance and significance all the more revealing in contrast with what the immediately preceding period had accomplished. It is quite true that Arcadism constituted the first great collective literary manifestation of any value in Brazil, when poetry really developed and a deep nationalist feeling became firm. It can be considered the first romantic manifestation or the forerunner of romanticism. In spite of its also coming from Arcadism, however, the germ of the exaltation of nature, with its rustic tendencies and allusions to local flora and fauna, would develop into one of the strongest characteristics of romanticism. Arcadism remained faithful, in form mainly, to classical and Portuguese models, leaving for romanticism the conquest of a nativism that was also based on emotion. In this way, there is evidence of the newness of romanticism, even more outstanding by the contrast with Arcadian elements, many of which had lasted in the shape of residue into the first phase of romanticism. The contrast is even more evident with the replacement of Portuguese influence by English and French.

Between the two movements there is, furthermore, a phase of transition, preromanticism, in which the new tendencies and the old spirit struggle. Such hesitation is expressed in the mixture and interpenetration of esthetic tendencies, of new forms with outmoded themes or new subjects with outdated genres, all showing the lack of definition and characterization of the period, dominated by a subarcadism or pseudoclassicism. Different currents are crossed and mixed; baroque, Arcadian, illuminist, neoclassical, rococo, romantic, the majority coming from European sources—Portuguese and French—others putting down roots in Brazilian soil, announcing traits that would mark the future literary physiognomy of Brazil. The transition is not chronological but formal.

Outstanding in the genesis of Brazilian romanticism is the contribution of Portuguese Arcadism, very active in the phase of transition, precisely, paradoxically, during the break with the mother country. By stirring up a reaction against decadent *cultismo;* by giving incentive to the imitation of the ancients by way of France; by initiating personal lyricism; by insisting upon the cult of nature, after which the transition to American exoticism was easy; by passing on to the preromantics the great heritage of blank verse; by elevating as poetic rules simplicity, naturalness, and fantasy; by these ways the Portuguese Arcadians—Correia Garção, Reis Quita, António Dinis da Cruz e Silva —to whom the Brazilians were linked, gained a position of influence that cannot be neglected. One must also note the influence of Bocage, himself already occupying a position of transition, as well as that of Nicolau Tolentino, José Agostinho de Macedo, Filinto Elísio, and others, some of whom, alongside Garrett and Herculano, had an influence that would last throughout Brazilian romanticism.

The outbreak of romanticism was not an isolated phenomenon, however, and was one of the aspects by which the consciousness of the nation was affirmed as it worked for autonomy.

The general progress of the country during the residence of the Portuguese court (1808–1821) and after independence (1822), had an indisputable cultural and literary expression. Rio de Janeiro became the literary capital as well as the seat of government, and, with freedom of the press, an intense journalistic movement was released throughout the country, in which literature and politics were merged in a product quite typical of the period. Intellectual agitation characterized the phase after independence; there was great curiosity concerning the country—its history, its social, economic, and commercial life, its ethnology, its flora and fauna—which resulted in the creation of the Brazilian Historical and Geographical Institute (1838). There was also an interest in the natural sciences, mineralogy, chemistry, medicine. Historical studies freed themselves from typical memoirs, chronicles, and genealogies, and headed towards the modern orientation. The role of the political and literary press was revealing in that phase. Its broad activities showed the growth of a public in Brazil; at the same time it established a link between the public and writers that would have a long life in the country, with ups and downs, but always present.

To this fusion of politics and literature are also owed many bad effects on literary production. It created or implanted among us the vogue of the "publicist," a mixture of journalist, politician, and man of letters, capable of flitting about all subjects without staying with any one. The primacy of such a "dilettante" over the "professional" in the exercise of letters was of grave consequences for the quality of production, whether in the field of literature of the imagination or that of ideas. It would not be unjust to hold this spirit responsible for the superficiality, the lack of restraint, content, and substance that are traits of our literature.

In any case, however, one cannot deny the role played by the literary and political press during the genesis of romanticism in Brazil. The press was represented above all by the following organs: *Correio Brasiliense* (1808–1822), of Hipólito da Costa Pereira; *Aurora Fluminense* (1827), of Evaristo da Veiga; *As Variedades ou Ensaios de Literatura* (1812), the first literary paper in Brazil; *O Patriota* (1813–1814); *Anais Fluminenses de Ciências, Artes e Literatura* (1822); *O Jornal Científico, Econômico e Literário* (1826); *O Beija-Flor* (1830–1831); *Revista da Sociedade Filomática* (1833); *Niterói-Revista Brasiliense* (1836); *Minerva Brasiliense* (1843–1845); *Guanabara* (1850).

As Virgínia Côrtes de Lacerda says so well,

observing the locale and the date of appearance, the more or less ephemeral duration, the philosophical, political, or literary orientation, the content of these organs of our press at the time, we can arrive at determined conclusions that are rather elucidative of our preromanticism: (*a*) foreign influence, political and literary, coming from London first, and from Paris second and with predominance; (*b*) the cultural centers of the period located in Bahia, Rio, and São Paulo; (c) the influence of secret or literary societies in the orientation of thought and action (masonic, literary, scientific, and artistic societies) (d) the stimulus coming from appeals for the nationalization of Brazilian letters begun by Ferdinand Denis and Garrett; (e) the persistence of Filintism and Elmanism in the literary expression of the time.

Through political or literary journalism, through news and translations the incipient and rarefied Brazilian cultural milieu kept in spiritual touch with the great foreign centers. There were also the translations, widely popular in the period, of the literature of ideas or of fiction done by illustrious hands. These translations powerfully influenced the intellectual renovation by spreading foreign culture, when, with the abrogation of the Portuguese prohibition on intellectual importation, the doors were opened wide to ideas. Illuminist, encyclopedist, revolutionary, and romantic ideas, therefore, were freely accessible to the country and rapidly produced their fruits.

Oratory was another important medium and was broadly cultivated in the period, helping to broaden horizons through pulpit and parliament. It was an extremely popular form, by means of which the new doctrines reached both high and low people who were attracted by the brilliance and eloquence of the preachers and politicians. The vogue of oratory lasted all through the nineteenth century and only in more recent years, after the modernist revolution, does it no longer awaken the same response. It left, however, a strong mark on the literary habits of the Brazilian mentality which reflects a taste for discourse, even in fiction and poetry. Situated properly in time, political and religious oratory played an important role in strengthening the Brazilian political and social structure. The eloquence of agitators in whom the affectations and yearning for nationality were concentrated emphasized liberal ideas and innovating nationalism, ideas spread largely by the Enlightenment and the French Revolution.

Lyric poetry, however, was the literary expression that dominated this phase of transition, during which, as Virgínia Côrtes de Lacerda reminds us, the poets of the group that Veríssimo called "the predecessors of romanticism," and Sílvio Romero "the last classical poets, after their time and transitional," and Ronald de Carvalho "the last Arcadians" were active.[7]

It is, therefore, in the preromantic period that one must place the seeds of Brazilian intellectual independence. Distinguished in this task were José Bonifácio, the promoter of literary independence, and Sousa Caldas. The revolutionary role that they played was in spite of their hybrid and transitional character. They were still neoclassical in certain aspects, and they adopted innovating attitudes and forms that either were inspired in preromanticism and European romanticism, or came from the life of the country itself.

It has already been recognized that our preromantics had superficial knowledge of the European preromantics [*Sturm und Drang*, Wieland, Young . . .], and of conservative and religious romantics [Scott, Wordsworth, Chateaubriand, Lamartine, the early Hugo, the medievalist poets . . .] and yet nothing of liberal and revolutionary romanticism [Shelley, Hugo, Heine. . . .] They were of nationalist inspiration, but conservative and religious.

The task of introducing romanticism into Brazil fell, however, to a figure who in addition, as José Veríssimo noted, was our first man of letters and who initiated the literary career among us: Domingos José Gonçalves de Magalhães, Viscount of Araguaia. It is singular that such a task was done by a man who was of conservative tendencies, as expressed in his first book of poems (1832), and still faithful to certain classical forms. These he revived long after the implantation of romanticism, in his clearly traditional poem, *A Confederação dos Tamoios* (1856). This hybrid nature is typical of the period of transition, however, and in Magalhães himself the classical remains are allied to traits and indications of a renovation. One can see the fusion of politics and literature, both working towards the cultural and political autonomy of the country; his intentionally revolutionary attitude for the total renovation of Brazilian literature, expressed in the manifesto with which he launched the magazine *Niterói* (1836); the anti-Portuguese intent, with France as the new source of literary and artistic inspiration, from where, symbolically, he published both the magazine and his book *Suspiros Poéticos e Saudades* (1836); the preference given to the Indian theme. These factors all justify the position of introducer of romanticism that Gonçalves de Magalhães holds in Brazilian literature.

The essential factor in the transformation in Brazil toward romanticism was the influence from France. To the name of Ferdinand Denis as the "father of Brazilian romanticism," one must add those of Chateaubriand, Victor Hugo, Lamartine, Musset, and other preromantic and romantic figures. The fact was already noted by Ferdinand Denis and afterwards by Ferdinand Wolf in *O Brasil Literário* (1863): "It was the French romantics who, in a large measure, fostered true romanticism in other neo-Latin peoples." This influence, as Paul Hazard stresses, instead of being oppressive, was exciting; and it freed them from their classicist chains.

In spite of the anti-Portuguese reaction of Brazilian romanticism right from the preparatory phase, it is necessary, nevertheless, not to forget the repercussion of Almeida Garrett, whose renovating work in the movement in Portugal comes before 1825, when he published his poem *Camões*. His ideas, set forth in the introduction to his *Bosquejo* (1826), favoring freedom and nationalization of Brazilian literature, run parallel to those of Ferdinand Denis in his *Resumé* (1826). The fact is, however, that the best spirits of the time (José Bonifácio and Gonçalves de Magalhães) already had urged a new form adapted to the new material.[8]

Romanticism in Brazil, then, is placed in the period between 1808 and 1836 for preromanticism, and from 1836 to 1860 for romanticism proper, with its high point located between 1846 and 1856. After 1860 there is a period of transition towards realism and Parnassianism.

The romantic movement in Brazil followed the path of the European one, with waves of successive generations constituting subperiods or groups more or less differentiated in ideological and thematic point of view.

One of the most complex problems is the classification and distribution of Brazilian romantic writers. This is a result of the very complexity of the movement, crossed by varying currents and tendencies which at times are also divergent. Commenting on the fruitless efforts of Sílvio Romero, José Veríssimo, and Ronald de Carvalho, Oto Maria Carpeaux confesses "that it is almost impossible to distinguish neatly the different phases of Brazilian romanticism." It is a difficulty that results, as he points out, from the number of writers appearing in a short period of time, and from the overlapping of chronology which completely ruins any scheme of grouping by generations.[9]

There are representatives of one generation who go beyond it spiritually and take part in another group. There are figures of transition; there are the dilettantes and marginal figures who are not fixed but adapt themselves to successive groups; the laggards, the ones who do not belong to any group, or who are linked to a group by spiritual and stylistic identity, but who are not of the generation; and in each group there are important figures, quite representative, and secondary ones who are linked to the principal ones in a pale, hesitant, and uncharacteristic way.

Following the evolution of literary tendencies and forms through romanticism, one can verify the progressive formation of an esthetic and a style, in which formal and spiritual elements are brought together. This evolution takes effect in various phases, in which groups or generations of poets participate along with writers of fiction and cultivators of other genres. In a general way, as Manual Bandeira notes, the form is the same, varying according to generation, theme, sentiment, and tonality. The new esthetic encompassed poetry, fiction, and drama, and formulated as well critical and literary theories concerning the nature and finality of literature and seeking the most convenient stategy for the realization of these ideals and the genres best-suited to their expression. The objective was to create a national literature in opposition to the Portuguese, considered imported and oppressive in that moment of the struggle for autonomy.

Without respect to strict chronology, already violated by reality, one can establish stylistic and ideological groups in the evolution of Brazilian romanticism. In the first place, it is necessary to distinguish preromanticism from romanticism proper, the last with four groups, using dates simply as flexible terms of reference.

PREROMANTICISM (1808–1836)

It is a body of tendencies, themes, ideas, without being a homogeneous literary doctrine, with leftovers from classicism and Arcadism, and new elements. Some specific notes of romanticism are already found. Now as precursors, now as figures of transition, they announce, prepare, or are vehicles for romantic qualities. Many of the figures of this phase, uncharacterized, pass through romanticism as dilettantes or marginal figures, utilizing the formal or thematic resources, without arriving at a total realization. The Portuguese influence is giving way to the French and English. Journalism (political and literary, mixed, for the most part) is cultivated intensely, along with sacred and profane oratory, lyric poetry, history, and natural sciences. It includes figures born before about 1820.[10]

ROMANTICISM

First group. Initiation was by the Rio group with the romantic manifesto of 1836: *Niterói-Revista Brasiliense.* Contradictory tendencies of conservatism with classical leftovers and the deliberate march towards the new esthetics place it in the preromantic phase and also play the role of initiation and introduction. There is religious and mystical poetry, nationalism, Lusophobia, and English and French influences (Marmontel, Chateaubriand, Hugo, Vigny, Lamartine). Romantic ideas attempt to impose themselves by means of new themes, spiritual and religious aspirations, a new sensibility; fiction is seen in outline; the liking for nature spreads; cultural interest is intensified (scientific, philosophical, historical, sociological). The preferred genre is lyric poetry, but fiction and theater take their first steps, and the intense cultivation of journalism continues.[11]

Second group (1840-1850). In spite of including figures belonging to the previous generation and also some retardatory figures, and in spite of the continuation in many of them of links to the classical and Portuguese past, a well-characterized group exists that is distinct from the previous one. What predominates is the description of nature, pantheism, Indianism, the idealization of the savage as the symbol of national spirit and civilization struggling against the Portuguese heritage. The influences are Chateaubriand, James Fenimore Cooper, Sir Walter Scott, Eugène Sue, Balzac. The most cultivated genres are lyric and narrative poetry, fiction, theater, criticism, history, and journalism. In the main figures born between 1820 and 1830 begin to be active in the decade of the forties.[12]

Third group (1850-1860). Prevalent were individualism and subjectivism, doubt, disillusionment, cynicism and bohemian negativism; *mal du siècle;* Byronesque or satanic poetry. The influence of Byron, Musset, Espronceda, Leopardi, Lamartine was felt. Fiction was established with Alencar, Macedo, Bernardo Guimarães, Franklin Távora, under Indianist, rural, and regional forms, using local material and a native environment, with nationalist intentions. Historical fiction also arose under the influence of Sir Walter Scott; and the urban variety was strong. Criticism, which had existed under the guise of biographical notes and anthologies, acquired an awareness of its mission and techniques. Lyric poetry, fiction, criticism, along with history and journalism were the genres most cultivated. It is made up of figures born around 1830 and who began working in the decade between 1850 and 1860.[13]

Fourth group (after 1860). Liberal and social romanticism were the elements; an intense politico-social, and nationalist impregnation were allied to the struggle for the abolition of slavery (especially after 1866) and the Paraguayan War (1864–1870). In lyric poetry, along with intimate and amorous lyricism, there is a tendency, under the influence of Victor Hugo, towards a lyricism of impetuous and daring metaphor which was called (Capistrano de Abreu) "condor poetry" or "condorism." Great formal preoccupations caused the group to make experiments that in a climate of literary and philosophical realism led in the direction of Parnassianism. It was almost a transitional "realistic romanticism," the forerunner of "art for art's sake," with a very strong erotic note. Some figures even went into Parnassianism or served as a link between the two styles. An open anti-romantic reaction comes in the decade of the seventies.

In this phase fiction went beyond the romantic formula, a formula that had run dry in sentimentalism and ruralism. The realistic form intruded after 1870 in the urban analysis of customs and characters, or in regionalism and naturalism. It is national fiction, Brazilian, established and autonomous.

The genres acquire greater esthetic autonomy, freeing themselves from politics and journalism. With the generation of 1870 there begins a new influence in letters, that of positivist and naturalist philosophy. It is comprised in the main by figures born around 1840.[14]

Characteristics. The romantic movement, very much in spite of being subdivided into stylistic nuances, shows unity in its fundamental characteristics. In Brazil, furthermore, it assumed a tonality of its own, shown through peculiarities of the milieu to which it was adjusted, although it conformed to the relative and the historical among its defining traits.[15] One could sum up its characteristics in the following ways:

With its appearance at the dawn of nationality, it adjusted itself to the spirit of the people, whose desires and qualities it felt and expressed. As a critic has stated quite well, "Brazilian romanticism is very much responsible for the fusion that came about between the personal moment and the collective moment." It was an instant of individual exaltation that was allied to collective exaltation; in the romantic esthetic was found the means adequate to the task. Hence, romanticism possessed various aspects such as literary and artistic, political and social, and involved varied genres such as lyric poetry, novel, theater, journalism, oratory, and essay. More than a strictly literary movement, it was first and foremost a national style of life, with all of the people living according to its forms, and feeling, singing, thinking in the same way, trying to affirm through it their individuality and their collective soul.

From the emphasis placed on inspiration as the supreme guide for literary creation, romanticism established a model which touched an innate quality in the Brazilian people, and was enthroned as an estheticliterary norm that was to dominate a large part of our literary activity. The Brazilian cult of inspiration, of improvisation, and of spontaneity as sources of creativity was most romantic, but it was also quite Brazilian, which illustrated a Brazilian soul in tune with the romantic soul. Quite Brazilian and quite romantic are sentimentalism and sensibility. A consequence of all this is the extreme popularity of romantic literature, which was then and still is a natural demand of the people, responding to a specific taste, to a permanent tendency, one might say, of its soul. The romantics are the most popular of Brazilian writers, the ones who arouse the most response in the people—Gonçalves Dias, Casimiro de Abreu, Álvares de Azevedo, Castro Alves, José de Alencar, Macedo.

The romantic norm of inspiration and improvisation, however, as it dislocated the rules and basic rhetoric of literary formation in its reaction against classicist postulates, introduced a disdain for the artisan and a subsequent carelessness, relaxation, and negligence in relation to all technical aspects of the art. Along with the romantic principle of freedom—literary, social, political—came the break with obligations to the tradition of the language. This enriched the vocabulary and broadened subject matter, but it also produced a certain anarchy and disorder that was called poetic license.

Brazilian romanticism had a strong political and social coloration. Its democratic-popular side is what becomes more visible and active, because, as Samuel Putnam states, "never was the relationship between art and society so intimate." Side by side it came with the bourgeois revolution and the movement for independence and democracy, all of which transformed it into a "powerful arm in the struggle and the literary vehicle of the nascent nationalism in Brazil and other Latin American countries." Here too the bourgeois revolution triumphed with independence and democracy, as a repercussion of the era that had begun with the French Revolution. Portugal represented everything the Brazilians abominated: political oppression, economic exploitation, literary conservatism. Romanticism sounded the trumpets of freedom in all sectors.

Parallel to political freedom, to autonomy of conscience, was the literary rebellion. In time it formed a new sensibility, trying to express itself in a different artistic form. With the materials of a new civilization in front of them, men of letters, after a long period of maturing, stopped looking to the Portuguese mother country for models of literary expression in poetry, fiction, and drama. There was an identity of ideas in politics and literature which brought about the elevation of José Bonifácio de Andrada e Silva as the patriarch of political independence and the foremost pioneer in the literary revolution.[16] An added fact is that many writers were also outstanding politicians which increased their popularity. This relationship between literature and politics made possible in Brazil—in spite of its being the only country in Latin America where the line of individual rebelliousness and *mal du siècle* flourished, as Henríquez Ureña has pointed out—greater success for the liberal and revolutionary over the conservative and the religious. Even among the clergy romantic idealism raged, politically and socially. After independence, therefore, romantic literature was an arm of political and social action.

Romantic nationalism assumed a character very much its own in Brazil under the form of *Indianism*. Linking Rousseau's doctrine of the "noble savage" to Lusophobic tendencies, Brazilian nativism found in the Indian and his civilization a symbol of spiritual, political, social, and literary independence. Capistrano de Abreu saw that Indianism was not an exotic plant, but had deep roots in popular literature. In addition, Indianism was for Alencar and Gonçalves Dias closely related to the revival of the myth of childhood and the return to childlike innocence, a general characteristic of romanticism. It was a theme which found in Álvares de Azevedo a different form of expression. The significance of Indianism is therefore deep. In the words of Clóvis Beviláqua, it was "the first step of Brazilian esthetics in search of its special and own type." It rose out of the raw material of national originality itself and became the most suggestive starting point of all later attempts to find peculiarly Brazilian materials for literary expression of the national consciousness. This is what brings out the cult of the backlands and its inhabitants, ruralism, the cult of the mixed-blood, and, above all, regionalism, which was, after all, the highest product that Brazilianism had yet produced.

The individualist and bohemian current flourished in the middle of the century even though its roots went back to Gonçalves de Magalhães, with his melancholy, pessimism, doubt, and religiosity, and his feeling of the uselessness of earthly things. It was with the group of Álvares de Azevedo, Junqueira Freire, and Casimiro de Abreu, however, that the *mal du siècle* reached its maximum force, with morbid states of doubt, negativism, and melancholy. This quite typical aspect of romanticism was widespread. It appeared in the heroes and heroines of romantic novels, the brothers and cousins of Werther and René, who constituted a populous gallery of morbid and melancholy dreamers in the novels by Macedo, Alencar, Taunay, figures like Lauro, Estácio, Cirino, Honorina, Raquel, Inesita, Isabel, Inocência, et al.

Out of the necessity for broadening the literary horizon, romanticism went to local or national sources of inspiration, as opposed to Greco-Roman sources that had dominated neoclassical poetics. The first step in this search for new dimensions was taken into the nature of the heart and the spirit, from which came the primacy of lyricism as the most natural and primitive form of poetry, and the establishment of a realism that was based on interior truth and on the outflow of the heart. The other step was oriented towards giving value to "local color" and the picturesque, following the relativist principle that man varies according to time and place in order to capture his truth in its external and internal diversity—customs, feelings, language—all that makes him typical. This theory found a ready climate in the novel especially, but it also served as a basis for the enhancement of local history and of popular creations and folklore.

The enhancement of history and the national past was one of the most important activities of Brazilian romanticism. History, ethnology, linguistics, all had a broad development, as can be seen by the founding of the Historical and Geographical Institute (1838) and the publication of numerous works that mark the beginning of Brazilian historiography on a modern basis, with Varnhagen as its great defender. History was an intellectual activity that enjoyed great favor under romanticism.

It also bore fruit in the vogue of the national historical novel patterned after Sir Walter Scott, the greatest writer of which was José de Alencar. It corresponded to the wish to value the national theme as opposed to the Portuguese. Instead of using material from the Middle Ages, which European romanticism generally did, Brazilian writers found in the records of local history, in the legends of our own past, and in the glorification of the Indian, suggestions for a yearned for return to the very beginnings. These were to be the sources of inspiration for art and literature as well as the whole spirit and civilization of Brazil.

The search for peculiar local color led to an understanding of popular literature, in which the romantics felt was the original character of literary creativity, and from which came the formative vein of literature. The traditional and folkloric forms, in the freshness of their lyricism and their veracity, were the differentiating factor of literature. In the place of classical mythology, to which the neoclassical and Arcadian imitators owed their ideological mold, the romantics preferred to populate their imagination with Amerindian myths and cosmogonies. There was a broad interest in all forms of popular creation. Men like Celso Magalhães, José de Alencar, Sílvio Romero, Araripe Júnior, Vale Cabral, Melo Morais, influenced by the importance that romanticism gave it, dedicated themselves to the collection and study of folklore, emphasizing the worth and significance of popular poetry as a form of tradition, at a moment when the search for a valid tradition was the objective of all Brazilian minds in their desire for autonomy and in reaction against the Portuguese tradition.

The feeling for nature, an essential characteristic of romanticism, was translated in Brazilian literature into an exalted thing, becoming almost a religion. The attraction of South American nature, its beauty, its hostile and majestic savagery, exercised a real fascination upon the minds of writers. They wanted to capture it through images and descriptions, and at the same time they allowed themselves to be taken by its enchantments and suggestions. In this way, a state of communion or correspondence grew up between the countryside and the writers, poets and novelists. This inclination had been introduced in Brazilian literature as the heritage of the period of discovery and the early colonization, and the Arcadians had accentuated it even though their imagination was still partly impregnated by classical visions. It was with romanticism however that the feeling for nature was transformed into a dogma and a cult, establishing itself in literature in prose and verse with its absorbing presence, raising to a distinctive category the descriptive power of the writer, and mobilizing the human capacity for admiring and being awed by the grandeur and mystery of tropical nature. Romanticism established an esthetic pleasure in the countryside, discovering it definitively for literature, and at the same time it made Brazil known with its descriptions.

Significance & legacy. Having established the specific qualities of Brazilian romanticism, it is fitting to raise the question of its legacy and importance.

From romanticism as an artistic style and as a literary movement, Brazilian literature received definitive contributions. For example, literary genres proper gained autonomy and consistency, in both thematic and structural aspects.

In a comparison with the literature of the baroque period, with neo-classicism, and Arcadism, and even with the preromantic production, it was clearly romantic literature itself that ceased to be an instrument of religious and moral action or of parlor jousts, and became the esthetic expression of the soul of the people, of their highest spiritual yearning. Even considering its fusion with politics, especially in the preromantic phase, there is in romanticism a superior esthetic sense that dominates its creation in evolution towards autonomy and specific activity and forms. It is literary consciousness itself that is taking shape.

Actually, the romantics brought forth the literary genres with a Brazilian make-up. Before them, poetry had been rekindling classical and Portuguese impregnations. It was Portuguese poetry written in Brazil by men who happened to live there, but poetry which had been shaped in the home kingdom and followed its ways. Romanticism destroyed that submission and introduced into literature a Brazilian way of feeling and facing the world, of translating feelings and reactions. Romanticism made for itself forums in the cities, it recognized the right of this new attitude to enter literature. Writers were no longer obliged to seek inspiration in the physical, social, and human landscape of Portugal. They only had to look around themselves, and the literature they produced would not necessarily be inferior to that of their Portuguese fellows. Leaving behind spurious expression, the new literature acquired the rights of citizenship, reaching a level of equality, thanks to the autonomist effort of the romantics.

Like Brazilian poetry, fiction was established during this period. Even beyond that, Brazilian fiction was created under romanticism. Even with the predominance of the descriptive and picturesque over the narrative, and in spite of the vogue for novelistic history, sentimental and idealized, the peculiar conditions of the Brazilian milieu favored the formation of the genre, in theme and in structure. This was so especially because of the highly conscious experiments of Alencar, who passed on the heritage, already shaped, to his successors. Machado de Assis particularly would only have to perfect the technique, great narrative writer that he was, and fashion it according to his own esthetic model. Alencar, therefore, deserves our thanks for understanding that the novel was a more adequate genre for Brazilian expression than was the epic (as Magalhães had thought), even though romantic poetics had induced him to idealize reality rather than reproduce it.[17]

With reference to criticism and to literary ideas, the romantic contribution was of the greatest significance. Leaving behind the biographical and anthological preoccupation, and the spirit of academic isolation which had characterized the first historians of Brazilian literature during the eighteenth and early nineteenth century, romantic writers courageously and conscientiously headed into the territory of literary ideas. The tendency reached its climax with the polemic concerning *A Confederação dos Tamoios* (1856) by Gonçalves de Magalhães, in which José de Alencar represented the most advanced thought, the polarizer of the desires and efforts of the national spirit for the possession of a technical consciousness in the treatment and understanding of the literary phenomenon. It was a crucial moment, therefore, in the evolution of Brazilian literary criticism, not only for the conception of its nature and ends, but also for an understanding of the structure and theme of the literary genres which could and should be cultivated in the Brazilian milieu. Alencar also tried to demonstrate the need for giving literature roots in Brazilian life. Out of this grew the basis of literary historiography, with the concept that literature is a social expression and as such must have its own history (Sílvio Romero et al.).

In matters concerning language too, the romantic movement played a revolutionary role, and here also the figure of Alencar stands out. Defending the rights of a Brazilian dialect, the romantics attempted a reform that, if it did not succeed completely, which would have been impossible without breaking linguistic unity, did point out the necessity of subjecting the manner of expression and pronunciation to the impositions of a Brazilian sensibility. To a new way of feeling an adequate expression had to correspond. There were the transformations through which Brazilian prosody and literary language were passing. These changes could no longer pass unperceived—the daring freedom of measure, caesura, "wrong" constructions, word order, placement of pronouns—and they were responsible for the freedom from the Portuguese classics and revolutionary approximation to the spoken language of the written, the colloquial language of the literary.

More than language as a literary expression, it was poetic language itself that romanticism created in Brazil. Getting farther away from the Portuguese, in spite of his still being too much their prisoner, Gonçalves Dias, paradoxically, with the strange experiment of going back to the primitive Portuguese language, formulated the problem of Brazilian poetic language. He offered at the same time the seeds of its solution, which, with his example, would be developed, free of its Portuguese chains, by Álvares de Azevedo, and would be definitively established by Castro Alves, in whom Brazilian lyricism reached its purest product as the tone and the vision and the feeling of our reality. In these poets one can feel the thread of an inner evolution that joins them to each other, moving the poetic form along according to an intrinsic impulse and through inner channels. Art is form, and a new form is born and develops by degrees from within, following the necessary stages as the material enters the new molds and adapts itself, and according to native experience and ideals acquires a new physiognomy. This is so true that in two poets one can find the seed of future styles: symbolism in the subjectivism of Álvares de Azevedo; Parnassianism in the objective vision of Castro Alves.

Also owed to the romantic movement is the beginning in Brazil of the literary career and an understanding of the man of letters in the community. Gonçalves de Magalhães embodied the position for the first time; José de Alencar raised it to its highest stature and dignified it as example and model for posterity, with the consciousness of a calling, the faithfulness of a vocation and a duty, with the understanding of its role in society. He is the prototype of the writer, the man of letters, the scholar, and Machado de Assis would find in him a figure, the greatest in Brazilian literature, on which to build personality and work.

A peculiar trait of the man of letters that is owed to the romantic movement and which attained a wide acceptance in Brazil, was that of the civilizing mission of the writer, who as seer and prophet was destined to influence the course of events, thanks to inspiration or supreme illumination. He had a responsibility, a particular vocation, a role in social and political reform, in the conduct of life in the community, an educative function, one to be exercised in conjunction with his contemporaries. This concept found a home in Brazilian society, and it prevails down to our own time. It made the writer more apt to act and be judged by his political or social activity than by the literary work that he produced. Political, journalistic, administrative activities have always been an attraction for the man of letters in Brazil, so often discontented and dissatisfied with a pure dedication to literary activity in the fields of imagination or criticism.

The improvement and growth of a public was another result of the romantic movement as it tightened the ties between the man of letters and society, creating greater bonds of interest between the two poles of activity, awakening stronger sympathy and even popularity for writers. A larger audience appeared for the novel, poetry and the theater, with the growth of a middle class, the creation and rise of the bourgeoisie, the growth of leisure, a greater respect for and cultivation of woman, the access of the mixed-blood, the reduction of illiteracy, the growth of secondary and higher, education, the improvement in the circulation of books through the business and through libraries, the growth of printing presses and publishers, the growing popularity of the newspaper. These and other factors gave a vitality to Brazilian intellectual life, and more particularly to literary life, and romanticism was the very nerve of this process which determined the autonomy of Brazilian literature.

For the first time, Brazil had a movement with roots deep in the national soil and its reality, inspired exclusively by great collective emotions. "Poets," Andrade Murici states, "embody, in effect, not the anguishes of an aristocratic and refined individual, but those of all the people." And elsewhere in his essay:

Romanticism provided the highest measure of the possibilities of the inspiration peculiar to the Brazilian race such as it is, mixed as it is. [He goes on to state that:] romanticism is one of the greatest and most Brazilian of our glories, showing something only possible among us; because it brought forth representations out of nature and the human soul and not from any view that had been gained through books; because then as in no other time, social and political events were reflected deeply in poetry and in turn they suffered the powerful and beneficial reaction of poetry.

Starting with romanticism, there comes into existence a real literature, in content and in form. It replaced the idealized vision of the world that held sway in classicism, in all of its varieties, with a real and direct image, even as it captured the inner and outer local atmosphere. Romanticism germinally possessed as an essential and primitive trait the realist principle, developed later as the highest form of Brazilian fiction.

It is during the period that passes from romanticism to realism that one must focalize the comprehensive study of Brazilian literature in order to interpret its nature and its qualities. It is especially necessary to stress, in spite of apparent opposition, the telescoping, the continuity, even the identity in many aspects of the two styles in Brazil. Many writers passed unknowingly from one form to the other, never freeing themselves from the first, and continuing with the same preoccupations and problems. It was Machado de Assis who stated that: "People who have suckled on romantic milk, may sink their teeth into the naturalist beef, but as they smell the Gothic and Oriental breast in it, they will abandon that fine piece of meat and run off after their childhood drink." [18] In that note of disenchantment we have the perfect picture of the state of the spirit that impregnated Brazilian writers during the second half of the nineteenth century, and what is typical of the awakening of Brazilian literature.

As the romantic imagination and the realities of Brazilian life in the middle of the century came together, a system was created of thought and feeling, deeply rooted in the native soil from which it drew its strength and its unity. The system confirmed the law pointed out by T. M. Greene, in *The Arts and the Art of Criticism,* of the relationship between style and the spiritual cohesion of the people: "In each case, the vitality of the style is intimately proportional to the spiritual cohesion and wisdom of the social group. The historic styles in art are, accordingly, accurate indices to the temper and spiritual atmosphere of the social group." [19] The lack of unity of style corresponds, therefore, to states of confusion and spiritual disorder. During romanticism, the unity of style and life showed that the Brazilian people had attained spiritual cohesion.

By bringing to the fore the Brazilian literary preoccupation with topics and types, romanticism gave it a Brazilian feeling, an intimacy with the milieu, that "instinct of nationality," notably defined by Machado de Assis and which since then has been its specific note. This preoccupation was its contribution, whether on the level of general esthetics and principles, or on that of a particular esthetic of genres, or on that of the strategy of realization. If the period was not always positive and perfect in the works that it handed down, considered as a body its contribution and message occupy an unequalled place in Brazilian literature. As Paul Hazard states:

Romanticism appears here less as a doctrine than as a vital impulse. Let us be clear: in Brazil, romanticism was a national religious and social force. It not only provided a most abundant flowering of novelists and poets, it did not only reestablish letters in the high dignity they deserved, but it took the side of freedom, at one with the very existence of the young nation.

From that time on, the literature that was produced in Brazil could no longer be considered as it had been before, as a simple branch of the Portuguese, despite the fact that they were expressed in the same language. The organic constitution of a new literature had come full turn, with the transplantation of a refined culture to a primitive area, with different necessities and a different view of the world. Brazilian literature had found its moment of definitive affirmation.

Realism, Naturalism, Parnassianism

❧

Three great literary movements in prose and poetry flourished during the second half of the nineteenth century and reached into the twentieth: realism, naturalism, and Parnassianism.

By adopting a literary criterion of periodic division based on movements and styles, the present work attempts to avoid the shoals of a simple chronological division, which is usually arbitrary or at most lacking any esthetic-literary meaning. Chronological divisions, when used here, are simply points of reference to show the advance of ideas and tendencies. What must be established above all are the specific characteristics of the movements, the style, the guiding ideas, the philosophical, esthetic, and poetical conceptions, the programs, their most typical representatives, their works. Without neglecting the spiritual content, the common denominator for a definition must be literary, that is, it must center upon the style that predominated and gave literary shape to an author or a school. The historical, social, and biographical elements, unless valuable for the explanation of the mental development of an author, are relegated to a secondary level as simple occasional accidents in relation to the work, whose analysis, interpretation, and judgment come before anything else. As a method, it aims to ally history and criticism, the former subordinated to the latter. This is the supreme finality of the study of the literary phenomenon.

Realism and naturalism should be looked upon as specific movements of the nineteenth century. Before they became concretized in a historical period they were esthetic categories or artistic temperaments, general tendencies of the human soul, as were classicism and romanticism. Realism arose whenever there was a union of the spirit and life by means of an objective picture of reality. Accordingly, there is realism in the Bible and in Homer, in classical tragedy and comedy, in Chaucer, Rabelais, and Cervantes before it appears in Balzac, Stendhal, and Dostoevsky. In the same way, naturalism exists whenever there is a reaction against excessive spiritualization, as in certain expressions of baroque eroticism or in naturalist fiction of the nineteenth century.

The nineteenth century was an era in which diverse esthetic and literary currents crossed and recrossed, advanced and retreated, acted and reacted one upon the other, now prolonging, now opposing. And even though the group studied here constituted a homogeneous bloc, the period was also crossed by the romantic-symbolist thread. If there is, therefore, a period which defies a precise periodization and the demonstration of clear frontiers between movements, it is the nineteenth century. Periods intermingle, and literary figures do not always present a clear esthetic coloration. They wear different garbs in the course of their literary evolution, when they do not show simultaneously the characteristics of diverse or opposing schools. This general phenomenon became commonplace in Brazil due to the circumstances of life there during the period. There is a tardiness with which spiritual movements leave their mark on us, and furthermore transformations here do not come about from inside outward, as the result of the evolution of national awareness, but as the reflection of idea-forces that are foreign in origin.

In fact, the nineteenth century was a great crossroads of literary currents. Romanticism was not yet over and traces of realism were already evident. Certain romantic manners made up realistic and naturalistic characteristics. On the other hand, symbolism prolonged romanticism in an effort to take literature more and more into human intimacy, in that long process of interiorization that characterizes literary evolution as it comes down to our times. The old oscillation between classicism and romanticism, between objectivity and subjectivity, with greater frequency than ever took place in that period. Realism-naturalism-Parnassianism, members of the same spiritual family, reacted against romanticism, taking at the same time many of their elements from it. In its turn, this other child of romanticism, symbolism, in the name of the individual against society, opposes the group. The oscillation and the crossing of these currents became markedly evident in Brazil in the work of many writers who had begun their literary careers under romanticism, and who developed into representatives of realism or naturalism, many without losing their original stamp. Not only in prose, but in poetry too this mixture can be seen: many Parnassians are faithful to romantic forms or go ahead to symbolism.

The group of currents studied here occupies a cultural period of greatest relevance in Brazil, the second half of the nineteenth century. National and international historical circumstances coincided with the advent of bourgeois, democratic, industrial, and mechanical civilization, and the new penetration of science came into the world of ideas and practice through biology. The values of that period produced a great impact on the Western spirit, and dominated it completely. In Brazil, it relegated the opposite tendency completely to a secondary level, to the point where the contemporary presence of symbolism, whose importance was noted and reported only in our own times, was almost unperceived.

The system of ideas and norms that characterized that period exercised such an influence in Brazil at the end of the nineteenth and the beginning of the twentieth century, that even today its mark can be noted in many spirits. Hence the importance of the period and the necessity of a general redefinition, indispensable to a proper understanding of its literary expression.

In a general way, 1870 marked a revolution in ideas and life in the world, one which led men to an interest in and devotion to material things. A single generation assumed control of the world, possessed by that special faith in material things. It was the "generation of materialism," as it was termed in a splendid book by the American historian Carlton Hayes. The revolution occurred first in the spirit and thought of men and from there it passed on to their lives, their world, and their values. Intellectually, the elite became impassioned with Darwinism and the idea of evolution (a heritage of romanticism). From a philosophy, Darwinism grew to resemble a religion; liberalism grew and bore fruit on the political and economic levels; the world and thought became mechanized, and traditional religion was fiercely attacked by free-thinking men.

This period of materialism (1870–1900) was a continuation of the Enlightenment and the encyclopedism of the eighteenth century, and the Revolution. It believed in indefinite and ascending "progress" and in the constant development of mechanical and industrial civilization. It believed in the humanitarian impulse, joining mass education and socialism to the cult of political power and military and national glory. The masses appeared historically, and achieved material and political progress. Science, the spirit of observation and rigor, furnished the models for thought and style of life since it judged all phenomena explicable in terms of matter and energy, and governed by mathematical and mechanical laws. The vast process of the "mechanization of work and thought" (Hayes) was reflected as much in material life as in the diverse sciences—physical, biological, social. Biology, with its determinist theory and its promise of the betterment of health and race, became a dominating vogue. Problems of heredity, embryology, cellular structure, and bacteriology intrigued men. Darwinism, evolution, and the doctrine of natural selection gave direction to research, not only in biology, but also in psychology and the social sciences. Another important factor was the rise of laboratory methods in scientific psychology, one more link in the chain between biology and physics and showed the physical base of thought and conduct, and of the affinity of man to animal (Hayes).

The repercussions of this spiritual climate were enormous in the social sciences. For the generation that was coming into its intellectual majority in 1870, the positivism (1830 to 1840) of Auguste Comte offered a singular attraction, in tune as it was with the spirit of the period. Rejecting any ultimate explanation, any theological or metaphysical finality, and concentrating on scientific factualism, positivism exalted social science or sociology as the queen of sciences, endowing it with the same method and principles that characterized the natural sciences. Sociological studies, under the direction of positivism, were oriented towards the collection of facts, their synthesis, and the formulation of laws and tendencies to explain the evolution and conduct of human society. Spencer saw society as an organism in evolution, and the struggle for existence as a constant antagonism among social forces. Historians adopted sociology's points of view and interpreted history as the result of social movements, as an evolution of forces and social institutions. Historians tried to emphasize the influence of economic phenomena and find the origin of modern societies in their roots.

From the moment in which social science, which Comte called

sociology and which Spencer emancipated, took shape, it received the impact of other sciences through a very common phenomenon, the application of methods and principles of one to the other. The social sciences allied themselves to the natural sciences. Economics, sociology, statistics, psychology, natural sciences, geography, anthropology, and ethnography; they were related in the study of human and social facts according to the postulates of Comte's positivism, and they generated the evolutionism of Spencer, the environmentalism of Taine, the psychological materialism of Wundt and Lombroso.[1]

The most important event in the history of culture in the nineteenth century, therefore, was the convergence of biology and sociology, which spread the evolutionist attitude everywhere. The revolution brought about by Darwin, which reinforced the historicizing tendency of the romantic spirit, placed biology in a dominant position over thought, bringing the concepts and methods of science to a naturalist sense: man was integrated into the natural environment, with a natural origin and history. From biology, thanks to Comte and Spencer, the social sciences took on their concepts and analogies. Scientific laws were deduced from the principle of evolution. The world was conceived of as a process of growth and evolution.

The idea of evolution spread widely as the greatest and most seductive of romantic beliefs. It was the new scientific ideal, the revolutionary notion of the century, that was constantly present in the intellectual life and the beliefs of men. Society was looked upon, under the influence of biology, as an organism composed of cells functioning harmoniously and obeying the biological laws of growth and death. To the interest in history and tradition, characteristic of romanticism, were added the biologist attitude and the evolutionist method, the idea of continuous change and development, of evolution and progress. The romantic's stress on the past and on origins led naturally to the notion of growth, evolution, and progress. In short, during the middle of the century biology and sociology were joined in the idea of evolution as a consequence of the work of Darwin, Comte, and Spencer. Biological and social Darwinism, in tune with mechanistic and materialistic theories in physics and chemistry, had their high point in Haeckel, whose popularity was enormous. The mechanistic principles penetrated the sciences of man and society, reducing the processes of life to chemical formulas.

Another result of this convergence of biology and the social sciences was the emphasis given to that other essential idea of Darwinism, that "external circumstances rigidly determine the nature of living beings, including man, and that neither will nor reason can act independently of their past conditioning" (Hayes). It is the notion of the omnipotence of environment, . . . the *milieu* of Comte and Taine. Man is an integral part of the natural order, and his body, like his spirit, develops and acts under total and inevitable conditioning. Environmentalism, a contribution of anthropogeography to social studies of the nineteenth century, influenced historians of civilization and culture, who followed the works of Lamarck, Buffon, and Cuvier, and the work of geographers like Ritter, Kohl, Peschel, Reclus, and Ratzel. It was through Buckle and Taine that the notion became popular and a commonplace of historical criticism and criticism of arts and letters. The influence of Taine in Brazil is overwhelming.

This, then, was the *Zeitgeist*, the spirit of the period. This was the general conception of life that formed a typical spiritual physiognomy: the cult of science and progress, evolutionism, liberalism, determinism, positivism, antispiritualism, naturalism. This is the spiritual complex that characterized the "generation of materialism."

The infusion of this concept into literature was through naturalism; in other words, naturalism was the movement that gave literary form to these theories. In the novel, Zola transformed the characters into puppets on whom environment and heredity invariably imposed character, actions, and fate. In criticism, Taine reduced the interpretation of works of art to an understanding of the milieu, the race, and the moment in which they were produced.

This scientificism gave a shape of its own to naturalism. Realism, Parnassianism, and naturalism, as revolts against romantic subjectivism, shared the same spirit of precision and scientific objectivity, of exactness in description, of an attention to detail, of the cult of the fact. The only thing that distinguishes realism from naturalism is the latter's scientific apparatus, its union with biology and the determinism by heredity and environment.

A knowledge of realist-naturalist esthetics and poetics will come from the determination of its characteristics. How can one define these two temperaments or artistic styles? First, let us look at the definition of the terms.

The word *realist* comes from *real*, originating in the vulgar Latin adjective *realis, reale*, derived in turn from *res*, thing or fact. Real-*ism* (a suffix denoting a party, sect, belief, genre, school, profession, vice, state, condition, illness, portion) indicates a preference for facts and a tendency to face things, as they are in reality. In literature, realism habitually stands opposite idealism (and romanticism), since it chooses reality as it is and not as it ought to be. Therefore, in literary criticism, as M. C. Beardsley points out in the *Dictionary of World Literature* (J. T. Shipley, ed.), the term designates literary works modeled in strict imitation of real life, performing in an objective, photographic and documentary way, without the intervention of the artist's subjectivism. The word came into literature through Champfleury, when in 1857 he published a volume of essays (which he had been working on since 1843) in which he expounded the realistic doctrine. About the same time, a new review of art by the critic Duranty called *Le Réalisme* was circulated. It was the publication of *Madame Bovary* (1857) by Flaubert, however, that assured the triumph of realism in France. Courbet made use of the term in the preface to the catalogue of his show (1885) confirming realism in French painting.

Western literature was already beginning to evolve, as Auerbach has shown, a gradual incorporation of reality. It is only in the nineteenth century however that, in its revolt against romantic idealism (which was related to the upper class), that realism was able to impose the true picture of the life for the humble and obscure, the common men and women always around us. Realism described a composite life made up of many opposites, good and bad, beauty and ugliness, crudeness and polish, without fear of being trivial and monotonous.

Even though opposites in many senses, as has already been stressed, realism and romantiscism head for the same target. They complement rather than oppose each other. Rousseau tried to show that nature was good and that man was naturally good. Consequently, no obstacle should be put in the way of the free exercise of his elemental virtues. All the fetters and organs of restriction should be abolished as non-human evils: society, laws, religion, state, institutions, reason, or any other kind of obstacle to the free manifestation of natural goodness and naturally good impulses.

Characteristics of realism. A complete definition of realism is impossible, because it is, first of all, a temperament, a tendency, a state of mind, rather than a finished type or division of literature. It exists whenever man deliberately prefers to face facts, to let truth dictate form, and to subordinate dreams to reality. It is possible, however, to describe its principal characteristics, and we shall do that according to the work by A. Hibbard already cited.

1. Realism attempts to present the truth. This treatment of the material, this verisimilitude in the arrangement of selected and unified facts, the pointing out of a direction, is essential. It can also be relevant in the use of emotion, which must avoid sentimentalism or artificiality. This quality also appears in the way the parts are presented: realism does not submit itself to a vision of life that is too well-ordered; it deems this artificial, because the rhythm of life is irregular.

2. Realism seeks truth through a faithful portrayal of characters. The characters in realism are first of all concrete, familiar individuals, rather than generic types. The plot occurs from the character of the people, and human motives dominate the action. They are complete, live human beings, whose motives and emotions are what realism portrays and interprets. In relating to psychology, realism had the good fortune to coincide with the development of the science of the human soul. Realism took two directions, therefore: towards the body and the external life, and towards the mind and the internal life.

3. Realism faces life objectively. There is no intrusion on the part of the author, who lets characters and circumstances work upon one another in a search for a solution. The author does not confuse his feelings and points of view with the emotions and motives of the characters.

4. Realism furnishes an interpretation of life. By objectively portraying life, realism gives it meaning, interprets it. The accumulation of facts through documentation is not everything in the realist attitude: selection and synthesis operate in search of a meaning for the concatenation of facts. Hence there is a preference for narration instead of description.

5. Realism portrays contemporary life. Its preoccupation is with men and women, emotions and temperaments, success and failure in the life of the moment. This sense of the contemporary is essential to the realist temperament, in the same way that the romantic turns to the past or to the future. The realist faces the present, in mines, in tenements, in cities, in factories, in politics, in business, in marriage.

Any theme whatever from the conflict of man and his environment or surroundings is material for the realist.

6. Realism draws the greatest sum of its effects from its use of specific details. Until now, we have seen realistic qualities as concerns subject and content. Realism also has a technique and a specific method. Precision and faithfulness in the observation and portrayal are therefore essential realist characteristics. Apparently insignificant details are used in the portrayal of characters and setting. These details must be brought together and harmonized in order to give an impression of reality itself. With the facts gathered, one must give them a certain arrangement in accordance with an artistic proposal to create a special unity.

7. A realistic narrative moves slowly. By the very nature of his technique, which is minute, and by a greater interest in characterization than in action, the realist gives an impression of slowness, hesitation, of an unhurried and gradual progress through the meanderings of conflicts, successes, and failures.

8. Realism leans especially on sensory impression; it picks the language closest to reality, simplicity and naturalness.

As for naturalism, it is realism with the addition of unmistakable distinguishing marks. It is not merely an exaggeration or a reinforced form of realism. It includes writers who cannot be confused with the realists. It is realism strengthened by a peculiar theory, scientific in origin, a materialistic view of man, life, and society.

The word naturalism comes from natural + *ism*, and in philosophy it refers to the doctrine by which nothing in reality has a supernatural meaning; therefore, scientific laws and not theological conceptions of nature can provide valid explanations. In literature, it is the theory that art should conform to nature, making use of scientific methods of observation and experimentation in the treatment of facts and characters.

The term came into literary criticism in France around 1850, but only around 1880 does it assume a definitive position when Émile Zola and his group adopt it in the *Soirées de Médan*. Because of Zola's great influence, it spread all over the world. The growth of science linking of man to "nature," political reforms, realistic tendencies in literature with Balzac, Stendhal, and Flaubert, the theories of Taine on environmentalism in the interpretation of the origins of art; all these helped naturalism achieve a place in the order of the day, with its social scientific vision of man in relation to his milieu and heredity. Enthusiastic after having read Claude Bernard's *Introduction à la médicine expérimental* (1865), Zola worked out an application of the theories to literature. In his book *Le Roman expérimental* (1880), he paralleled the ideas of the master with his theory of the naturalist novel, asserting that the scientific method should be used by the writer. "The experimental novel . . . replaces the study of abstract and metaphysical man with that of natural man, subject to physico-chemical laws and determined by the influence of his milieu." In this way, determinism was established as a dominant theory in naturalist literature. "Moral deliberations are determined by or are the direct result of psychological and other conditions" of a physical nature. Man was nothing but a machine driven by the action of physical and chemical laws, by heredity and by the physical and social environment.

Like the realists, however, the naturalists sought the truth, disdained sentimentalism, were preoccupied with the contemporary period, and constructed their books on the foundation of precisely observed and faithfully collected facts. At the same time their plots and narratives moved slowly along. They increased the interest in society, especially at its lowest levels, and they put more emphasis on freedom of expression.

The critic M. C. Beardsley notes three meanings for the term: (*a*) it refers to works that exhibit an accentuated interest and love for nature and natural beauty; (*b*) it refers to works that have as a model a strict faithfulness to nature, and in this sense it is the same as realism; (*c*) it refers (and this is the most generalized meaning) to works that, in an implicit or explicit way, express a naturalistic concept of life (in opposition to the humanistic and religious) and, as a consequence, these works accentuate the physiological aspect of man, his kinship to the animal, the temporality and futility as well as the irrational and selfish origin of his ideals, and man is portrayed in an ironic way, as morbid, sordid, and vile.

There are, then, fundamental differences between the two, as Hibbard goes on to point out. The vision of nature in naturalism is more deterministic, more mechanistic: man is an animal, the prisoner of fatal and superior forces and propelled by physiology in the same measure as by the spirit or reason. The naturalist observes man by means of the scientific method, impersonally and objectively, as a "case" to be analyzed. The naturalist shows a reformist inclination: his preoccupation with the aspects of inferiority envisage a betterment of social conditions that gave birth to it. The naturalist, with his scientific preoccupation, declares himself to have broad and universal interests, that nothing is lacking in interest and meaning as material, nothing in nature is unworthy of literature. This universality and faithfulness to fact, to all facts, leads naturalism to a certain amorality, a certain indifference. Opinion concerning the acts is not important, only the acts themselves.

In conclusion, realism is the literary tendency that tries to represent truth above all, that is, the true as it is, using for this the techniques of documentation and observation, which are opposites of romantic invention. Interested in the analysis of character, it faces man and the world objectively in its interpretation of life. Making use of sensory impressions, it tries to portray reality through the use of specific details, which makes the narrative long and slow and gives a clear impression of faithfulness to facts. The realist esthetic tries to reach beauty under the guise of the common and the familiar, in a local environment, and on the contemporary scene.

From the point of view of structure, realist fiction is distinguished by the predominance of character over plot, of characterization over action, of the portrayal of individuals and the chronicle of their lives over incidents, and an interest in human motivations.

Realism pays particular attention to the technical, structural, and formal aspects of narration and composition. In the particulars of form, the realist reiterates the classical ideal of purity, measure, and restraint. The realist exalts beauty of expression, like the "*écriture artiste*" of Flaubert and some representatives of the second French realist generation. This was the counterpart of the Parnassian ideal of art for art's sake.

Naturalism accentuates the qualities of realism, adding a conception of life that sees it as the dominance of mechanical forces over individuals. For naturalism acts, character, and destiny come from activity, hereditary, and environment. The spirit of scientific objectivity and impartiality leads the naturalist to introduce into literature all matters and activities of man, including the bestial and repulsive aspects of life, giving preference to the lowest levels of society. By means of a documentary method, by means of language that is direct, natural, colloquial, even vulgar, and of the dialects of the sciences and professions, naturalism tries to represent all of nature, the life which is close to nature, natural man.

As for Parnassianism, it was the poetic movement corresponding to realism-naturalism. It appeared in France as a term to designate poets who came together for the publication of poetry anthologies called *Le Parnasse contemporain,* published in three phases, in 1866, 1871, and 1876. The most famous poets of the school were: Gautier, Baudelaire, Leconte de Lisle, and Baville. The name *Parnasse* (in English, Parnassus, Parnassian, Parnassianism) comes from Parnassus, a mountain in Phocis, in Greece, where, according to legend, the poets lived. By extension, it is a symbolic dwelling place of poets; it also takes in the poets of a single nation. Inspired by the "art for art's sake" esthetic of Gautier, Parnassianism reflects the pendular movement of an objectivist and classicizing current following romantic subjectivism. It subordinates itself to the scientific ideal of objectivity and even to philosophical positivism. It likes to portray historical incidents and natural phenomena in impassive and perfect verses, with rigorous and classical form, and with motives that are classical. The poetry is descriptive, with exactness and economy of images and metaphors. This classic realism in poetry flourished, particularly in Brazil, no doubt from the facility which versifiers found in its poetics, more a technique than an inspiration, more a form than a content. Parnassianism in Brazil went far beyond its chronological limits, contemporary to symbolism and even modernism, making up, in the main, a subschool of poetry that was widespread in the provinces.

The penetration of the "modern" ideas of the nineteenth century in Brazil is due to French influence. French influence was broad and deep. The ideals of the century, its libertine and seditious principles, the French mania stirred up by the Revolution, the Enlightenment, the critical movement of the Encyclopedia were translated into doctrines of philosophical liberation, rationalism, materialism, political and social emancipation, in a nationalist, abolitionist, and republican sense. These swept the country from north to south early in the century. The channels for circulation of ideas in that period functioned efficiently everywhere. Among them, Freemasonry was a powerful and tenacious instrument for the propagation and agitation of doctrines. It was Masonry which helped in the clandestine circulation of forbidden "seditious" books. Despite the vigilance of the censorship, circulation took place all over Brazil, and even formed the basis of rich and famous libraries, including that of Father Agostinho Gomes in Bahia and that of Canon Luís Vieira da Silva in Mariana (described by Eduardo Frieiro in *O Diabo na Livraria do Cônego*).

Thus, as far as ideas were concerned, it was French influence which marked the life of the century, touched here and there with certain English notes in harmony of course with general French tonality.

Three great questions agitated the country during the second half of the century: the slavery question, the religious question, and the military question. In all three, one can feel the influence of those ideas that constituted the spirit of the time, of that intellectual agitation that stirred up men of thought. Ideas of laicization, materialism, rationalism, anticlericalism, naturalism were the intellectual patrimony of the "generation of materialism" and of the period that opened around 1870.

On the truly intellectual level, although one cannot separate it from the political, religious, and social, for all were intertwined, agitation took shape in all of the provinces. At the beginning of the seventies, all Brazil felt itself swamped by the wave of ideas that was agitating the period. Certain established focal points had a role of greatest importance: the academies. It would be well to examine the social and intellectual action undertaken in the provincial Empire by the law schools established in 1827 in São Paulo and Olinda (the latter moved to Recife in 1854), a role identical to that played by the medical school of Bahia, founded in 1808 and reorganized in 1815. Those centers of culture in a country that lacked intellectual life, subordinated as it was to centers in the mother country, "were not sufficient to bring about deep transformations in the colonial mentality." [2] They did serve as poles of attraction and of intellectual fervor through which the intelligent and restless youth of the country could come in contact with the great European centers of cultural production. At the same time the academies shaped the awareness of intellectual unity and autonomy.

Expressions of this fervor were the "French Academy" of Ceará and the "Recife School." The French Academy lasted from 1872 to 1875. It was founded by young intellectuals of the northern province; Rocha Lima, Capistrano de Abreu, Tomás Pompeu, Araripe Júnior, Xilderico de Faria, Lopes Filho, et al. Ceará is rich in academies, associations, and clubs that play an active role in its intellectual life. The "Academy" came from the development of a different association in 1870, "Student Phoenix," and was followed by others. Among these others was the "Reading Cabinet" (1875), the same group with the addition of Paula Nei, Domingos Olímpio, Rodolfo Teófilo, Guilherme Studart, Clóvis Beviláqua; still later came the "Spiritual Bakery" (1892). These are the high points in the intellectual ferment in Ceará, a ferment of philosophical and literary character.[3]

The "Recife School," as Sílvio Romero called it, developed in the northeastern capital around the Faculty of Law, having as its main proponents Tobias Barreto and Sílvio Romero. It was active through the second half of the century as a center of vigorous intellectual agitation, with three phases as set forth by Romero: the literary and poetical, in the sixties, the critico-philosophical from 1870 to 1877–78, and the juridical, from 1878 on.[4]

Other intellectual focal points were São Paulo, Rio de Janeiro, and Bahia.[5]

In all there was a predominance of the "modern" thought that was agitating all of Spanish America and Portugal. The Portuguese reaction was led by Antero de Quental, Eça de Queiroz, Ramalho Ortigão, and Teófilo Braga in 1865, and the famous Coimbran polemic of Good Sense and Good Taste.[6]

As José Veríssimo stresses, the period is witness to an uncommon flourishing of studies and a preoccupation with education. Thus everything favored that vast revision of values and postulates that would place "modern" thought on the highest level: the positivist doctrines, orthodox and heterodox, of Littré, the biology of Darwin, the evolution of Spencer, the determinism of Taine, the historical conception of Buckle, the monism of Kant, Schopenhauer, and Haeckel.

One must underline at this point one of the deepest and broadest influences working on the Brazilian literary mind of the time: that of the Portuguese writer José Maria Eça de Queiroz (1845–1900). The struggle of realism against romanticism had begun in Portugal in 1865 with the Coimbra Question, and continued in 1871 with the lectures presented by the Casino Lisbonense. In a Brazil dominated by sentimentalism, by the sometimes refined, sometimes rustic style of romanticism, and with a literary life that still lacked the necessary links, his repercussion was enormous and was one of the factors in the transformation that took place here at that time. In 1875, Eça de Queiroz published O Crime do Padre Amaro, and a short time later O Primo Basílio (1878). It was a realization of the realist-naturalist esthetic in fiction. Through these books and the constant link that he had with Brazil (through the press and by his relationships with the literary world), the fascinating Eça became one of the chief mentors of Brazilian intellectual life. His influence in literature was felt in all the works being published at the time, and it was seen for many years after in theme, manner, style, and irony.

In this atmosphere, literature evolved in Brazil out of romanticism and towards realism-naturalism. Around 1880, the transformation was effected, and the first fruits began to appear. O Mulato, by Aluísio Azevedo, is from 1881. Afterwards it is sometimes the line of realism, sometimes that of naturalism, by which short story or novel is written. Sometimes, in writers like Machado de Assis, who never allowed himself to be carried away by exaggerated naturalist tones, and who even reacted against Eça's formula in the critical study that he did of him, many doctrinaire points of view and certain esthetic arrangements found a home. In a general way, however, naturalism as a school did not last beyond the eighties. What is more commonly found in the fiction of the period are its impregnations here and there.

If it were not for an occasional book done by Aluísio Azevedo, Adolfo Caminha, Domingos Olímpio, a short story here and there (regional or not), and scattered pages everywhere, it might be said that naturalism was a frustrated movement in Brazil. On the other hand, there were earlier attempts through costumbrismo and the picaresque novel of Spanish origin, which took the form here of feuilleton novels. This was obvious in the works of Martins Pena and Manuel Antônio de Almeida, of Lima Barreto and Cardoso de Oliveira, and in that of Machado de Assis himself, an influence in our fiction that has not yet been given the attention that it merits. Having appeared in transitional forms, naturalism was interspersed in the novels of Taunay and Franklin Távora, and even under the coloration of a small or minute romanticism in the colloquial language and the observation of everyday life and customs of the environment that Antônio Cândido points out in Joaquim Manuel de Macedo.[7] It was realism, mitigated, more balanced, without exaggerated compromises with science and determinist biology, and it produced, starting with the decade of the eighties (the *Memórias Póstumas de Brás Cubas* are from 1881) our most elevated and independent expressions in fiction, lasting far beyond the strictly naturalistic phase, and giving Brazilian literature a new vigor.

An identical phenomenon occurred in France. The naturalism of Zola and the Goncourts did not smother the older lineage of the realists Balzac, Stendhal, and Flaubert, which was, in the end, the one that prevailed as the fullest manifestation of French fiction. In England, strict naturalism did not find a propitious climate; realism predominated, more in keeping with the English spirit and the Victorian mentality. Sometimes the realist form, sometimes the naturalist appeared in Russia, Germany, Italy, Spain, Portugal, and the United States.

In our century, both outside and inside Brazil, realism constitutes the principal tendency of literature. The use of realistic techniques is a generalized convention, whether in their purer and more moderate forms, or in forms that are combined with the technical and thematic elements of symbolism, impressionism, and expressionism, whether under the manifestations of populist, socialist, and existentialist neonaturalism or neorealism.

In the second half of the nineteenth century, the social, economic, and political elements which made up the framework of Brazilian life, the very structure of society, suffered a frank and radical transformation. From an agrarian, landowning, slave-holding, aristocratic society, Brazil became an urban and bourgeois civilization in a phase preparatory to industrialization, but already responsible for a new marginal population, if not a small urban proletariat. Parallel to this socio-economic revolution there was taking place, as Gilberto Freyre shows, an identical transformation in social psychology and anthropology: the attainment of certificates of whiteness by the mixed-blood population and its rise to active and broad participation in social, political, and intellectual life.

An intensely political period, political, parliamentary, and religious oratory was the most outstanding and popular form of intellectual activity. For the truly literary mentality, however, while poetry had been the favorite form of the romantics, prose fiction constituted the best means of literary realization now, as it demanded the investigation of content and methods in the realist spirit.

In conformity with the general esthetic of realism, Brazilian fiction writers placed greater emphasis on the portrayal of characters and the description of their lives than on the organization of the plot. Within this general principle, however, they follow diverse patterns. In the biographical pattern, in which a character, male or female, stands out above the others and the life that involves him, everything served to emphasize the essential traits of the protagonist or to portray him in tragic or comic situations; for example, family history and the private social group (collective residences, small agglomerations, groups of relatives and friends). In the regional pattern, individuals of different occupations or social castes in the same region were brought together. In the environmental pattern, relationships were accentuated between a geographical picture and the population that inhabits it. In the psychological pattern, elements were analyzed that combined to produce and resolve a subjective situation.

It could be affirmed that two directions marked the evolution of realism in Brazil: the social current, attracting social problems, urban and contemporary themes, the common material of everyday life. According to this current realism sometimes slides off into naturalism as it assumes a philosophical position and submits itself to the light of a "theory." The regionalist movement brings to the fore local color, the role of the land, which is the real protagonist of this literature. In regionalism, too, realism frequently comes together with naturalism. The difficulty and melancholy of Brazilian rural life brought on pessimism, disillusionment, and despair, which easily led to the acceptance of geographical determinism and the uselessness of a mean struggle against inevitable and irreducible forces. This in turn led to the negation of free will. There came about the conviction of a determinist link between the land and human conduct, between it and human destiny itself, which was a Brazilian formulation of realist-naturalist bent to the problem of the relationship between man and his environment. Brazilian regional literature is a true saga of the land and its victory over man.

Brazilian realism had yet another role in the process of nationalization of the language. The evolution came from afar and was accented by romanticism and consolidated by realism. It incorporated into literature areas of professional, popular, and regional expression. Unlike the French masters of artistic writing, who were more inclined towards the reproduction of the real experience in its immediate freshness without classic fetishisms and with relative formal indifference, the realist (Machado de Assis for example) was responsible for the development of a style in native speech. Enriching independent expression, it continued, through the hand of its masters, the nationalization of literature. Coinciding with the beginning of evaluation, analysis, and interpretation of Brazilian reality (thanks to anthropological, ethnographic, folkloric, sociological, historical, and linguistic studies), realism looked to the Brazilian world. It taught the Brazilian writer to deal esthetically with native material rather than sentimentally, and with it literature put roots down definitively into the native soil and attained what modernism (1922) was able to ratify once and for all.

At the end of this chapter in the history of ideas and literature, it is licit for us to look back. If the configuration of the period does not appear to us with precise contours, and if it seems closed to us, like a stagnant room, nevertheless, when its diverse coordinates are known, one has a confirmation of the unity of style which dominates it. There was a uniform style marked by a system of thought, which directs, in addition, all the manifestations of culture, by means of a specific body of values and ideas and a form proper to art. It was above all the phase in which a literary temperament, realism, in a state of fullness, created a flexible and plastic literary genre, the novel. This form was adopted as the one best suited to the esthetic aims of the period.

Study of the material must begin with the forerunner of realistic fiction, the work of Manuel Antônio de Almeida, a precursor, out of time, deserving the tribute paid him. (There is no rigorous chronology to respect, because naturalist or realist works arose together.) Afterwards we have the group of typical naturalist novelists: Aluísio Azevedo, Inglês de Sousa, Júlio Ribeiro, and Adolfo Caminha. In a unique position are Machado de Assis and Raul Pompéia, who, although they reveal naturalist impregnations here and there, are independent realists; in the case of Pompéia this independence is marked by the impressionistic half-tones that peculiarly mark his work. There follow Lima Barreto and Coelho Neto, who are part of the naturalist spirit.

Realism-naturalism in Brazil found excellent ground for realization in regional material. Through contact with the techniques and skills of the realist-naturalist spirit, some creations were produced that occupy a definitive place in our literary history. Thus it is necessary to study in detail the diverse regional varieties of fiction and the contributions that gave local flavor to our literature.

Among literary genres, the short story is an instrument of great utility in the hands of our realistc and naturalistic writers. Many began with this form, or even reached fame with it, and elevated it to the most pure and perfect of creations, along psychological lines or as an analysis of customs. Since it was freed historically, the genre owes much to the principles of realism even in our days, as it attempts to incorporate or absorb other techniques and experiences, impressionistic or expressionistic.

In addition, the Brazilian theater, with its origins in the colonization, more or less stationary during the colonial phase, rose up in the dawn of the realist-naturalist period. Theater did not receive a doctrinaire esthetic outline, which a marked influence would characterize in it. Nevertheless it is joined to realism at several points of articulation.

Lastly, the poetic form of realism-naturalism, called here Parnassianism from the French model, is too important among us, because of the large number of cultivators and the high value of some of them, not to merit special attention. One must include in the study the figures of Rui Barbosa, Euclides da Cunha, and Joaquim Nabuco, quite representative of the realist and Parnassian spirit.

In respect to criticism, the work of the positivist and materialist period was vast and important in Brazil. Sílvio Romero, José Veríssimo, Araripe Júnior, Capistrano de Abreu, and other lesser critics, such as Valentim Magalhães, Artur Orlando, and Rocha Lima, construct a whole body of criticism, representative of the period and influential through the years in our literature. The study of the criticism and literary ideas that illustrate and shape the period deserve special attention, therefore.

Regionalism in Prose Fiction

❦

Ever since romanticism, with its recognition of the *genius loci,* the growing importance of regional Brazil was a fact of major significance. The geographical, economic, folkloric, and traditional influences that left marked traces and distinctive characteristics in the life, customs, temperament, language, artistic expressions, and ways of being and feeling, acting and working, were evident in Brazilian intellectual life after a national awareness of political and cultural independence had arisen. There is, however, an essential difference between regionalism as it was seen by the romantics and that practised by the realist generations. In José de Alencar, Gonçalves Dias, and Bernardo Guimarães, regionalism was a form of escape from the present to the past, a past idealized by sentiment and made artificial by compensation and representation in dreams, in a manner of speaking. This mood of regionalism occurs as a contradiction since it over-emphasizes the picturesque and typical local color; at the same time it attempts to dissimulate, attributing qualities, sentiments, and values that do not belong to the locale, but to the culture that has been imposed upon it. It has already been noted that Alencar's Indian was a European with a breechclout and tomahawk.

As was stressed in the introduction of this work, regionalism, as it coincided with the movement for the evaluation, analysis, and interpretation of Brazilian reality, encouraged that introspective advance that came out of romanticism. Regionalism plunged into the national magma in search of understanding of values and motives of life, and at the same time it sought there the sources of intellectual nutrition and inspiration. The mentality of the country under realist influence, however, divested itself of that romantic nostalgia and escapism, to consider contemporary existence and its environment.

From mere localism to broad literary regionalism, there are several ways of interpreting and conceiving regionalism. There are those who see it allied to mediocrity and narrowness, confusing it with provincialism in the pejorative sense; this is a deformation in the same way that cosmopolitanism is a counterfeit of universalism. It is a confining, self-sufficient regionalism, one which provokes rivalry among regions and has both limitation and opposition.

A related conception is one that reduces regionalism to a synonym for literary localism, with regional literature failing to reach beyond exploration and exposition of the picturesque forms and special color of the regions. It is another form of romantic escapism; or else it is the mark of tired periods and civilizations that take refuge in the past or in local color.

With George Stewart,[1] we can define regionalism in two ways. In a broad sense, every work of art is regional when it is woven from the cloth of some particular region or seems intimately to germinate on that base. In that sense, a novel can take place in one city and deal with a universal problem, so that the localization is incidental. More strictly, to be regional, a work of art not only has to be localized in a region, but also must derive its substance from that locale. That substance comes about primarily from the natural background (climate, topography, flora, fauna, and so forth) as elements that affect human life in the region; and also from the manners peculiar to human society established in that region. This is the meaning of authentic regionalism.

By involving itself in the truth of realism, the Brazilian literary mind lost its sentimentalism in the consideration of regionality. It went on to understand that literary regionalism consists, to paraphrase Howard W. Odum,[2] of presenting the human spirit in its diverse aspects in correlation to its immediate environment, of portraying man, language, countryside, and the cultural wealth of a particular region, considered in relation to the reactions of the individual who inherits certain peculiarities of race and tradition. It was with realism that people became aware that regional culture, as B. A. Botkin stresses,[3] could offer literature "a subject [physical and cultural landscape, local customs, legends, myths, types, language, etc.], a technique [native and popular manners of expression, style, rhythm, imagery, symbolism], a point of view [the social idea of groups and of cultural values moved by tradition, which plays a liberating and not a confining role]."

In this way, the Brazilian regional mass furnished realist writers with an ample source of subject matter, native language, human types, forms of social and moral conflict.

At this juncture, with Brazilian literature part of a culture that is regionally differentiated and interregionally related, one finds an implicit recognition of the importance of the concept of regionalism in literary criticism and history, even though it had earlier been applied, as Viana Moog has pointed out.[4] One must also remember the studies of Gilberto Freyre and what he has to say about sociological interpretation;[5] and there were the older studies by Euclides da Cunha, Capistrano de Abreu, and Tavares Bastos. One must also keep in mind, in addition to this important tradition of regionalist studies in Brazil, the new science of regionalism as a powerful instrument for research and historical studies and its development during the past few years in the United States.

The fact is that Brazil did not escape the general law of the development of civilizations and cultures evolving "logically from regional starting points, growing from domain to domain, from the elemental unity or the regional group." The application of the theory to a study of Brazil's national organization, and history (including cultural and literary history) is therefore natural. The penetration and expansion of the land; independence; federalism and municipalism; economic cycles; rivalries among the various states for control of federal power; the alternating domination of different provinces with the vicissitudes of economic power; the opposition of North and South, province and metropolis, interior and coast; the regional specialization of culture and civilization, with even a human type, psychologically and socially differentiated; a type of frontier man, the mixed-blood, who struggles to expand his area of participation, rising to a position of political, social, and cultural visibility; these are examples of what it would be proper to call the action of the "frontier" and "sections" or "regions" (the terms are those of American historian Frederick J. Turner, a pioneer in this theory of historical interpretation), examples in Brazilian organization and evolution of economic, political, social, or intellectual regionalism.

With no other basis but the spirit of rivalry and revenge, Franklin Távora outlined in 1876, in the preface to *O Cabeleira*, the manifesto of what he called "Literature of the North." His struggle to divide Brazilian literature into two sections, North and South, had a basis in that small and narrow regionalist spirit referred to above, the product of self-sufficiency, isolationism, complacency, and pride in the inferior and mediocre aspects of a region, which is best termed provincialism. The attitude of Franklin Távora, however, contained an awareness of the problem, and Távora arose to face Alencar's romantic regionalism.

Thenceforward, a whole literary production surges out of the regional laboratory. From north to south of the country, writers appear who attempt to capture in prose, with a maximum of veracity, the themes, customs, types, and language of the various geographic regions which make up the country. A hero is even created, the regional hero of almost epic stature, a superman, struggling against a fatal destiny laid down by the superior forces of the environment.

One must not forget yet another typically Brazilian aspect of regionalism: ruralism, the rise in value and idealization of the backlands and the backlands type. After the romantic movement, and following Indianism, this vein goes all through our regionalism. In the beginning, there was idealization and optimistic sentimentalism, through which the backlands were seen only in their rosy aspect, as the good and healthful backlands, peopled by good, healthy, and vigorous creatures, with pure souls. It was supposedly the most Brazilian Brazil. In a more laggard phase, this ruralism became corrupted into *caipirismo*, rusticism caricatured and grotesquely represented, whose types made up an enormous gallery in our novel and theater, even down to the present time. Juca Mulato is the poetic symbol of this sentimental idealization, while Jeca Tatu is the realist representation of the rural man or rustic, corrupted by despair and illness. In any case, the cult of the backlands is a nativist reaction that is more vigorous than Indianism, and above all more authentic, because, based on a national reality, it is more in tune with the history of our civilization.

However, this regional literature did not put the growing unity of the country in check. The common Portuguese origin is blended here with the Indian and Negro contributions, and later with the various foreign influences. Regionalism is a collection of patches that cover the whole nation. It is variety seen in the unity, the identity of spirit, of feelings, of language, of customs, and of religion. The regions do not produce isolated literatures, but rather they contribute their differences to the homogeneity of the literary landscape of the country.

The divisions based on the criterion of natural regions is of no interest to literary study. What matters here are cultural regions, marked by their importance as regional centers of literary production. Of course the divisions that result from the application of this criterion are not far from those established by the National Council of Geography in 1944 as the basis of geographical research.

The cultural or literary regions, as seen in the study of the theme, are the following, and they seem very well characterized: Northern group; Northeastern group; Bahian group; Central group; São Paulo group; Rio Grande do Sul group.

One could add a sort of subregion, consisting of Rio de Janeiro and its suburban zone, really a small literary province, from which Lima Barreto, Macedo, and even Machado de Assis drew their material.

From an analysis of the broad influence that the regional province had in the formation and development of Brazilian literature, and of the regionalist contribution to realism, one reaches the conclusion that literature becomes more vigorous whenever it is closer to its roots, and all the more as these go deeper into the soil. These focal points act as fertile sources of culture, of variety, and of spiritual and artistic stimuli. Literature in Brazil dies out, or writers do whenever they get too far away from those local sources.

Furthermore, it is through the particular that art arrives at the general, from the individual that it broadens into the human. This is what André Gide affirms: by particularizing themselves, great creative artists arrive at a common humanity. Commenting on this thought of Gide's, the Spanish critic José Bergamín, in confirmation of this philosophy of universality through the regional and the individual, quotes a Spanish proverb which sums it all up: "My courtyard is private, but when it rains, it gets wet like all others."

Symbolism, Impressionism, Modernism

‹§›

A LITERATURE IN CHANGE

The Brazilian artistic scene was dominated by esthetic ideas and norms implanted by the powerful generation of 1870, and which made up the stylistic complex of realism-naturalism-Parnassianism. Until 1890, the domination of this esthetic was uncontested. It was one in which prose and poetry worked together in the objective portrayal of reality, an expression of the general interest in material things during the period. Then, however, new ideas began to circulate, to influence restless spirits. It was a change that did not pass unperceived by the wise critic Araripe Júnior.[1] The weariness and decrepitude of the old school was already visible; there was an obvious decline of production and creativity along naturalist lines. The truth was that the victory over romanticism had not been complete, and the period was crossed by a romantic vein. The realist-naturalist esthetic itself had inherited certain characteristics of romanticism.

If the romantic elements had some life in that phase, however, it was of a latent nature until it reappeared in symbolism as a revenge of subjectivity on objectivity, of interiorization on exteriorization, of the individual on society. This crossing of esthetic currents made up the dynamics of the last quarter of the nineteenth century. The appearance of symbolism did not do away with the naturalist-Parnassian current. On the contrary, symbolism was muffled by it in certain aspects, and barely managed to make itself known to criticism. Its importance was recognized only much later. The result was that as poetical movements, Parnassianism and symbolism were different literary phenomena in spiritual attitude, in generational language, and in style of expression. They remained together for a long time, sometimes parallel, sometimes mingled. There were writers who were characterized by both Parnassianism and symbolism. Since neither had succeeded in doing away with the other, both lasted into the twentieth century, Parnassianism continuing on in isolation, with certain outstanding figures; or mixed with elements of symbolism, making up a poetry of transition and syncretism. From 1910 to 1920 this poetry laid the way for the coming of modernism.

But, in addition to its own importance as an independent movement and the significant figures that it inspired during the last days of the nineteenth century, symbolism played an important role as a stimulant for the literary spirit in general, and it promoted a singular transformation in prose, even in fiction. It was Araripe Júnior who first noted this tendency at the end of the century:

This coming together of the last efforts of the poet of O Guarani with the first attempts at literary mysticism in Brazil, forces me to reveal an idea that may pain many enthusiasts of realism and of Zola.

The poetry that naturalism had expelled from the national novel in the name of analysis and the study of characteristics, seems to have been reconquering its abandoned redoubts for some time. Coelho Neto, in some of his studies, has already given a characteristic note to the new phase. And this return to a love of nature, to the lyricism of life, to the waking dream, to the natural tendency of man towards legend and the confusion of the real with the ideal, probably comes about so easily among us because there is a lyric poet in every national writer, normally little inclined towards labors of persistent observation, and who is always obliged to reshape his urges in order to undertake analytical studies if the microscope should not offer him the illusions of the infinitely small. If, however, it is easy to foresee the influence of the poetic imagination in the works that are to be produced in the near future, it would be very difficult to determine from here the form that would be taken by works in prose destined to describe Brazilian life concretely, dependent as we still are and at this time upon the capricious currents of European thought.[2]

As a critic with sharp eyes, Araripe Júnior immediately pointed out to the new generation in Brazil the path to broader horizons; it should seek inspiration in the new examples furnished by the Russians and the Scandinavians, Tolstoy, Dostoevsky, Ibsen, and Bjornson, in whom they could escape the morbid tendencies of the old esthetic and of the "dreary books of the French psychologists." The advice was heeded by authors recognized later as guiding lights of the new esthetic, and who would have so much influence in the later development of the literary art.

This transformation, which took place in prose and which was glimpsed so well by Araripe Júnior, was the result of an esthetic process joining symbolism and naturalism. A prose was produced that today we call impressionism, a type that will in turn influence the genesis of modernism. Instead of disappearing and being born anew, the esthetic styles fertilize each other and are transformed, with resulting new forms that are never completely new because they integrate many elements of the previous ones.

Clear in literature after 1890 is this reaching beyond naturalism-realism through introspection and symbolism, in spite of its being a fact that took place more or less unperceived until a short time ago. In this respect, even the position of Machado de Assis is quite significant. Although he may have received impregnations of positivist ideology and naturalist technique, Machado never let himself be conquered, a confessed drinker of "romantic milk." He produced, furthermore, the best criticism of the naturalistic novels of Eça de Queiroz, masterful pages, still valid today as models of criticism of an esthetic type. The absolute realist-naturalist doctrine was not the ideal climate for a writer like Machado de Assis who transfigured reality rather than simply painting it. He created a work that is similar to life rather than a copy of reality. He uses some of the procedures of the school, such as the autobiographical method, the organic structure, a certain slackness of plot, keeping in mind an approximation of reality and a portrait of man. But Machado had a clear awareness of the difference between art and life, which therefore put him at a distance from orthodox realists and naturalists. In contrast to them, Machado knew how to face literature as a body of symbols and conventions, without which, use of the elements of life became unartistic. He knew that the mission of the artist was, by means of those symbols, artifices, and conventions, to create a special world, similar to the real one, that would awaken an illusion of life without being life. It is clear that this world had to be realistic, but of a deeper realism, more intense. It was enough to capture and represent life by showing reality through small representative snapshots, properly selected and structured, which would communicate the impression of the total effect.

There is a difference of grade and material as well as treatment in the work of Machado as compared to the typical naturalist. Above all, the dominating landscape is that of the human spirit, the mysterious and varied region, which his art specialized in plumbing, transfiguring its perspectives into myths and symbols. Machado followed a tendency of the literature of those closing decades, the tendency to ransack the inner life of the individual by using, furthermore, the realistic techniques of exact observation. Introspective psychological fiction had placed in the lists a new kind of reality, from which the inventive faculty and fantasy were not far removed, and to which Machado allied a basic tragic vision of existence.

The evolution of Machado de Assis in the progress of literature, became evident in the transfigured realism, a realism broadened by symbolism and mythology. The fact is all the clearer as the writer reaches the end of his career, freeing himself by conscious effort from naturalist chains. This was shown precisely by Eugênio Gomes[3] as the "forest of symbols" that the novelist has used ever since *Brás Cubas*, accented in *Esaú e Jacó* (1904). Machado continues "in a significant and exciting way to think in images or metaphors, and . . . even when subtle, could dissimulate with picturesque elements the metaphysical or allegorical meaning of the artistic creation," his universe enriched with a moral idealism, peopled with symbols of good and evil. Thus it was in *Esaú e Jacó* and in many of his short stories: a world of symbols and allegories. Machado's faithfulness to the realistic technique obliged him to immerse himself in the contemporary in order to gather the material of life which, as it reached the unconscious, would be transformed into a symbol of art. His chronicles documented this fact: many matters observed in daily life, gathered in the reading of the *fait divers* of the newspapers, served as material for chronicles, were later unfolded into short stories or were introduced into his novels, losing in reality along the way and gaining in artistic intangibles through different levels of meaning. Fact was thus hidden, rejected as fact, transformed into an esthetic substance. It was life being saved through art, acquiring permanence, changing in form and structure, revealing through art its intimate secrets, the eternal and deep truth of human nature.

This religion of art or this victory of life through art achieved a true apotheosis in the final message written in the *Memorial de Aires*

(1908). Art saved him here, redeemed him, humanized him. "Suffering became art in the *Memorial*," Graça Aranha said. Machado became converted to humanity, to life, and reconciled himself with the poetical meaning of existence, with the moral world, with spiritual life.[4]

If prose was leaving the naturalistic esthetic behind and was heading towards impressionism, poetry felt the transforming process just as unmistakably. In prose, in addition to the final works of Machado de Assis, the transition brought forth the works of Raul Pompéia, and Graça Aranha, and a whole gallery of fiction writers whose books were impregnated with the same esthetic values that would lead to modernism.

In poetry, after the symbolism of the first phase, the new current multiplied into various movements filled the period with syncretism and transition at the beginning of the twentieth century.

At the beginning of the decade of the nineties, restless and discontented young men, bearing the dominant literary stamp, which was that of naturalism-Parnassianism, met in Rio de Janeiro to discuss new esthetic and literary ideals. These were known as "decadent" and were French in inspiration. The meeting was the advent of Brazilian symbolism. The group, made up of B. Lopes, Oscar Rosas, Cruz e Sousa, and Emiliano Perneta, among others, issued the first manifesto of renovation in the newspaper *Fôlha Popular* (1891), using a faun as a Mallarmean emblem. As Araripe Júnior points out in the essay mentioned above, the best record of the change at its inception, since 1887 there had been a penetration among us of the "decadent" ideas that came from France, and they could be seen in the "subtleties of a grammatical hieraticism, in which syntax passed through capricious truncations in order to obtain certain and determined effects." There was a taste for mythology, for metaphysics, for the occult, and for the invisible, expressed by the poet as though he were a magician. This tendency was received as a "tool for the demolition of the naturalist school of Zola," Araripe continues, and thus the current came into the news.

In addition to the group in Rio de Janeiro in 1891, another pleiad of young men founded in 1892 a literary society called the "Spiritual Bakery" in Ceará, dedicated to the cultivation of the eccentricities of the new art. The symbolist movement was launched in Brazil in this way, and in 1893, Cruz e Sousa inaugurated it with his books *Missal* and *Broquéis*.

UNDER THE SIGN OF THE SYMBOL

Origins of symbolism. Not all literature that uses symbols is symbolist. Universal poetry is essentially symbolic. Symbols have been used in literature since its beginnings. It was sufficient for man to attempt to express himself in an indirect way and through figurative representation, avoiding practical language and the establishment of the visible.[5] During the decade beginning with 1890, however, there developed in France an esthetic movement that was first called "decadent" and later symbolist.[6] Linked to romanticism in many aspects, and having a common beginning with Parnassianism,[7] symbolism came about as a reaction against the Parnassian esthetic formula which had dominated the literary scene during the decade of the seventies. Along with realism and naturalism the older form defended the impersonal, the objective, a pleasure in detail and in the precise representation of nature, a preference for form over content, an emphasis on the descriptive exterior, on the factual, on the portrayal of the commonplace and everyday.

Although it was not a unity of methods but rather of ideals, symbolism did attempt to set up an esthetic credo based on the subjective, the personal, suggestion and vagueness, on the mysterious and the illogical, on indirect and symbolic expression. As Mallarmé preached, one should not give an object a name, or present it directly, but should suggest it, evoke it little by little. It is a process of enchantment characterized by the symbol.

The cradle of symbolism, as well as of *Parnassianism*, Cornell affirms,[8] is the first volume of the *Parnasse contemporain* (1866). Not only are some of its collaborators among the ancestors common to both movements, but also it gave room to the first wails of that "intimate emotion" that was to be one of the most typical of symbolist elements. Quite curious is this phenomenon of modern literary history wherein two movements, united in their origins, identified or mingled in their formal and ideological elements, diverge as they advance in time and become parallel and inimicable.

Baudelaire (1821–1867) is the great precursor of symbolism, that

Baudelaire whom Rimbaud in 1871, as he inaugurated the Baudelairean cult that was to become a new literary religion, affirmed to be the "first seer, king of poets, a true God." [9] Before Baudelaire, however, it was to Edgar Allan Poe (1809–1849) that the paternity of the movement was attributed because of his influence on Baudelaire. One must add Verlaine (1844–1896), Rimbaud (1854–1891), and Mallarmé (1842–1898) to those most responsible for the poetical transformation. There were also, according to Chiari,[10] the remote sources and philosophical antecedents of the movement, which for a long time had been preparing "the mystical and idealistic approach to literature." Accordingly art would not be communication or information, but the "source of strong emotional experiences and the revelation of the mystery of the world." [11] Schopenhauer and Hegel formed its principal philosophical base; both Wagner and the Russian novel were other decisive influences.

The decade of the seventies was realist and Parnassian, while that of the eighties became decadent and symbolist, cultivating a poetry of suggestion and musicality, correspondences and interrelations of the senses, and a literary life marked by eccentricity, artifice, and insanity. The change was gradual and became evident with the growing influence of Baudelaire, Mallarmé, Verlaine, and Rimbaud as the great masters of a nonobjective and nondescriptive poetry. Around 1880, the idea of decadence spread, characterized by Paul Bourget in 1881 who identifies the state of decadence with Baudelaire, the mystic, libertine, and analyst. Baudelaire was typical of a series of individuals "incapable of finding their proper place in the work of the world," with a clear view of "the incurable mask of their destiny," extreme pessimists and individualists, wishing to submit the world to their intimate necessities and feeling the period as one of crisis and boredom, fatigue and degeneration, dissolution and guilty conscience. Decadence, as it was portrayed in *À Rebours,* by Huysmans, with its famous hero Des Esseintes, constituted a state of revolt against bourgeois society and its concept of family morality.[12] After the article by Moréas in 1885, the term came to be replaced by "symbolism," which finally prevailed in current usage, even though here and there the first continued in use.

Along with the great pioneers, Baudelaire, Verlaine, Mallarmé, and Rimbaud, symbolism has the following names: Laforgue, Corbière,

Samain, Le Cardonnel, Guérin, Moréas, Ghil, Maeterlinck, Villiers de l'Isle Adam, Régnier, Huysmans, Stuart Merrill, Dujardin, Fontainas, Moekel, Francis Jammes, Vielé-Griffin, Paul Fort, Verhaeren. A phenomenon typically French in origin, it had, however, a centrifugal character, radiating throughout the Western world, impregnating other literatures. Above all, it left a very strong heritage, analyzed by C. M. Bowra,[13] in five poetical personages who since the end of the nineteenth century have had an impact: Valéry, Rilke, George, Blok, and Yeats. One might add as heirs to this or that form of symbolism Proust, Apollinaire, and Claudel. In England, a similar movement was the estheticism of Rossetti, Pater, and Wilde. In Scandinavia there was Ibsen (1828–1906). As a movement, symbolism lasted until the last years of the nineteenth century, with symptoms of decline clear after 1896.

Its contribution to literature was imperceptible. There were those who gave greater importance for its positive aspect and for the heritage that it gave to modern poetry. Bowra underlines the change that took place in European poetry after 1890 due to symbolism. Cornell points out the new possibilities and powers given poetry after the experiences of the period between 1885 and 1898, an experience that enriched many forms of expression, with prose poems, free verse, and metaphorical prose. Romantic sentimentalism had been completely extirpated from poetry, along with didacticism, banality, and pure description. It was, therefore, a movement of singular importance with international repercussions.

Definition and characteristics. It is not easy to define symbolism or reduce it to a formula, since the movement did not constitute a body of doctrines with a program of defined and coherent propositions and unity of methods. Its representatives were united by certain common ideals and other disparate elements of independent meaning.

First of all, symbolism was a reaction against realism, naturalism, and positivism, and against Parnassianism in poetry. As Martino observes, it was a revolt against the positivist spirit in all sectors: art, morality, philosophy. Furthermore, symbolism represents

the final result of a development that began with romanticism, that is, with the discovery of the metaphor as a germinal cell of poetry, a discovery which led to the richness of impressionistic imagery; but thus, as it drew away from impressionism because of its materialistic view of the world, and from Parnassianism by virtue of its formalism and rationalism, it rejected romanticism because of its emotionalism and the conventionalism of its metaphorical language.

[And Hauser adds:] In certain aspects, symbolism could be considered the reaction against all previous poetry; it discovered something that had not yet been known or emphasized before: "pure poetry," the poetry that grew out of the irrational spirit, non-conceptual in language, opposed to all logical interpretation. For symbolism is nothing more than the expression of those relationships and correspondences, which language, abandoned to itself, creates between the concrete and the abstract, the material and the ideal, and among the different spheres of the senses.[14]

Symbolism was, therefore, a form of the romantic spirit, one of its continuations, an indirect and extreme romanticism since it fled the external world to believe that the only reality is what is reflected in the individual consciousness. In this way, what matters for the symbolist are the states of the soul and of those, only the ones that can be known, one's own. Hence its cult of the ego which was a strong individualistic note in opposition to social philosophy, and the cult of sensations in the place of a philosophy of esthetics. A natural result of the egoism was the antirational and mystical attitudes, the idealistic and religious tone, the tendency towards isolation, the respect for music, the theory of sensory correspondences, the cult of beauty. Poetry was separated from social life and mixed with music as it explored the unconscious through symbols and suggestions, preferring the invisible world to the visible, wishing to understand life through intuition and the irrational, exploring the reality located beyond the real and beyond reason.

With life being mysterious and inexplicable, as the symbolists thought, it was quite natural that it be represented in an imprecise, vague, nebulous, illogical, and unintelligible way. The thing by itself was not the main element to be expressed; rather, it was the symbol of the thing and its inherent essences, of its particular aspects instead of the whole.

In the place of direct expression, incapable of capturing the internal essences and the most personal feelings, symbolism used indirect processes, associations of ideas represented by clusters of metaphors and symbols. The poet, Hauser asserts, must express something that escaped a defined form and could not be reached by a direct route.

What they sought, says Bowra, was the capture of a supernatural experience in the language of visible things; hence, every word is a symbol, used not by common proposal, but for the associations that a reality situated beyond the senses can evoke. Therefore, Hauser insists, the poet must become a "seer," one whose senses abandoned their normal function. The essence of symbolism, Bowra states further, is the emphasis on a world of ideal beauty and the conviction that it is attained through beauty. Hence the religious attitude of the symbolist, who finds in the practice of his calling an ecstasy identical to that of contemplation and prayer.

Symbolist poetry drew a great effect from musical (tonal and rhythmic) elements as well as from color. One of the characteristics of the symbolist period was the fusion of music, painting, and literature. To reintroduce music into poetry, to realize through words what notes accomplished in music using suggestion and evocation, creating an atmosphere; that is what the symbolist idealized.

The primacy of the individual ego, of intimate impression, the flight of common emotions, the concentration on interior visions, constitute, as Bowra among others points out, a typical trait of symbolism, responsible for the attitude of isolation from society, of an intellectual aristocracy, and for a refusal of action. The symbolist ideal is the ivory tower, and its typical hero is Des Esseintes of *A Rebours* by Huysmans, who was looking for a retreat to which he could flee from the baseness of the world.

Summing up, with Hibbard,[15] we can characterize symbolism by the following elements:

a. A content related to the spiritual, the mystical, the subconscious.

b. A mystical concept of life.

c. A greater interest in the particular and the individual than in the general or universal.

d. A highly poetical tone.

e. An attempt to escape from reality and from contemporary society.

f. An intuitive rather than logical knowledge of things.

g. An emphasis on imagination and fantasy.

h. Nature is disdained for the mystical and the supernatural.

i. Art for art's sake.

j. A scant interest for plot and action in narration.

k. The characters are human beings at uncommon moments, so that interest reverts to the intimate spirit of the people.

l. It tries to select the elements that contribute to fantasy or those that present essence instead of reality.

m. An ornate, colorful, exotic, and poetical language in which words are chosen for their sonority, rhythm, and color, making artificial arrangements of parts or details to create sensory impressions, suggesting rather than describing and explaining.

Having appeared in a world dominated by positivism, mechanism, and naturalism, a world based on the realistic ideal of objectivity, symbolism constituted a reaction against the mechanical and scientific order in the name of the individual, his intrinsic value, and his subjective reality. It was a new revolt of the individual, a new romanticism. Its work was of the greatest importance, having reformed subsequent poetry, and perhaps all literature. In this respect, Edmund Wilson declares, "the literary history of our time is in a large part that of the development of symbolism and of its fusion or conflict with naturalism." [16] And Oto Maria Carpeaux: "Like all modern poetry, it has its start in symbolism." [17]

Symbolism in Brazil: chronology & characteristics. A movement of idealistic origin, symbolism in Brazil had to face opposition and hostility created by the realist and positivist *Zeitgeist* that had been dominant since 1870. The prestige of Parnassianism (which even conditioned the foundation of the Brazilian Academy of Letters (1896) left no margin for the recognition of the symbolist movement or for its evaluation, important as its repercussions and influence would be in relation to modernist literature. Thus, among us (in the words of Oto Maria Carpeaux), "symbolism, in spite of having produced a Cruz e Sousa and an Alphonsus de Guimaraens, was suffocated." [18] Elsewhere, the same critic states:

Only today does Brazilian symbolism receive its due consideration, neglected as it had been under the artificially prolonged regime of Parnassianism, which meant the retreat of poetry from the world of artificially prolonged colonialism. Modernism, an unconscious symbolism, as I see it, made possible the transformation of private symbolism into public poetry. [19]

In any case, symbolism in Brazil had strong opposition, and its adepts were pejoratively called cloud worshippers. [20]

It is necessary to mention here the advent of an identical movement in Portugal; in a completely Parnassian-realist climate, there appeared after 1890 the symbolist works of Eugênio de Castro, Guerra Junqueiro, António Nobre, Cesário Verde, and João Barreira, who had an influence on Brazilian symbolism, as Andrade Murici points out.

The entry of symbolism into Brazil, however, came directly from France, as Araripe Júnior states, through Medeiros e Albuquerque, who, from 1887 on, had received books of the French decadents. In 1891, the manifesto of the *Fôlha Popular* brought together the principal cultivators of the new esthetic ideas. Criticism during the period reacted in diverse ways to the new tendencies. Araripe Júnior tried to understand them with detachment; this was not the case with José Veríssimo; Adolfo Caminha, Sílvio Romero, and Nestor Vítor sensed the singularity and importance of Cruz e Sousa, but Alphonsus de Guimaraens and the rest had to wait many years for a judgment at a level that understood the significance of their work.

The Brazilian symbolist movement developed through waves of successive generations, which Andrade Murici has noted and classified.[21] Besides influencing the movement as it is properly defined, and the groups to which it gave origin, such as "shadowism" and "dandyism," symbolism inspired artists of later periods. It even impregnated certain of its Parnassian enemies such as Alberto Oliveira and Coelho Neto and the neoparnassians of greatest significance such as Augusto dos Anjos and Raul de Leôni. To symbolism is also owed the initial impulse of many poets of the transitional generation who finally came to full flower in modernism, men like Manuel Bandeira, Mário de Andrade, and Onestaldo do Pennafort, not to mention the spiritualist line of modernism, the *Festa* group, including Cecília Meireles, Tasso da Silveira, and others.

Around 1910, symbolism as well as Parnassianism had become stagnant, with a subsequent phase of transition and syncretism, during which certain representative figures still made an effort to write poetry according to the worn-out and superseded canons. There reigned an atmosphere of doubt and hesitation. A certain restlessness, however, made one sense that radical reforms were in the air.

FROM REALISM TO IMPRESSIONISM

Throughout the decade of the eighties, naturalism declined as a literary movement, and the decline was accompanied by the crisis of positivism and materialism. At the same time, there was growing a wave of idealistic reaction; humanism and religiosity were generated by a boredom with the crude picture of reality and with the belief that art and nature are the same. The period of naturalism came about, as Huysmans' character says, as if the state of the spirit needed to be synthesized.

A new style emerged from this collision of esthetic tendencies, one that was to become common to all of the arts and would predominate in all of Europe during the last decade of the nineteenth century. Painting was ahead of the other arts; it passed on its own characteristics and elements—light, color, air—and gave over recourse to pictorial forms of expression. Impressionism[22] was the style that dominated Western arts during the period in question. In painting and music there has been ample study, and impressionism has been recognized as the last great style with universal unity. In literature, however, the phenomenon has only recently been characterized as a stylistic period with a well-marked individuality. This has been done in spite of the difficulty of completely divorcing it from realism-naturalism at its start and from symbolism at its end.

Its genesis as a literary phenomenon occurs deep within realism-naturalism of which it is a product. Actually, impressionism is a form of realism, the result of its transformation by turn of the century esthetic and cultural variations and by the idealist reaction. It is the product of the fusion of symbolist and realist-naturalist elements. The reproduction of reality in an impersonal, objective, exact, and minute way was the realist norm; for the impressionist, reality persisted as a center of interest, but it sought to record the impression that reality provoked in the artist at the very moment when the impression is made. The most important element in impressionism is the instantaneous and the unique reaction of the observer. It is not the object itself, but rather the sensations and the emotions that it arouses at a given moment in the mind of the observer which are reproduced by him capriciously and vaguely. It is not a question of presenting the object as it is seen, but as it is seen and sensed at a given moment.

The opposite of realism, however, impressionism is a collaboration of subjectivity, and it was through this element that impressionism stood apart from realism as a peculiar style of art, blending finally with symbolism in a tendency towards the respiritualization of art. In impressionism, reality is seen through a temperament and noted by the sensations and impressions that it arouses at a single passing moment. By putting the record of external relationships in the place of that of internal relationships, that is, using the impressions aroused in the mind by contact with things, scenes, landscapes, or people, the impressionists introduced a new world into literature.[23]

Characteristics. If one wishes to synthesize the essence of the impressionist attitude in a philosophical formula, this must be, as suggested by Arnold Hauser, Heraclitus' idea that man does not dive twice into the same river of life because of its eternal forward movement. Phenomena never remain the same in this constant flux. Hence, as Hauser stresses, the domination of the moment over continuity and permanence, for reality is not a coherent and stable state, but a becoming, a process that grows and declines, a metamorphosis. Out of this theory comes the impressionist method of grasping the moment, the fragmentary, the unstable, the mobile, and the subjective. The notion of time was at the center of impressionist thought and art, as Hauser stresses, but it was a new conception of time which found expression in the philosophy of Bergson and the novel of Proust. It is the complete experience of reality that is modified, because through the flow of time and the sum of the diverse moments of our mutable existential reality we attain the integration of our spiritual life. The present is the result of the past, hence the necessity to remember, relive, and revive the lost past.

The impressionist artistic technique is "pointilism." It captures restless reality that uses impressions and affective knowledge of aspects of the real.

According to Addison Hibbard in his book *Writers of the Western World,* we can sum up the characteristics of impressionist literature in the following way:

1. It is a record of the impressions and emotions awakened in the soul of the artist by his senses from scenes, incidents, and characters. Emotions and states of soul are more important than plot and narrative, and the effect supplants the structure. Instead of the external causal relationship between individuals and events, what matters is the internal relationship evoked in the mind of the artist; instead of an

objective sequence of cause and effect, a different logic prevails, subjective, personal, vague, and inconsequential. Instead of things, the sensations of things are used.

2. There is emphasis on the revelation of the moment. What it attempts to capture, thanks to an instantaneous exposition, is the essence of the moment, of the incident, or landscape, interpreted by the artist's mind and state of soul. In this way, there is more of the spirit of the observer than of the exterior world.

3. There is an appreciation of color, of tonal effects, and of atmosphere. This trait reveals the influence of painting. Scenes and situations are broken up and put together again, with only the details that pertain to the desired effect standing out. On the other side, episodes are not presented as they might be known, but rather as they are seen or felt. It is the visual perception of the instant.

4. The reproduction of individual emotions, sentiments, and attitudes is of interest. The impressionist is a poet coping with states of the soul, momentaneous emotions, colors, and sounds. It is the interior life in its most refined shades that he wishes to portray.

5. The traditional structure and conventions of the narrative technique are violated. The plot is twisted, subordinated to the state of mind, which thus yields to a narrative technique of its own. Events are not what matter has especially created, but the pleasure of the sensations and emotions; unity, coherence, and suspense are conditioned to the atmosphere, to the sensations, to the colors and tonal qualities from which the total effect derives. Literary elements give way to the pictorial aspects. Masses break up into details. Hence there is an impression of vagueness, diffuseness, obscurity, lack of meaning, and lack of beginning and end.

6. Nature is interpreted; the landscape is invented rather than seen and described objectively.

7. The truth of the impressionist is his truth at a determined moment. Life being a constant change (the same landscape is different at different hours of the day) to the artist falls the task of capturing the states of mind created by contact with this flux, the people and episodes of its continuous slipping away.

8. Feelings, emotions, and sensations supplant intellectual aspects. Reason gives way to sensations.

Having these general qualities, impressionist art created the techniques of expression adequate to the reproduction of such states. The impressionist reproduction of reality consists of the attempt to capture the instantaneous and the unique. There is, in addition, a linguistic conception of impressionism that was studied quite well by Amado Alonso and Raimundo Lida.[24] If, as those students of the problem stress, there is no such thing as impressionist language,[25] there is, however, a language used by impressionist writers that expresses an impressionist content.

The following preferential traits stand out in its style, syntax, and figures, the conjunction of which, and not their isolated use, characterizes impressionism: (*a*) Impassivity and impersonality, even in the reproduction of subjective observations and aiming at the objective capture of sensory and instantaneous perceptions. (*b*) A schematic syntax, opposed to a structured and classical syntax, in which, as Alonso and Lida affirm, regular sentence structure, logical order, subordinate and coordinate conjunctive ties are abandoned. (*c*) An inverse sentence order (anacoluthon). (*d*) The suppression of the conjunction, in order to free and to enliven the sentence. (*e*) The use of the imperfect mood, to give the reader the impression that he is witnessing the facts described, with the action being, in a manner of speaking, "mobilized in the eyes of the reader" (Brunetière). (*f*) A wide use of metaphor and simile. (*g*) Expressive, colorful, and sonorous language. (*h*) Language of fantasy and imagination, freedom of expression, animation, richness of imagery. This combination of formal qualities of the tendency was known by the expression *écriture artiste*.

With the esthetic of the Goncourts (1851–1870), the transformation of realism-naturalism into impressionism came about; they were the founders and typical representatives of the new style. Exhibitions of impressionist painting took place between 1874 and 1886, even though the signs of renovation had begun earlier. Pissarro (1830–1903), Manet (1832–1883), Degas (1834–1917), Monet (1840–1926), Renoir (1841–1919), and Rodin (1840–1917) are some of the most famous impressionist painters; composers include Debussy (1862–1918), Ravel (1875–1937), and Respighi (1879–1936).

Originally a pictorial art, impressionism for the writer included the dominant technique in painting, "pointilism," and also "divisionism," accumulating isolated sensations, details, for the capture of a world of ephemeral appearances. The reader must grasp and later synthesize the accumulating patrial aspects. The impressionist "invents" landscapes which seem more authentic than reality.

At the end of the century, impressionism became the richest literary movement in prose fiction, and as such reached into the twentieth century. Its highest voices are: Henry James (1843–1916), Pierre Loti (1850–1923), Joseph Conrad (1857–1924), Anton Chekhov (1860–1904), Stephen Crane (1871–1900), Marcel Proust (1871–1922), Katherine Mansfield (1888–1923), and Thomas Wolfe (1900–1938). In the nineteenth century one can catch the impressionist technique in the style of Flaubert, Baudelaire, Verlaine, Rimbaud, and especially in the Goncourt brothers and Daudet. In Portugal, Fialho de Almeida (1875–1911) is the typical representative, particularly in his short stories.

Mixing the forces unchained by impressionism, symbolism, and the idealistic and anti-materialist reaction, the atmosphere had become by the end of the century impregnated with artistic currents and philosophical attitudes that gave the period a well-defined physiognomy. On one side was the estheticist movement, which approached a work of art as an end in itself:

not just a self-sufficient combination, whose spell could be broken by an external extra-esthetic proposal, not just the most beautiful present moment that life has to offer, for the pleasure of which man must be initially prepared, but also, by means of its autonomy, its lack of consideration of everything beyond its jurisdiction, a model for life, for the life of the dilettante.[26]

This became the ideal of the period. Estheticism implies, still following Hauser, an effort to make a work of art out of life, something useless, superfluous, extravagant, and dedicated to pure beauty, to passive contemplation, to "art for art's sake."

At the same time, the spirit is invaded by a feeling of distaste, tedium, rejection of the real world, of nature, of material things. There is yearning for an ideal and fictitious world, subjectivism and mysticism, a reaction against bourgeois society with its narrow morality. This complex of feelings was called "decadence," and the men who expressed it were "decadents." Decadence brought about the appearance of "bohemia," the incarnation of the anti-bourgeois reaction, and "exoticism," the search for new worlds to which one could escape.

There was the impression that one was living at the end of an age, in a state of crisis, degeneration, and fatigue. But unlike other ages of decadence, the men of the time took pride in the abyss in which they felt they were living. Baudelaire, Verlaine, Gautier, Nerval, Huysmans, Wilde, Rimbaud, and Barbey d'Aurevilly were the models and inspiration for this fashion which gave such a singular coloration to the artistic life of the end of the century.

Thus, the picture of literature during the century shows impressionism as the heir and continuation of realism; symbolism the prolongation of romanticism into which "decadentism" had penetrated; Parnassianism an expression of realism-naturalism in poetry. It is worth stressing that realism did not disappear. On the contrary, it was the movement that laid the basis for contemporary literature, for the modern literary spirit, as it penetrated the twentieth century with impressionism, with expressionism, and, in certain countries, with regionalism. It will often be difficult to separate or identify impressionist, expressionist, and symbolist forms in certain literary expressions of the period, since the elements mixed and mingled in them are so many.

In Brazil, the first great example of impressionism can be found in Raul Pompéia. A disciple of the Goncourts, an adept of the *écriture artiste* and poetical prose, after forming his spirit in the doctrine of naturalism he came under the influence of the symbolist esthetic and found full and satisfactory expression only within the canons of impressionism. The evolution of Machado de Assis reveals an independence of the postulates of positivist naturalism which leads him to the same impressionist climate that is characteristic of his final phase. Graça Aranha shows the same impressionist impregnation in *Canaã*. Aranha and other writers of the period could not escape the dualism —the ties on one side to realism (or even naturalism), on the other to the symbolist influence. Coelho Neto, Afrânio Peixoto, and many others who in certain aspects escape ordinary classifications, use an impressionist form. The case of Adelino Magalhães cannot be explained and interpreted in any other way.

Impressionism, therefore, is a literary concept of recent use and understanding that aids in the interpretation of various writers otherwise unclassified, and of a period that was considered marginal or secondary, but which offered a lasting contribution to modern Brazilian literature. Writers like Pompéia, Graça Aranha, and Adelino

Magalhães form the limits of an esthetic current that formerly lacked classification.

Since Brazil did not have the social conditions and economic transformations generated by industrialization until much later, naturalism did not find an environment propitious for its great flowering in the nineteenth century. The period did not offer the conditions necessary for its development. It was a frustrated movement, therefore, which only produced a few results, and those not of high quality. Furthermore, there was no preoccupation with applied and technical science, hence only biological theories found a place among Brazilian naturalists. Only after 1930, with a full climate of industrial transformation, did social circumstances propitious for naturalism arise. In that period, however, the ideology that was at the base of naturalism, or neo-naturalism, was nothing except scientific positivism, coming out of the social struggle that resulted from industrialization. The literary form that attempted to express it was socialist realism or naturalism.

In short, the disappearance of naturalism of the Zola school did not imply the end of realism, which unfolded and changed into impressionism, and later on had a rebirth in a form related to positivist naturalism or socialist realism. One must take note, furthermore, that realism found the Brazilian regionalist movement an ideal thematic situation in which to develop during the last decades of the nineteenth century.

At the beginning of the twentieth century, Brazilian literature plunged into a phase of transition and syncretism, in which elements of Parnassianism, symbolism, and impressionism were blended. This style of transition, to which one owes the uncharacteristic tone of the 1910–1920 phase, reveals traits that are sometimes predominantly Parnassian, sometimes symbolist, sometimes impressionist. But the importance of this phase is undeniable; it brought about the transformation that resulted in modernism. Other esthetic tendencies are included in the transition; expressionism, futurism, dadaism, and surrealism, all leading to the modernist revolution.

Without having had the neat limits of the Spanish modernist period, the Brazilian symbolist-impressionist decadent phase, from 1890 to 1910, revealed the same esthetic values: intimism, mysticism, estheticism, individualism, a liking for mystery, and interiorization. On the other hand, this tendency cannot be separated from the Parnassian current, which goes through the period with such a tight grip that its elements are mixed in the work of various authors. The Parnassian line resists and dominates, prolonging itself through a whole gallery of figures right up to the threshold of modernism.

In Brazil, Parnassianism supplanted other tendencies to such a degree that during this period the symbolist movement passed unperceived. Its importance was recognized only much later thanks then to the influence it had on certain aspects of modernism. The lack of appreciation or, at least the lack of attention, with which the period treated symbolism (recognized exceptionally only by a great critic, Araripe Júnior), is seen clearly in the fact that the Brazilian Academy of Letters did not receive at its foundation (1896) any of the representatives of symbolism, who were relegated to a secondary plane. It was from the heart of the great Parnassian generation, then at its apex, and in control of literary life, that the founders of the Academy were recruited.

Symbolism and Parnassianism, therefore, in poetry, were prolonged with minor changes in characteristics by neo-parnassian and neo-symbolist waves that prepared for the advent of modernism.

THE INCORPORATION OF THE NATIONAL

The period studied during this step, between the last decades of the nineteenth century and the middle of the twentieth, witnessed, among other things, a movement toward the integration of intellectual life, of culture, arts and letters into Brazilian reality. This movement corresponded to the attainment of mental maturity and the coming of age of Brazilians as an autonomous people. The independence of 1822 had not completely severed the links with the mother country. Portugal continued to exercise colonialist action through the social and economic aristocracy, more or less Lusophile, which dominated the monarchy; through the powerful Portuguese financial colony which dominated commerce, the banking system, and the press; and through intellectual influence, because Portuguese culture still exercised a strong attraction during the nineteenth century in spite of the new styles coming from France. The Regency (1830–1841), the first hint at a republican movement, was an attempt at autonomy that did not succeed, and it was only with the Republic (1889) that a definitive break between Portugal and Brazil came about. The Republic, with "its capacity to create a Brazil within Brazil," to use Gilberto Amado's fortunate expression,[27] made clear our awareness of being Brazilians, gave us the capacity to establish self-definition after a century of questions and investigations concerning what it was to be Brazilian and the characteristics of a nationality and a national literature.

The search for nationality in Brazilian literature was a theme that absorbed our men of letters, especially during the second half of the nineteenth century, when it became a constant of criticism, as Soares Amora has already pointed out.[28] This movement toward literary nationality attempted to find "symbols that could make a literary translation of our social life," as Araripe Júnior has so well defined it,[29] and it found in José de Alencar its interpreter of genius, as he made an effort to give body to its tendencies.

This was the search for elements that would differentiate the new country from the colonizer. It was the problem of being Brazilian, a problem new to literature; the problem of a new country, of a culture that came from the transplantation of a traditional culture to a new region. It was the search for an answer to the question of national self-definition, self-identification; that is, of the body of qualities that made the Brazilian different from other peoples and at the same time one with all other Brazilians.

Such questions were common in nineteenth-century man, and were naturally expressed in the voice of all conscious and responsible artists and thinkers. From Joaquim Nabuco to Sílvio Romero and Araripe Júnior, from José de Alencar to Raul Pompéia and Afonso Arinos, all felt the necessity of imprinting a national Brazilian stamp on the literature being produced in Brazil, whether by means of Indianism, ruralism, or regionalism. The symbol of that "instinct of nationality," so well characterized by Machado de Assis as being the literary ideal of the moment (1873), might be any one of these.

The result, as Araripe Júnior said, "was the most energetic movement of differentiation that we have had." Contemporaries did not always properly understand its aim. But reactionaries, nostalgic Portuguese and Brazilians economically and mentally chained to Portugal, were never deceived as to their duty to mobilize against the tendency and to defend their own cause and interests. From the start, therefore, they attacked Alencar, denying him completely; especially did the pens of imported scribes. Towards the end of the century, however, especially after the Republic, the nativist wave was already spreading in spite of the strength of the Lusophile bastions. Araripe Júnior comments: "It was indispensable for there to be some victim, so that a new world of Brazilian ideas could arise." The colonial spirit had not died, but "at each silent defeat, its camp would mask its operations and, in the end, it would always be the one to gather the spoils, and through its finances it was able to keep its conscience in a state of siege." Only with the change of regimes was there a definitive consolidation of gains over colonialism. Yet the latter's resistance was prolonged until the first years of the twentieth century through newspapers and publishers who were still looking to the Portuguese intelligentsia to exercise pressure on Brazilian intellectual life.[30]

In 1902 an unequalled event became the cry of intellectual freedom. When he published *Os Sertões* that year, Euclides da Cunha was able with one blow to pull us into Brazil, to force our eyes onto Brazilian reality, which some "cosmopolites" had tried to disguise in order to keep us prisoners of the European mirage. There were feelings of colonial inferiority to which as many Europeans as Brazilians were subject.

It is true that the event did not occur in a vacuum; it resulted rather from a long evolutionary process. There was not, perhaps, any other line of thought that was more coherent, more constant, and more ancient than the nationalist one, nor any that brought together a larger number of great figures of our intelligentsia—Gregório de Matos, the first voice of our New World baroque movement, who defended the people of the land against greedy exploiters and sham colonists; Father Vieira, the great Brazilian voice, who defended our rights before the owners of the world; Botelho de Oliveira, Rocha Pita, and Vicente do Salvador, the first to speak of our products, our deeds, and our habits; members of the academies, who already considered themselves "Brazilic," "forgotten" by the Portuguese; the conspirators in Minas Gerais, neoclassicists and romantics, the latter already expressing themselves in independent form and language, and thinking autonomously (Alencar). Thenceforth the wave could no longer be held back. It included the great architects of political independence and the Regency, the great journalists and orators of the period, the founders of Abolition and the Republic. The realist ideology of the last three decades of the nineteenth century, the period of our "renaissance," was the moving force for our coming of age with its extraordinary importance for our mental and historical life. This was followed by Euclides da Cunha and later the great modernist outpouring in the decade of 1920 that culminated in the Revolution of 1930.

If we follow this evolution with care, we will see a constant march in the direction of the integration of the country and its people among themselves, a deepening of national roots, a search into the reality of our civilization, a civilization differentiated in the tropics by the peculiar action of its own elements. One characteristic, however, of Brazilian nationalism, whether translated into the spiritual or physical order, is that it did not turn, unless it was during the so-called heroic phase of our life, "against" any country or people. On the contrary, it is essentially assimilating. All outside contributions were welcomed and transformed through acculturation and miscegenation into elements that dissolved into the whole. Our nationalism is affirmative, therefore, in that instead of opposing things, it attempts to turn towards itself, seeking to define itself, to deepen the awareness of its strengths and weaknesses, virtues and defects, in order to affirm itself positively instead of becoming immobile in a negative and reactionary attitude worthy of wornout peoples. What Brazilian nationalism aims to do is to affirm Brazil.

In synthesis, Brazilian cultural nationalism finds expression in various theses defended intermittently throughout our history: to think about Brazil, interpret it, to integrate the culture into the Brazilian reality, to emphasize the values of our civilization and the regional qualities of our culture, to underline our racial, social, and cultural characteristics, to defend the rights of a speech that became unique out of contact with rugged reality; these are some of the themes that are true constants of our intellectual history.

In what concerns literature, the central thought has been very well defined by Araripe Júnior: [31] to nationalize literature without demeaning the foreign contribution, classical and modern. Out of this fusion of elements there will arise a new culture, with its own characteristics, thanks to the incorporation of the native qualities of the people who bring to life an imported cultural heritage. In this part of the globe, the masses developed into a peculiar civilization, with emotions and sentiments, thoughts and aspirations generated in a specific historical and geographical situation. It could not help but be a different culture, even though it was enriched by the cultural heritage of the West.

This effort at differentiation existed in Brazil since the dawn of its civilization, and the literature that was produced here, beginning with that of Gregório de Matos, is different from the Portuguese. Regarding the problem of what Brazilian literature is and when it began, two theories characterize our literary history. In one of them, dominant during the colonial period of our civilization, the productions of Brazil and Portugal were not separated, but were taken as a bloc, as if there were a single "Portuguese literature," within which were small chapters or "cases" that took place in Brazil. Such a perspective accustomed people to look upon the Portuguese literary past as common to Portugal and Brazil, Luso-Brazilian "classics," having patrimony of a common culture, cast in the same language.

The other theory, the nationalizing and differentiating concept that existed in Brazil from the earliest times, arising with the first man who set foot here, was not unnoticed. The Portuguese thought that Brazilian literature of the colonial period was lacking in individuality. They could not see the substance of revolution that was at work in the minds of the men who had settled in the colony or had been born there, a revolution so important that from the very first moment it had transformed the mentality of the inhabitants, their sensibilities, motivations, interests, and reactions; ways of being and acting had been provoked by the new historical and geographical situation.

The romantics, especially Alencar, in what concerns the adoption of a doctrinary awareness of the problem, tried to locate the dike; and it could be said that this problem is a constant of romantic criticism and literary theory. Later Araripe Júnior made it one of his main preoccupations, establishing the investigation of the nativist trait as a criterion of Brazilian literary historiography. His companions in realist and naturalist criticism, Sílvio Romero and José Veríssimo, are noted for their appreciation of the nationalist criterion as applied to the gauging and evaluating of Brazilian literature. Araripe Júnior created a theory to explain the phenomenon of differentiation. It was what he termed, in an original way, the principle of *obnubilação*,[32] which attempted to apply to the study of the formation of Brazilian character and literature a law which he said was quite strong and active during the first two centuries. The colonists, as they withdrew from the coast and the small settlements, reverted to their primitive condition, and forgot their status as civilized men in order to adapt themselves to their milieu and habituate themselves to the struggle with the forest-dwellers. Such a process could not help but profoundly modify the man, creating a new man in every aspect. Could we, perhaps, consider him a simple continuation of the European? As Ortega y Gasset stated, a new man was being born from the very first instant in which a colonist set foot in the New World. He was an American, a Brazilian. His speech, sensibility, emotions, poetry, and music had to be, and were, different, differentiated from the beginning. They had nothing in common with what was being produced in Europe at the same moment. From the first century, the second at most, one spoke, felt, and sang in a different way in Brazil. From the seventeenth century on, the Portuguese and the Brazilian were no longer one literature. Our writers were few, but they were ours, different from the Portuguese. Portuguese writers were no longer ours. There were two distinct literatures.

This current of nationalist thought, which immediately recognized the autonomy of Brazilian literature, was a thread that was always alive and present, but it had been repressed by economic forces, by the propaganda of intellectual interests, by the anti-Brazilian prejudices of those who denied their homeland in the name of bogus civilized values (identifying civilization with Europe).

It was necessary for us to reach the twentieth century and the capacity of the Republic to "create a Brazil within Brazil" and make a definitive conquest, forcing the intellectual "return" of the exiles who, although living here, had existed outside. As a consequence, the conviction spread that Brazil could be "lived" intellectually and recreated artistically out of the raw material that it offered. It was done by artists of the stature of Vila Lôbos, Portinári, Pancetti, Monteiro Lobato, Jorge Amado, José Lins do Rêgo, Mário de Andrade, Manuel Bandeira, or, in the past, Gonçalves Dias, José de Alencar, Castro Alves, Machado de Assis, Cruz e Sousa, and Alberto de Oliveira.

Thus, "to nationalize literature without completely losing classical culture and the noble emulation of foreign monuments" (Araripe Júnior), is the ideal of nationalist literary thought. And by nationalizing, one understands the absorption and grasp of the peculiarities of the socio-historico-geographical situation, making them live as "symbols which [translate] our social life into a literary form" (Araripe Júnior).[33] This was what our major writers did in the past and what those in the present are doing.

Euclides da Cunha channeled this whole tradition in favor of upgrading the national in literature into Os Sertões. From the investigation of the origins, the ethnic factors, the characteristics and habits of social life, the dialectical modulations, the myths and legends in the popular imagination that came from the Indian and Negro cosmogonies and from the Christian and Iberian tradition, from the cosmic vision and aspirations of the man who lives here, his meditations as he faces life and the world, a whole body of data, facts, studies, essays, and theories was being accumulated, making up what was very properly called "Braziliana" or Brazilian studies. It would be difficult to point out in any other important culture such a vast and substantial sum of studies as that offered by our "Braziliana;" it occupies a relevant sector of our cultural history, on a level where literature, philosophy, history, sociology, anthropology, ethnography, geography, linguistics, economics, and so on interact among themselves, creating an intellectual genre that was unknown among other peoples. From Frei Vicente do Salvador to Varnhagen, to Nina Rodrigues, to Batista Caetano, to Euclides da Cunha, to Alberto Tôrres, to Oliveira Viana, to Artur Ramos, to Roquete-Pinto, to Gilberto Freyre there is a whole lineage of thought and investigation concerning the Brazilian land and people, in order to know and reveal the country and the people, in order to give Brazilians an awareness of their civilization and culture and consolidate its physiognomy.

This investigation, this interpretation, this rediscovery, this definition of Brazil, which is the function of "Braziliana," and, at the same time, the essence of our nationalism (to know Brazil in order to affirm it such as it is) reached its high point in the twentieth century, paralleling the mental coming of age which Brazil had reached.

With Os Sertões, all barriers to the full affirmation of Brazilian nativism were down, and art especially became nationalized as the result of the impregnation and incorporation of the environment in which it was produced, without any acceptance of Taine's determinist notion that art is a product of the milieu and the race.

Since then, literature has lent itself more than ever to the search for the national and its incorporation. The regionalist movement, which had had a growing importance ever since the end of the nineteenth century, supplied an interesting tool, placing at the disposition of fiction and poetry the material peculiar to the various Brazilian regions. Its importance cannot be underestimated, keeping in mind especially the fruitful utilization of realist techniques by regionalism.

Whatever the esthetic colorations might be by which it can be distinguished, Brazilian literature in the twentieth century is crossed by a central current—the preoccupation with Brazilianness, the search for it, its artistic representation. This feeling of Brazilianness, the strongest Brazilian cultural heritage, became the central theme of contemporary literature, especially after modernism. The whole modernist movement was characterized by this nationalist preoccupation, with the matter being explored in all of its various coordinates.

The other essential quality of Brazilian nativism is the respect for the cultural ties that link Brazilian culture to Western culture. No responsible writer has asked for a break in these ties, always advocating, on the contrary, the maintenance of the interchange, of the relationship with foreign sources of culture, because in no way can genuine national art thrive in an environment of ignorance and supposed virginity of the soul. What makes a great artist—a Machado de Assis, a José Lins do Rêgo—is the full use of local raw material according to that "instinct of nationality" which Machado defined, subjecting it to the transfiguring process in accordance with great masters and models. True nationalism results from the fertilization of the national soil by the universal spirit. No one is more English than Shakespeare, and no one more universal. The artist's secret is the realization of this in a superior way. His mind is a laboratory where the meeting is processed and out of which the work of art comes. An original literature is thus formed, one with peculiar qualities in theme, form, meaning, and imagery, which make it different from all others, even though related in its cultivation of the same traditional genres. It is, therefore, through intercommunication that literatures are able to mutually enrich themselves, as long as peculiar national characteristics are respected by the foreign influence, which is always stimulating when it is legitimate and when the spirit that receives it is genuine.

Such a doctrine and its corresponding practice have been the privilege of the generations that filled the ranks of Brazilian literature during the twentieth century to apply and develop. Within the scope of this evolution figure the names of Euclides da Cunha, Monteiro Lobato, Mário de Andrade, and José Lins do Rêgo, to mention only those no longer alive.

DISINTEGRATION & ADVENTURE

European antecedents. When Brazil reached the impasse that characterized the post-symbolist and post-Parnassian period of 1910 to 1920, a period of syncretism and transition which produced such important figures as Augusto dos Anjos, José Albano, Raul de Leôni, and Hermes Fontes, literature came under the sign of disintegration and adventure, making nonconformist spirits and those in the vanguard sound their revolutionary trumpets.

Tristão de Ataíde defined this moment of transition very well, recording with precision the continuity of the symbolist line through some figures who penetrated into modernism:

Ribeiro Couto began during the dawn of modernism, in the year before the São Paulo "Week." He came, like Raul de Leôni, to lead the generation that was emerging from the last rays of the symbolist sun that was dying on the horizon. It was the farewell of a moribund world. It was the farewell to the subtle, interior, nostalgic poetry that had represented on the poetical level the breakdown of a historical world. In the following year, the fanfare of the literary revolution was heard. The voices of a dying symbolism, Raul de Leôni, Filipe de Oliveira, Guilherme de Almeida, Álvaro Moreira, Marcelo Gama, Ribeiro Couto, Manuel Bandeira, Ronald de Carvalho, Hermes Fontes, and Olegário Mariano, seemed condemned to remain shut up in the urns of forgetfulness. They were voices of a world of silence, while a world of violent clamor is what seemed to be entering upon the scene, definitively, replacing forever the voices of silence. Poetry, however, whether in its infancy or not, is also silence, mystery, and purity, or it is not poetry. And those who had a real poetical message to bring to the new world, which the clangor of the modernists had announced in 1922, had easily been conquered by the wave of fashion. But they reappeared on the other side of the wave, swimming in the open sea. . . . [34]

Everywhere, in addition, the demolishing fury was sweeping Western literature at the same time. Idols were broken, canons were destroyed, models held as traditional were discredited. The spiritual and moral crisis, accompanied by the rumble from the old social and political order as it collapsed with World War I brought on the testimonies of a mankind profoundly shaken in its spiritual foundations and in its conception of life, world, and destiny. Art could not help but reflect this state of *désarroi*, of demolition, of inner perplexity and trembling.

The old confidence in reason and pure knowledge gave way to a restlessness and a tragic sense of life, an agonic concept of existence in which there is a coming together of the thought of a Nietzsche, an Unamuno, a Péguy, a Spengler,[35] witnesses of the break provoked at the end of the nineteenth century by the spiritualist reaction against scientificism and positivism. The period of peaceful confidence in the scientific and technical order had been harshly challenged and then destroyed by the reality of the war. The superiority of "civilization" in the optimistic and absolute meaning as conceived by nineteenth-century enlightenment and progressivism was also deceptive, and, in the words of Paul Valéry, it had been proven that civilizations too were mortal. Worlds were opened or reopened to the investigation of sciences that had not been foreseen by the exacting spirit of the nineteenth century—the world of the unconscious (Freud), of intuition and the facts of consciousness (Bergson), of religious unrest, of ethical and esthetic values.[36]

A new ideological and literary complex was developing when World War I accelerated its process of gestation. Out of it there grew restlessness and nihilism, a state of imbalance, which, according to Crémieux, found expression in the most diverse forms: "dadaism" (Tzara, 1916); "super-realism" or "supra-realism" (Breton, 1924); an antirealism, an aspiration for the absolute, a recourse to the unconscious, a rejection of intelligence, a logic in order to attain the authenticity of the being—these are the principal qualities attributed to it by Benjamin Crémieux;[37] literature of evasion, with journeys, adventures, and dreams; a search for the profound ego through psychological introspection which led to the dissociation of the personality; the cult of total sincerity through reconstitutions of the memory.

Outside of France, "futurism" was another of the vanguard movements that characterized the period of negation and rebellion and which had international repercussions. Created in Milan by Marinetti's Manifesto of 1909, it was the one which unleashed the most agitation and influence, defending the cult of danger, energy, movement, audacity, and velocity as sources of lyricism. To attain that, futurism judged it necessary to destroy traditional syntax, defending the use of the noun, alongside the infinitive verb only, doing away with the adjective and the adverb and replacing punctuation with mathematical and musical signs. It advocated the dehumanization of the work of art, the renovation of images and metaphors for poetry. Futurism came close to dadaism and surrealism and other vanguard tendencies of the period such as cubism and ultraism.[38] All of these "isms" that infected the Western literary scene from 1910 to 1930 were reactions against the drying up and the fatigue of the Western literary tradition. They were windows which opened on the future, a preoccupation that absorbed minds. They were attitudes of violent destruction and the negation of the past which they considered dead and useless; they were attempts at a return to primitive or childlike innocence. They were glorifications of the technical and mechanical world, the only source of dynamism. They were freedom from all traditional hindrances and forms.

In addition to Marinetti (1876–1944), one must name at the head of the renovating movements Tristan Tzara (1896–1964), Guillaume Apollinaire (1880–1918), André Breton (1896–1966), Louis Aragon (1897–   ), and Paul Eluard (1895–1953).

Another esthetic tendency of great relevance during this revolutionary phase was expressionism, which came as a continuation of impressionism (post-impressionism). Originating with a German school of painting, in which "the painter should attempt a direct expression of his emotions," the current spread out to other countries and other art forms, especially to music and literature. Its principle is expressive insurrection; it is not the artist who expresses, rather the elements express themselves. Cézanne (1839–1906), Gauguin (1848–1903), Van Gogh (1853–1890), Matisse (1869–1954), and Picasso (1881–   ) in painting, Schönberg (1874–1951) and Darius Milhaud (1892–   ) in music are figures who manifest themselves through expressionism. In literature, the expressionist esthetic found great realization, especially in Germany.

Expressionism consists of a total subjectivism. In contrast to impressionism, in which the origin of inspiration is external, provoking in the artist the impression that is immediately reproduced, expressionism places in relief the personal awareness that comes from any consideration of action, characters, or environment. Instead of reproducing the impressions aroused in his spirit by the exterior world (impressionism), the expressionist represents his own visions, feelings, emotions, and intuitions. Instead of imitating, he "expresses" what he has inside of himself. In expressionism, the motion is outward; the poem, the play, or the narrative contain the artist's own vision; impressionism paints what it sees in a given moment, on that state of mind, while the expressionist represents the state of mind itself, the associations and responses that reside in his spirit, which constitute it, which are his spirit. What interests him is not exterior reality, but the personal interpretation his spirit makes of that reality. The external world is disdained; preferred is the individual reaction to that world. His realization is "dictated" by his soul. Plot and characters, as externals, are not important to the narrative. As for characterization, what is of interest is not the exterior of the characters, but what happens in their spirit.

An extreme subjectivism, expressionism is a highly intellectualized form of art, tending towards the abstract, towards intellectualism, in which intelligibility is not always a characteristic, given the difficulty for the reader to penetrate the recondite world of the artist, which is not always accessible to verbal representation. One of the techniques most in vogue among expressionists is the stream of consciousness, an uninterrupted interior monologue, a type of narrative in which the spirit portrays itself in its mutations, in its flow, as is the case with James Joyce's *Ulysses*. Literary expressionism, therefore, is a form of psychological literature in which the subconscious depths of the soul are dissected and portrayed in great detail. The prose style is abstract, and symbolic, twisted, associative, and suggestive.[39]

Impressionism and expressionism often find themselves associated in the same writer or in the same work. James Joyce (1882–1941), Virginia Woolf (1882–1941), T. S. Eliot (1888–1965), and Eugene O'Neill (1888–1953) stand out as the most famous and influential expressionists. One could add the names of Karel Capek (1890–1938), Franz Kafka (1883–1924), and Nikolai Yevreinov (1879–   ).

From revolt to renovation. When the battle was over, the post-war process of liquidation done, there began the construction of a new order in which the results of the experimentalism of the previous period were capitalized upon. With a contemporary balance, the period gave itself unity with the participation of the various arts— painting, architecture, sculpture, engraving, music, and literature—in a web of reciprocal interrelations and influences. Certain general characteristics, certain constants, certain elements that were left over, certain new balances between tradition and change were the indications of a continuity between the old and the new. At the same time, they did not conceal the existence of a new form of art and literature, of a new style or period.

This body of traits is what can be defined as the "modern" in literature, or as modern literature.

In our time, furthermore, everything seeks the mark of the period of "modernity" so that it can be defined as a "modern" piece in opposition to "old" works. Like every new period, it is preoccupied more with the demolition and replacement of values and convictions of the previous period. It stays turned towards the future instead of becoming immobilized in conformity by contemplating the past and its acquisitions as if the world were fixed and definitively structured. Progress stands opposed to tradition, and is a constant renovator in arts, sciences, culture, and philosophy. To the imitation of models and the rule of authority, it prefers the rights of reason, free examination, investigation, and personal creation; mistrustful of science, in the name of the primacy of literary or humanistic knowledge, it substitutes the supremacy of intelligence for the scientific domination of nature, in order to broaden the benefits of technology in all fields of mechanical progress. In spite of an idea of superiority to previous periods, the modern is dominated by a feeling of being provisional and transitory, which makes it unstable and restless.

Particularizing this description of the "modern" attitude, especially with respect to the artistic and literary spirit, we will find a valuation of various categories that place it in antithesis to "old" periods. Instead of universality and the absolute, what it considers important are the particular, the local, the circumstantial, the personal, the subjective, the relative, details, and multiplicity; instead of permanence, it is change, diversity, and variety; to the absolute, it prefers the relative, to Truth, many truths; to absolute norms, relativism and the diversity of artistic experience and individual cases; to stability, movement; to nature, human nature (after the nineteenth century had placed man in nature, it returned to man himself); to description and the revelation of the exterior world, the feeling of subjective existence; avoiding the tradition of nobility, dignity, and decorum, it incorporated low and earthy subjects, everyday reality, the circumstantial and particular. Quite typical of this is the phrase of Proust's in which, during a conversation with H. Nicholson, the novelist demanded that he be more precise with his facts, that he particularize them.[40]

Having fixed in this way the concept of the modern, and shown the evolution of arts and letters up to this time, we can now verify whether in this evolution under the sign of modernity it is possible to point out certain distinctive characteristics or definitive acquisitions of its literature. Enriched by the romantic and realist heritages and by the contribution of symbolism, and revived by the experiments of the phase of the "ism"—dadaism, surrealism, futurism, and expressionism—Western literature reached a stage in which one can point out certain structural and ideological constants that give homogeneity to its physiognomic traits. These qualities of contemporary literature can be summed up, according to A. Hibbard,[41] in the following categories:

1. The author absents himself from the narrative. Unlike fiction writers of the eighteen hundreds, authors try to be impersonal, keep out of the work, although they are very much in the spirit of their characters.

2. Action and plot lose importance in favor of emotions, mental states, and the reactions of the characters.

3. The theme passes from universal matters to the particular, individual, and specific.

4. The basis of the selection of material is expanded to include all motives and matters.

5. Characterization varies, with growing interest in mental states, in the inner life of the ego, instead of in external actions. Also, the manner of presentation is different, the analysis and construction of characters being made by accumulation, with quick, significant, instantaneous moments, or with a presentation of the consciousness itself in operation (stream of consciousness). Instead of the author's making a portrait, the character lives, and this is how the reader comes to know and judge him.

6. Literature becomes more and more subjective, internalized, and abstract, constructed from mental and interior experiences, the life of the spirit.

7. Suggestion and association, and indirect expression are the means of showing experience.

Another important characteristic of contemporary literature is pointed out by Gaetan Picon: literature ceases to be provincial, and the diverse literatures tend towards a unity, each one revealing the necessity for entering into contact with the whole of what is being done all about and what was done in the past, making up a total and universal order as defined by T. S. Eliot.

When he describes "this new style of literature," Gaetan Picon, after outlining the conditions of the new literature, analyzes the novel, showing the metamorphosis through which the narrative genre passed. In spite of survivals, as the century passes the evolution is clear. First, the appearance of an artistic prose, the *écriture artiste*, and of a novel in which things have less importance than the manner of telling them; "compensating for the insufficiency of the object with an excess of form." Symbolism appeared to create a magical and symbolic conception of reality, which ceased to be "the material appearance and the concatenation strictly determined by social and physical phenomena," in order to construct a profound or transcendental world. Hence this other aspect of the contemporary novel, psychological investigation, the dissection of motives and characters, the investigations into the depths of the ego and the unconscious. The modern novel, Picon says finally,

is an investigation and an experiment in language, a certain order among words and not the illusory reflection of the real that is furnished us. The novelist knows now that he is working with words, not things. Of course, with those words, he must speak of things. . . . He does not get [his view of the world] either from listening to inner voices or from the contemplation of real things: he attains it by creating a language.[42]

As for the style of the new poetry, which has its main source in symbolism, certain defining traits can also be pointed out.

It too is made up of words, it is the poetical creation of language; it incorporates total reality into the poetical. Selden Rodman sums up the traits of modernity in poetry in this way:[43]

1. Images increasingly modeled on everyday language.

2. An absence of inversions, bombastic apostrophes, and conventional rhymes.

3. A sequence of images free of logic and cause and effect, based rather on association.

4. An emphasis on the habitual and not on the cosmic.

5. An interest in the unconscious.
6. An interest in the common man.
7. An interest in the social order, as opposed to heaven and nature.

THE MODERN REVOLUTION IN BRAZIL

Definition. "Modern" literature in Brazil is what is called modernism, a term that is becoming established in literary historiography to designate the stylistic period that began with "Modern Art Week" (1922) and comes down to the present. Modernism, therefore, is not only the movement restricted to that Week in 1922, but it takes in the whole contemporary period.[44]

The word "modernism" had already been used by José Veríssimo in his *História da Literatura Brasileira*, but the body of ideas thus characterized is that made up of the currents of positivism, transformism, evolutionism, and materialism of the realist and naturalist period. The expression "modernism" did not take at the time, and the terms realism and naturalism still designated that period, while "modernism" came to be used in reference to the period beginning with the movement of 1922.[45]

At the beginning, the movement was called "futurism" and its initiators futurists, with the words circulating in Brazil from 1915; in 1921, Oswald de Andrade, in a resonant article, was still calling Mário de Andrade "My futurist poet." [46] This word which was used at first, as can be seen in the articles of 1920 and 1921 by Menotti del Picchia and Oswald de Andrade, aroused the opposition of the followers of the movement, who did not want to confused with followers of Marinetti.[47] They reacted against the epithet, which was used subsequently, especially by their adversaries, with an intent to ridicule.[48] The designation of the Week of 1922 itself, including the word "modern," is already an indication that the other term was not acceptable. "Modern art" and "modern spirit" also appear in the titles of the lectures given by Graça Aranha in 1922 and 1924. But the irritation, especially that of Mário de Andrade, reached its height in 1925 with modernist collaboration on the newspaper *A Noite* of Rio de Janeiro. The title of the first section was to be "The Futurist Month," against which Mário de Andrade protested, forcing the newspaper to change it to "The Modernist Month That Was to Have Been Futurist." A new protest by Mário de Andrade led to the heading, "The Modernist Month," and the great figures of the movement collaborated in the supplement. In that way, the terms "modernism" and "modernist" became definitively established.

An important distinction must be made between the word "modernism" as it is understood in Brazil and Portugal and its use in literatures of the Spanish language. Among Portuguese-speaking peoples, "modernism" is the movement that came after World War I, born as a reaction against the state of Parnassian decay. In Spanish and Spanish-American literatures, however, modernism designates the movement that arose during the last two decades of the nineteenth century in the New World and spread to Spain, combining symbolist and Parnassian tendencies, individualists and decadents, realists and idealists, intimists and mystics, provincials and cosmopolites, and which dominated a great portion of those literatures with Rubén Darío at the fore. It corresponds to English pre-Raphaelism and French impressionism.[49]

Antecedents. Opposed to the state of conformity, stagnation, and apathy in certain sectors during the decade between 1910 and 1920, a desire for renovation can be noted then in certain avant-garde and non-conformist spirits. In a world reduced by modern and rapid means of communication, Brazil could not escape the contagion of universal restlessness.

The phase preceding modernism has also been somewhat underestimated. Actually, it was during this period that the seeds of the 1922 movement began to germinate. Modernism did not arise all at once and massively in 1922. This is a fact that has been pointed out by those who have watched the rise of the movement most closely, men like Tristão de Ataíde and Wilson Martins. There had been preparation for it during all of those years. The important phase of transition, that Tasso da Silveira so properly characterized as one of "syncretism," included all the seeds that would develop into modernism, and it is to precisely that spirit of syncretism that one owes the capacity to have generated the movement.[50] A syncretism of symbolist and Parnassian elements clearly went beyond the official representatives of literature exemplified by a Bilac and an Alberto de Oliveira; these men were responsible for the domination of Parnassianism even after the outbreak of modernism, and, with Coelho Neto, they set up the barrier against which the revolutionary vanguard of modernism would have to hurl itself.[51]

Syncretism did not have the strength to create a movement, but it did generate the environment that allowed the outbreak of modernism. Without the widespread spirit of dissatisfaction with established conventionalities, and without the opening of the Brazilian mentality to the wind of artistic newness that was sweeping the European atmosphere, modernism might not have come to term at the proper time. The phenomenon was very well described by Tasso da Silveira when he refers to the inability of the most authentic artistic vocations of the period to find any possible realization in a unifying esthetic movement, one that would "spin about itself, making its own synthesis, blending into the unity of its art the elements that had the deepest affinity with its own temperament." [52] It is precisely there that the syncretist or synthetic inclination begins, and it is often because of this that there is difficulty and hesitation in classifying certain figures such as Raul de Leôni (sometimes listed as Parnassian, sometimes as symbolist) because elements from both schools are mingled in their art.

And there is another fact: among those who will occupy outstanding positions in modernism, there are those who began by attempting that synthesis, and those who came out of a Parnassian heritage, like Mário de Andrade, or a symbolist legacy like Manuel Bandeira, or those who tried a new line based on symbolism that took on an intimist direction, like the "shadowism" of the early Ribeiro Couto. And there were even those like Ronald de Carvalho who from the symbolism of *Luz Gloriosa* (1914) would turn to the Parnassianism in *Poemas e Sonetos* (1919), a "retreat from symbolism to Parnassianism," as Tristão de Ataíde said in "Ano Zero," a characteristic of that moment of confusion and hesitation "in which surprises in content [are] rectified by parnassian form." One must keep in mind, therefore, the capital importance of the syncretist phase, without doubt the vehicle of many innovating tendencies that made up the pre-modernist climate.

But there are other facts that prepared the modernist revolution or which contributed to its advent. They were isolated facts, embodied in writers who in this or that way sowed the seeds of revolt or nonconformity, in opposition to the taboos and established postulates of the "past-ists" as the opponents of renovation came to be called.

Relying on the studies of Mário da Silva Brito, published in *An-*

hembi, Antônio Soares Amora offers the following succession of significant moments prior to Modern Art Week in 1922, and which already showed the deliberate path of renovation.

From 1912 to 1915, Oswald de Andrade, in São Paulo, tried, through the press and his own personal action, to arouse an awareness of the European modernist renovation; in 1913, Lasar Segall had his first exhibition of expressionist painting in São Paulo, still unable to influence public opinion; in 1914, the same thing happens with the first showing, also in São Paulo, of Anita Malfatti, influenced by German impressionism; in 1914, *O Estado de São Paulo* publishes the first article in Brazil on futurism by Prof. Ernesto Bertarelli, "As Lições do Futurismo;" in 1915, in Rio, Luís de Montalvor, a Portuguese, and Ronald de Carvalho plan the review *Orfeu,* a Luso-Brazilian magazine that is clearly modernist in spirit; in 1916, Alberto de Oliveira, in the Brazilian Academy of Letters, affirms the consciousness of the new tendencies of the spirit and in art, including futurism; in December 1917, recently returned from the United States, Anita Malfatti puts on her second show in São Paulo; now already frankly modernist, she is unjustly and severely criticized by Monteiro Lobato (*Paranóia ou Mistificação?*), who represents conservatism; at this point, only Oswald de Andrade and Mário de Andrade defend and support the renovating spirit of the young painter; still in 1917, several new poets begin to come to the fore: Mário de Andrade, *Há uma Gôta de Sangue em cada Poema*; Manuel Bandeira, *A Cinza das Horas*; Menotti del Picchia, *Moisés* and *Juca Mulato*; Guilherme de Almeida, *Nós*; Murilo Araújo, *Carrilhões*; still in 1917, the first manifestations of the influence of the Russian Revolution: a workers' strike in São Paulo; pronouncements of sympathy with the new ideology and the beginning of its propaganda; in 1918, in Rio, Andrade Murici in his critical essay *Alguns Poetas Novos,* calls the attention of the public to the renovation that was taking place in Brazilian poetry; in 1920, in São Paulo, the renovating meaning of the work begun by Brecheret "is discovered"; at the end of 1921, in the Livraria de Jacinto Silva, where a group of young writers and artists habitually gathers (Guilherme de Almeida, Oswald de Andrade, Di Cavalcanti), a literary meeting takes place to hear the reading of *Era uma Vez . . .* by Guilherme de Almeida. At this meeting the idea of "Modern Art Week" is raised.[53]

One must still consider, however, other facets of this premodernist evolution, by means of which esthetic restlessness was preparing the terrain for the movement. In an essay on the origins of the movement, Brito Broca records with great precision the transformation that was taking place:

The modernist rebellion—although assuming a radical aspect that separated it from what went before—was already being announced in 1910 by the work of certain writers who rose up against routine, the lack of awareness of Brazilian reality, everything that the modernist movement would tenaciously fight against.[54]

From the publication in 1909 of the *Recordações de Isaías Caminha* by Lima Barreto, one sign succeeded another, Brito Broca stresses, marking the appearance of new values with an obviously nonconformist spirit in letters. Gilberto Amado (1887), beginning in 1912 with the essays and chronicles collected later in the books *Chave de Salomão* (1914), *Grão de Areia* (1919), and *Aparências e Realidades* (1922), sketches out "frequently, lucid analyses of the Brazilian social phenomenon, in an Attic style, without dross, and not excluding certain shows of emotion." Antônio Tôrres (1885–1934) and Lima Barreto (1881–1922) struggled "against everything that showed artificiality, foreign imitation, frivolity, scribbling among us."

On the truly artistic level, "the spirit of investigation and the desire for new forms, new esthetic dimensions, could already be seen in the years just before Modern Art Week." This was how, in the field of fiction, Adelino Magalhães (1887) would antedate the modernists by many years with "the disarticulation of the classical forms of narration, the daring syntheses, the fragmentary style" of his *Casos e Impressões* (1916) and *Visões, Cenas e Perfis* (1918), with which he took his place as a legitimate forerunner.

As for poetry, the search was an anguished one; legitimate poets were undecided between Parnassian and symbolist forms. Another forerunner, Manuel Bandeira (1886) tried free verse, and with *A Cinza das Horas* (1917) and *Carnaval* (1919), in which he included the poem "Os Sapos" that the modernists later "fell in love with," as he himself said in *Itinerário de Pasárgada*, he creates a kind of esthetic crossroads between the past and the modern. Murilo Araújo brought out *Carrilhões* (1918) and *A Cidade de Ouro* (1921), and Ribeiro Couto (1898) led a reaction of symbolist inspiration, of intimist stamp, subtle, nostalgic, "shadowist," with rain, mist, and shadows, of which his *Jardim de Confidências* (1921) is evidence. As part of the group of those who were inspired initially in symbolism, and who played an important role in modernism, one must point out: Álvaro Moreira (1888–1964), Filipe de Oliveira (1891–1932), Ronald de Carvalho (1893–1935), and Rodrigo Otávio Filho (1892–).

Among the members of the old guard, there are those who also show signs of dissatisfaction: João Ribeiro (1860–1934) in 1917 attacked Olavo Bilac and Alberto de Oliveira, describing their art as "past its time." [55]

The national and regionalist line of modernism did not arise in such an abrupt fashion, but rather as the prolongation of a previous tendency that included, among others, Afonso Arinos (1868–1916), Simões Lopes Neto (1865–1916), Monteiro Lobato (1882–1948), and Gastão Cruls (1888–). "Brazilian reality" had already been discovered and to modernism fell the task of giving it value, using a revolutionary tone, responsible for its definitive integration.

The case of Monteiro Lobato is curious; he had never been a part of modernism, and was even hostile in the beginning to the founding figures in São Paulo (he protested against Anita Malfatti's show in 1917, classifying it as "paranoia or mystification"). Yet Lobato must be included among the precursors of the esthetic renovation by virtue of the feeling of nationalization in his work, by the regionalist stamp of the *Revista do Brasil*, which he edited; he gave value to the Brazilian of the backlands, the rustic, Jeca Tatu, and the novelty of this did not even escape Rui Barbosa, who, along with Coelho Neto and Alberto de Oliveira, was a symbol of the past in the mind of the followers of the modern revolution. It was in his famous speech of 1918 that Rui Barbosa brought to the fore the literary dimension that Lobato had introduced, thus concurring indirectly in the victory of ideas opposed to his.

But the problem of giving value to Brazilian reality was one of the touchstones of modernism, and one which would be reflected in the creation of a true cultural genre—that of "Brazilian studies" (historical, sociological, linguistic, ethnographic, economic, and political). It was not a creation of the 1922 movement alone. Notable figures in historical and social thought had laid its bases, authentic pioneers along lines that would be developed later. It is therefore necessary to name, in addition to Gilberto Amado already cited above, Alberto Tôrres (1865–1917), Oliveira Viana (1883–1951), as well as Nina Rodrigues (1862–1906), and Euclides da Cunha himself, whose *Os Sertões* (1902) is the modern starting point for these preoccupations. [56]

The necessity for a renovation of Brazilian literature did not escape many. According to the testimony of Tristão de Ataíde and of Rodrigo Otávio Filho, in 1913, from Europe, Graça Aranha was speaking of nothing else but a renovation of the Brazilian literary scene.[57]

To sum up, in the words of Tristão de Ataíde, "the esthetic restlessness was bubbling along in silence." All that remained to happen was the maturation of the artistic climate, which was taking place gradually, according to concomitant and successive causes (Tristão de Ataíde). The signs of change are found—he insists—in isolated manifestations ever since 1910.

In the phase preceding modernism, two currents faced each other: that of the archaics, the prisoners of the magic spell of the past, faithful to the consecrated canons; and that of the forerunners, who announced and prepared for change. The first, characterized according to Wilson Martins by a literature of evasion and flight,[58] whether through stylization, imagination (fantasy), or symbolization, made up the model of "literature 1900." It was a cult of form, verbalism, pompous phraseology, scribbling, a Parnassian heritage aggravated in certain aspects by symbolism, in which a Coelho Neto[59] sinned so much, idolizing a literature in which the things said have less value than the way in which they are said, in which an excess of form compensates for the thinness of the content, a superstition of style and florid skills masks the poverty of ideas and emotions, and a wordiness disguises artistic ineptness.

It is against this esthetic conception that the most serious artistic vocations come to rebel, consciously and unconsciously. Many are unable to escape the impasse of a choice of directions, the Parnassian or the symbolist, others unable to overcome their hesitation as they seek a conciliatory and syncretic solution.

The esthetic reaction of the reformers had been fermenting for a long time without coordination, even though in silence and in the recesses of individual aspirations it stirred up isolated spirits. It did not come about all at once, but was the product of a slow and surreptitious germination and evolution prior to 1922.

The Week of 1922 is, therefore, a coronation more than a starting point, a result (Wilson Martins), a point of convergence and agglutination of forces that had been struggling to manifest themselves. It was, in the words of Sérgio Buarque de Holanda,[60] "a contact, even though ephemeral. And it marked, as a matter of fact, the first meeting between 'modernism' and the public." Antônio Bento has pointed out that "the Brazilian public was almost completely ignorant of the movement that had been taking place in the field of plastic arts in Europe since the beginning of the century." [61]

As it approached the Week of 1922, the movement acquired coordination and a collective spirit. The Week was therefore only a signpost. Furthermore, interpreted in this way, modernism is not reduced, as Cassiano Ricardo has stressed very well, "to an event of only seven days, but [it is] something that was born previously and which, if it had been limited to a week, would not have come down to 1952." [62] The Week was only the final touch in the establishment of a movement that was more of a general state of mind and in which numerous young intellectuals and artists who had not been present at the Week and who came to play an important role in modernism participated out of "historical necessity" (Tristão de Ataíde).

Among the causes still to be considered are the foreign movements. Modernism too arose according to the law of repercussion that Tristão de Ataíde finds in the origins of all literary movements in our history. It is a repercussion of foreign currents.

Unlike the previous ones, however, foreign influence in this case did not have a character of importation or imitation so much as one of contamination of the "modern" spirit that was sweeping Europe. Also, the foreign stamp was not very strong, nor was the imported idea extensive, but was limited to some futurism, dadaism, and surrealism. The European vanguard influence had its origins most especially in the plastic arts, and the dynamic force of the movement comes from them. It has already been noted above that the first symptoms of renovation in Brazil were furnished by painting and sculpture, by Lasar Segall, Anita Malfatti, Di Cavalcanti, and Brecheret; even the idea and make-up of the Week originated here.

One must consider also the case of Portuguese literature and the relations between Brazilian and Portuguese modernism. In the twentieth century, the distance between Brazil and Portugal has been greater than that between Brazil and France. Portuguese influence, still alive at the end of the nineteenth century, had been replaced by the French and has tended to disappear gradually as the present century advances. Implicit in this was the recognition that the Portuguese capacity for supplying us with valid and fertile contributions was running out.

What has remained is the effect of the symbolists—Eugênio de Castro and António Nobre—not to mention the lasting influence of Eça de Queiroz, Antero de Quental, and Camilo Castelo Branco, as well as the older writers.

At the beginning of the century, however, what was left was a rancid classic influence in the literary language, still finding a vehicle in the mirage of the Portuguese past which had had so much effect during all of Brazilian history in spite of nativist reactions. The weight of that influence was quite harmful, and it contributed to the retardation of literature and language in the new country. The weakness of a Coelho Neto, a Rui Barbosa, a Euclides da Cunha, along with their high qualities, was this taste for inflated wordiness, the difficult, unusual, and archaic. It was a travesty that hindered the growth of Brazilian expression, prolonging the divorce between the spoken and written language.

The struggle against this vice, which had already been attacked along with the whole Portuguese heritage by the sarcasm of Antônio Tôrres, was one of the main features of the battle of modernism. It is possible that this fact brought on the disdain, lack of attention, and the progressive rejection of contemporary Portuguese culture, to the point where the two modernisms—the Portuguese and the Brazilian—had practically no contact, and, in addition, the Portuguese version was almost unknown in Brazil.

Actually, there is a concomittance or contemporaneity between the two movements, both influenced by the same foreign sources but having had independent developments. There was, however, during the phase of gestation that began in 1910, coexistence, with certain points in common, as in the conception of the Luso-Brazilian review *Orfeu* in Rio de Janeiro in 1915 by the Portuguese Luís de Montalvor and the Brazilian Ronald de Carvalho. It was the beginning of Portuguese modernism. For the most part, the two movements followed parallel paths, and only in more recent years has there been a greater receptivity in Brazil for the highest voice of Portuguese modernism, especially Fernando Pessoa, whose extraordinary lyrical work had awakened a singular resonance in the hearts of the new generations in Brazil.[63]

But the foreign contribution was counterbalanced from the beginning by the nationalist tendency, by the "conscious and systematic search for Brazilianness" (Wilson Martins), for a Brazilian reality, to the point of demanding a certain affinity of ideals for complete receptivity in the Brazilian milieu.[64]

Reference is still made to factors foreign to literature as responsible for modernism. Some of these would be related to World War I, to the industrialization of São Paulo, even to the Russian Revolution. Without denying the interrelation of facts in the history of human life, however, we can say that it is not the task of literary criticism to investigate the causes of esthetic transformations outside its own artistic realm. These causes are found in the exhaustion of forms, which prevents artists from finding conformity in them for the representation of their view of reality, a new conception of life and the world which takes care of them. Modernism, a new concept of esthetic style, occupying a new stylistic period, corresponds, thus, to a moment in Western esthetic history and, in our case, in Brazilian artistic consciousness. It is the result of an internal evolution in literary forms according to the laws of esthetics, which realize aspirations and sentiments, emotions and ideals, in tune with a different cosmovision.

Modern Art Week. The history of the Week (February 13, 15, and 17, 1922, were the dates of its programs in the Teatro Municipal in São Paulo) is not the object of the present study. There is room here only for some considerations of a general nature.

The Week was an explosion. With the literary spirit long prepared for a radical renovation, some vanguard spirits gathered together because of common anxieties and points of view and laid plans for the real battle in which they would assault the bastions of "past-ism." It was most of all a destructive blow against the old order. It originated in the suggestion made by the painter Di Cavalcanti to Paulo Prado that they organize a week of scandals in São Paulo just like "the series of scandals of Elegance Week in Deauville."

Still a question of controversy is whether the initiative for the movement came from São Paulo or Rio de Janeiro. The fact is that Rio de Janeiro, like São Paulo, had been following the line of renovation for some time, with groups in both cities developing new ideals, and various people came from Rio to participate in the Week in São Paulo.[65] The climate for the outbreak of the movement that had been created in Rio was perhaps more accentuated in the literary field, in São Paulo in the artistic field, Rio leaning more to an evolutionary transformation and São Paulo to revolution. The final impulse, however, came from São Paulo, more up to date, as Mário de Andrade pointed out, farther along the path of revolution, and it was there that the great battle was joined, "the great surgical operation necessary for the definitive emergence of Brazilian modernism." [66]

Circumstances of the moment, however, in the main the support that it found at once in high circles of São Paulo aristocracy, whose salons gave it prestige, was responsible for São Paulo's being the seat of the rebellion. Although the atmosphere was no different from that found in other regions, the development of the modern spirit in São Paulo was rapid and it took the lead, especially in the number of adherents.[67] Special mention should be made, concerning the formation of this climate, of the press campaign begun around 1920 by Oswald and Mário de Andrade and Menotti, "with a great uproar and scandal," as they spread the artistic changes that were taking place in Europe and called upon intellectuals for their realization in Brazil.

It was in São Paulo especially that the movement found a group awareness (the Week was the "great collective roar," Mário de Andrade said) that was more decisive and vigorous,[68] artistic in stamp. It did not have either a popular or politico-social sense, having been consolidated already at that time in a union between artists and intellectuals that would be one of the characteristics of the movement after Anita Malfatti's show and after Mário and Oswald de Andrade discovered Brecheret in 1920. Then Oswald de Andrade published his article "O meu Poeta Futurista," pointing out and extolling the *desvairismo* or "hallucinationism" of Mário de Andrade.

1922 was more than a date. It showed that the revolutionary situation had come to a high point of maturity, and it was not by casual chance that the esthetic and political revolutions coincided, the latter having begun with the uprising of the Eighteen in Copacabana Fort in the same year, showing that the conscience of the country had reached an acute stage of revolt against the old order in all of its sectors. It is not a question of seeking the precedence of one fact over the other, the intellectual and artistic, the political, the economic, but of recognizing that it was the structure of Brazilian civilization, it was the whole national organism that was mobilizing its forces to break the fetters of subjection to mental, political, and economic colonialism, firmly entering an era of maturity and self-possession.

On the intellectual level, there appeared in 1922, as Tristão de Ataíde has pointed out, certain works that accentuate the great divide: "*Luz Mediterrânea,* by Raul de Leôni, a farewell to the symbolist spirit; *Epigramas Irônicos e Sentimentos,* by Ronald de Carvalho, a transfer from symbolism to modernism; *Paulicéia Desvairada,* by Mário de Andrade, the bomb of modernism; *Pascal e a Inquietação Moderna,* by Jackson de Figueiredo, the dawn of the spiritualist renovation; *A Igreja, a Reforma e a Civilização,* by Leonel França, the revelation of the new Thomism as the basis or the movement for spiritualist restoration."

One must study here the controversial role of Graça Aranha in the movement. On his return to Brazil in October of 1921, as a retired ambassador, the author of *Canaã* came imbued with the renovating aspirations that he had already revealed to Tristão de Ataíde and Rodrigo Otávio Filho in 1913, as was pointed out above. He had finished *A Estética da Vida,* which he published in 1921, and he considered the book a kind of revolutionary manifesto. His impression, aggravated now by contacts he had made upon arrival, was that the country was completely bound up in intellectual and political apathy, and this impression he translated into a speech at a gathering of writers and artists on November 12, 1921. He joined decisively at that time with the young people who represented the new spirit.

With respect to his participation, modernist groups disagree. Mário de Andrade was the most contrary to this position, thinking that the revolution would have occurred with him or without him, and his hostile attitude is expressed in the letter he wrote Graça Aranha in 1926.[69] Manuel Bandeira affirms that Aranha was the one who was closest to the young people, sustaining that modernism still damaged his most important qualities. Others, like Renato Almeida, attribute to him the leadership of the movement, which would not have had the impact that it had obtained if it were not for the prestige and fascination of his glorious presence.

The reaction, especially on the part of the São Paulo group, was provoked most of all by Graça Aranha's intention of imposing unity and a doctrinaire coherence based on his theories, to which they would not submit, as they did not agree with his esthetic and philosophical postulates. It was what Sérgio Buarque de Holanda explained very well, observing that Graça Aranha "was assimilating the ideas of true modernism into his ideas." [70] But in spite of this attitude of Graça Aranha and the lack of unity in the movement, Holanda goes on to say,

one would fall into error . . . if he tried to reduce the considerable, truly decisive role which fell to him in the development of modernism. One can think that with him, with the leadership he was attempting to impose, and was unable, that the movement would have been condemned to perish. But it is necessary to state that without him, without his arresting presence, it would have been difficult for it to have gained a truly national scope as it did.

In short, without having been the guide or leader of the movement, even having aroused reactions, Graça Aranha did lend it his courage in breaking with the past, with his generation, in joining with the young people, lending them his name and prestige, calling public attention to them. In this sense, it is possible to recognize a certain intellectual heroism in him, as Renato Almeida did. He was an animator, to whose enthusiasm much is owed by the movement during its phase of demolition. [71]

What are the characteristics, objectives, and results of the Week?

The central idea of the Week is that of destroying, making scandals. The principal direction is critical. "We do not know how to define what we want, but we can discern what we do not want," was the phrase of Aníbal Machado that could have been their platform. Everything that made up the "past-ist" patrimony was rejected: oratorical emphasis, eloquence, Parnassian hieraticism, the cult of rich rhymes, perfect and conventional meters, classicizing and Lusifying language; it advocated a greater faithfulness to Brazilian reality.

Mário de Andrade, twenty years later, would outline what he thought the initial directions of the movement had been: 1. The break with academic subordinations; 2. The destruction of the conservative and conformist spirit; 3. The demolition of taboos and prejudices; 4. The permanent adherence to three fundamental principles: (a) the right to esthetic investigation; (b) the up-dating of Brazilian artistic intelligence; (c) the stabilization of a national creative consciousness. [72]

And there is no doubt but that the objectives envisioned were reached. The movement gushes out of the Week and nothing will hold it back. In 1924 it gains even greater repercussion and prestige with Graça Aranha's battle against the Brazilian Academy of Letters, a typical battle of the type in which the loser comes off victorious.

And if there was a certain grouping of participants around the Week, which might induce the observer to believe in a homogeneity and unity of doctrine—which there never was, for the movement lacked a "philosophical and psychological content" as Peregrino Júnior has pointed out, or as Prudente de Morais Neto said, "it was never a school, much less a body of doctrine"—after the Week was over, that apparent unity slowly broke up, mainly because of the figure of Graça Aranha. One could even establish, with Sérgio Buarque de Holanda, the number of the review *Klaxon* (January 1923) dedicated to Graça Aranha as the great divide after which the modernists separated. With the battle won, the adversary, if not destroyed, was at least rejected, ridiculed, reduced to silence, to the loss of positions of publicity and command of literary life, to public discredit, to solitude; the victors then fell out and divided up into groups which took divergent directions.

The esthetic revolution had been made, however, and the consequences would be deep and broad in the Brazilian artistic and literary mentality.

After the Week: groups and currents.   Modernism is not just the Week, however, and after the Week the relatively united front of the group and the unitarian character of the movement, which by then had been attained by various destructive objectives, were giving way and differences were arising. Around 1925, according to Prudente de Morais Neto, modernism began to divide up into groups and successive generations and divergent currents. Graça Aranha was the principal cause of the beginning of this break-up. Modernism was disappearing as a unified group.[73]

The movement continued, however, through the numerous groups into which it was subdivided, in the two cities where it had begun and from there into the whole country. In many of these places, where ideals of esthetic renovation had also been at work, groups had already arisen coincidentally with those of Rio de Janeiro and São Paulo; in others, the groups that appeared originated from the repercussion that the central movement had unleashed. The new generations enlisted in the movement in all regions of the country, each one naturally obeying the local imperatives and varients along with the general characteristics.

The principal groups and currents of the movement were the following, for which we take advantage of the studies by Tristão de Ataíde and Peregrino Júnior,[74] along with the observations of other critics:

1. *Dynamist:* Rio de Janeiro; around Graça Aranha, bringing together Ronald de Carvalho, Guilherme de Almeida, Teixeira Soares, Filipe de Oliveira, Renato Almeida, Álvaro Moreira, Vila Lôbos, Paulo da Silveira, Agripino Grieco, et al. Its theses: the cult of *movement* and *velocity*, material progress, technical greatness, called "dynamic objectivism" by Graça Aranha. The book *Velocidade*, by Renato Almeida, is the synthesis of their theories.

2. *Primitivist:* São Paulo; with Oswald de Andrade, Raul Bopp, Osvaldo Costa, Antônio de Alcântara Machado, the *Pau-Brasil* (brazilwood) Manifesto, and the review *Antropofagia*, "two inventions of genius by Oswald," as Cassiano Ricardo said. They sought renovation by seeking inspiration in the primitive motifs of the Brazilian land and people. "Anthropophagy is the cult of the instinctive esthetic of the new land," as Oswald de Andrade defined it.

3. *Nationalist:* São Paulo; with the *green and yellow* movement (1926), that of the *tapir* (1927), and that of the *bandeira* (1936), with Plínio Salgado, Cassiano Ricardo, Menotti del Picchia, Cândido Mota Filho, et al., defending the "nationalization" of literature, according to motives that are Brazilian, indigenous, folkloric, native, and American, as opposed to the inspiration of European themes. These currents aspired to create a Brazilian epic, begun with *Pau-Brasil* (1925) by Oswald de Andrade, and followed by *Raça* (1925) by Guilherme de Almeida, *Vamos Caçar Papagaios* and *Martin Cererê* (1927–1928) by Cassiano Ricardo, *República dos Estados Unidos do Brasil* (1928) by Menotti del Picchia, and *Cobra Norato* (1931) by Raul Bopp.

4. *Spiritualist:* Rio de Janeiro; around the review *Festa*, with Tasso da Silveira, Andrade Murici, Murilo Araújo, Barreto Filho, Adelino Magalhães, Brasílio Itiberê, and, later on, Francisco Karam, Cecília Meireles, Murilo Mendes, the heirs of symbolist spiritualism, linked to the critic Nestor Vítor, very sympathetic to the group and its ideas; also called "dynamic traditionalism" by Carlos Chiacchio of Bahia in

opposition to the "dynamic objectivism" of Graça Aranha. They defended tradition and mystery, blending past and future.

5. *Desvairista* ("Hallucinationist"): This is the line inaugurated and inspired by Mário de Andrade, which is linked to many intellectuals all over the country. It fights for the freedom of esthetic investigation, for the renovation of poetry, for the creation of a national language.

Along with these currents, one should mention: that of *intimist and estheticist sentimentalism*, with Ribeiro Couto, Guilherme de Almeida, and the Minas Gerais group; the group of *independents*, such as Manuel Bandeira, Tristão de Ataíde, Jackson de Figueiredo, Sérgio Milliet, Rubem Borba de Morais, Sérgio Buarque de Holanda, and Prudente de Morais Neto (with the review *Estética*), Rodrigo Melo Franco de Andrade (with the *Revista do Brasil*). One must also remember the São Paulo reviews *Terra Roxa e Outras Terras* and *Klaxon*, which followed this independent path.

It was the renovation practiced by the most diverse directives and following directions that were at times discordant. The tendencies described almost never appeared in a pure form, however; on the contrary, in most cases, they were mixed in the same person, even in the case of an independent. Elsewhere, the primitive and nationalist tendencies came together under different aspects, both being a reaction against the primacy of Western civilization and its religious concept, and against Mário de Andrade's urban tendency in the name of Brazilianness, an attitude that Oswald de Andrade symbolized in Bishop Saldanha's being swallowed by the Indians.

Along with these, sometimes inspired in them, were simultaneous or subsequent movements in the states. In Minas Gerais, there was the *Verde* group in Cataguases, with Rosário Fusco, Ascânio Lopes, Guilhermino César, Francisco Inácio Peixoto, Camilo Soares, Martins Mendes, and Humberto Mauro; in Belo Horizonte that of *Revista*, with Carlos Drummond de Andrade, Emílio Moura, João Alphonsus, Ciro dos Anjos, Abgar Renault, Pedro Nava, Aníbal Machado, Martins de Almeida, João Dornas Filho, Mário Matos, Enrique de Resende, et al. In Bahia, Godofredo Filho, back from Rio in 1926, in the pages of the press introduces the poetical fashion plates, and at once, drawn by the exuberant personality of the critic Carlos Chiacchio, other young people like Eugênio Gomes, Carvalho Filho, Pinto de Aguiar, Hélio Simões, Ramaiana de Chevalier, Pereira Reis Júnior, and Queirós Júnior came together to create the review *Arco e Flecha* along the lines of the "dynamic traditionalism" of *Festa*. Another group was made up of Jorge Amado, Sosígenes Costa, Pinheiro Viegas, Edson Carneiro, Alves Ribeiro, and Clóvis Amorim, and it followed an independent line. In Ceará, modernism arose with the review *Maracajá* in 1929, and in Pará with the Flaminaçu group and Abguar Bastos. In Rio Grande do Sul, the *Madrugada* group, with Augusto Meyer, Teodomiro Tostes, Vargas Neto, Miranda Neto, Paulo Gouveia, and Moisés Velinho.

A point of fundamental importance in the consideration of modernism is that of its relationship to regionalism. In spite of those who affirm that modernism has been "the enemy of all types of traditionalism and all forms of regionalism," [75] the tendency during the period to blend and conciliate modernism and regionalism is obvious.

Regionalism, it is quite true, came earlier, as has been pointed out above. It was joined to a traditional current in Brazilian culture, that of the worth of the land and the people, and nativism, which after having been worked on by the romantics and the realists took on forms that were more artistically finished with Afonso Arinos, Monteiro Lobato, Valdomiro Silveira, and others in fiction. Modernism, from early times, showed itself ready to consolidate this tradition. Its preoccupation was with Brazilian things, with national, folkloric, historical, and regional motives and themes, and with the Brazilian language.

The intensification of the regionalist movement, however, came to give an even deeper character to the tendency, broadening its dimensions and reach. In two areas of especially strong regionalist tradition, this conciliation took on a greater drive and a clearer sense of modern esthetic evaluation of the regional element: the Northeast and Rio Grande do Sul.

In the Northeast, after the arrival in 1923 of Gilberto Freyre from five years of study abroad, his inspiration and direction brought about an intensive regionalist movement with the foundation of the Regionalist Center of the Northeast in 1924, and the meeting of the First Regionalist Congress of Recife in 1926.[76] The ideas spread by this movement had repercussion in the poetry of Jorge de Lima and Ascenço Ferreira, in the novels of José Lins do Rêgo and José Américo de Almeida, in the painting of Cícero Dias, M. Bandeira, and Luís Jardim, and in several other manifestations.

The position of Gilberto Freyre is therefore of the greatest importance, not only in what concerns this aspect, but also in relation to the whole movement of modern cultural renovation. By contributing to the change in molds and methodology in historical and social studies by broadening the perspective facing the past, by giving value to local or regional elements of culture, by spreading an attitude of sympathy for Brazilian values, for historical and popular matters, he exercised an effective leadership that went beyond the limits of "Brazilian studies," of which he is an unquestionable master, to literary and artistic areas, with a marked influence which makes him one of the principal figures of contemporary Brazilian culture.

In Rio Grande do Sul, where regionalism was "the only characteristic movement in literary production," as Augusto Meyer has said, the terrain was prepared for the task to be done by the generation of the moderns, Darci Azambuja, Vargas Neto, Ciro Martins, and Nogueira Leiria, in whom, still quoting Augusto Meyer, "one can see the point of convergence between modernism and the regionalistic tradition," "an awareness of motives and a certain convergence of aims." [77]

Therefore, the literary and artistic renovation found the necessary elements for its execution in regional inspiration, in local traditions, in motifs of the Brazilian land and its life, in the *genius loci*. It was a very special direction of modernism, and one of the more fortunate realizations, according to the ancient esthetic slogan that in regional diversities one can find the eternal foci of the rehumanization and renovation of art.

Modernist groups generally tried to present their ideas and divulge the production of the new art in vanguardist reviews. Of these, the main one are the following: *Klaxon* (São Paulo, 1922), *Estética* (Rio de Janeiro, 1924), *Terra Roxa e Outras Terras* (São Paulo, 1926), *Revista de Antropofagia* (São Paulo, 1928), *Papel e Tinta* (São Paulo), *Revista do Brasil* (Rio de Janeiro, 1925–1926), *Festa* (Rio de Janeiro, (1927–1929, 1934), *Movimento* (Rio de Janeiro, 1928–1930, later *Movimento Brasileiro*), *A Revista* (Belo Horizonte, 1925), *Verde* (Cataguases, 1928), *Elétrica* (Itanhandu, 1928–1929), *Novíssima* (São Paulo, 1926), *Arco e Flecha* (Bahia, 1928), *Maracajá* (Fortaleza, 1929), *Madrugada* (Pôrto Alegre, 1929), *RASM* (São Paulo, 1939), and others.

In spite of the absence of a marked philosophical preoccupation, which might even have given a certain unity of point of view, there were several texts in which the leaders or groups tried to defend their peculiarities of orientation. They are manifestos, program-articles, prefaces, even books of doctrine-poetry, all of which are real declarations of principle. One could make the following list of the principal item:[78]

The lectures of Graça Aranha: "A Emoção Estética na Arte Moderna" (1922), "O Espírito Moderno" (1924), now included in *Espírito Moderno*.

The "Prefácio Interessantíssimo" to the book *Pauicéia Desvairada* (1922) by Mário de Andrade.

The *Manifesto da Poesia Pau-Brasil* (1924) by Oswald de Andrade (reprinted in *Letras e Artes*, Lit. Supl. of *A Manhã*, Rio de Janeiro, Feb. 17, 1952).

The review *Estética* (1924), with program-articles by Prudente de Morais Neto and Sérgio Buarque de Holanda.

"A Revolta dos Anjos," an article by Ronald de Carvalho.

Natalika (1924) by Guilherme de Almeida.

"As Bases da Arte Moderna," a lecture by Ronald de Carvalho (1925).

A Escrava que não é Isaura (1925) by Mário de Andrade, the modernist *ars poetica*.

Manifesto Regionalista do Recife (1926) by Gilberto Freyre.

Manifesto Verde-Amarelo (São Paulo, 1927), signed by Plínio Salgado, Cassiano Ricardo, Cândido Mota Filho, and Menotti del Picchia.

Manifesto Antropofágio (São Paulo, 1928), signed by Oswald de Andrade, Antônio de Alcântara Machado, Raul Bopp, and Osvaldo Costa.

The *Verde* manifesto of Cataguases (1928).

"Ensaio sôbre Estética Moderna" or "Diálogo do Bárbaro com o Alexandrino" (1928), a lecture by Ronald de Carvalho (reprinted in *Estudos Brasileiros*, 2nd series, Rio de Janeiro: 1931).

Definição do Modernismo Brasileiro (1932) by Tasso da Silveira, containing articles from *Festa* (1927).

Modernistas e Ultramodernistas (1951) by Carlos Chiacchio, containing the theories of *Arco e Flecha* (1928).

Domingo dos Séculos by Rubens de Morais.

Chronology & characteristics of modernism. As has been stated above, contrary to what some critics think, modernism was not restricted to the Week of 1922, nor to the heroic phase between 1922 and

1928 or 1930. *Modernism,* in the growing consensus of the most authorized interpreters of contemporary literature, is the period that, inaugurated by the Week, has come down to our times, giving value to the modern spirit, the present, and the new to the detriment of the past.[79] The name is losing the strict character or meaning of its origins —a revolutionary meaning of the modern, transitory, present—and is assuming the tone of a definition of the whole stylistic period. It tends, therefore, to become stratified and conventionalized as a general term.

Thus, it is not proper to say that modernism has died. In 1942, in answer to a questionnaire by Osório Nunes in *Dom Casmurro,* Manuel Bandeira and Ribeiro Couto replied to the assertion by Menotti del Picchia in his speech to the Brazilian Academy of Letters that modernism had died, as they affirmed correctly that, first, "modernism has evolved," and second, that "it did not die, it became transformed." It continued on with differences from one generation to the next, from phase to phase.

Studying its evolution, one can clearly distinguish a succession of phases in modernism, to which differences in various generations in their attitude towards life and art corresponded. In spite of the diversity of the groups who had lived through the movement during these phases—regional or doctrinary divergencies—each group or phase, seen in perspective, offered a certain general unity.

For Tristão de Ataíde, the movement was divided into three phases: premodernism, modernism, and postmodernism,[80] with the Week of 1922 located at the beginning of the second phase which, in turn, extended to the neighborhood of 1930.

In accord with the conception adopted in this study, modernism is the whole of the modern movement in Brazilian letters. Before modernism, one must record the phase of the forerunners or precursors, or premodernism, studied in a previous subdivision (*Antecedents*). During this phase, which lasted from the beginning of the century, more precisely from 1910, to 1922, the date of the Week, the preparation of the movement was taking place.

Modernism, properly speaking, is made up of three phases, marked by three different and successive generations, those of 1922, 1930, and 1945: The first phase, from 1922 to 1930, which corresponds to the term modernism as used by Tristão de Ataíde, The second phase, from

1930 to 1945, which corresponds to the designation postmodernism. The third phase, from 1945 on, which corresponds to the label neo-modernism by the same critic.

It does not seem, however, that there is any discrepancy of such an order as to justify the prefixes *post* and *neo* before the word modernism, which would give one to understand radical changes. What stands out in an examination from the relative distance in which we find ourselves, is the temporal unity of the movement, in spite of the regional, group, or generational differences. It is the "modernist" character of the various Brazilian literary generations since 1922, as Wilson Martins has observed so well.[81]

Each generation that made up the movement contributed its marked vocation, its coloration, and it was natural that the various phases should offer a special esthetic physiognomy in conformity with the tendencies and preferences of the dominant generation.

Therefore, the first phase is one of a break, executed by the generation of 1922. It is a revolutionary generation, in art as well as in politics. Its objective is the demolition of a fictitious social and political order, a colonial one, an artificial art and literature produced by imitation of the foreign, unconnected with the national reality. It is a "modern" generation, which is rebelling against all kinds of "past-ism" in the name of interests of the present and aspirations for the future. It is a critical and anarchistic generation, a combative generation, whose weapons were the wisecrack, ridicule, scandal, agitation, and clowning, and it is not surprising that it awoke a reaction of insults, catcalls, jeers, and invective.

In this way, the first phase is heroic, adventurous, romantic, polemical, destructive, and chaotic. Its most fertile years were, as Manuel Bandeira says, from 1924 to 1930, "the years of greatest strength and courage." [82] It opened the way with its urge for esthetic investigation and creative liberty to the splendor of the movement in its second phase. It was a predominantly "poetical" phase, in which the principal formal and esthetic victories of the movement in the field of poetry were established. Its agents were those who had formulated the Week or had arisen out of the whirlwind it produced, and they are related in diverse groups during the Week and after it.

The second phase reaped the results of the preceding one, replacing the destructive nature with a constructive intent "for the recomposition of values and the configuration of the new esthetic order" (Cassiano Ricardo). With the battle over, the waters became calm, and the members of the new generation could gain the effects of the dismantling and apply the esthetic formulas obtained from the revolution to attempts at new syntheses. Poetry follows the task of purification of means and forms that had been earlier initiated, broadening its themes in the direction of philosophical and religious unrest with Vinícius de Morais, Jorge de Lima, Augusto Frederico Schmidt, Murilo Mendes, and Carlos Drummond de Andrade. At the same time prose was broadening its area of interest to include new preoccupations of a political, social, economic, human, and spiritual order. The wisecrack was followed by a graveness of spirit, a seriousness of soul, proposals and means. A serious generation, preoccupied with the destiny of man and with the sorrows of the world, for which it considered itself responsible, it gave the period exceptional activity.

It was mainly in prose, however, that its greatest effect lay, since 1928, with *A Bagaceira* by José Américo de Almeida and *Macunaíma* by Mário de Andrade. The "decade of the modernist novel" [83] began, a noisy beginning of a period of extraordinary splendor, in which a cluster of artists endowed with a powerful creative power stood out. On one side, the line of study and the essay, with Gilberto Freyre, Afonso Arinos de Melo Franco, Otávio de Faria, Almir de Andrade, and Euríalo Canabrava. On the other side, the group of the renaissance of the novel, working towards a regionalist and social neo-naturalism, the land placed ahead of everything else, with José Lins do Rêgo, Graciliano Ramos, Jorge Amado, Raquel de Queirós, and Amando Fontes, or along the line of psychological investigation, the interior world, overwhelming preoccupations, with Cornélio Pena, José Geraldo Vieira, Otávio de Faria, Lúcio Cardoso, Ciro dos Anjos, João Alphonsus, Eduardo Frieiro, and Érico Veríssimo.

The third phase, which began around 1945, witnesses a purification in form of greater and greater precision, an effort at disciplinary recuperation, emotional containment, severity of language in the field of poetry, thanks to the work of the generation of 1945. In fiction there is a certain stagnation of the novel, while there is an attempt to revitalize the short story by means or new experiments on the level of language, with psychological investigation, expressionist technique. The great event here is the revelation of João Guimarães Rosa.

The great contribution of the phase, however, is in the field of criticism, with the surpassing of the old impressionist methods and the debate over the new criticism of esthetic cast. This could be called the *esthetic* phase of modernism.

Certain reviews played an important role in this phase: *Clã* (Fortaleza), *Edifício* (Belo Horizonte), *Joaquim* (Curitiba), *Orfeu* (Rio de Janeiro), *Revista Branca* (Rio de Janeiro), *Sul* (Florianópolis), *Planalto* (São Paulo), among others.

One of the most important movements in Brazil, modernism, the exaltation of the modern psyche, did not limit itself to the literary and artistic sphere, but covered the whole complex of the culture, and if literature and the arts were radically renovated, the whole of Brazilian culture was affected by a profound transformation. As Graça Aranha said in his speech to the Academy, the modern spirit "should not limit itself to arts and letters, but it should have a total identification with the people and the country." Furthermore, by including all forms of life and cultural activity, it had a national scope. It was a movement of integration.[84]

This sense of totality of the movement and the period, this multifaceted structure, made the same spirit affect all sectors of Brazilian life, unleashing a vast transformation. It was in this way that, in addition to literature (short story, novel, poetry, theater, chronicle, essay, and criticism) and the arts (music, painting, sculpture, architecture, decoration, and printing), there were other entries in the cycle of reforms unleashed by modernism: education, with the new education movement of Fernando de Azevedo, Anísio Teixeira, and Lourenço Filho; historical and sociological studies, with Gilberto Freyre, Roquete-Pinto, and Sérgio Buarque de Holanda, following the interest in Brazilian studies; economic and political studies, thanks to which a new scientific and technical mentality came to apply itself to the reality of phenomena of government and public administration; urban studies, responsible for a new way of approaching the formation, reform, and beautification of Brazilian cities. Modernism was a whole concept of life which generated a new style of facing Brazilian reality, whether in the process of dominating it, or representing it artistically.[85] Brazilian civilization, in this contemporary phase, goes through a profound crisis in its structure, a crisis in the sense of spiritual restlessness, moral and intellectual, of cultural effervescence in search of solutions for the problems brought on by the stage that it had reached. This crisis is manifest in politics, in social life, and in the arts. Modernism was the new style that arose out of the national conscience to face and express the new Brazilian attitude in arts and letters, life and culture.

In the panoramic view of the modernist period, among the personalities that participated in it Mário de Andrade stands out as the central figure. Active in the forefront from the very beginning, endowed with uncommon qualities of intellectual leadership, with an extremely lucid and dynamic intelligence, with a strong will to action, a great passion for literary matters, and the mental courage indispensable to innovators, he grew in such a way until his death in 1945, that it would be difficult to find another man of letters in Brazilian literary history with the influence which he exercised—literary influence, not political or religious. In these events, and, afterwards, he influenced younger writers by means of an intense intellectual activity and production, not to mention the vast correspondence he maintained for a quarter of a century in all national fields, debating esthetic, literary, and technical problems. This influence is broad, its role is not limited to the poet, to the prose writer, to the animator, being relevant in each of these aspects notwithstanding.

But it is as an indoctrinator, as an esthete, as a "writer," as a guide, that he became an uncontested master. Let one look at his *A Escrava que não é Isaura* (1925), the poetics of modernism.[86] If there were others who were greater as poets or novelists, no one surpassed him in importance as a total personality, so much one of his characteristics. "There has never been among us, however, an act of intellectual presence as great as that of Mário de Andrade," Paulo Mendes Campos asserts very well.[87] And by this act of presence he occupied his period intellectually, and he marked it in an indelible way. If the movement owes a significant part of its success to a great personality, it is undeniable, in the case of modernism, both in its destructive period and its heroic phases and in its more constructive period, that this guiding personality was that of Mário de Andrade. In the short story, in his epic of *Macunaíma*, in poetry, in literary criticism and theory, in language, in folkloric studies, not to mention the various other sectors where his action made itself felt, he left the seal of his creative and innovating capacity in definitive conquests of the Brazilian intelligence, conquests important as positive realizations, as lessons and examples of the genuine and correct attitude of the Brazilian spirit from then on in everything concerning literature, whether in the thematic or formal aspect, in inspiration or technique.

Balance & legacy. As a consequence of the dynamism released by modernism and its work of giving density and depth to the Brazilian theme, as well as all the efforts towards the technical perfection of the literary art that it brought about, literature achieved a position that showed the degree of maturity and conscious integration of the Brazilian mind and soul.

Modernism brought about a complete change in the literary mentality and climate. An examination of the present state of literature reveals the definitive achievements in a large part due to its generative or transforming drive.

1. The modernization of Brazil. Modernism bridged the time gap between Brazil and the rest of the world that had been responsible for Brazil's mental retardation and for the remoteness of the Brazilian spirit, which had always been placed in a position back in time in relation to the march of intellectual events in the world.

2. Freedom from mental colonialism. There is in Brazil today a healthy autonomy of the spirit, which does not mean an absolute isolation from universal culture, but a capacity to think for one's self, to reflect on problems without being servile in the light of Brazilian interests. Brazilian intelligence came of age, without denying foreign intellectual nutrition, which is normal. There is a proper way of reacting, of thinking, of formulating problems and solutions, without subservience to foreign models and recipes.

3. Nationalism. Without adopting "anti" nationalism in the Jacobin sense, the present-day Brazilian conscience is focused on Brazil, its problems, its reality, the Brazilian man. Peregrino Júnior asserts correctly:

. . . the modernist movement brought about the orientation of our art and our literature in a clearly nationalist sense, with a human and social base, the roots of which are deep in the sources of the people, in the heart of nationality, in the purest traditions of our land and our people.[88]

Present-day Brazilian literature and art are essentially national in their make-up, in motives, themes, and atmosphere. It is the result of more than a century of nativist effort on the part of Brazilian intellectuals.

Having arisen under the sign of the national, modernism took this direction and produced a true rediscovery of Brazil, creating an awareness of Brazilian reality, freeing the country from the colonial mentality and fascination with Europe. Formerly, the Brazilian intellectual had lived with his eyes turned towards Europe, an exile in his own country, as it were. The exiles returned, proving that they could experience the land and give it artistic representation by means of its special material in speech and not that of an artificial language following Portuguese models. Brazilian intelligence became integrated, matured, took possession of itself and its country, rooting itself in the land, coming to have "active participation in national life," thanks to a total identification with the social, political, and economic problems of Brazil (Peregrino Júnior).

4. This discovery of the Brazilian land and environment, this movement of "national introspection" (Peregrino Júnior), brought, as the same critic stresses, a revitalization of regionalism, traditionalism, and folklore. Indian and Negro traditions, regional legends, popular language with Indian and Negro contributions, came to have unchallenged freedom in literature, in both poetry and fiction.

There was also a great investigation into Brazil and the Brazilian man, his past, his formation, his way of life, not only in fiction, but also in historical, social, ethnographic, and linguistic studies. Brazilian music and plastic arts were given value for example in the recognition of Aleijadinho and colonial architecture and the use of the large quantity of folkloric material in the great musical art of Vila Lôbos, Camargo Guarnieri, Francisco Mignone, and others, as well as popular and historical motives in the painting of Portinári, Pancetti, and Guignard. The present-day artistic movement in Brazil is one which most elevates the name of the country in the eyes of the world.

In all sectors of intellectual life and culture, the concept of Brazilianness is the touchstone of creativity. And the artist keeps alive a sense of presence of the Brazilian milieu, not creating, as formerly, an art that is unconnected to the reality of the environment, a Europeanizing art. It is a peaceful demand that artistic material should come from the Brazilian milieu.

From modernist inspiration, and the valuation of the Brazilian past, out of which the movement rose, one faces folkloric, historical, and social studies with a scientific spirit, which is due to a complete modification of the Brazilian mentality in relation to Brazilian problems and the store of cultural material. Consequently, the Service of National Historical and Artistic Patrimony in the Ministry of Education and Culture was created (1936), a typically modernist initiative, with the object of defending and safeguarding our historical and artistic patrimony in conformity with the ideal of synthesis between renovation and tradition. Equally eloquent indications of this tendency are the collections of "Brazilian studies," put out with great success by various publishing houses: Brasiliana, Documentos Brasileiros, Biblioteca Histórica Brasileira, for example.

5. Intellectual decentralization, with growing value given to the provinces (Peregrino Júnior). This is a consequence of the rediscovery of the land and regionalism. Brazilian literature, which was always being revitalized by contact with peripheral movements of regional inspiration, lived under the spell of the mirage of the center, however, believing that intellectual life could not exist outside the compensating environment of the metropolis. The center in Lisbon was succeeded by that in Rio de Janeiro, the colonial court by the imperial and republican court, in both cases a form of imperialism of the center over the regions, on which it acted like a suction pump as it drew off the creative reserves and left the provinces consequently drained. There was a general belief that it was possible to lead an intellectual life only in the metropolis.

Modernism broke this prejudice, rich as it was in local independent movements and groups, with their own characteristics and which knew how to gain public recognition for their accomplishments. Since then, the various provinces are continually consolidating their positions as regional centers, with their own intellectual life, capable of self-sufficiency, no longer seduced by the mirage of the metropolis. Great intellectuals live in their provinces, which they would not for an instant think of leaving, men like Gilberto Freyre, Luís Câmara Cascudo, Érico Veríssimo, and Eduardo Frieiro, not to mention many residents of São Paulo who have always been satisfied to live in their native state.

A decisive factor in the gradual growth, from this time on, of this decentralization can be found in the regional universities and faculties of philosophy, especially as they stress their capacity to polarize local intellectual life by progressive improvement in teaching attitudes and cultural creativity, especially, and of most interest here, in the teaching of literature at the university level.[89]

6. To an autonomous sense in Brazilian literature and to an awareness of Brazilianness, the products of modernism, one must add an understanding of its esthetic character and the autonomy of the work of art, a notion that dominates the third period of modernism, as Wilson Martins has stressed.[90] The esthetic preoccupation was constant among the champions of modernist reform, who joined it to a combative stance. The problems of art and literature, which with few exceptions had been erroneously located before, were reformulated— form, technique, the literary phenomena, the problems of poetics, form and lyrical structure, themes and structure in the novel, in all of its aspects modernism remade the awareness of literary problems. One can feel that the Brazilian writer of today dominates his trade by skill with advantage, with greater precision in the arrangement of material collected from the milieu in an obligatory way and increasingly subjected to the fundamental disciplines of the art that are indispensable to the fullness of accomplishment. Discipline will be the motto of good production, with especial thanks to the best type of literary teaching that comes from the faculties of letters.

7. Professionalism and dilettantism. Brazilian generations tend more and more to renounce the amateur and dilettante spirit in the exercise of literature, taking on professional methods and attitudes in the conception and production of literary works. There is an end to self-teaching, improvisation, lack of method, lack of discipline, scattering, imprecision, disdain for the rules of composition or structure, including material; to a falsely romantic attitude of believing only in a telluric, instinctive inspiration, in improvisation, paying no attention to the duties of apprenticeship in the trade, an attitude that in most cases tried to cover up weaknesses, theorizing by means of the error itself as an attempt was made to change it into a general norm. This theory was typical of a milieu that had no organized intellectual life, no existence of its own, no normal agents of cultural production and distribution.

Responsible for this defect was the absence of a university tradition in Brazil, with the result that the exercise of literature was marginal, a parasite of other activities, with the intellectual living in dependence on professions that were foreign to his calling—law, medicine, bureaucracy, politics, and unspecialized teaching. In general, men of letters were professionals in those various activities and cultivated literature in moments of leisure; that is, when they were not climbers who found in literature a vehicle of access or a pass for their entry into politics or administration. Or then, as José Veríssimo has pointed out, literature was created by young men still in school, especially those who studied law and who would abandon literature as soon as they entered practice, which explains the adolescent character of much of our production, an immature literature, with no technical rigor, no specific and conscious terminology, characterized by a bohemian spirit and dilettantism.

It is the university experience that stamps a technical awareness on a literature. All of the great European literatures are linked together by the university tradition and the literary instruction received there. From this instruction, writers habitually emerge. From this instruction they live and draw their sustenance. It is so in France, Italy, Spain, and England. In France, alongside the university tradition, there is a strong current of the independence of literature in relation to teaching; writers make up a kind of clergy with its own professional life, explained by the solidarity of the economic resources of the literary life, thanks to the prestige of literature and to the publishing industry, which is a source of wealth in the country.

In the United States, the great recent novelty has been the penetration of university environments by writers, including some of the most advanced. The fusion of writers and professors of literature is therefore normal. And what deserves emphasis is that it is not only the scholar who dedicates himself to studies of literary history who lets himself be drawn to teaching. This was a current accusation against the influence of teaching on literary production: that professors dedicate themselves to a past, so they have created a mentality of the past, impermeable to an understanding of contemporary and living literature. For them, only literature of the remote past possesses any value. They have a rigid, inflexible, dead spirit, and they turn their backs on the present. Literary worship of the past, however, must not be confused with teaching.

Today, this attitude, if it has not disappeared completely, for there will always be spirits turned to stone, even outside of teaching, has been affected by the penetration of the teaching environment by a fresh breath of genuine literary spirit, one not identified with an incorrigible worship of the past. We find everywhere in the exercise of literary teaching the figures of poets, novelists, playwrights, and critics, some of whom are responsible for the renovation of the literary atmosphere of their time, exercising the teaching of literature, teaching the secrets of their craft to young people who want to become writers, trying to reveal to them the mysteries and techniques of poetry, the novel, or the theater, or transmitting their experience in literary phenomena as scholar or creator, or even spreading the experience of others, the efforts of their comrades past and present in their search of literary forms. Nothing could be more proper for a man of letters. And in the United States we find a team like Allen Tate, R. P. Blackmur, Kenneth Burke, Robert Penn Warren, Cleanth Brooks, and innumerable others rubbing elbows with historians and scholars in the university teaching of literature, some of whom are major exponents of the literature of their country that is most alive. We can see too in Spain a Dámaso Alonso, a Carlos Bousoño, a Rafael Lapesa, university masters who, along with others, have also built the literature of their period. The majority of outstanding literary critics at the present time have contributed to literary education. The most important work of creative criticism, published in the past few years was *Mimesis*, by Erich Auerbach, a university professor who produced it in a university environment.

In Brazil, the situation tends to change with the consolidation of faculties of philosophy. It is their place, like few others, to take possession of the literary leadership of the country, not only drawing to literary life those properly prepared and endowed with a technical and professional awareness, the innumerable cultivators of letters, but also, through secondary and upper-level teaching (with the teachers who have separated the secondary teaching of literature from that of Portuguese) working together toward critical and scholarly production along modern lines. From the faculties of philosophy could come a profound modification of the Brazilian literary scene, giving literary life and literature a sense and a content that until now they have not had, a result of the beneficent influence of education, an efficient and renovated teaching of literature in which there would not be the slightest conflict between criticism and historical scholarship, between the literary past and the present.

The time has now passed when literature was produced at the tables of cafés and bars.

In Brazil, within thirty years, nothing will be done of importance in the literary field which will not be linked to the university, to the faculties of letters, putting the country into step with the universal and illustrious tradition of the identification of the university with literature.

8. This professionalization of literature will bring as a consequence an invasion of the ancient formula which used to characterize Brazilian literature: the primacy of literary life over literature proper. It has already been observed that this phenomenon was general in our literary history, in which literature lived as the prisoner of the dilemma of "literary life" and "literary work." [91] Instead of making literature, one preferred to live "literarily" according to that phrase of Oscar Wilde's by which he explained that he had given only his talent to his work, while he had put "all of my genius into my life." Therefore, in Brazil, literary life is more important than literature, it supplants the works, because men of letters are less interested in constructing than in living as curious men, men of the spirit, spending capacity, energy, and talent in coteries, circles, arguments, intrigues, and literary politics.

There is, nevertheless, an inclination to go beyond that situation, with a progressive professionalization and the acquisition of a university consciousness and a scientific spirit for the treatment of the literary phenomenon.

9. The problem of language. One of the richest consequences of modernism has to do with the problem of language and Brazilian style as a legitimate instrument for the literature produced here. Until now, the powerful Portuguese norm had ruled, with writers like Rui Barbosa and Coelho Neto using a language completely out of touch with the object they wish to describe or present, a vice in Coelho Neto pointed out so many times by Veríssimo and other critics.[92]

This archaic and Lusifying esthetic in language was one of the elements of "past-ism" most violently attacked by the modernist barrage, with their having thought even of "a little grammar of Brazilian speech" (Mário de Andrade), which never came to fruition. The revolutionary impact of modernism in the field of language was, as Peregrino Júnior says, a useful consequences:

It freed Brazilian writers from an immemorial and voluntary subordination to the classic canons of Portugal, permitting them to adopt a language that was freer, looser, more natural, of regional and popular inspiration, which doubtless represented an enrichment and a liberation of our literary language, turning into reality what the romantics, with Alencar in the lead, had tried to do with a complete lack of success.[93]

As for the problem of language and the purification that came after modernism, Rubem Braga has shown how that work resulted from the freedom from ghosts populating the minds of our writers that had been created by a subordination to Portuguese canons and which were hampering their freedom of expression.[94] Modern writers took advantage of this cleansing operation by developing a language that, if it could not be called "Brazilian," at least was increasingly distinct and farther away from traditional Portuguese models.

The studies of language, within this same preoccupation of giving value to the Brazilian linguistic genius as a force capable of use in our expressive capacity, found an interpreter who placed himself, without being aware of it, in the same modernist line. He gave cover to the modernist revolution in language, and he made of his life an apostolate of combat in favor of an understanding of living Brazilian speech, of its incorporation into literature and its integrated study in the Brazilian cultural complex and in the social reality. Herbert Parentes Fortes prophesied the "gradual victory of the Brazilian sense of language," [95] a sense developed through our historical evolution, in tune with the milieu, climate, social reality, influences of other languages, and Indian and Negro contributions,[96] social, biological, geographical, and sentimental exigencies which gave rise to new forms of expression and to the development and differentiation of the existing ones. It was the character of the mother tongue, the Brazilian, that modernism recognized.

The verification of this fact drew Herbert Parentes Fortes, with his background as sociologist, psychologist, and humanist, to investigate the constants of our speech, many of which had been held as mistakes in the light of Portuguese tradition, in the intention of preparing scholars of the phenomenon of language for recognizing our peculiar linguistic reality and defending the legitimacy of the use that was made and is continuing to be made of it by our writers. It was the work of modernism that linguistics, in the light of scientific criteria and rigorous argumentation, applauded and justified, a work that will remain as a starting point, leaving out certain exaggerated polemics of the past, for linguistic studies of Brazilian orientation and for a philosophy of a national language, the resistance of the traditionalist and historicist school which still carries weight in our philological circles notwithstanding.

10. The revisionist spirit of the modern period also favored the formation of an environment for a reaffirmation of spiritual values, in counterposition to the rule of materialism and positivism, a heritage of the nineteenth century and even recently still in effect. As a consequence, prejudices were down and we witnessed a strong movement for the respiritualization of elites and masses, with the participation of intellectuals, professors, and writers, and even touching fiction and poetry. The uncontested leader of the movement Jackson de Figueiredo, with an act of initiative, created the Centro Dom Vital, which was to have a wide influence in the country, especially after his death in 1928 when direction of the movement passed on to Alceu Amoroso Lima (Tristão de Ataíde), who, like many others, had been converted to Catholicism by him.

This movement is described in detail in the chapter "A Reação Espiritualista" in *A Literatura no Brasil,* Vol. III. It is also studied by Renato Rocha in the collective volume *Modernismo: Estudos Críticos* (1954).

11. Poetry.[97] Leaving the order of general, historical, and esthetic considerations for the more specific orbit of poetics, in what concerns literary forms modernism was also quite profitable.

If we scan the history of Brazilian poetry, we will see that the romantics freed the language from classical and neoclassical stiffness, without succeeding, however, to refine it sufficiently, for they were bound by survivals from the past and Portuguese influences that were still quite close, even to the influence of a Portuguese romanticism that was so markedly neoclassical. Only the Parnassians were able to purify the vocabulary, reaching a poetical language with structural value, architectural sense, and musicality. The symbolists inherited from the Parnassians a taste for the perfect word, a sense of rhythm and the plasticity of verse, and they also broadened the musical resonance of the word, placing more value on its suggestibility and rhythmical capacity.

Modern poetry at first mixed and disdained genres; it put value on the free association of ideas, everyday themes, pedestrian, colloquial, and familiar expressions, vulgarity, and logical disorder. It was completely the domain of adventure and intuition, of poetry-experience. Afterwards, however, its contribution to the field was of the greatest importance, as Cassiano Ricardo stresses as he enumerates the steps of that renovation:

The victory of free verse, which should not be confused with polymetric verse; the incorporation of the subconscious, with the lesson of the surrealists; the liberation of rhythm, which had been a slave of metrics; the recreation of words, which would make up the new lyrical dialect; a free esthetic investigation, which today is the touchstone of the very new, are facts that might serve to characterize the importance of the modern movement in poetry.[98]

Within this order of principles, there is a whole gallery of great names of Brazilian poetry: Manuel Bandeira, Mário de Andrade, Cassiano Ricardo, Jorge de Lima, Oswald de Andrade, Raul Bopp, Carlos Drummond de Andrade, Ribeiro Couto, Guilherme de Almeida, Cecília Meireles, Menotti del Picchia, Ronald de Carvalho, Murilo Araújo, Murilo Mendes, Mário Quintana, Augusto Meyer, Augusto Frederico Schmidt, Tasso da Silveira, Abgar Renault, Vinícius de Morais, Dante Milano, Joaquim Cardoso, Emílio Moura, Henriqueta Lisboa, Américo Facó, Alphonsus de Guimaraens Filho, and Mário da Silva Brito from the generations of 1922 and 1930, who were followed by the so-called "generation of 1945," which includes João Cabral de Melo Neto, Lêdo Ivo, José Paulo Moreira da Fonseca, Geir Campos, Darci Damasceno, Péricles Eugênio da Silva Ramos, Domingos Carvalho da Silva, Afonso Félix de Sousa, Moacir Félix de Oliveira, Paulo Mendes Campos, Marcos Konder Reis, Bueno de Rivera, Mauro Mota, Ciro Pimentel, José Escobar Faria, Osvaldino Marques, Geraldo Vidigal, et al.[99]

With the generation of 1945, poetry deepened the formal purification, returning to certain disciplines that had been broken by the revolt of 1922, restoring the dignity and severity of language and themes, policing the emotions, with an effort at objectivism and intellectualism, and reestablishing certain fixed genres, such as the sonnet and the ode.[100] It is interesting to note that this greater preoccupation with form and the rigorous treatment of words is not restricted to those of the generation of 1945, but is also revealed among figures of the previous generation, like Drummond, Jorge de Lima, and Cassiano Ricardo, a general characteristic of the phase, therefore, even reaching certain formalist exaggerations that in the end attempted to counterbalance a humanistic tendency.

After 1950, showing influences of Mallarmé, Pound, Cummings, Joyce, Apollinaire, and Gomringer, there arose a poetical movement that was inspired by pictorial concretism, characterized by the reduction of expression to concrete signs, which sought a direct presentation of the object by an organization of the basic elements of language into graphic representations. It is an effort at a visual deepening of the word, of its isolation in relation to possible content (it draws away from "content" poetry); as an experiment in form, the movement is destined to produce beneficial results. Among the most typical practitioners and students of the tendency are: Haroldo de Campos, Décio Pignatari, Augusto de Campos, Ronaldo Azeredo, Vladimir Dias Pino, Ferreira Gular, Mário Faustino, Oliveira Bastos, Reinaldo Jardim, José Lino Grunewald, Pedro Xisto, Edgard Braga, et al.[101]

Recapitulating the evolution of modernist poetry, one can point out the following tendencies or currents up to the present time:

(a) Remnants and residues of the poetry previous to modernism, and which passed through it and came to be reflected even today in a certain universalist and spiritualist tendency: from symbolism and post-symbolism, with Tasso da Silveira, Onestaldo de Pennafort, Murilo Araújo, Cecília Meireles, and Augusto Frederico Schmidt, it comes to Emílio Moura, Vinícius de Morais (first phase), Henriqueta Lisboa, Alphonsus de Guimaraens Filho, and Mário Quintana, up to the last phase of Jorge de Lima.

(b) Tendencies developed in the bosom of modernism itself, such as surrealism and free verse.

(c) Nationalist and regionalist poetry of the phase from 1922 to 1930, with Cassiano Ricardo, Menotti del Picchia, Oswald de Andrade, and Raul Bopp.

(d) Humorous poetry, an expression of non-conformity and a tragic sense of the world, with Oswald de Andrade in the first aspect, and Carlos Drummond de Andrade in the second.

(e) Socializing, compromised, and dogmatic poetry, also with a tendency of its own, with Carlos Drummond de Andrade, Vinícius de Morais, Afonso Félix de Sousa, Osvaldino Marques, and João Cabral de Melo Neto.

(f) Estheticist, formalist poetry, out of time, a hermetic tendency, with Péricles Eugênio da Silva Ramos, Darci Damasceno, José Paulo Moreira da Fonseca, Lêdo Ivo, and Olímpio Monat da Fonseca.

One must add that this classification is not absolute, as many poets pass from one group to another, or begin by following one esthetic and then change their direction.

12. Fiction.[102] In fiction, Brazilian literature reached a stage which shows how much it had profited from the liberating reform of modernism. While the first phase of the movement was characterized by the domination of poetry, even then the revolutionary pioneering was able to open paths that were broadened in the second phase, from 1930 on. It is a period of splendor in prose fiction, in which the fruits of the previous experimentalism of a Mário de Andrade, an Oswald de Andrade, and an Antônio de Alcântara Machado are gathered, not to mention the line that came from impressionism, with an Adelino Magalhães and an Andrade Murici.

One can place the golden period of modernist fiction between 1930 and 1945. Afterwards it falls into sudden death, lacking the same creative vitality, with the main authors repeating, in the great majority, the same processes with which they managed to come to flower and achieve fame. Only in more recent years, after 1950, have there been certain signs of attempts at renovation.

It can be affirmed that Brazilian fiction has attained a well-defined physiognomy, which places it among the highest expressions of literature in the Americas.

Created in romanticism, consolidated in realism, in its technical and thematic aspects, in the portrayal of characters and environments, in story-telling and the construction of the narrative, in the selection and development of themes, in structural planning, in stylistic characterization, the differentiation is so clear at this moment of the evolutionary process following the modernist contribution, that one can speak of a "Brazilian" fiction with its own, unmistakable, and peculiar structure.

Owing much to models of the eighteen hundreds, especially those of the French, English, and Portuguese, its technical processes were still of the nineteenth century and very much under the effect of those influences. In the thematic area, however, the advance was direct, towards incorporation of Brazilian material, with a series of attempts using such elements as Indianism, ruralism, and backlandsism, until it reached the great synthesis of regionalism. Excluding the line of the psychological novel, it can be affirmed that all Brazilian fiction is basically regionalist or regional, in a broad sense, whether based on rural or country areas, deliberately manipulating local types, or on the fixation of urban scenes, of suburbs and small cities. What stands out in both directions is the frame, the environment, the land or the city, the two elements in frank hostility to man, devoured by the problems which the milieu has put before him. It was due to the techniques of realism that Brazilian fiction managed to succeed in this incorporation of the regional and give it a universal value and meaning.

Constituting a true heritage, however, one that began with romanticism and reached modernism, we have, on one side, regionalism, more or less strict, which uses the material furnished by the urban or rural area.

On the other side, there is a parallel evolution (with the two often mixed as one furnishes an environmental base on which the other can create its human situations), a psychological line, with a preoccupation with problems of behavior, dramas of the conscience, meditations on fate, searching into acts and motivations as it seeks a view of human personality and life. This form was powerfully influenced by symbolist and impressionist techniques.

The two thematic lines of Brazilian fiction—the regional and the psychological—developed through the esthetic styles from romanticism to modernism, receiving a special contribution from each movement. Thus, from Alencar and Manuel Antônio de Almeida, to Machado de Assis, to Aluísio Azevedo, to Raul Pompéia, to Afonso Arinos, to Coelho Neto, to Graça Aranha, to Afrânio Peixoto, to Xavier Marques, to Domingos Olímpio, to Simões Lopes Neto, to Lima Barreto, to Monteiro Lobato, to Adelino Magalhães, Brazilian fiction reaches modernism, gaining definitive subsidies along the way and giving mid-century writers, after the shake-up of modernist experimentalism, a powerful instrument for artistic realization with Brazilian molds that they would know how to use.

On reaching modernism, however, Brazilian fiction, originating in romanticism, had received realist, symbolist, and impressionist contributions, and was ready to absorb revolutionary experiences.

In that way, diverse currents developed within modernism, some a prolongation of previous tendencies, others the result of the establishment of new forms in universal fiction to which the modern spirit had given birth.

The outbreak of the modernist movement, which brought on an intensification of nationalist feeling, had intense repercussions in fiction, giving it a definitively Brazilian coloration, an ideal towards which it had been struggling ever since romanticism. All currents of modernist fiction share this Brazilian stamp, and even the psychological tendency in many aspects reflects preoccupations or impregnations of the Brazilian environment; there is the example of Machado de Assis himself, for whom human problems existed in a determined historical "situation," studied so well in this part of his work by Astrojildo Pereira.

Two great principal currents of modernist fiction stand out, with various subcurrents.

(*a*) The national and regional current. The nationalism of 1922 invaded documentary, regional, and social fiction that was founded on realist techniques. Actually, it attempts a kind of neorealism and, at times, neonaturalism.

Neorealism—the urban-social documentary of realist stamp—was especially preoccupied with the recording of simple reality through the observation of problems and customs of middle-class urban life. Prominent here are the names of Érico Veríssimo, Telmo Vergara, Amando Fontes, Galeão Coutinho, Dionélio Machado, Guilhermino César, Amadeu Amaral, Oswald de Andrade, Ribeiro Couto, Guilherme Figueiredo, Alcântara Machado, Orígenes Lessa, Amadeu de Queirós, Afonso Schmidt, Rosalina Coelho Lisboa, Diná Silveira de Queirós, Joel Silveira, Osvaldo Alves, Luís Martins, Dalcídio Jurandir, Atos Damasceno, Viana Moog, Luís Jardim, Rosário Fusco, and Lígia Fagundes Teles.

Next to this current and mingling with it at times, is neonaturalism, different from the naturalism of Zola and his followers, as instead of founding its image of reality on presuppositions of deterministic, mechanistic, and positivistic philosophy, it makes use of a political ideology as the substratum of its conception of reality, with the objective of doing violence to it and subverting it, using fiction as a weapon of propaganda and action. It belongs to the family of socialist realism or naturalism, an instrument of revolutionary action through the novel, which in this way does not have a literary individuality, but is a mere vehicle for political values and messages. Part of Jorge Amado's work belongs to this tendency.

Another aspect of neorealism, however, is that of the regionalist documentary novel, which furnished the most important and most original harvest of modernist fiction. Included in this category is the neoregionalist line, which includes the modern "cycles" of Brazilian fiction, many of which sink roots into the past and have the participation of some nonmodernist authors like Gustavo Barroso and Mário Sete: the cycles of drought, of the backlands, of banditry, of sugar cane, of cacao, of coffee, with Raquel de Queirós José Américo de Almeida, José Lins do Rêgo, Jorge Amado, Graciliano Ramos, Jorge de Lima, Clóvis Amorim, and Nestor Duarte. To these one can add the cycle of the southern rancher, with Darci Azambuja, Ciro Martins, Ivan Pedro Martins, et al.

It is necessary to mention also, another current of pure regionalism, without social implications, which includes Amadeu de Queirós, Guimarães, Rosa, and others.

(b) The subjectivist and introspective or psychological current. Showing an accentuated estheticist impregnation, the obvious heritage of symbolism and impressionism, this tendency develops in the direction of inner investigation, around problems of the soul, of destiny, of conscience, in which the human personality faces itself or is analyzed in its reactions to other men. In this group are Cornélio Pena, Lúcio Cardoso, Otávio de Faria, Jorge de Lima, José Geraldo Vieira, Lúcia Miguel-Pereira, Josué Montello, Andrade Murici, Barreto Filho, Rodrigo Melo Franco de Andrade, Fernando Sabino, Murilo Rubião, Waldomiro Autran Dourado, and, in one aspect of his work, Graciliano Ramos, who combines introspection and the interior monologue with social documentation and the analysis of human destiny, as is also the case with Adonias Filho.

Combining urban documentation with a relative introspection, that is, not rejecting an observation of the episodic and social side, with moderate subjectivism, there is the group in urban and subjective fiction, which should be placed apart: João Alphonsus, Ribeiro Couto,

Ciro dos Anjos, Marques Rebêlo, Osvaldo Alves, Luís Jardim, Rosário Fusco, Aníbal Machado, and some others included in the previous group.

In some cases, as in that of Cornélio Pena, Otávio de Faria, Lúcio Cardoso, and Gustavo Corção, a religious and metaphysical direction is added to the psychological delving, reaching beyond tangible reality in search of the supreme essences and values of spiritual life, with a tone of classical tragedy.

Another variant of this group places value on the products of dreams and fantasy, creating an "atmosphere" without any real density, but with a strong emotional content, using a metaphorical language. This is the case of Clarice Lispector.

The short story underwent radical transformations in modern fiction. To the naturalist and exterior experience of the line of Maupassant, and to the psychological esthetic, the moderns brought new dimensions, with a thematic enrichment from regionalism and its various types. The technical aspect, which until then had been hampered by traditional canons in its structure of beginning, middle, and end, with its narration conditioned to maintaining interest through manipulation of suspense and intrigue, was deeply affected by modernism. A continuous and objective telling of stories gave way to simple evocation, to snapshots, to episodes rich in suggestion, to intensely poetical slices of atmosphere. This renovation took place beginning with Adelino Magalhães, through Antônio de Alcântara Machado, Mário de Andrade, and João Alphonsus, to reach the short-story writers of the more recent period, people like Clarice Lispector, Waldomiro Autran Dourado, Lígia Fagundes Teles, Osman Lins, Samuel Rawet, Homero Homem, Carlos Castelo Branco, Dalton Trevisan, and numerous others.

In a general way, in the novel and the short story, there is a difference among the periods of modernism as concerns the problem of language. By a dominant preoccupation with the narrative, there was neglect during the first phase of formal and structural care, a neglect in which some of the most original creators of the period sinned. Quite the contrary, following the general tendency of current literature in all sectors, fiction writers of the new generation reacted against the lack of care that had characterized their predecessors in favor of workmanlike discipline, a respect for the rules of the trade, rigor of form, sureness and awareness in the manipulation of expression.

Having reached this stage of evolution, Brazilian fiction is ready to produce the great synthesis of the elements that had been furnished equally by regional themes and psychological investigation. It will go beyond local limits and become integrated, still Brazilian, however, in the broad picture of world fiction, giving an image of Brazilian man and reality that is universal in meaning and scope.

13. The chronicle[103] is a genre that in Brazil, especially in the present century, has assumed, along with the personality of a genre, a development and a status which make it a literary form of refined esthetic worth, a specific and autonomous genre, so much so that Tristão de Ataíde created the term "chroniclism" for its general designation.

In truth, if there is something in our literature that can be taken as a significant example of our literary and linguistic differentiation, it is the chronicle. It would be difficult to point out anything similar, even in Portuguese literature, to a chronicle by Rubem Braga. This author also presents another singularity: he is a great writer who will go down in literary history exclusively as a writer of chronicles. A unique fact in contemporary Brazilian literature, and a very significant one, is the position of the chronicle, its importance, the degree of perfection it has attained through a long evolution by means of which it has become specialized and has developed a specific literary form, including a style of its own and a very peculiar manner.

In the first place, it is necessary to emphasize the literary nature of the chronicle. The fact that it is published in newspapers does not imply any lack of worth for the genre. While journalism has its own objective, the dealing with facts, for the chronicle, facts only have value insofar as they can be used as a means or pretext from which the artist draws the maximum advantage for the virtuosities of his style, his spirit, his wit, his inventive faculties. The chronicle is essentially a form of art, the art of the word, to which is joined a strong element of lyricism. It is a highly personal genre, an individual and intimate reaction to the spectacle of life, things, and beings. The chronicler is a solitary person with an urge to communicate. And no one communicates better than he, through that living, gay, insinuating, and agile means which is the chronicle. Literature is an art, one whose means is the word, and originating therefore in the creative imagination, with the aim of arousing an esthetic pleasure. There is nothing more literary than the chronicle, which does not pretend to inform, teach, or orient. And it is not so indissolubly linked to the press that its pleasures cannot be tasted in a book, as is the case with the chronicles of Machado de Assis, Rubem Braga, Henrique Pongetti, Lêdo Ivo, Manuel Bandeira, Ribeiro Couto, Carlos Drummond de Andrade, Álvaro Moreira, Elsie Lessa, Fernando Sabino, and Eneida, to name a few masters of the genre.

Another characteristic is the essayistic naturalness of the chronicle. It is clear that in order to understand it one must distinguish between the formal, critical, biographical, historical, philosophical, and discursive essay, which among us is becoming synonymous with a study, and the informal, familiar, and colloquial essay for which the English are noted. This second type shares characteristics with our chronicle. One only has to compare the small essays of Steele, Addison, Hazlitt, Lamb, Chesterton, and others of the large English family, to the pages of our chroniclers in order to see their kinship. We will not have to change the name, because the specialization of the word "chronicle" as it is used in Portuguese to designate the genre is interesting. As is well known, the old meaning of the word, which obtained during the Renaissance, for example, and is still current in other romance languages, made the chronicle a historical genre. Chronicle and chronicler (from the Greek *chronos,* time) were related to the chronological story of events that had happened in a place. This sense disappeared and the word came to designate a small piece in prose, of a free nature, in a colloquial style, brought on by the observation of everyday or weekly events, reflected through an artistic temperament.

What should be emphasized is the importance that the genre has been taking on in our literature. Following its historical development, from romanticism on, one can see the effort with which it was opening the way until it achieved the personification of a genre; it is well individualized today in literature thanks to the work of artists of superior quality. The contribution of the chronicle to the differentiation of the language in Brazil is an especially relevant fact, as Álvaro Moreira stresses, to the point where in Portugal it became necessary to translate a Brazilian chronicle by Elsie Lessa so that it would be understandable to the overseas public. This shows that as it is linked to daily life, the chronicle must make use of the spoken and colloquial language, even acquiring a certain dramatic expression from its contact with daily life.

The difficulties of classifying the chronicle result, as Eduardo Portella has stressed, from the fact that it "must be characterized not by its order or coherence, but precisely by its ambiguity," which "quite often leads it to the short story, to the essay, at times, and frequently to the prose poem." [104] The chronicle, the same critic insists, is held down by the dilemma of transcendency and the environment. Its journalistic conditions and its urban base must be overcome if it is to achieve transcendency, whether by constructing "a life beyond the news," whether by enriching the news "with elements of a psychological or metaphysical type," or with humor, as with Carlos Drummond de Andrade, or by having "the artist's subjectivism," "his inner universe," impose itself "on the objective preoccupation of the chronicler," as with Rubem Braga or Lêdo Ivo.

14. Modernism was also beneficial to dramatic literature, and we could assert that some of the most original literary products of the past few years have come from the field of the theater. Not having gone beyond isolated attempts until then,[105] thanks to a series of experimentations brought about by the spirit of modernist renovation, dramatic production has been acquiring a definite form, in which the names of certain writers who dedicate the best of their creative activity to it stand out. Nélson Rodrigues, Guilherme Figueiredo, Raimundo Magalhães Júnior, Joraci Camargo, Henrique Pongetti, Ernâni Fornari, Silveira Sampaio, Lúcia Benedetti, Ariano Suassuna, Pedro Bloch, Abílio Pereira de Almeida, Edgard da Rocha Miranda, and José Paulo Moreira da Fonseca are some of the authors who turn their plays over to various theatrical organizations of good quality, which in turn find a most enthusiastic support from an avid public.

15. Criticism. Without being a literary genre, but rather a body of methods of approach for the analysis, interpretation, and judgment of the literary phenomenon, criticism accompanies the development of literature.

Traditionally tied to journalism, Brazilian criticism, when not incorporated into the historiographical schemes of a Sílvio Romero, with its scientificist and philosophical pretensions, was evidence of the impermanent character and superficiality of journalism. This helped keep it under the sway of impressionism; there were, however, exceptional qualities of some of those who exercised criticism, or the deliberate efforts at a sociological or psychological interpretation of literature.

The deep modernist subversion could not leave criticism untouched. The constant preoccupation with esthetic and technical problems of literature (very clear in Mário de Andrade, and one of the reasons why his figure as esthete, theoretician, and indoctrinator, has occupied center stage in the modernist period), the forces unleashed by the dogma of esthetic liberation, the spirit of investigation and the search for esthetic values and the renovation of literary forms, the preoccupation with the esthetic object in a literary work (which led Tristão de Ataíde to formulate his theory of "critical expressionism" [106]); all of this prepared the way so that in the later phase of modernism, there would be efforts at the renovation of literary criticism.[107]

This renovating tendency arose principally in opposition to the historicist, sociological, or psychological orientation, determinist in origin, to which one owes the principal works of previous Brazilian criticism. It was the study of literature as a *document* of a period, society, race, or great individual, never as an esthetic *monument*. It was the legacy, above all, of Sílvio Romero, whose ideas still had primacy.

The reaction against this tradition had begun with some critics linked to symbolism, men like Nestor Vítor, Henrique Abílio, Tasso da Silveira, Andrade Murici, and Barreto Filho, not to mention the vigorous action of Mário de Andrade, the work of spiritualist and expressionist reevaluation by Tristão de Ataíde, and the essays of Eugênio Gomes, which placed emphasis on investigation through comparative criticism.

The movement would have to wait a few years, however, to bear more significant fruit. In opposition to the theory that literature was but an epiphenomenon of political and social life, and that criticism consisted of its genetic interpretation, that is, of its roots and its extra-literary elements, there developed a movement of the esthetic reevaluation of literature which favored an understanding of the autonomy of the literary phenomenon and of an esthetic criticism, founded on the analysis of the work by itself and in its intrinsic elements, with the application of esthetic criteria in evaluating works and planning a stylistic periodization of literary history. This movement is linked to foreign movements of a similar nature, Slavic formalism or structuralism, German-Swiss and Spanish stylistics, Anglo-American new criticism, Italian esthetic autonomy, and its presence in Brazilian literature has already produced obvious results, as seen in the new generation of active critics: Péricles Eugênio da Silva Ramos, Eduardo Portella, Heron de Alencar, Osvaldino Marques, Franklin de Oliveira, Fausto Cunha, Waltensir Dutra, Mário Faustino, Oliveira Bastos, Barreto Borges, Afonso Ávila, Fábio Lucas, Othon Moacir Garcia, Darci Damasceno, Bráulio do Nascimento, José Guilherme Merquior, not to mention the studies of Lêdo Ivo, Cavalcânti Proença, and Eurálio Canabrava.

Criticism, therefore, reaches a phase of self-awareness, of methodological and technical domination, of professionalism, of the repudiation of self-education, amateurism, and improvisation, with a preference for university training. It is evident that the new group does not have the field to itself. Against it and the new orientations are the remains of outmoded journalistic impressionism, which have struggled to keep criticism on the level of irresponsible commentary, wandering, and subjectivism.

In this way, in spite of misrepresentations,[108] with modernism the principal literary genres and criticism establish physiognomies of their own, sharpen their tools, perfect their techniques, reevaluate their craft, consolidate a critical and professional consciousness, incorporate Brazilian themes in a definitive way, giving to the body of literature an esthetic and national autonomy and an undisguised coming of age. Modernism was a great collection of tendencies, and its results show that there has been a reconquest of the balance between continuity or the heritage of the past and change and innovation, between tradition and revolt.[109]

Notes

☙❧

GENERAL INTRODUCTION

1. "There are, without doubt, among them some fortunately endowed who without any need for explicit reflection on method and concepts, can produce good and innate criticism and literary history. But such good fortune is not only rare, it is also unstable and dangerous, because when later on an unforeseen difficulty arises for which such reflection is necessary, they seem to be disarmed and they become confused and baffled, and can even lose heart." B. Croce, "Osservazioni sullo stato presente della metodologia della storia letteraria," Proceedings of the First International Congress of Literary History, *Bulletin of Historical Sciences*, IV, No. 14 (1932), p. 31.

2. Paul Van Tieghem, "Le Prémier Congrès International d'Histoire Littéraire et la crise des méthodes," *Modern Philology*, XXIX, No. 2, November 1931.

3. Lanson has pointed out that "the best preparation for the student of letters . . . must be the *Introduction aux études historiques*, by Langlois and Seignobos."

4. Paul Van Tieghem, "La Question de méthodes en histoire littéraire," in *Bulletin*, p. 7.

5. See René Wellek, *The Revolt against Positivism*. This study is now included in the author's work *Concepts of Criticism*, New Haven, Yale University Press, 1963.

6. Philippe Van Tieghem, *Tendances nouvelles en histoire littéraire*, Paris, 1939.

7. For this problem of the concept of literary history, see the studies by René Wellek; see also *Comparative Literature*, III, No. 1, Winter 1951, and "The Aims, Methods, and Materials of Research in the Modern Languages and Literatures," *PMLA*, LXVII.

8. Committee on Research Activities, *The Aims and Methods of Scholarship in Modern Languages and Literatures*, New York, Modern Language Association, 1963.

9. Wellek, "Six Types of Literary History," *English Institute Annual: 1946*, New York, Columbia University Press, 1947, p. 123.

10. Gustave Lanson, *Méthodes de l'histoire litteraire*, Paris, Belle Lettres, 1925, pp. 237–40.

11. The studies by Wellek are indispensable and definitive for the proper understanding of the problem, and many of the inspirations put forth here have been based on them. The study by H. Cysarz is also useful.

12. Oto Maria Carpeaux, "A Querela da História Literária," *O Jornal*, Rio de Janeiro, July 1943, *passim*.

13. Written especially for this work.

14. Paul Van Tieghem, *Le Romantisme dans la littérature européenne*, Paris, A. Michel, 1948, pp. 1 and 120.

15. From the preface to the study by Jean Hankiss, *La Littératura et la vie*, p. vii.

16. For these matters consult further: Afrânio Coutinho, *Correntes Cruzades*, Rio de Janeiro, A. Noite, 1953; *idem, Conceito de Literatura Brasileira*, Rio de Janeiro, Livraria Acadêmica, 1960. Consult also the books by Fidelino de Figueiro.

17. Consult in addition to the bibliography at the end of this book the following studies: A. Mota, bibliography of a general nature in *História da Literatura Brasileira*, Vol. I, São Paulo, 1930, pp. 267–86. Simões dos Reis, *A Bibliografia da História da Literatura Brasileira de Sílvio Romero*, Rio de Janeiro, Z. Valverde, 1944. M. L. Voiglaender, "Bibliografia da história da literatura brasileira," *Boletim Bibliográfico*, No. 14, São Paulo, 1950. G. M. Moser, "Histories of Brazilian Literature: A Critical Survey," *Revista Interamericana de Bibliografia*, Vol. X, No. 2, Washington, Pan-American Union, 1960.

18. Consult the introductory chapters of the literary histories by Sílvio Romero, José Veríssimo, Artur Mota, Ronald de Carvalho, Afrânio Peixoto, and Mozart Monteiro.

19. Soares Amora, *História da Literatura Brasileira*, p. 12.

20. Gilberto Amado, *Minha Formação no Recife*, Rio de Janeiro, 1955, pp. 353–55.

21. See P. Henríquez Ureña, *Literary Currents in Hispanic America*, Cambridge, Harvard University Press, 1945.

22. J. A. Portuondo, "Períodos y generaciones en la historiografía literaria hispanoamericana," *Cuadernos Americanos*, 1948, pp. 231–52.

23. Henríquez Ureña, *Literary Currents*, p. 38.

24. Viana Moog, *Uma Interpretação da Literatura Brasileira*, 1943, pp. 19 and 22.

25. See Gilberto Freyre, *Continente e Ilha*, Rio de Janeiro, 1941; *idem, Manifesto Regionalista do Recife*, Rio de Janeiro, 1955.

26. Fidelino de Figueiredo, "Características da Literatura Espanhola," *Espanha*, 1945, pp. 17–18.

27. "Twisting the meaning of the words a little, perhaps it is proper to say that in art, just as in social life, we passed from the Middle Ages into the Baroque without ever having known the Renaissance." Sérgio

Buarque de Holanda, "Literatura Jesuítica," *Diário de Notícias*, January 16, 1949.

28. On the legacy of ancient literatures see: R. R. Bolgar, *The Classical Heritage*, Cambridge, 1954. E. R. Curtius, *European Literature and the Latin Middle Ages*, New York, Pantheon, 1953 (Spanish translation, Mexico, 1955, Brazilian translation, Rio de Janeiro, 1957). W. P. Friederich, *Outline of Comparative Literature*, Chapel Hill, 1954. G. Highet, *The Classical Tradition*, Oxford, 1949 (Spanish translation, Mexico, 1954). M. Menéndez y Pelayo, *Horacio en España*, Madrid, 1877. H. O. Taylor, *The Classical Heritage of the Middle Ages*, New York, Macmillan, 1929. J. A. K. Thompson, *The Classical Background of English Literature*, New York, Macmillan, 1948. *Idem, Classical Influences on English Poetry*, London, Allen and Unwin, 1951.

29. See Coutinho, *Correntes Cruzades*.

FROM BAROQUE TO ROCOCO

1. Fidelino de Figueiredo, *Características da Literatura Portuguêsa*, Lisbon, Liv. Clássica, 1923, p. 13. *Idem, Literatura Portuguêsa*, Rio de Janeiro, Liv. Acadêmica, 1954. *Idem, História da Literatura Clássica*, 3 vols., Lisbon, 1922–1931. See also: Hernâni Cidade, *A Literatura Portuguêsa e a Expansão Ultramarina*, Lisbon, 1943.

2. "The Portuguese mentality of the sixteenth century, seen as a whole, appears to be the result of two lines of influence; one which comes from overseas activities, the other one derived from contact with cultured Europe . . . . The stimulus that humanists received from contact with foreign countries was continued by scientists and men of action in the overseas adventure. Nautical activity played the same role among the Portuguese of the period of discovery as industrial activity did among Italians in the period that followed. It was what necessitated a realistic analysis of the phenomena of nature as well as their interpretation and domination. Without its demands and suggestions, perhaps we would not have rectified the astronomical and natural knowledge of the ancients, nor perfected nautical instruments, nor developed mathematics, nor acquired the custom of observing and reasoning in the light of facts. From their voyages and wanderings through the world, as sailors, administrators, apostles, or traders, our grandparents plucked the delicious fruit of a direct and experienced knowledge of the phenomena of nature, of different flora and fauna, different customs, lands, and people. This knowledge, derived from practice and not from books, was like a dagger aiming at the heart of ancient science, inviting it to confess its chimeras and contradictions of reality." J. S. da Silva Dias, *Portugal e a Cultura Européia*, offprint from *Biblos*, Coimbra, 1952, pp. 203 and 216.

3. C. E. Whitmore, "The Validity of Literary Definitions," *PMLA*, XXXIX, September 3, 1924.

4. R. Lebègue, "La Poésie baroque en France," *Cahiers de l'Association Internationale des Études Françaises*, No. 1, Paris, 1951.

5. A. Adam, *Histoire de la littérature française au XVIIe siècle*, 4 vols., Paris, 1949–1954.

6. H. Peyre, *Le Classicisme français*, New York, Maison Française, 1943.

7. "The French classics are not like those of any other nation. Only some few rare Latin classics have points of contact with them. One could even say that we alone have true classics. We also have a certain difficulty in assimilating them before we have personally acquired the experience of life." E. Jaloux, *Nouvelles Littéraires*, November 18, 1939.

8. In addition to the books by Henri Peyre and A. Adam, for the problem of classicism, consult: E. B. O. Borgerhoff, *The Freedom of French Classicism*, Princeton, 1950. R. Bray, *La Formation de la doctrine classique en France*, Paris, Payot, 1931. T. S. Eliot, *What Is a Classic?*, London, Faber, 1945. J. E. Fidao-Justiniani, *Qu'est-ce qu'un classique?*, Paris, Didot, 1930. G. Highet, *The Classical Tradition*, Oxford, 1949. D. Mornet, *Histoire de la littérature française classique*, Paris, Colin, 1947. *Idem, La Clarté française*, Paris, Payot, 1920. G. Murray, *The Classical Tradition in Poetry*, Harvard, 1937. G. Reynold, *Le XVIIe siècle*, Montreal, L'Arbre, 1944. J. A. K. Thompson, *The Classical Background of English Literature*, New York, Macmillan, 1948. M. Turnell, *The Classical Moment*, London, Chatto and Windus, 1950.

9. H. Wölfflin, *Conceptos fundamentales en le historia del arte*, Madrid, Espasa-Calpe, 1945. *Idem, Classic Art*, London, Phaidon, 1952.

10. The books cited below give evidence for this principle of literary theory of the period as well as the role of rhetoric in Renaissance education and its ties with poetics: T. W. Baldwin, *William Shakespeare's Small Latin and Lesse Greek*, 2 vols., Urbana, University of Illinois Press, 1944. M. L. Clark, *Rhetoric at Rome*, London, Cohen and West, 1953. A. Reyes, *La antigua retórica*, Mexico, Fondo de Cultura Económica, 1942. E. Tuve, *Elizabethan and Metaphysical Imagery*, Chicago, Chicago University Press, 1947. R. Wallerstein, *Studies in Seventeenth-Century Poetic*, Madison, University of Wisconsin, 1950. B. Weinberg, *Critical Prefaces of the French Renaissance*, Evanston, Northwestern University Press, 1950.

For the problem of imitation particularly, in addition to the studies of commentators on the *Poetics* of Aristotle, especially as they deal with the concept of *mimesis*, which has produced such a vast bibliography, see: J. W. H. Atkins, *Literary Criticism in Antiquity*, 2 vols., Cambridge, 1934. *Idem, English Literary Criticism. The Renascence*, London, Methuen, 1947. C. S. Baldwin, *Ancient Rhetoric and Poetic*, New York, Macmillan, 1924. *Idem, Medieval Rhetoric and Poetic*, New York, Macmillan, 1928. *Idem, Renaissance Literary Theory and Practice*, New York, Columbia University Press, 1939. A. P. Basto Ferreira, "Breves considerações sôbre classicismo e medievalismo," *Brotéria*, May 1939. R. Bray, *La Formation de la doctrine classique en France*, Paris, Payot, 1931. S. H. Butcher, *Aristotle's Theory of Poetry and Fine Arts*, London, Macmillan, 1895 (4th ed., 1927). J. F. D'Alton, *Roman Literary Theory and Criticism*, London, Longmans, 1931. I. Jack, *Augustan Satire*, Oxford, 1952. R. McKeon, *Thought, Action, Passion*, Chicago University Press, 1954. *Idem*, "Literary Criticism and the Concept of Imitation in Antiquity," *Modern Philology*, XXXIV, August 1, 1936. J. C. Piguet, "La Voye royale de l'imitation," *Revue d'Esthétique*, January-March 1953. J. E. Spingarn, *Literary Criticism in the Renaissance*, New York, Macmillan, 1899. H. S. Wilson, "Imitation," *Dictionary of World Literature*, J. T. Shipley, editor, New York, 1943.

Addenda, 1964: B. Hathaway, *The Age of Criticism*, Ithaca, Cornell University Press, 1962. W. S. Howell, *Logic and Rhetoric in England, 1500-1700*, Princeton University Press, 1956. G. dalla Volpe, *Poetica del Cinquecento*, Bari, Latenza, 1954. B. Weinberg, *A History of Literary Criticism in the Italian Renaissance*, 2 vols., Chicago University Press, 1961. *Testi Umanistici su la Retorica*, Rome-Milan, Fratelli Bocca, 1953.

11. "You observe I am a mere imitator of Homer, Horace, Boileau, Garth, etc. (which I have the lesse cause to be ashamed of, since they were imitators on one another)." Alexander Pope, quoted by Ian Jack, *Augustan Satire*, p. 11, note.

12. "Discounting very rare exceptions, the southern continent continues to produce a literature of low level, one of reflection, lending itself to themes and expressive forms. . . . The two greatest ills of literary production in the southern Americas: the lack of originality in conception, the absence of a formal technique in expression." F. Diez Medina, "El problema de una literatura nacional," *Cuadernos Americanos*, March-April, 1953, pp. 135, 136.

13. A. Peixoto, *Panorama da Literatura Brasileira*, São Paulo, Cia. Editôra Nacional, 1947, p. 69.

14. H. Wölfflin, *Conceptos fundamentales en la historia del arte*, Madrid, 1945.

15. Wellek, "The Concept of Baroque in Literary Scholarship," *Journal of Aesthetics and Criticism*, Vol. II, December, 1946. This is the basic study for the evolution of the concept in criticism and literary history. For further details see also: Afrânio Coutinho, *Aspectos da Literatura Barroca*, Rio de Janeiro, 1951. The present chapter is in many ways a shortened or slightly modified version of this book.

Wellek's study now appears in *Concepts of Criticism*, New Haven, Yale University Press, 1963.

16. W. P. Friedrich, *Outline of Comparative Literature*, p. 45.

17. "And therefore the labels Renaissance and classicism have too long prevented us from viewing clearly French works that appeared between 1580 and 1640; after the word *baroque* was admitted to the terminology of literary history, it became undeniable that many secondary authors emerged

from the shadows and that the poetic débuts of a d'Aubigné, a Corneille are much better understood than formerly." R. Lebègue, "La Poésie baroque en France," *Cahiers.*

18. The following work, the first to present a masterful total picture of the baroque period, is indispensable for a study of the matter: Carl J. Friedrich, *The Age of the Baroque, 1610–1660,* New York, Harper, 1952.

19. Studying the baroque character in Racine, Spitzer shows that the vital forces, in a state of conflict of polarities in the baroque, are submitted to a violent effort to produce a balance, expressed in classical rules and guide-lines, which he calls the *"klassische Dampfung."* Spitzer, *Linguistics and Literary History, passim.*

20. "And it is partly at least for this reason that the period (1575–1675) between the Renaissance, properly so called, and the neoclassical age has never been clearly differentiated in literary history, although in the other arts, in sculpture, painting, and architecture its character has been recognized and described." Morris W. Croll, "Attic Prose," *Studies in Philology,* XVIII, April 2, 1921, pp. 123–24.

21. "But while in the countries of northern Europe the baroque spirit was repressed in the visual arts, it found free and complete expression in music, poetry, and science. The baroque is a European style, with fundamental qualities in common from north to south, even though, as with other previous styles, it is subject to national variations." M. M. Mahood, *Poetry and Humanism,* London, 1950, p. 133.

22. "Therein lies a conflict between strict literary history and criticism or esthetics. For the strict historian, *préciosité* is a determined and unique phenomenon, limited in space (a few Parisian salons and their provincial imitations), limited in time (from 1654 to 1661, one might say). For the critic, *préciosité* is a permanent tendency of literature, the manifestation of which is favored by certain circumstances, but which accommodates itself to different social and spiritual states, even though they resemble each other. Therein lies a debate on words, just as with the terms romanticism, classicism, realism, etc., that is not worth lingering over." René Bray, "La Préciosité," *Cahiers,* p. 51.

"The problem of the baroque is with its age, and it is all the more interesting within those limits, where there is still so much to be clarified before criticism can agree on a precise position." F. Neri, *Poesia nel tempo,* Turin, 1948, p. 57.

23. T. M. Greene, *The Arts and the Art of Criticism,* Princeton, 1940, p. 379.

24. For bibliography on the baroque in general and the literary baroque, see Wellek, *Concepts of Criticism,* which is the indispensable starting point. Wellek has brought his bibliography up to 1963. See also Afrânio Coutinho's *Bibliografia para o Estudo da Literatura Barroca,* Rio de Janeiro, 1951. The book by Carl J. Friedrich, *The Age of the Baroque,* offers a good bibliographical outline. The same is true of the studies by C. Calcaterra

and G. Getto. See also H. Hatzfeld, *Estudios sobre el barroco*, Madrid, Gredos, 1964.

25. "If the baroque is a spirit that is expressed by a style, one must find its nature by psychology and by stylistics." P. Kohler, "Le Baroque et les lettres françaises," *Cahiers*, p. 13.

26. This problem of the survival of the Christian heritage and of anti-national and anti-humanistic movements in the period is masterfully studied in: H. Haydn, *The Counter-Renaissance*, New York, 1950. On the Counter-Reformation and the Council of Trent see: L. Cristiani, *L'Église à l'époque du Concile de Trente*, Paris, 1948. E. Quaza, *Preponderanze straniere*, Milan, 1938. Daniel-Rops, *L'Église de la Renaissance et de la Réforme*, Paris, 1955. Imbart de la Tour, *Les Origines de la Réforme*, 3 vols., Paris, 1914. On its influence in the arts see: C. Dejob, *L'Influence du Concile de Trente sur la littérature et les beaux-arts*, Paris, Thorin, 1884.

27. On the question of the Spanish origins of the baroque, see the studies by Hatzfeld, Weisbach, Weibel, McComb, Sommerfeld, Gilman, Hume, Lanson, and others. On the Spanish influence in Italy, see various studies by B. Croce, especially *La Spagna nella vita italiana durante la Rinascenza*, 4th ed., Bari, 1949. Also to be consulted are the works of A. Farinelli and that of Quaza.

28. "The baroque is a period in which the most striking contrasts exist at the same time. An enormous progress in rational thought, in a knowledge of nature, alongside crass superstition, astrology, alchemy, chiromancy, spells, and witchcraft; the appearance of criteria of tolerance alongside religious fanaticism; a military zeal for the faith alongside mystical quietism; a skeptical, ironical, and satirical view of the world alongside an unshakable belief in miracles; a manifest delight in magnificence and splendor alongside a denial of external ostentation and reflective resignation. It is not that such contrasts did not exist in other periods, but that at that time they appear in a specially characterized form that defines the whole. This gives the baroque its complex character, dual and varying. We feel ourselves transported into the midst of a fervent mass shaken by incessant waves, palpitations, and flashes. In the interior of this fluctuating movement, Catholicism tries to preserve its prerogatives, affirm and consolidate its domain by means of a propaganda directed at the soul and the spirit, at the eyes and the ears, as it attracts and chooses from the spiritual structure of the period everything that seems appropriate and useful for its objective of exercising a suggestive action on the masses." Weisbach, *El barroco arte de la Contrarreforma*, p. 88.

29. H. Hatzfeld, "A Clarification." The recently published work by H. Hatzfeld, *Estudios sobre el barroco*, Madrid, Gredos, 1964, brings together the studies on the subject of this great Romance scholar.

30. On the fusion of Aristotle and Horace in this phase see: A. H. Gilbert, and H. L. Sangs, "On the Relations of Horace and Aristotle," *Journal of English and Germanic Philology*, XLVI, No. 3, July 1947. M. T. Her-

rick, *The Fusion of Horatian and Aristotelian Literary Criticism, 1531–1555*, Urbana, 1946. B. Weinberg, "From Aristotle to Pseudo-Aristotle," *Comparative Literature*, II, Spring 1953. *Idem*, "The Problem of Literary Aesthetics in Italy and France in the Renaissance," *Modern Language Quarterly*, XIV, No. 4, December 1953. *Idem*, "Scaliger versus Aristotle on Poetics," *Modern Philology*, May 1942. *Idem*, "Robortello on the Poetics; Castelvetro's Theory of Poetry," *Critics and Criticism*, Evanston, 1950. See also the works referred to in note 10 on critical theories of the Renaissance.

31. "It is true, as Curtius maintains, that no stylistic device is new; but, contrary to this thesis, as Spitzer correctly observes, the device, emerging again in a totally different cultural climate, represents something spiritually different within the new complex phenomena it helps to form. Admitting this much, one must admit also, that it is the more individual compound or constellation of these devices found in an author which reveals the breadth and depth of his originality." M. J. Maggioni, *The Pensées of Pascal*, pp. vi–vii.

"But here they assume a special value by their very coming together. One must admit in esthetics that certain characteristics or certain effects, from the fact that they predominate during a moment in history, acquire a greater meaning by that very reason." M. Raymond, quoted by Kohler, in *Cahiers*, p. 20.

32. See A. Coutinho, *Aspectos da Literatura Barroca*, pp. 120 and following. Recent studies are those by M. Gotaas and Belchior Pontes.

33. "When it wishes to praise a culteranist writer, Brazilian and Portuguese criticism has a mania for saying that 'he is not as Gongoristic as the rest.' Therefore, what is necessary to note, at least in the case of Brazil, is that they did not know that they were Gongoristic, because in the almost absolute majority, they were mediocre . . . bad poets, not because of *cultista* imitation, but because of their own poetical insufficiency. When we find one of greater capacity, like Matos, we note that of his lyric poems, the best are precisely those where more Gongorism is visible." Antônio Cândido, *O Jornal*, September 8, 1946.

34. "It is an accepted point today, the conclusion of which has been acquired by impartial criticism, that our literary sixteenth century, besides being a brilliant period, does not present (if we except the *Lusiads* and the lyrics of Camões), any classical genres that had begun then except in a kind of embryonic state. The seeds of classicism did not develop completely in that century, nor could they in so brief a time; in the following century there was, certainly, notable progress in the perfection of prose, but in general, one can feel the lack of a complete and sequential evolution of the literary genres of the new esthetic." Paulo Durão, "O Seiscentismo Literário," *Brotéria*, XIV, April 4, 1932, p. 221.

35. On Brazilian colonial art, whose importance is universally recognized today, see: Lúcio Costa, "A Arquitetura dos Jesuítas no Brasil," *Revista SPHAN*, No. 5, Rio de Janeiro, 1941. L. Gomes Machado, "O Barroco e o

Absolutismo," *Estado de São Paulo*, April and June 1949. *Idem*, "Viagem a Ouro Prêto," *Revista do Arquivo Municipal*, São Paulo, CXXIV, 1949. P. Kaleman, *Baroque and Rococo in Latin America*, New York, 1951. J. Mariano Filho, "O Pseudo Estilo Barroco-Jesuítico," *Estudos Brasileiros*, IX, Rio de Janeiro, 1939. P. F. Santos, *O Barroco e o Jesuítico na Arquitetura do Brasil*, Rio de Janeiro, Kosmos, 1951. R. dos Santos, *Conferência de Arte*, Lisbon, 1943. *Idem*, "A Arte Luso-Brasileira do Século XVIII," *Belas Artes*, No. 1, Lisbon, 1948. R. Smith, "Minas Gerais no Desenvolvimento da Arquitetura Religiosa Colonial," *Boletim do Centro de Estudos Históricos*, III, Rio de Janeiro. *Idem*, "As Igrejas Coloniais do Brasil," *Boletim da União Panamericana*, Vol. 72, No. 1, Washington, 1938. *Idem*, "A Arte Barroca de Portugal e do Brasil," *Panorama*, No. 3, Lisbon, 1949. *Idem*, *As Artes na Bahia*, Salvador, 1954. D. Vasconcelos, *A Arte em Ouro Prêto*, Belo Horizonte, 1931.

36. On "mannerism" see: E. B. O. Borgerhoff, "Mannerism and Baroque," *Comparative Literature*, IV, 1953. C. Calcaterra, in A. Momigliano, *Problemi*, p. 427; E. R. Curtius, *European Literature and the Latin Middle Ages*, Chapter 15; A. Hauser, *The Social History of Art*, I, p. 353; M. Maggioni, *The Pensées of Pascal*, p. 49; W. Sypher, *Four Stages of Renaissance Style*, p. 100.

37. In recent years there have been developed studies on mannerism which tend to characterize it as a style of its own. See the following recent studies: *Manierismo, barocco, rococó: Concetti e termini*, Rome, Academia Nazionale dei Lincei, 1962. G. Briganti, *Italian Mannerism*, London, Thames and Hudson, 1963. Roy Daniels, *Milton, Mannerism, and Baroque*, Toronto University Press, 1963. H. Hatzfeld, *Estudios sobre el barroco*, Madrid, Gredos, 1963. G. R. Hocke, *El mundo como laberinto: El manierismo en el arte y en la literatura*, 2 vols., Madrid, Guadarrama, 1961–1964. J. Legrand, "À La découverte du maniérisme européen," *Critique*, No. 152, Paris, January 1960. R. Scrivano, *Il Manierismo nella letteratura del Cinquecento*, Padua, Liviana, 1959. F. Würtenberg, *Mannerism: The European Style of the Sixteenth Century*, London, Weidenfeld and Nicolson, 1963. N. Pevsner, "The Architecture of Mannerism," *The Mint*, London, 1946. *Idem*, *An Outline of European Architecture*, London, Pelican, 1963. D. B. Rowland, *Mannerism: Style and Mood*, Yale University Press, 1964.

38. The word "Enlightenment" is a translation of the German *Aufklärung*, having come into use, alongside "illustration," to designate the mentality, dominant in the eighteenth century that was made up of rationalism, scientific investigation, an optimistic concept of the world, a belief in ascensional progress, the encyclopedia spirit, scientific and experimental, and which was defined by the metaphor of the "light" of reason, the reason that "illuminates," illustrates, clarifies. Thence the philosophy of light, enlightenment, illustration, an illuminated or luministic mentality.

39. On Portuguese academies, beginning with that of the Singulars

(1628) and that of the Generous (1647) of the seventeenth century, see the outline presented by Fidelino de Figueiredo in *História da Literatura Clássica*, Vol. II, and for the literary ideas they defended, consult the *História da Crítica em Portugal* by the same author.

40. Nuno Marques Pereira, *Peregrino da América*, II, p. 53.

41. On the supposed theoreticians of neoclassicism see: J. W. H. Atkins, *English Literary Criticism, 17th and 18th Centuries*, London, Methuen, 1951. W. J. Bate, *From Classic to Romantic*, Cambridge, Harvard University Press, 1946. A. Bosker, *Literary Criticism in the Age of Johnson*, Groningen, 1953. M. Menéndez Pelayo, *Historia de las ideas estéticas en España*, Vol. III, Buenos Aires, Espasa-Calpe, 1943. S. H. Monk, *The Sublime*, New York, MLA, 1935. H. A. Needham, *Taste and Criticism in the Eighteenth Century*, London, Harrap, 1952. G. Saintsbury, *A History of Criticism and Literary Taste in Europe*, Vol. II, Edinburgh, 1900. R. Wellek, *A History of Modern Criticism*, Vol. I, New Haven, Yale University Press, 1955. W. J. Hipple, *The Beautiful, the Sublime, and the Picturesque in Eighteenth-Century British Aesthetic Theory*, Carbondale, 1957.

42. C. Calcaterra, *Il Parnaso in revolta*, p. 223 *et passim*.

43. Basil Willey, *The Eighteenth Century Background*, London, 1946.

44. There is no propriety in the use of the formulas "Bahian School," "Minas School," "Rio School," or "Maranhão School," as various Brazilian literary historians do to designate the groups of writers who lived in seventeenth-century Bahia, Minas Gerais in the period of the *Inconfidência*, in Rio de Janeiro, and in Maranhão. They are nothing but circumstantial groups who did not constitute schools in the strict sense, justifying only the term "group," or, as José Veríssimo calls them, "pleiad."

45. A. Faria, *Aérides*, Rio de Janeiro, 1918, pp. 88–99.

46. On the subject see: A. Faria, *Aérides;* J. Veríssimo, *Estudos da Literatura*, Vol. IV, pp. 157–200. T. Braga, *Filinto Elísio e os Dissidentes da Arcádia*. F. Figueiredo, *História da Literatura Clássica*, Vol. III, pp. 205–38. A. Mota, *História da Literatura Brasileira*, Vol. II.

47. M. Fabini, "Arcadia e illuminismo," in A. Momigliano, *Problemi ed orientamenti critici*, Vol. IV: "Questioni e correnti di storia letteraria," Milan, Marzorati, 1949, p. 595.

48. Wylie Sypher, *Four Stages of Renaissance Style*, New York, 1955, p. 7.

49. T. M. Greene, *The Arts and the Art of Criticism*.

50. "Outside of architecture, rococo should involve manifestations as unlike in appearance as are the paintings of Watteau and Tiepolo, Louis XIV style, frivolous arcadism, the music of Jomelli, Gluck, Cimarosa, Mozart, the melodrama, the comedies of Marivaux and Goldoni, the Encyclopedia, freemasonry, the anti-mechanicalism of Berkeley, the mechanicalism of Condillac, the experimentalism of Hume and of the heirs of Locke, the economic and social tendencies that will redound in the so-called in-

dustrial revolution of England and the social, economic, and ideological tendencies that will break forth in the American Revolution and the French Revolution.

"Forms of the pragmatic and etiquette, furniture and household utensils, preference given to determined materials over others (silk, glass, porcelain, mother of pearl, wood, widely substituted by stone in northern countries), styles of ornamentation and gardening, religious movements (Methodism, pietism), mystical charlatanism (Cagliostro), a reordering of classes, ideas, values, inspired in part by the growing affirmation of the bourgeoisie, the coexistence of contrasting attitudes and principles, of aulicism with revolt, of weepy sentimentalism with ethical epicureanism, of sensualism with rationalism, of pagan mythology and *chinoiserie*, all of this was to be brought together and given kinship under the same label. What subtleties of ratiocination would be necessary to forge a common denominator among elements where some are so adverse to others?

"Extreme attention is not necessary, however, to verify how among these distinct and opposed forms there do exist certain zones of contact and even secret links that might justify and even seem to demand a common treatment. When they cannot be explained by kinship, they can be explained, not rarely, by the very contrariety. Also, it will be advantageous, perhaps, to understand them better, to try to consider these discordant forms as a single one and in the same perspective, able to unify them and momentarily verify them, provided that, immediately following, they can recoup their freedom and that the provisional artifice does not become a fatal armor for the historian." Sérgio Buarque de Holanda, "Domínio Rococó," *Diário Carioca*, September 6, 1953.

51. In *Filosofía de la ciencia literaria*, E. Ermatinger, editor, Mexico, 1946, p. 130.

52. H. Hatzfeld, *Literature Through Art*, Oxford, 1952, p. 102 *et passim*.

THE ROMANTIC MOVEMENT

1. Hatzfeld, *Journal of Aesthetics and Art Criticism*, December 1955, p. 156.

2. For the problem of periodization, especially stylistic periodization, particular attention should be given the studies of R. Wellek, H. Hatzfeld, P. Frank, and C. Friedrich. The studies by Frank and Friedrich describe the theoretical postulates of stylistic periodization in rather clarifying terms.

3. F. Baldensperger, "Romantique, ses analogues et équivalents," *Harvard Studies and Notes in Philology and Literature*, XIV, 1937, pp. 13–105. A. Lovejoy, "On the Discrimination of Romanticisms," *Essays in the History of Ideas*, Baltimore, 1948. L. P. Smith, *Words and Idioms*, Boston, 1925. P. Van Tieghem, *Le Romantisme dans la littérature européenne*,

Paris, 1948, pp. 2–5. R. Wellek, "The Concept of Romanticism in Literary History," *Comparative Literature*, I, No. 1, Winter, and No. 2, Spring 1949, reprinted in *Concepts of Criticism*.

4. For greater details see Wellek, *Concepts of Criticism*.

5. Paul Van Tieghem, *Le Romantisme dans la littérature européenne*, Paris, A. Michel, 1948. *Idem, Le Préromantisme*, 3 vols., Paris, Alcan, 1924–1947. *Idem, Histoire littéraire de l'Amérique*, Paris, Colin, 1941. *Idem, Le Sentiment de la nature dans le préromantisme européen*, Paris, Nizet, 1960. M. Magnino, *Storia del Romanticismo*, Rome, Mazara, 1950.

6. Hibbard, *Writers of the Western World*, Boston, Houghton Mifflin, 1942, p. 389 *et passim*.

7. The lyric poetry of the period is defined, still according to Virgínia Côrtes de Lacerda, in this way: "Lyric poetry, meant to be sung and therefore strophic in its primitive meaning, still preserved in those days its most remote forms, the Greco-Roman heritage dressed up as neo-Latin; they are *odes* (religious, heroic, philosophical, or comic), *cantatas* (odes put to music, so much to the taste of the eighteenth century), epistles, eclogues, sonnets, idylls, epitaphs, epithalamia, forms found in almost all poets of the period. The various types of Greek odes (alcaic, asclepiadic, sapphic) were used very much in the eighteenth century, especially in Germany and England, and they infiltrated all literatures of the time as the most noble genre until romanticism came to banish them. Even though the imitation of the classics continues, translation of romantic poets begins (José Bonifácio); even though the ancient genres are still cultivated, the preoccupation with the renovation of poetic forms begins; even though the literary formation of the poets has been Greco-Roman, some proceed consciously and intentionally towards the abandonment of mythology (Sousa Caldas, S. Carlos . . .); even though the eternal poetical themes are still dealt with in the ancient way, new motives are adopted (Borges de Barros) and new paths of renovation are already being tried (Gonçalves de Magalhães). Hence this disproportion between content and form, this eclecticism of literary genres, this incoherence between thought and action, which make difficult a neat characterization of the period. There are, for that very reason, different degrees of romantic initiation in the poets of this period of transition since José Bonifácio first presented us with his romantic translations until Gonçalves de Magalhães came to indicate 'a new path for future minds,' making 'the strings of the heart vibrate' and elevating 'thought on the wings of harmony up to archetypical ideas.' To this new finality of poetry there must correspond, according to Magalhães himself, a *reform of genres*, an abandonment of the 'ancient and jaded ornaments,' and of *form*, which is that of not following 'any order' in the material construction of stanzas, and of fleeing from monotony by abandoning 'the equality of lines, the regularity of rhyme, the symmetry of stanzas,' without forgetting that as far as language is concerned, 'a new idea calls for a new term.' There, in essence, is the whole romantic revolu-

tion that Magalhães and Pôrto Alegre preached but could not fully attain. The official introducers of romanticism into Brazil, they are, by their works, only pre-romantics, lacking in their poetry that truly romantic strain which was to vibrate so strongly later on, identified with the collective and personal state of the Brazilian spirit of the time, bringing about the fusion verified later of the inspiration of the individual calling of our great romantic poets (who at the time were going through adolescence and early youth, the romantic moments of life and of every individual) and of the collective inspiration, for, as a people, we were experiencing the great exaltation of nationality which was established and affirmed by autonomy. The adolescence of Brazil coincided with the adolescence of many of its literary lights of the time (Álvares de Azevedo, Castro Alves, Casimiro de Abreu . . .), hence the complete acceptance by the public of the poetry that only then was truly new and truly romantic. This fact, singular in all of our literary history, can only be truly and deeply understood when we analyze carefully the literary production of that period, so little studied until today, which was our pre-romanticism; when we try to penetrate the core of this poetry, of such little worth as poetry, but so full of proposals of renovation, we can see what the task of our pre-romantics was." Virgínia Côrtes de Lacerda, *O Pre-Romantismo Brasileiro* (unpublished study).

8. "Now, everybody is familiar with the great influence of Ferdinand Denis on our first romantics and remembers his famous statement written in 1826, ten years before Magalhães' book: 'Brazil already feels the necessity of drinking in its poetic inspiration from a spring that actually belongs to it, and in its nascent glory it will not delay in presenting the first fruits of this enthusiasm that certifies the youth of a people. If this part of America adopted a language that had been perfected by our old Europe, it must reject the mythological ideas owed to the fables of Greece . . . because they are not in harmony with its climate, nor with its traditions. America, glowing with youth, must have new and energetic thoughts. . . . America must, at last, be free in its poetry as it already is in its government.' Ferdinand Denis was the father of our romanticism." Tristão de Ataíde, *Estudos*, 3rd series, II, Rio de Janeiro, A Ordem, 1930, p. 156. Concerning the role of Ferdinand Denis in the origins of romanticism in Brazil, particularly his influence on the *Niterói* group, see the study by Paul Hazard, *Revista da Academia Brasileira de Letras*, No. 69, 1927.

On the other hand, the influence of Garrett cannot be dismissed or diminished. Based, furthermore, on an error of date, Sérgio Buarque de Holanda judges unfounded the suspicion of José Veríssimo that Gonçalves de Magalhães had read the nationalizing advice of Garrett in *Bosquejo*, "published ten years after the *Discurso* of Magalhães." In truth, however, the *Bosquejo* dates from 1826, ten years before the *Discurso* (1836), and not 1846 as he affirms. See the preface to *Suspiros Poéticos e Saudades*, Rio de Janeiro, M.E.S., 1939, p. xx.

NOTES: THE ROMANTIC MOVEMENT

In this respect one must also point out the testimony of J. S. Queiroga, in *A Literatura no Brasil,* Vol. I, Part 2, p. 643.

9. These were the principal attempts at the classification of romantic writers:

Sílvio Romero, in *História da Literatura Brasileira,* speaks of six phases, which he reduces later in *Evolução da Literatura Brasileira* (1905) to five moments: 1st, from 1830 with the second Rio school and the second Bahian school; 2nd, from 1848 with the first São Paulo school; 3rd, from 1855; 4th, from 1858 with the Maranhão school; 5th, from 1862 to 1870 with the condor poets. Along with these moments, he refers to divergent writers, precursors, laggards, and so forth.

José Veríssimo, faced with the problem and without a sure methodology, opts for a simplification and selection of romantic values, which he divides into two phases or generations, outside of the precursors and a third group of "late romantics."

Ronald de Carvalho establishes four groups or phases, characterized by dominant tendencies: (*a*) religious poetry (Gonçalves de Magalhães et al.); (*b*) poetry of nature (Gonçalves Dias et al.); (*c*) poetry of doubt (Álvares de Azevedo et al.); (*d*) social poetry (Castro Alves et al.). He also adds some minor poets and points out others as figures of transition between romanticism and Parnassianism (Machado de Assis, Luís Guimarães).

Oto Maria Carpeaux (*Pequena Bibliografia Crítica da Literatura Brasileira*) adopted the criterion of a stylistic division, establishing the following groups: preromanticism (Gonçalves de Magalhães, Pôrto Alegre, Borges de Barros, Varnhagen, Dutra e Melo), a current parallel to others of neoclassicism and trivial and dilettante romanticism which followed that of preromantic classicism (Minas Gerais Arcadism). In romanticism proper, he distinguishes the groups of: national and popular romanticism (Gonçalves Dias, Alencar, et al.), individualist romanticism (Álvares de Azevedo et al.), and liberal romanticism (Castro Alves et al.).

10. Representatives of the preromantic period: Manuel Aires do Casal (1754?–1821); Father Domingos Simões da Cunha (1755–1824); José Joaquim Azeredo Coutinho (1743–1821); José de Sousa Azevedo Pizaro e Araújo (1753–1830); José Arouche de Toledo Rendon (1756–1834); José da Silva Lisboa (1756–1835); Baltasar da Silva Lisboa (1761–1840); Antônio Pereira de Sousa Caldas (1762–1814); Cipriano José Barata de Almeida (1762–1825); José Bonifácio de Andrada e Silva, pseud. Américo Elísio (1763–1838); José Elói Otôni (1764–1851); Luís Gonçalves dos Santos, "O Pererecа" (1767–1844); Lucas José de Alvarenga (1768–1831); Frei Francisco de São Carlos (1768–1829); Silvestre Pinheiro Ferreira (1769–1846); Mariano José Pereira da Fonseca, Marquis of Maricá (1773–1848); Antônio Carlos Ribeiro de Andrada (1773–1845); Hipólito José da Costa (1774–1823); José Feliciano Fernandes Pinheiro (1774–1847); Joaquim José Lisboa (1775–1811); Manuel de Araújo Ferreira Guimarães (1777–1838); Frei Francisco de Santa Teresa de Jesus Sampaio (1778–1830);

Domingos Borges de Barros (1779–1855); Frei Joaquim do Amor Divino Caneca (1779–1825); Januário da Cunha Barbosa (1780–1846); Caetano Lopes de Moura (1780–1860); Joaquim Gonçalves Ledo (1781–1847); José Lino Coutinho (1784–1836); Frei Francisco de Mont'Alverne (1784–1859); José Rodriques Pimentel Maia (1785–1837); Frei Francisco de Xavier Baraúna (1785–1846); Dom Romualdo Antônio de Seixas (1787–1860); Father Francisco Ferreira Barreto (1790–1851); José Joaquim Machado de Oliveira (1790–1867); Miguel do Sacramento Lopes Gama (1791–1852); Cândido José de Araújo Viana (1793–1875); Francisco Muniz Tavares (1793–1876); Miguel Calmon du Pin e Almeida (1794–1865); Antônio Joaquim de Melo (1794–1873); Francisco de Montesuma (1794–1870); Bernardo Pereira de Vasconcelos (1795–1850); José da Natividade Saldanha (1796–1830); José Inácio Abreu e Lima (1796–1869); Manuel Odorico Mendes (1799–1864); Evaristo Ferreira da Veiga (1799–1837); Francisco Sotero dos Reis (1800–1871); Ladislau dos Santos Titara (1801–1861); Antônio Peregrino Maciel Monteiro (1804–1868); Francisco Muniz Barreto (1804–1868); João de Barros Falcão (1807–1882); Álvaro Teixeira de Macedo (1807–1849); Inácio Acióli de Cerqueira e Silva (1808–1865); Joaquim Caetano da Silva (1810–1873); João Salomé de Queiroga (1810–1878); Francisco de Paula Meneses (1811–1857); José Maria Velho da Silva (1811–1901); Justiniano José da Rocha (1812–1862); Antônio Augusto de Queiroga (1812?–1855); João Francisco Lisboa (1812–1863); José Maria do Amaral (1813–1885); Francisco Bernardino Ribeiro (1815–1837); Firmino Rodrigues da Silva (1816–1879); José Maria da Silva Paranhos (1819–1880); Father José Joaquim Corrêa de Almeida (1820–1905); Agostinho Marques Perdigão Malheiros (1824–1881); Manuel Joaquim Ribeiro (c. 1822); Father Silvério Ribeiro de Carvalho, called Silvino Paraopeba (?–1843).

11. Representatives of the first romantic group: Manuel de Araújo Pôrto Alegre (1806–1879); Domingos José Gonçalves de Magalhães (1811–1882); Antônio Gonçalves Teixeira e Sousa (1812–1861); Luís Carlos Martins Pena (1815–1848); Francisco Adolfo Varnhagen (1816–1878); João Manuel Pereira da Silva (1817–1898); Emílio Adet (1818–1867); Joaquim Norberto de Sousa e Silva (1820–1891); Francisco de Sales Tôrres Homem (1822–1876); Cândido M. de Azeredo Coutinho (?–1878).

12. Representatives of the second romantic group: Francisco de Paula Brito (1809–1861); João Duarte de Lisboa Serra (1818–1855); Vicente Pereira de Carvalho Guimarães (1820–?); Joaquim M. de Macedo (1820–1882); Antônio Gonçalves Dias (1823–1864); Antônio Francisco Dutra e Melo (1823–1846); Joaquim Caetano Fernandes Pinheiro (1825–1876); Bernardo Joaquim da Silva Guimarães (1825–1884); João Cardoso de Meneses, Baron of Paranapiacaba (1827–1915); Joaquim Felício dos Santos (1828–1895); José Martiniano de Alencar (1829–1877); Trajano Galvão de Carvalho (1830–1864).

13. Representatives of the third romantic group: Francisco Otaviano de

Almeida Rosa (1825–1889); Laurindo José da Silva Rabelo (1826–1864); José Bonifácio de Andrada e Silva, the Younger (1827–1886); Aureliano José Lessa (1828–1861); Luís Gonzaga Pinto da Gama (1830–1882); Antônio Joaquim Rodrigues da Costa (1830–1870); Manuel Antônio de Almeida (1831–1861); Manuel Antônio Álvares de Azevedo (1831–1852); Francisco Pinheiro Guimarães (1832–1877); José de Morais e Silva (1832–1896); Luís José Junqueira Freire (1832–1855); Vítor Meireles (1823–1903); Antônio Ferreira Viana (1833–1903); José Alexandre Teixeira de Melo (1833–1870); Agrário de Sousa Meneses (1834–1863); Quintino Bocaiúva (1836–1912); Carlos Gomes (1836–1896); Franklin de Meneses Dória (1836–1906); Juvenal Galeno da Costa e Silva (1836–1931); Júlio César Leal (1837–1897); Casimiro José Marques de Abreu (1837–1860); Francisco Inácio Marcondes Homem de Melo (1837–1918); Bruno Henrique de Almeida Seabra (1837–1876); Joaquim Maria Serra Sobrinho (1838–1888); Antônio Joaquim Macedo Soares (1838–   ); Aureliano Cândido Tavares Bastos (1839–1875); Luís Nicolau Fagundes Varela (1841–1875); José Joaquim Cândido de Macedo Jr. (1842–1860); Veríssimo José do Bom Sucesso (1842–1886).

14. Representatives of the fourth romantic group: Joaquim de Sousa Andrade, Sousândrade (1833–1902); Luís Delfino dos Santos (1834–1910); Joaquim José da França Júnior (1838–1890); Joaquim Maria Serra Sobrinho (1838–1888); Tobias Barreto de Meneses (1839–1889); Pedro Luís Pereira de Sousa (1839–1884); Joaquim Maria Machado de Assis (1839–1908); Vitoriano José Marinho Palhares (1840–1890); Salvador de Meneses Furtado de Mendonça (1841–1913); João Barbosa Rodrigues (1842–1909); João Franklin da Silveira Távora (1842–1888); José Carlos do Patrocínio (1842–1905); Pedro Américo (1843–1905); Alfredo d'Escragnole Taunay (1843–1890); Apolinário Pôrto-Alegre (1844–1904); Rosendo Muniz Barreto (1845–1897); Júlio César Ribeiro (1845–1890); Luís Caetano Pereira Guimarães Jr. (1847?–1898); Antônio de Castro Alves (1847–1871); Pedro de Calasans (1837–1874); Melo Morais Filho (1844–1919).

15. On Brazilian romanticism, its characteristics and meaning, see among others: C. Alves, "A Sensibilidade Romântica," *Revista da Academia de Letras*, No. 73, 1928. Mário de Andrade, *O Aleijadinho e Álvares de Azevedo*, Rio de Janeiro, R. A. Editôra, 1935. J. Andrade Murici, "Elógio do Romantismo Brasileiro," *Suave Convívio*, Rio de Janeiro, Anuário do Brasil, 1922. Manuel Bandeira, Preface to *Antologia dos Poetas Brasileiros da Fase Romântica*, 3rd ed., Rio de Janeiro, Instituto Nacional do Livro, 1949. *Idem, Apresentação da Poesia Brasileira*, Rio de Janeiro, C.E.B., 1946. C. Beviláqua, "Esbôço Sintético do Movimento Romântico Brasileiro, *Esbôços e Individualidades*, Rio de Janeiro, Garnier, 1888. J. Capistrano de Abreu, *Ensaios e Estudos*, 1st series, Rio de Janeiro, Briguiet, 1931. R. de Carvalho, *Pequena História da Literatura Brasileira*, Rio de Janeiro, Briguiet, 1919 (ref. 4th ed., Rio de Janeiro, Briguiet, 1929). V. Côrtes de Lacerda, *Unidades Literárias*, São Paulo, Cia. Editôra Nacional, 1944. J. C. Fernandes

Pinheiro, *Literatura Nacional,* Rio de Janeiro, Garnier, 1893. P. Hazard, "As Origens do Romantismo no Brasil," *Revista da Academia Brasileira de Letras,* No. 69, 1927. P. Henríquez Ureña, *Literary Currents in Latin America,* Cambridge, Harvard, 1945. F. Magalhães, "O Romantismo Liberal," *Revista da Academia Brasileira de Letras,* No. 69, 1927. C. Monteiro, *Traços do Romantismo na Poesia Brasileira,* Rio de Janeiro, 1929. A. Orlando, "Teorias Literárias no Brasil," *Filocrítica,* Rio de Janeiro, Garnier, 1886. H. Paranhos, *História do Romantismo no Brasil,* 2 vols., São Paulo, Cultura Brasileira, 1937–1938. Afrânio Peixoto, "O Romantismo e seu Significado," *Pepitas,* São Paulo, Cia. Editôra Nacional, 1942. *Idem, Noções de História da Literatura Brasileira,* Rio de Janeiro, Alves, 1931. S. Putnam, *Marvelous Journey,* New York, Knopf, 1948. S. Romero, *História da Literatura Brasileira,* Rio de Janeiro, Garnier, 1888. J. Veríssimo, *História da Literatura Brasileira,* Rio de Janeiro, Alves, 1916. F. Wolf, *O Brasil Literário,* Brazilian edition, São Paulo, Cia. Editôra Nacional, 1955.

16. Afrânio Peixoto considers José Bonifácio as the "father of romanticism" more than a "scholar, politician, statesman, poet, the greatest and most cultured Brazilian of his time." *História da Literatura Brasileira,* pp. 154, 177. The same author propounds the theory of the precedence of José Bonifâcio, with his poems of 1825, in relation to Magalhães (1836). He states that the *Poesias* of Américo Elísio is "the first book in Brazil that subscribed to romanticism" (See "O Primeiro Livro do Romantismo no Brasil," the preface to the *Poesias,* Rio de Janeiro, Publicações da Academia Brasileira, 1942.). It seems more correct to attribute to José Bonifácio the position of a preromantic precursor, in light of the very arguments of Afrânio Peixoto, because, in spite of his romantic tendencies, he was faithful to the classical credo (See S. Buarque de Holanda, preface to the *Poesias* of Américo Elísio, Rio de Janeiro, Instituto Nacional do Livro, 1942, p. xiii.). This position of transition—Arcadism, neoclassicism, preromanticism—is the one which José Bonifácio best fits, not simply because of his poetical production, but also because of his poetical doctrine. It was what Antônio Soares Amora has shown further in his two articles: "Um *Alter Ego* Comprometedor," and "Américo Elísio Desagravado," *Estado de São Paulo,* Suplemento Literário, March 30, 1963, and April 27, 1963. Josué Montello also puts himself in a position of understanding with respect to the poetry of the patriarch, stressing his character of syncretism and transition, as he recognizes all the while its documentary value as an interpretation of his personality (See "O Poeta José Bonifácio," *Jornal do Comércio,* Rio de Janeiro, July 11, 18, 25, 1964.).

17. "As we reduce the history of the national novel, from Teixeira e Sousa and Escragnole Taunay to a general law of evolution, we shall see that in its first phase, that is, with *O Filho do Pescador,* the *Romances e Novelas* (Norberto), and other inferior productions, there was a predominance of local character, merely descriptive, without other preoccupations that did not arise out of the author's fantasy; in the second phase, with *A Moreninha*

and *O Guarani*, there is already the sketch of a feeling of a thesis, the style becomes smoother, the narration becomes more complicated; finally, in the third and last phase, with the *Memórias de um Sargento de Milícias, A Escrava Isaura, O Cabeleira*, and *Inocência* one can perceive a movement of reaction against the purely idealistic genre, a construction of types and scenes is more evident, reality passes on to the first level, as much in the description of scenes as in that of characters, and there is already a hint of the psychological intentions of Machado de Assis and Aluízio de Azevedo.

"Two tendencies, however, were dominant during the romantic period: the back country or Indianist ruralism of Alencar and the anecdotal, descriptive, or realistic tendency of Machado. The national novel took place within them, dividing itself between forest and city, among Indian, mixed-blood, peasant, middle-class bourgeois, business man, civil servant, and military man. We still had not come to know either the ironical doubt of a Dom Casmurro or the amoral paradoxes of a Brás Cubas." Ronald de Carvalho, *Pequena História da Literatura Brasileira*, 4th ed., Rio de Janeiro, Briguiet, 1929, p. 293.

18. Machado de Assis, Chronicle of December 25, 1892, *A Semana*, Rio de Janeiro, Garnier, 1910, p. 40.

19. T. M. Greene, *The Arts and the Art of Criticism*, p. 386.

REALISM, NATURALISM, PARNASSIANISM

1. See Ogden and Goldenweiser, *The Social Sciences and Their Interrelations*, Boston, 1927. H. E. Barnes, editor, *The History and Prospects of Social Sciences*, New York, 1925.

2. F. de Azevedo, *A Cultura Brasileira*, p. 212.

3. See J. Barreira, *História da Literatura Cearense*, Fortaleza, 1948.

4. See S. Romero, *História da Literatura Brasileira*, 5 vols., 5th ed. Rio de Janeiro, 1954. H. Lima, *Tobias Barreto*, São Paulo, 1939. C. Beviláqua, *História da Faculdade de Direito de Recife*, 2 vols., Rio de Janeiro, 1927. J. Veríssimo, *História da Literatura Brasileira*, Rio de Janeiro, 1916.

5. See J. Veríssimo, *História da Literatura Brasileira*. S. Vampré, *Memórias para a História da Academia de S. Paulo*, São Paulo, 1924. G. Muniz, *A Medicina na Bahia*, Salvador, 1922. *Idem, Memória Histórica da Faculdade de Medicina da Bahia*, Salvador, 1940.

6. See J. Veríssimo, *História da Literatura Brasileira*, p. 343. F. de Figueiredo, *História da Literatura Realista*, Lisbon, 1914. Forjaz de Sampaio, A. M. P., *História da Literatura Portuguêsa Ilustrada*, Vol. IV, Oporto, p. 185.

7. See J. M. Macedo, *A Moreninha*, Prefâcio de Antônio Cândido, São Paulo, Liv. Martins, 1952 (Biblioteca de Literatura Brasileira, No. 7).

REGIONALISM IN PROSE FICTION

1. G. Stewart, "The Regional Approach to Literature," *College English*, April 1948.

2. H. W. Odum and H. E. Moore, *American Regionalism*, New York, 1938. *Regionalism in Transition*, offprint from *Social Forces*, 1942–1943.

3. B. A. Botkin, "Regionalism: Cult or Culture?" *English Journal*, XXV, No. 3, March 1936.

4. See Viana Moog, *Uma Interpretação da Literatura Brasileira*, Rio de Janeiro, 1943.

5. See especially G. Freyre, *Região e Tradição*, Rio de Janeiro, 1941. *Idem, Continente e Ilha*, Rio de Janeiro, 1943. *Idem, Manifesto Regionalista de 1926*, Recife, 1952.

SYMBOLISM, IMPRESSIONISM, MODERNISM

1. Araripe Júnior, *Movimento de 1893: O Crepúsculo dos Povos*, Rio de Janeiro, Tipografia da Emprêsa Democrática Editôra, 1896.

2. Araripe Júnior, *Movimento*, pp. 151–52. The reading of these pages is quite worthwhile, an eloquent testimony of superior criticism.

3. Eugênio Gomes, "À Margem de *Esaú e Jacó*," *Correio da Manhã*, Oct. 5, 19, 1957; reprinted in *Machado de Assis*, Rio de Janeiro, Liv. São José, 1958.

4. See Afrânio Coutinho, *A Filosofia de Machado de Assis*, Rio de Janeiro, Vecchi, 1940, pp. 192–96; new edition, Rio de Janeiro, Liv. São José, 1959.

5. The following works stand out on the problem of the symbol in literature: *Art and Symbol*, special number, *The Kenyon Review*, Summer, 1953, Vol. XV, No. 3. R. P. Basler, *Sex, Symbolism, and Psychology in Literature*, New Brunswick, 1948. M. Bodkin, *Archetypal Patterns in Poetry*, Oxford, 1934. E. Caillet, *Symbolisme et ames primitives*, Paris, 1936. E. Cassirer, *The Philosophy of Symbolic Forms*, 3 vols., Princeton, 1953–1958. J. Delanglade, H. Schmalenbach, P. Godet, and J. L. Leuba, *Signe et symbole*, Neufchatel, 1946. C. Feidelson, *Symbolism and American Literature*, Chicago, 1953. M. Foss, *Symbol and Metaphor in Human Experience*, Princeton, 1949. N. Fry, *Anatomy of Criticism*, Princeton, 1957. S. K. Langer, *Philosophy in a New Key*, Cambridge, Massachusetts, 1942. *Idem, Feeling and Form*, London, 1953. M. Loeffler-Delachaux, *Le Symbolisme des contes de fées*, Paris, 1949. *Idem, Le Symbolisme des légendes*, Paris, 1950. J. Maritain, *Quatre essais sur l'esprit*, Paris, 1939. *Symbol and Symbolism* (a symposium), *Yale French Studies*, No. 9. *Symbolism and Values: An Initial Study* (a symposium), New York, 1954. *Symbolism and Creative Imagination* (special number), *The Journal of Aesthetics and Art Criticism*, Vol. XII, No. 1, September 1953. W. Y. Tindall, *The Literary Symbol*, New York, 1955. *Polarité du symbole* (special number), *Études Carmélitaines*, Paris, Desclée, 1960. H. A. Murray, editor, *Myth and Mythmaking*, New York, Braziller, 1960. B. Slote, editor, *Myth and Symbol*, Lincoln, Nebraska, 1963.

6. "After 1890 the word 'decadence' loses its suggestive note and people

begin to speak of 'symbolism' as the leading artistic trend." A. Hauser, *The Social History of Art*, Vol. II, p. 895.

But it is from 1885 and after the manifesto of *Figaro Littéraire*, on Sept. 18, 1886, that we have the date of the change in names at the suggestion of Moréas, in reply to an article by Paul Bourdée, "Les Décadentes," in which the latter characterized the "decadents" as perverted, using mysticism, satanism, morphinomania in order to reach the morbid state from which literary creation would emerge. Concerning the origin of the term see: K. Cornell, *The Symbolist Movement*, p. 41; J. Chiari, *Symbolism from Poe to Mallarmé*, p. 60; G. Michaud, *Méssage poétique du symbolisme*, Vol. IV, p. 99.

7. Concerning this see Cornell, *The Symbolist Movement*, Chapter I.

8. *Ibid.*, p. 2.

9. *Ibid.*, p. 5.

10. J. Chiari, *Symbolism from Poe to Mallarmé*, Chapter II.

11. *Ibid.*, pp. 41–42.

12. A. Hauser, *The Social History of Art*, pp. 888 ff.

13. C. M. Bowra, *The Heritage of Symbolism*, New York, 1943.

14. A. Hauser, *The Social History of Art*, Vol. II, p. 896.

15. A. Hibbard, *Writers of the Western World*.

16. E. Wilson, *Axel's Castle*, New York, 1942, p. 25.

17. Oto Maria Carpeaux, *Origens e Fins*, Rio de Janeiro, 1942, p. 313.

18. Carpeaux, "Uma Crítica do Simbolismo," *O Jornal*, Rio de Janeiro, May 24, 1953.

19. Carpeaux, *Origens e Fins*, p. 327.

20. The fundamental source and outline for the study of Brazilian symbolism, where the rehabilitation of the movement is definitively reached in critical terms is: J. Andrade Murici, *Panorama do Movimento Simbolista Brasileiro*, 3 vols., Rio de Janeiro, Instituto Nacional do Livro, 1952.

Other studies worthy of consultation: T. A. Araripe Júnior, *Movimento de 1893: O Crepúsculo dos Povos*, Rio de Janeiro, 1896. R. Bastide, *A Poesia Afro-Brasileira*, São Paulo, 1943. O. M. Carpeaux, *Origens e Fins*, Rio de Janeiro, 1943, pp. 313–38. Frota Pessoa, *Crítica e Polêmica*, Rio de Janeiro, 1902. J. A. Murici, "Curso Sôbre a Estética do Simbolismo e o Movimento Simbolista no Brasil," *Revista da Universidade do Rio de Janeiro*, II, No. 3.

21. The first group, the oldest, was the inaugural one, gathered around Emiliano Perneta on the *Fôlha Popular*: Emiliano Perneta (1866–1921), Cruz e Sousa (1861–1898), B. Lopes (1859–1916), Oscar Rosas (1861–1925), Virgílio Várzea (1862–1941), Artur de Miranda (1869–), Gonzaga Duque (1863–1911), José Henrique de Santa Rita (1872–1914), Alves de Faria (1871–1899), Lima Campos (1872–1920).

The second group gathered around Cruz e Sousa: Carlos D. Fernandes (1875–1942), Tibúrcio de Freitas (?–1918), Nestor Vítor (1868–1932), Maurício Jubin (1875–1923), Artur de Miranda.

The third group, meeting until the death of Cruz e Sousa (1898), was made up of: Cruz e Sousa, Nestor Vítor, Tibúrcio de Freitas, Maurício Jubin.

With the death of Cruz e Sousa, his followers divided into two opposing groups: that of the magazine *Rosa-Cruz*, made up of: Saturnino de Meireles (1878–1906), Félix Pacheco (1879–1910), Maurício Jubin, Carlos D. Fernandes, Gonçalo Jácome (1875–1943), Narciso Araújo (1876–1944), Pereira da Silva (1876–1944), Paulo Araújo (1883–1918), Cassiano Tavares Bastos (1885–?), Castros Meneses (1883–1920).

The other group, headed by Nestor Vítor, was made up of: Tibúrcio de Freitas, Rocha Pombo (1857–1933), Gustavo Santiago (1872–?), Oliveira Gomes (1872–1917), Colatino Barroso (1873–1931), Silveira Neto (1872–1942), Neto Machado, Antônio Austregésilo (1876–1960), Carlos Fróis, Artur de Miranda.

Lastly, the group which founded the magazine *Fon-Fon*: Gonzaga Duque, Mário Pederneiras (1868–1915), Lima Campos, to whom are joined the neosymbolists of Rio Grande do Sul Eduardo Guimarães (1892–1928), Álvaro Moreira (1888), Felipe d'Oliveira (1891–1932).

In Curitiba, the group of the *Cenáculo*: Dario Veloso (1869–1937), Silveira Neto, Júlio Perneta (1869–), Antônio Braga, J. Itiberê (1870–).

In São Paulo, around Adolfo Araújo and *A Gazeta*: Alphonsus de Guimarães (1870–1921), Father Severiano de Resende (1871–1931), Viana do Castelo, Freitas Vale (1870–1958), Adolfo Araújo (1875–1915).

In Belo Horizonte, the group of the "Pilgrims of the Ideal": Álvaro Viana (1882–1936), Viana do Castelo, Horácio Guimarães, Alfredo de Sarandi Rapôso, Carlos Rapôso, Eduardo Cerqueira, Batista Santiago, Edgard Mata (1878–1907), Archangelus de Guimarães (1872–1934).

In Bahia, the groups of the *Nova Cruzada* and the *Anais*: Álvaro Reis (1880–1932), Pedro Kilkerry (1885–1917), Pethion de Vilar (1870–1924), Francisco Mangabeira (1879–1904), Domingues de Almeida (1888–?), Galdino de Castro (1882–1939), and, later, Durval de Morais (1882–1948), Artur de Sales (1879–1952), Carlos Chiacchio (1884–1947).

In Rio Grande do Sul: Eduardo Guimarães, Álvaro Moreira, Marcelo Gama (1878–1915), Filipe d'Oliveira, Homero Prates (1890–), Alceu Wamosy (1895–1923).

This outline is taken from Andrade Murici, *Panorama do Movimento Simbolista Brasileiro*, III, pp. 298–300. In the same place there is a vocabulary of themes, types, and legends, a liturgical vocabulary, and a glossary of typical terms of symbolism, which brings into relief the techniques of Brazilian symbolist style.

22. The name impressionism comes from the title of the painting *Impression*, by Claude Monet, exhibited in 1874. With the book by Louis Duranty, *Les Peintres impressionistes* (1878), the designation became official. Thus, coming from painting, the term spread out into other artistic forms that had been touched by the movement.

23. On impressionism in literature, see the following studies: A. Alecrim, "A Técnica da Prosa Impressionista," *Cultura*, Rio de Janeiro, No. 4, December 1954. C. Bally, E. Richter, A. Alonso, and R. Lida, *El impresionismo en el lenguajae*, Buenos Aires, 1942. J. W. Beach, *The Twentieth Century Novel*, New York, 1932. F. Brunetière, *Le Roman naturaliste*, Paris, 1883. E. Carter, *Howells and the Age of Realism*, Philadelphia, 1954. M. E. Chermovitz, *Proust and Painting*, New York, 1945. B. J. Gibbs, "Impressionism as a Literary Movement," *The Modern Language Journal*, XXXVI, April 4, 1952. H. Hatzfeld, *Literature through Art*, Oxford, 1952. A. Hauser, *The Social History of Art*, 2 vols., London, 1951. A. Hibbard, *Writers of the Western World*, Boston, 1942. R. Moser, *L'Impressionisme français*, Geneva, 1952. R. Ricatte, *La Création romanesque chez les Goncourt*, Paris, 1953. P. Sabatier, *L'Esthetique des Goncourt*, Paris, 1920. P. Tyler, "The Impressionism of M. Proust," *Kenyon Review*, Winter 1946; W. Falk, *Impresionismo y expresionismo*, Madrid, Ed. Guadarrama, 1963.

24. Alonso and Lida, *Impresionismo en el lenguaje*, Buenos Aires, 1942. See also the study by B. J. Gibbs referred to above.

25. "The experience represented can be impressionistic, but not the experience of representing it and expressing it, which we call idiomatic form." Alonso and Lida, *Impresionismo*.

26. A. Hauser, *The Social History of Art*, II, 883.

27. Gilberto Amado, *Minha Formação no Recife*, Rio de Janeiro, 1955, p. 355; and *Grão de Areia*, Rio de Janeiro, 1948, p. 170.

28. A. Soares Amora, *Históra da Literatura Brasiléira*, São Paulo, 1955, p. 12.

29. Araripe Júnior, "Cantos Populares do Ceará: A Propósito do Livro do Sr. Sílvio Romero," *Gazeta Literária*, Rio de Janeiro, March 31, 1884. See *Obra Crítica de Araripe Júnior*, Vol. I, Rio de Janeiro, 1958.

30. On this question see Araripe Júnior, *Movimento de 1893: O Crepúsculo dos Povos*, Rio de Janeiro, 1896. The quotations are from chapters I and II. See *Obra Crítica de Araripe Júnior*, Vol. III, Rio de Janeiro, 1963.

31. Araripe Júnior, *Don Martín García Merou*, Rio de Janeiro, 1895, prefácio, p. ii; *idem, Obra Crítica*, Vol. III.

32. On various occasions, Araripe Júnior expounds this law of *obnubilação brasílica*, a theory of his own to explain the genesis of the differentiation and originality of Brazilian life and character, and consequently that of their history and literature. Along these lines see: *Gregório de Matos*, Rio de Janeiro, 1894, pp. 37 and 179; *idem*, "Literatura Brasileira," *A Semana*, No. 154, December 10, 1887; *idem, Obra Crítica*, Vol. III.

33. The two quotes from Araripe Júnior belong to: *Don Martín García Merou*, and *Gazeta Literária*.

34. Tristão de Ataíde, "O Incrível Sexagenário," *Jornal do Brasil*, Rio de Janeiro, March 16, 1958.

35. See in this respect: B. Crémieux, *Inquiétude et reconstruction*, Paris, 1931; Daniel-Rops, *Notre inquiétude*, Paris, 1927; idem, *Carte d'Europe*, Paris, 1928.

36. "To the desire for pure knowledge, there is opposed the desire for a knowledge which at the same time can be a direction of life: religious values, esthetic values, moral values, social values, heroism and revolt, the cult of the self or the cult of 'the land and the dead'—values of life more important than 'the relations of similarity and succession' among things." Gaetan Picon, *Encyclopédie de la Pléiade: Histoire des littératures*, Vol. II, Paris, 1958, p. 190.

37. Crémieux, *Inquiétude et reconstruction*, pp. i–v.

38. See Guillermo de Torre, *Literaturas europes de vanguardia*, Madrid, 1925.

39. For greater detail concerning expressionism in modern art and literature, see the following studies: J. Warren Beach, *The Twentieth Century Novel*, New York. S. Cheney, *A Primer of Modern Art*, New York, 1932. F. W. Chandler, *Modern Continental Playwrights*, New York, 1931. J. E. Cirlot, *Diccionario de los Ismos*, Barcelona, 1949. C. Dahlstrom, *Strindberg's Dramatic Expressionism*, New York, 1930. L. Riding, and R. Graves, *A Survey of Modernist Poetry*, London, 1927. J. T. Shipley, editor, *Dictionary of World Literature*, New York, 1943. *Idem, Trends in Literature*, New York, 1949. W. Falk, *Impresionismo y expresionismo*, Madrid, 1963.

40. On the modern spirit, see, among others, the following studies: C. Baudoin, *Le Mythe du moderne*, Geneva, 1945. N. Berdiaeff, *Destin de l'homme dans le monde actuel*, Paris, 1936. B. Crémieux, *Inquiétude et reconstruction*, Paris, 1931. Daniel-Rops, *Notre inquiétude*, Paris, 1927. *Idem, Le Monde sans Âme*, Paris, 1932. *La Formation de l'homme moderne*, Entretins de Génève, No. 5, Paris, 1935. H. Keyserling, *La Révolution mondiale*, Paris, 1934. *Idem, El mundo que nace*, Madrid, 1930. J. W. Krutch, *The Modern Temper*, New York, 1933. L. Romier, *L'homme nouveau*, Paris, 1929. F. Strowski, *L'homme moderne*, Paris, 1931.

41. A. Hibbard, *Writers of the Western World*, pp. 1128–235.

42. G. Picon, *Encyclopédie de la Pléiade*, pp. 210–11.

43. Selden Rodman, *A New Anthology of Modern Poetry*, New York, 1938, pp. 23–24.

44. The bibliography on Modern Art Week and the modernist movement is vast and scattered. There is a good bibliography of modernist works in the volume *Modernismo: Estudos Críticos*, Org. Saldanha Coelho, Rio de Janeiro, Revista Branca, 1954.

The following list of studies is not absolutely complete. One must refer to the works of critics of the period, Tristão de Ataíde, Mário de Andrade, Sérgio Milliet, Sérgio Buarque de Holanda, Álvaro Lins, Antônio Cândido, et al. One should consult the bibliography on the great figures in modernist fiction and poetry. Consult also the book of Oto Maria Carpeaux, *Pequena Bibliografia Crítica da Literatura Brasileira*, and see especially Mário da Silva Brito, *História do Modernismo Brasileiro*, São Paulo, 1958.

Almir de Andrade, *Aspectos da Cultura Brasileira*, Rio de Janeiro, 1939. Carlos Drummond de Andrade, "Aquêles Rapazes de Belo Horizonte," *Correio da Manhã*, Rio de Janeiro, July 6, 13, 1952. Mário Andrade, *O Movimento Modernista*, Rio de Janeiro, C.E.B., 1942. *Idem, O Empalhador de Passarinho*, São Paulo, Martins, n. d. Oswald de Andrade Letters to the *Jornal do Comércio*, São Paulo, February 1922; Manuel Anselmo, *Família Literária Luso-Brasileira*, Rio de Janeiro, 1943. Murilo Araújo, "Evolução e Revolução Modernistas," *Jornal do Comércio*, Rio de Janeiro, May 10, 1953. Manuel Bandeira, "O Modernismo Brasileiro," *Jornal do Comércio*, Rio de Janeiro, March 10, 1940. *Idem, Apresentação da Poesia Brasileira*, Rio de Janeiro, C.E.B., 1957: *Idem, Itinerário de Pasárgada*, Rio de Janeiro, 1957. Antônio Bento, "As Artes Plásticas e a Semana de 1922," *Diário Carioca*, Rio de Janeiro, April 27, 1952. Brito Broca, "Salões e Ambientes do Modernismo," *Letras e Artes*, supl. of *A Manhã*, Rio de Janeiro, February 3, 1952. *Idem*, "A Semana da Arte Moderna," *Letras e Artes*, supl. of *A Manhã*, Rio de Janeiro, February 10, 1952. *Idem*, "A Margem do Modernismo," *Letras e Artes*, supl. of *A Manhã*, Rio de Janeiro, February 17, 1952. *Idem*, "Quando Teria Começado o Modernismo," *Letras e Artes*, supl. of *A Manhã*, Rio de Janeiro, July 20, 1952; Sérgio Buarque de Holanda, *Cobra de Vidro*, São Paulo, Martins, 1944. *Idem*, "Em tôrno da Semana," *Diário Carioca*, Rio de Janeiro, February 17, 1952. *Idem*, "Depois da Semana," *ibid.*, February 25, March 3, 9, 1952. Antônio Cândido, *Brigada Ligeira*, São Paulo, Martins n. d. Oto Maria Carpeaux, *Origens e Fins*, Rio de Janeiro, 1943. Manuel T. de Carvalho, "Alguns Aspectos da Poesia Moderna," *Personalidade*, November 1946. Ronald de Carvalho, *Espelho de Ariel*, Rio de Janerio, 1923. *Idem, Estudos Brasileiros*, 3rd series, Rio de Janeiro, 1930–1931. José Aderaldo Castello, "Uma Definição do Modernismo," *O Estado de São Paulo*, March 9, 1957. Povina Cavalcânti, *Auséndia da Poesia*, Rio de Janeiro, 1943. Edgard Cavalheiro, *Testamento de uma Geração*, Pôrto Alegre, Globo, 1944. Carlos Chiacchio, *Modernistas e Ultramodernistas*, Bahia, Progresso, 1951. "Como Nasceu o Modernismo no Brasil?" *Jornal de Letras*, Rio de Janeiro, May 1950. Roberto Alvim Correia, *Anteu e a Crítica*, Rio de Janeiro, 1948. *Idem, O Mito de Prometeu*, Rio de Janeiro, 1951. Fausto Cunha, "O Movimento de 22," *A Manhã*, Rio de Janeiro, June 19, 1949. Pedro Dantas, and W. Lousada, "Modernismo: Romances e Idéias," *Cultura Politica*, Rio de Janeiro, No. 1 ff. *Idem*, "Meninos, Eu Vi," *Jornal de Letras*, Rio de Janeiro, May 1952. Eneida, "1922: Revolução Modernista," interview with Di Cavalcanti *Jornal de Letras*, Rio de Janeiro, February 1952. *Idem*, "No Trigésimo Aniversário da Semana de Arte Moderna," *Diário de Notícias*, Rio de Janeiro, February 10, 17, March 2, 1952. *Idem*, "Na Infância do Modernismo," *Diário Carioca*, Rio de Janeiro, February 10, 1952. "Um Escandaloso Tumulto na Academia,"

Letras e Artes, supl. of *A Manhã*, Rio de Janeiro, February 12, 1950. Hugo de Figueiredo, "Retrolâmpago do Modernismo," *Correio da Manhã*, Rio de Janeiro, March 8, 15, 1952. Augusto Fragoso, "Breve História da Semana de Arte Moderna em 1922," *Jornal do Comércio*, Rio de Janeiro, February 17, 1952. Antônio França, "O Modernismo Brasileiro," *Diário de Notícias*, Rio de Janeiro, December 3, 1944. Gilberto Freyre, "Modernismo e Suas Relações com Outros Ismos," *O Jornal*, Rio de Janeiro, June 29, 1952. Rosário Fusco, *Vida Literária*, São Paulo, 1940. *Idem, Política e Letras*, Rio de Janeiro, 1940. Graça Aranha, *O Espírito Moderno*, São Paulo, 1932. "Graça Aranha Defendido dentro da Própria Academia," *Letras e Artes*, supl. of *A Manhã*, Rio de Janeiro, March 5, 1950. Agripino Grieco, *Caçadores de Símbolos*, Rio de Janeiro, 1923. *Idem, Vivos e Mortos*, Rio de Janeiro, 1931. *Idem, Gente Nova do Brasil*, Rio de Janeiro, 1935. Vera Pacheco Jordão, "Há alguma Analogia entre Modernismo e Romantismo?" *Corréio da Manhã*, Rio de Janeiro, August 9, 1952. *Lanterna Verde*, special number, Rio de Janeiro, November 1936 (articles by: Afonso Arinos, Gilberto Freyre, Jorge de Lima, Lúcia Miguel-Pereira, Manuel de Abreu, Murilo Mendes, Otávio de Faria, Renato Almeida, Tristão de Ataíde, Filipe de Oliveira). Múcio Leão, "Roteiro de Duas Gerações," *Autores e Livros*, Rio de Janeiro, IV, No. 6, March 21, 1943. "Lembrando a Semana de Arte Moderna," *Jornal de Letras*, Rio de Janeiro, February 1957. "Letras Brasileras" *Ficción*, special number on Brazilian literature, Buenos Aires, February, 1958. Alceu Amoroso Lima, *Quadro Sintético da Literatura Brasileira*, Rio de Janeiro, Agir, 1956. *Idem*, "O Premodernismo," "O Modernismo," "O Posmodernismo," *O Jornal*, Rio de Janeiro, December 4, 11, 19, 1938. *Idem*, "Ano Zero" *Diário de Notícias*, Rio de Janeiro, August 24, 31, 1952. *Idem, Contribuição à História do Modernismo, I, O Premodernismo*, Rio de Janeiro, José Olympio, 1939. *Idem, Estudos*, 5th series, Rio de Janeiro, 1929–1933. *Idem, Primeiros Estudos*, Rio de Janeiro, Agir, 1948. Álvaro Lins, *Jornal de Crítica*, 6th series, Rio de Janeiro, J. Olympio, 1941–1951. Wilson Martins, *Interpretações*, Rio de Janeiro, J. Olympio, 1946. Lúcia Miguel-Pereira, *Cinqüenta Anos de Literatura*, Rio de Janeiro, M.E.C., 1952 (Cal. Cultura). *Idem*, "Tendências e Repercussões Literárias do Modernismo," *Cultura*, Rio de Janeiro, M.E.C., No. 5). Sérgio Milliet, *Ensaios*, São Paulo, Brusco, 1935. *Idem, Diário Crítico*, 9 vols., São Paulo, 1943–1957. *Modernismo: Estudos Críticos*, Org. Saldanha Coelho, Rio de Janeiro, Revista Branca, 1954 (a reproduction of the special number dedicated to the thirtieth anniversary of *modernismo; Revista Branca*, Rio de Janeiro, May and June, 1952). J. Andrade Murici, *A Nova Literatura Brasileira*, Pôrto Alegre, Globo, 1936. Mário Neme, *Plataforma ad Nova Geração*, Pôrto Alegre, Globo, 1945. Peregrino Júnior, *O Movimento Modernista*, Rio de Janeiro, M.E.C., 1954 (*Cadernos de Cultura*, No. 69). "Quem Foi o Dono da Semana?" *Diretrizes*, Rio de Janeiro, June 17, 24, 1943. "Inquérito sôbre Modernismo," *Revista do Brasil*, Rio de Janeiro, March 1940. Cassiano Ricardo, "Discurso de Recepção a Menotti del Picchia," *Discurso Acadêmico*, Vol. XI, Rio de Janeiro, 1944. Tadeu Rolha, "O Modernismo na Província," *O Jornal*, Rio de Janeiro, August 31, September 7, 14, October 19, 1952. "A Semana da Arte Moderna," *Letras e Artes*, supl. of *A Manhã*, Rio de Janeiro, February 5, 1950. Homero Sena, *República das Letras*, Rio de Janeiro, 1932. *Idem*, "Tradicionalismo Dinâmico, o Sentido do Grupo de *Festa*," *Jornal de Letras*, Rio de Janeiro, May 1952. Silveira Peixoto, *Falam os Escritores*, 2 vols., São Paulo, 1940–1941. René Thiollier, "Depoimento Inédito sôbre a Semana de Arte Moderna," *Habitat*, No. 12, São Paulo. "Trigésimo Aniversário da Semana de Arte Moderna: Série de Reportagens com Escritores," *Diário Carioca*, Rio de Janeiro, February 10 (Manuel Bandeira), March 2 (Renato Almeida), March 9 (Lasar Segall), March 16 (Augusto Meyer), March 30 (Cassiano Ricardo), April 6 (Rosário Fusco, Ian Almeida Prado), April 13 (Guilherme de Almeida), April 20 (Augusto Frederico Schmidt), May 4 (Peregrino Júnior), May 11 (Rodrigo M. F. Andrade), May 18 (Américo Facó), May 25 (Pedro Dantas), 1952. "Trinta Anos de Modernismo no Brasil: Série de Reportagens com Intelectuais," *Tribuna das Letras*, supl. of *Tribuna da Imprensa*, Rio de Janeiro, February 9–10 (Lourival Gomes Machado), February 16–17 (Prudente de Morais Neto), 1952. Moisés Velinho, *Letras da Província*, Pôrto Alegre, Globo, 1944. *Idem*, *O Estado de São Paulo*, February 2 and April 14, 1962.

45. See Veríssimo, *História da Literatura Brasileira*, 1916 ed., Chapter XV. Veríssimo says there: "These ideas, not always coherent, sometimes even incompatible with those pointed out, we shall call modern, an expression of 'modern thought' " (p. 338).

46. See the chapter "A Revolução Modernista" of *A Literatura no Brasil*, Vol. III.

47. The little or no sympathy on the part of the modernists for Marinetti is reflected in the lack of attention and catcalls given him during his trip to Rio de Janeiro and São Paulo in 1926. In a letter, Mário de Andrade gave the following impression of him: "Lacking in vivacity, maniacal, a bad reader, a shouter, and most Italianly 'francesescabertini,' still repeating the same things that he has been saying since 1900, thus giving the impression of a person reciting by rote."

In an interview in 1952, Cassiano Riccardo remembers how from the beginning there was a group of those who disagreed with the initial tendency of the movement "that smelled of futurism. A futurism imported with the same methods, the same hooting, etc." And he goes on: "Marinetti, in Brazil, could only be a personage who worships the past, a mere item of importation, nothing but a copy of European 'isms.' We wanted, those in the group and I, an art that would be genuinely Brazilian and still would reflect the sign of the times." Cassiano Ricardo, *Diário Carioca*, Rio de Janeiro, March 30, 1952.

As a presentation of the doctrinary aspect, the most important reaction of the period to futurism was that of Tristão de Ataíde in an article entitled "Marinetti," and included in *Estudos,* 1st series, Rio de Janeiro, 1927.

48. "And also the name 'futurists,' which very few accepted in the early days and did not take long to reject. The only one, if I remember correctly, who some years after the Week I still saw admitting willingly to the label imported from Marinetti's Italy was Graça Aranha. Not that the author of the *Estética da Vida* found any particular affinity between his own doctrines and those preached by the famous buffoon. It was just that the word 'futurism' seemed singularly apt for the optimistic philosophy that Graça Aranha would have liked to have seen embraced by all of the adepts of the renovating movement." Sérgio Buarque de Holanda, "Em Tôrno da Semana," *Diário Carioca,* Rio de Janeiro, February 17, 1952.

"Bad faith comes crawling along and I must publicly kill the word 'futurism.' It is time. Whoever has gone along with the campaign for esthetic renovation, and I have been doing that for nearly a year in São Paulo, alongside the eminent spirits of Menotti del Picchia and Mário de Andrade, would see that a dozen times at least we have rejected the strict meaning of the term 'futurism,' giving it, when we have used it, either a broad and universal meaning that took in the whole modern revolution in the arts, or the São Paulo meaning, innovation within our closed provincial ranks. In one case or the other, we cannot bear any longer the idiotic blemish given us by certain hacks who like to call us F. T. Marinetti's bandit gang. That we are not. What we well might have been [. . . before the return of Graça Aranha and before the merger with the intellectuals and artists of Rio] was 'São Paulo futurists,' very personal and independent, not only of the petty dogmas of Marinettism but of all mean little yokes. Futurists only because we are aiming towards a constructive future, in opposition to the melodramatic decadence of the past on which we did not wish to depend. . . . To call us futurists still is to change criticism into mule kicks, discussion into hairy cretinism." Oswald de Andrade, letter to the *Jornal do Comércio,* São Paulo, February 19, 1922. See also Augusto Fragoso, "Breve História da Semana de Arte Moderna em 1922," *Jornal do Comércio,* Rio de Janeiro, February 17, 1952.

49. On Spanish and Spanish-American modernism see: J. Chabas, *Literatura española contemporánea (1898–1950),* Havana, 1952. G. Díaz-Plaja, *Modernismo frente a noventa y ocho,* Madrid, 1951. Luis Alberto Sánchez, *Balance y liquidación del novecientos,* Santiago de Chile, 1941. Max Henríquez Ureña, *Breve historia del modernismo,* Mexico, 1954.

50. "There are, beginning with the turn of the century, and in particular beginning in 1910, numerous indications of a change in the collective mentality and, consequently, in the literary mentality: Modern Art Week . . . is more a coronation than a starting point, it presupposes the maturity of a 'modernist spirit,' indispensable for the later creation of a modernist literature." Wilson Martins, "Antes do Modernismo," *O Estado de São Paulo,* Lit. Supl., March 8, 1958.

"In effect, Modern Art Week, which took place in São Paulo in February

1922, and from which it is customary to date the beginning of modernism, is not only a starting point, as is generally thought, but also a coronation. With it, modernism *became aware* of itself, which means having understood its true nature, the scattered anxieties and manifestations that were being repeated with more and more insistence ever since the first years of the century. When Modern Art Week takes place, modernism is already *mature*, if not for the general public, at least among the intellectuals who at that moment made up the movement, the liveliest and most creative sector of Brazilian intelligentsia. The Week 'officially' introduced a new state of spirit and was, in all certainty, the most profound of all of our literary revolutions. . . . But this state of mind did not come about all at once, nor even come about in the months which had preceded it: one can find it in the first signs of progressively accentuated dissatisfaction accentuated by a Parnassianism that was more and more 'mechanical' and a symbolism that was not very dynamic that had been provoked among literary youth." Wilson Martins, "Introdução à Literatura Brasileira Moderna," *O Estado de São Paulo*, Lit. Supl., November 23, 30, December 7, 1957. The quote is from the first article.

With respect to pre-modernism see also: Tristão de Ataíde, *Contribuição à História do Modernismo, I, O Premodernismo*.

The reference by Tasso da Silveira is in: "50 Anos de Literatura," *Revista Branca*, Rio de Janeiro, May 1952; reprinted in *Modernismo: Estudos Críticos*, Rio de Janeiro, Revista Branca, 1954. See also: Tasso de Silveira, *Definição do Modernismo Brasileiro*, Rio de Janeiro, Ed. Forja, 1932.

51. "A complete and very interesting movement, of symbolist origin, was taking place in the country, with some of our greatest poets, without its having had any kind of repercussion on the national collectivity. Even by 1922 the 'new ones' who had been sublimated by Brazilian life were Hermes Fontes and Martins Fontes. Coelho Neto was the great and glorious standard of our prose, carried off on the shoulders of the crowd in opposition to Graça Aranha when he left the disorder provoked by the latter in the Academy. And Tristão de Ataíde himself, who later on would be the lucid critic of modernism, still extolled Tarde, dazzled, without perceiving the general mediocrity of thought in the book and the vast technical deficiency, the clichés, the crutches, and the facile scaffolding with which the great lyricist of the *Via Láctea* had constructed almost all of those verses. Let Ascendino Leite review the newspapers of the time and he will see that modernism had something and someone to react against." Mário de Andrade, "Modernismo," *O Empalhador de Passarinho*, São Paulo, Martins, n. d.

And the reaction was violent against the Week in São Paulo, with Mário Pinto Serva and Oscar Guanabarino, and in Rio with Osório Duque Estrada among others. See: Augusto Fragoso, "Breve História da Semana de Arte Moderna de 1922," *Jornal do Comércio*, Rio de Janeiro, February 17, 1952.

52. "The moment of the syncretists . . . was different from that of the

Parnassians and symbolists. The Republic had been consolidated. The political genius of Prudente de Morais and later on that of Rodrigues Alves and their aides in government had created, with the construction of the docks and the sanitation and beautification of Rio de Janeiro, an atmosphere of tranquility, optimism, and a fervent hope in the future of Brazil. We were heading towards the first centenary of our political independence with the unshakable certainty that in a short time we would dominate the world. Since political and social interest had not been awakened in us and since none of us understood administration and finance, no one perceived the grave mistakes that were hiding under illusory appearances. And no one heard the slow rumble of collective anxieties (mysteriously announced, furthermore, by symbolism) that would lead us to unrest and suffering.

"In an atmosphere of doldrums and ingenuous happiness, with no strong wind to blow spirits in a determined direction, in the interregnum between symbolism and modernism, no current of unifying esthesia could be formed. The consequence: every genuine vocation that arose, and there were many (there were immense possibilities for leisure), had to rotate back onto himself, elaborating his own synthesis, blending in the unity of his art those elements that had the deepest affinity with his own temperament. It was in this way that we have the appearance of Hermes Fontes, Augusto dos Anjos, Pereira da Silva, Martins Fontes, Gilka Machado, Raul de Leôni, da Costa e Silva, Ronald de Carvalho, Murilo Araújo, Manuel Bandeira, Raul Machado, José Oiticica, Amadeu Amaral, Cecília Meireles, Guilherme de Almeida, Humberto de Campos, Cleômenes Campos, and Paulo Setúbal—to mention only a few. It can be seen from the list that several of these poets eventually worked in modernism—when the strong wind that formed currents came up.

"This syncretist movement was, I repeat, one of the most highly curious phenomena of our spiritual life, by the surprising results that it produced." Tasso da Silveira, *Definição do Modernismo Brasileiro.*

53. A. Soares Amora, *História da Literatura Brasileira*, São Paulo, Saraiva, 1955, pp. 147–48. See Mário da Silva Brito, *História do Modernismo Brasileiro*, São Paulo, Saraiva, 1958 (2nd ed., 1964).

54. Brito Broca, "Quando Teria Começado o Modernismo?" *Letras e Artes,* Lit. Supl. of *A Manhã*, Rio de Janeiro, July 20, 1952, p. 9.

55. See the preface by Múcio Leão to the *Obras de João Ribeiro: Crítica: Os Modernos*, Múcio Leão, editor, Rio de Janeiro, 1952. But Alberto de Oliveira himself, in a lecture given in 1916 to the Academy, spoke of the necessity of renovation.

56. See the chapter "A Literatura e o Conhecimento da Terra" in the author's *A Literatura no Brasil*, Vol. I, Book 1.

57. "It is from that same year, 1913, in Paris, that I recall my most remote memory of modernism. We were ready to leave for Brazil to continue or finish our studies, Temístocles Graça Aranha, today Ambassador in Cairo, and I. And Graça Aranha, the father, brought us to the garden of

the Hotel Ritz for tea, in order to give us a real appeal, the same, in the end, except in more intimate words, that he would offer the Academy eleven years later. '—Brazilian literature is dying of academicism. It does not renew itself. There are the same sonnets, the same novels, the same words of praise, the same negligence, that I have heard ever since the Academy was founded, when José Veríssimo did not want to let me in and Nabuco forced my admission. We must reform all of that. Give life to that cemetery. You are young. You are students. Stir up the schools. Move with your schoolmates. Do mad things. But do try to clear away those cobwebs.' And he made us an amusing proposal which showed quite clearly how even then a Tobias Barreto-like seduction by German culture was still at work in his mind: 'Why don't you found a Goethe Club?' " Tristão de Ataíde, "Ano Zero," *Diário de Notícias*, Rio de Janeiro, August 24, 1952. See also on the same subject: "Posição de Graça Aranha," *Estudos*, 5th series, Rio de Janeiro, 1933.

"We were in Paris at the time, in the year 1913, on the eve of World War I. In that year our meetings with the writer became frequent, and I was able at that time to feel and understand all of the vitality of his intelligence, the power of his imagination, based on a solid philosophical and literary culture. It was when, judging himself predestined, he began to feel in his discontented soul the desire or the necessity to make a revolution in the Brazilian literary environment. He was in the full swing of premeditation.

"He was frightened, he said, by our literary apathy, and he wanted newness, enthusiasm, revolution, freedom, much freedom, complete freedom! No shackles on the spirit. No static forms or attitudes.

"He was dreaming of a new esthetic of life, in whose philosophical depths the principles of a modern spirit would stand out." Rodrigo Otávio Filho, *Nova Conversa sôbre Graça Aranha*, Rio de Janeiro, M.E.C., 1955 (a lecture delivered to the Brazilian Academy of Letters, November 20, 1952).

On the state of Brazilian literature in 1910, consult the book by João do Rio, *O Momento Literário*, Rio de Janeiro, n. d.

58. Wilson Martins, "Antes do Modernismo," *O Estado de São Paulo*, Lit. Supl., March 8, 1958.

59. "And the fact is curious: the fine heritage of symbolist poetry was accepted by very few, while the bad heritage of its prose found fertile and propitious terrain in which to develop among us. The beginning of the century brought to our literary and fashionable reviews vignettes and illustrations, a kind of poematical chronicle, a sort of fantasist musing on abstract motives, a mere playing with words, where the verbal ability and ingenuity of the author was exercised. It was the assimilation of the worst kind of symbolism by the worst kind of Parnassianism, and the perfect example of that evil of scribbling, which became one of the principal targets of the modernists." Brito Broca.

60. Sérgio Buarque de Holanda, "Em Tôrno da Semana," *Diário Carioca*, Rio de Janeiro, February 17, 1952.

61. A. Bento, "As Artes Plásticas e a Semana de 1922," *Diário Carioca*, Rio de Janeiro, April 27, 1952.

62. Cassiano Ricardo, replying to a questionnaire on the thirtieth anniversary of the Week: *Diário Carioca*, Rio de Janeiro, March 30, 1952.

63. On Portuguese modernism see: Manuel Anselmo, *Família Literária Luso-Brasileira*, Rio de Janeiro, 1943. Hernâni Cidade, *O Conceito de Poesia como Expressão de Cultura*, São Paulo, 1946. *Idem, Tendências do Lirismo Contemporâneo*, Lisbon, 1938. Fidelino de Figueiredo, *Depois de Eça de Queiroz*, São Paulo, 1943. A. Casais Monteiro, *Sôbre o Romance Contemporâneo*, Lisbon, 1940. *Idem, De Pés Fincados na Terra*, Lisbon, 1941. *Idem, O Romance e seus Problemas*, Rio de Janeiro, 1950. José Régio, *Pequena História da Moderna Poesia Portuguêsa*, Lisbon, 1941. João Gaspar Simões, *Novos Temas*, Lisbon, 1935. *Idem, Tendências do Romance Contemporâneo*, Lisbon, n. d. *Idem, Liberdade do Espírito*, Oporto, n. d. *Idem, Crítica I.*, Oporto, 1942. *Os Modernistas Portuguêses*, 3 vols., Petrus editor, Oporto, Textos Universais, 1957.

The history of Portuguese modernism is centered about a series of reviews: *Orfeu* (1915), *Portugal Futurista, Contemporânea, Atena, Presença* (1927), *Cadernos de Poesia, Novo Cancioneiro, Poesia Nova* (1940), among others.

64. "Primitivism was the door through which the modernists penetrated into Brazil and is their certificate of Brazilian naturalization." Mário Pedrosa, *Correio da Manhã*, Rio de Janeiro, June 6, 1952.

65. The São Paulo group was made up of: Oswald de Andrade, Mário de Andrade, Menotti del Picchia, Guilherme de Almeida, "the four knight errants of the crusade," and also Sérgio Milliet, Luís Aranha, Agenor Barbosa, Plínio Salgado, and Cândido Mota Filho.

In the Rio group, among *cariocas* and adopted *cariocas*, were: Manuel Bandeira, Álvaro Moreira, Ronald de Carvalho, Renato Almeida, Ribeiro Couto, and others, who were joined by Graça Aranha upon his return from Europe in 1921 with an urge to lead it.

66. Di Cavalcanti, in reply to the questionnaire on the thirtieth anniversary of Modern Art Week: *Diário Carioca*, Rio de Janeiro, February 3, 1952.

67. ". . . it was a spontaneous idea which came forth naturally, without manifestos, or chiefs, or anything. The Week came about all by itself, because it came, because it had to come, or, rather, it did not come: it appeared, it showed itself. We, the 'boys' of 1922, did not have any awareness then of what we were trying to do, just as right now we are not aware of what we are doing." Guilherme de Almeida, *Revista Anual do Salão de Maio*, São Paulo, 1939.

"But when a balance is made of the work accomplished by the modernists, it is easy to see that the enthusiasm was born in Rio, the organization belonged to São Paulo, while the creative impulses came from Minas Gerais, the Northeast, and Rio Grande do Sul." Peregrino Júnior, *O Movimento Modernista*, Rio de Janeiro, M.E.C., 1954, p. 20 (Os Cadernos de Cultura, No. 69).

68. "Brazilian modernism was born out of the meeting and awareness of certain dissatisfactions. Arts and letters had come to a blind alley. The very necessity for movement and life was what dictated a destruction of barriers, something that is not attained by individual efforts, but by collective force. When a group of writers and artists, even though not very numerous, became aware of this, modernism was born, seeking a way of affirming and living. Its first public manifestation was Modern Art Week. The second, the review *Klaxon*, had enormous importance." Prudente de Morais Neto, in reply to the questionnaire of *Tribuna das Letras*, Lit. Supl. of *Tribuna da Imprensa*, Rio de Janeiro, Feb. 16, 17, 1952.

69. In that letter, Mário de Andrade said:

"In the statement that the modernists of São Paulo drew away from you, I see a misconception. It was not those of São Paulo who drew away, it was practically all those in Brazil. . . . In the first place, there is the mistake of vanity, in which you confused the function of guide with that of petty tyrant and local political boss. This is proof that you are a Brazilian. . . . I will neglect the zeal with which you protested to *A Noite* concerning the leadership of modernism, which in some mistaken moment they had thought to award me with, while you did not protest when they awarded you the same leadership for so many mistaken moments. It is of no importance and it is only a painfully comic episode. I was one of those who had the hardest time convincing himself that you, just back from Europe, became involved in Brazilian modernism out of personal interest and not from the desire of being helpful." de Andrade, *Corréio da Manhã*, Rio de Janeiro, February 16, 1952. For Mário de Andrade, Graça Aranha had missed his calling, because he believed himself to be one thing, while he was really another; he does not represent an orientation as varied and as widespread as that of modernism, and therefore he failed too as a guide of the movement; he does not even represent Brazilianism; his arrogant indiscretion made him want to be marshal of Brazilian youth and all he could make was colonel. Youth could not accept him and they abandoned him.

As for Manuel Bandeira, this is how he expressed himself:

"Therefore, neither he nor I agreed to take part in the homage that the review *Klaxon* gave to Graça Aranha by publishing a number dedicated to him. My refusal did not imply any end to the admiration and esteem that I have always accorded the author of *Canaã*. It did seem to me, however, that the homage would give Graça Aranha, at least in the eyes of the general public, the position of leader of the modernist movement in Brazil. What happened later showed that I was right: the movement came to be considered the work of Graça Aranha, and even though 'the dates are there, and the books,' as Mário de Andrade said to me in a letter of 1924, we have not managed even today to make the truth clear, to wit, that we were never the disciples of Graça Aranha. The movement was already in full force when Graça Aranha returned from Europe in October 1921, bringing us his *Estética da Vida*, which none of us accepted. But, as Mário de Andrade wrote, 'what no one will deny is his importance to the acceptance of the movement and his personal courage. It is logical: even if Graça Aranha did not exist, we would still be modernists and others would come after us, but he did bring greater facility and rapidity for our implantation. Today we are accepted by almost everybody.' " Manuel Bandeira, *Itinerário de Pasárgada*, Rio de Janeiro, Liv. São José, 1957, p. 63.

70. Sérgio Buarque de Holanda, "Depois da Semana," *Diário Carioca*, Rio de Janeiro, February 24, March 2, 9, 1952.

71. The attitude of Graça Aranha can also have a psychological interpretation, such as that of Peregrino Júnior: "It is necessary to keep in mind the drama of the retired diplomat . . . who after having enjoyed all of those privileges, returns home . . . to be more or less forgotten, still suffering the consequences of adjustment, of a lack of relationships and of a sympathetic entourage, for having lived abroad most of the time. Such would be the case of Graça Aranha, after a brilliant existence in the great European centers: growing old all alone in the Hotel dos Estrangeiros. The modernist movement arises and he finds companions among the young and new people, the entourage he needed. He joins them and wants to lead them; his prestige grows from one moment to the next, he becomes the name on people's lips, discussed, attacked, praised, and there is popularity at last—popularity to a degree that he had never enjoyed until then. Of a combative nature, and exuberant and romantic temperament, even though he was forever rising up against romanticism, Graça Aranha could not conform to the inactivity to which he seemed condemned. Modernism gave him his means to pick up the thread again of a full, brilliant, and lively existence, prolonging it into an intellectual action that he extended into the political field." Peregrino Júnior, in an interview with Brito Broca, "Salões e Ambientes do Modernismo no Rio," *Letras e Artes*, Lit. Supl. of *A Manhã*, Rio de Janeiro, February 3, 1952.

72. Mário de Andrade, *O Movimento Modernista*, Rio de Janerio, 1942. This formulation of Mário de Andrade's theses was done by Peregrino Júnior in *O Movimento Modernista*, Rio de Janerio, M.E.C., 1954.

73. This subject was studied very well by Sérgio Buarque de Holanda in "Depois da Semana."

74. Tristão de Ataíde, "O Modernismo," *O Jornal*, Rio de Janeiro, December 11, 1938. Peregrino Júnior, *O Movimento Modernista*.

75. Gilberto Freyre, *Região e Tradição*, Rio de Janeiro, 1941, p. 24.

76. See Gilberto Freyre, *Região e Tradição. Idem, Manifesto Regionalista*

de 1926, Rio de Janeiro, M.E.C., 1955 (Os Cadernos de Cultura, No. 80). Tadeu Rocha, "O Modernismo na Província: Dois Regionalismos," *O Jornal*, Rio de Janeiro, August 31, September 7, 21, October 19, 1952.

77. Augusto Meyer, in reply to the questionnaire on the thirtieth anniversary of the Week: *Diário Carioca*, Rio de Janeiro, March 16, 1967.

78. ". . . Modernism, a movement bursting with theories and ideas, a revolution that was, in its early times, a revolution of manifestos, brought out a group of programs that were realized little by little, in pieces, without any apparent connection among themselves." Wilson Martins, "Introdução à Literatura Brasileira Moderna," *O Estado de São Paulo*, Lit. Supl., November 23, 1957.

Tasso da Silveira announced a series of essays on these various documents, but only the first one, on *Natalika*, has been published: in *Letras e Artes*, Lit. Supl., of *A Manhã*, Rio de Janeiro, July 20, 1952.

79. "Our century only begins, then, in 1922, if we want to date it, as is necessary, from its first (and, until now, only) literary movement of importance. All contemporary Brazilian literature has lived and still lives under the sign of modernism. . . . This is due, in a great part, to the fact that the modernist generations (understanding by this expression all of those who followed from then until now) have all appeared with a clear literary vocation." Martins, "Introdução," November 23, 1957.

80. See the essays with these titles in *O Jornal*, Rio de Janeiro, December 4, 11, 18, 1938; and further: *Quadro Sintético da Literatura Brasileira*, Rio de Janeiro, Agir, 1956.

81. Martins, "Introdução."

82. Manuel Bandeira, *Itinerário*, p. 82.

83. "The year 1928 still has, however, the value of a crucial instant in the history of modernism: it is a decisive 'turning point' with the books of José Américo de Almeida, Mário de Andrade, and Paulo Prado, *Retrato do Brasil*." Wilson Martins, "Introdução," II, *O Estado de São Paulo*, Lit. Supl., November 30, 1957.

84. ". . . for Brazilian intelligence, it was the beginning of these victories that can no longer be lost, and, once incorporated into the assests of the spirit, they constitute a definitive enrichment for it." Prudente de Morais Neto, "Meninos Eu Vi," *Jornal de Letras*, Rio de Janeiro, May 1952.

85. "In their paths and their by-ways, the modernists sought, for better or for worse, and each one in his own way, broader terrains where their efforts would finally be revealed at work in the most varied sectors of Brazilian life. And this is one of the circumstances that must be listed among its assets today." Sérgio Buarque de Holanda, "Depois de Semana," *Diário Carioca*, Rio de Janeiro, March 9, 1952.

86. The great importance of this work as a text of poetical theory was very well emphasized by Luís Santa Cruz: "Jubileu d'*A Escrava*," *Diário Carioca*, Rio de Janeiro, November 26, 1950, and "Atualidade d'*A Escrava*," *Idem*, September 2, 1951.

87. In *Jornal de Letras*, Rio de Janeiro, February, 1952, p. 9.

88. Peregrino Júnior, *O Movimento Modernista*, p. 41.

89. See, concerning the problem of literary education: Afrânio Coutinho, *O Ensino de Literatura*, Rio de Janeiro, M.E.C., 1952. *Idem, Correntes Cruzadas. Idem, Da Crítica e da Nova Crítica*, Rio de Janeiro, Civilização Brasileira, 1957.

90. Martins, *Introdução*, Dec. 7, 1957. With respect to the tendency towards an understanding of the esthetic character of literature, see the studies by Afrânio Coutinho cited above.

91. See Afrânio Coutinho, *Correntes Cruzadas*, pp. xvi–xx.

92. José Veríssimo, in several essays on Coelho Neto; consult: "O Sr. Coelho Neto," *Estudos de Literatura Brasileira*, 6th series, Rio de Janeiro, Garnier, 1910.

93. Peregrino Júnior, *O Movimento Modernista*, p. 40.

94. "Let us consider pronouns. Even modernism, which wrote in the Portuguese language, had a phantom before it: *pronouns*. One of the preoccupations of the writer was to place them all well. A sterile preoccupation for a writer, because it diverted his attention to a problem that did not have the slightest esthetic interest, a fruitless problem. And the modernists? They had apparently freed themselves from this preoccupation, but only apparently. Actually, what they did was to free the post-modernists from it. Just like the academician, the modernist was confused by pronouns. He worried about misplacing them—according to Portuguese grammar. His was the task of placing them in the Brazilian way, or in Brazilian ways, and even to invent ways of placing them. In any case, he was strongly preoccupied with pronouns. In certain sentences of academic writers, we can see how a pronoun placed in accord with the best rules will ruin the sentence, upset the reader, be painful. In sentences by modernist writers, we see pronouns so abusively and deliberately misused that they too make one uncomfortable, also hurt the eyes. Reacting against stiff-collar language, many modernists even descended to hoodlum speech. Fighting against a false dignity of language, at times they wrote a language lacking in dignity.

"Now, the post-modernist had this advantage: he was unfamiliar with pronouns. He went on writing pronouns in a way that seemed to be the easiest to him, paying no attention to how he was writing, not worrying whether he was correct or mistaken. The pronoun for him was still just another element in the sentence, like an adverb, for example. Therefore: the post-modernist no longer had any pronoun problem.

"The written language before modernism was uncomfortable and backward. It was a situation in which, to write with simplicity, a writer with the obligation to be correct faced very complicated problems of style. The majority preferred to write without simplicity. What did the modernists do? Reacting against the language of Portugal, they took refuge in vulgarisms. Just as the others had been preoccupied with embellishing the sentence with classical and sometimes archaic high-sounding words, the modernists were preoccupied with filling it with Brazilianisms and plebeian words. They opened the gates of the language, and they were confused by the invasion. They acted like children, who have learned a few dirty words and repeat them at every moment, even without occasion, to show that they knew those words and that they could say them. They put on a show. A show, and, in many cases, exhibitionism, deliberate abuse, a *nouveau riche* ostentation of the language they had sought in the mouth of the people, sometimes out of books on folklore, to put into the written language. Naturally, in this detail, as in others, the evil varied according to personal temperament. In many cases it reached a populist *préciosité* more precious than any academic *préciosité*. In this way the modernists did well . . . for those who came after. They did badly for themselves, because by worrying so much about language, about their tool, they prejudiced the work itself. The post-modernists no longer needed to worry about pure or impure expressions. When they began to write, they were writing, thinking only about saying what they wanted to say, about giving their message. They were writing in a language that seemed most comfortable to them, the easiest to write and in which to be understood." Rubem Braga, "O Trabalho do Modernismo," *Diário de Notícias*, Rio de Janeiro, June 28, 1942.

95. The important work of Herbert Parentes Fortes (1897–1953) is being published posthumously: *Filosofia da Linguagem*, Rio de Janeiro, G.R.D., 1956. *Idem, A Lingua que Falamos*, 1957. *Idem, A Questão da Língua Brasileira*, 1957. *Idem, Euclides, o Estilizador de nossa História*, 1958.

96. A century ago, Gonçalves Dias said, quoted by Herbert Parentes Fortes in *Filosofia da Linguagem*: "It also happens that in distances as considerable as those of Brazil, the tenor of life changes, and the men who adopt this or that manner of living have formed a language of their own, more expressive and varied. Cowboys, miners, fishermen, and river men fit the case. Well, is the Brazilian novel unable to portray any of these types because the proper terms are lacking in classical Portuguese?"

97. On modern poetry in general see: Academia Brasileira de Letras, *Curso de Poesia*, Rio de Janeiro, 1954. Alceu Amoroso Lima, *Quadro Sintético da Literatura Brasileira*, Rio de Janeiro, Agir, 1956. *Idem, Estudos*, 5th series, Rio de Janeiro, 1929–1933. *Idem*, "Poesia Moderna," *O Jornal*, Rio de Janeiro, 1929–1933. *Idem*, "Poesia Moderna," *O Jornal*, Rio de Janeiro, November 20, 30, December 7, 1941. *Idem, Poesia Brasileira Contemporânea*, Belo Horizonte, 1941. Afonso Ávila, "Aspectos da Poesia Posmodernista," *Correio da Manhã*, Rio de Janeiro, January 12, 19, 1957. Manuel Bandeira, *Apresentação da Poesia Brasileira*, 3rd ed., Rio de Janeiro, C.E.B., 1957. Jaime de Barros, *Poeta do Brasil*, Rio de Janeiro, J. Olympio, 1944. Domingos Carvalho da Silva, *Introdução ao Estudo do Ritmo na Poesia Modernista*, São Paulo, Rev. Bras. Poesia, 1950. Adolfo Casais Monteiro, *A Moderna Poesia Brasileira*, São Paulo, Clube de Poesia, 1956. Clube

de Poesia de São Paulo, *Antologia da Poesia Brasileira Moderna, São Paulo,*
1953. Mário Faustino, "A Poesia Concreta e o Momento Poético Brasileiro," *Jornal do Brasil,* Rio de Janeiro, February 10, 1957. Otávio Freitas
Júnior, *Ensaios de Crítica de Poesia,* Recife, 1941. Agripino Grieco, *Evolução
da Poesia Brasileira,* Rio de Janeiro, April 1932. Álvaro Lins, *Jornal de
Crítica,* 6th series, Rio de Janeiro, J. Olympio, 1941–1951. Edson Lins,
História e Crítica da Poesia Brasileira, Rio de Janeiro, Ariel, 1937. Wilson
Martins, "Poesia de Ontem e de Hoje," *O Estado de São Paulo,* April 19,
26, 1958. Dante Milano, *Antologia de Poetas Modernos,* Rio de Janeiro,
Ariel, 1935. Sérgio Milliet, *Panorama da Moderna Poesia Brasileira,* Rio de
Janeiro, M.E.C., 1952. *Modernismo: Estudos Críticos,* Saldanha Coelho,
editor, Rio de Janeiro, Revista Branca, 1954. José Osório de Oliveira,
Pequena Antologia da Moderna Poesia Brasileira, Lisbon, 1944. Ciro
Pimentel, *Breve Antologia da Poesia Nova Brasileira,* Braga, 1956–1957.
Eduardo Portella, "A Poesia Brasileira de Hoje," *Jornal do Comércio,* Rio
de Janeiro, September 29, October 16, 1957. Miguel Rio Branco, *Etapas
da Poesia Brasileira,* Lisbon, 1955. Luís Santa Cruz, "Cinqüenta Anos de
Poesia," *Correio da Manhã,* Rio de Janeiro, June 15, 1951. Roger Bastide,
Poetas do Brasil, Curitiba, 1947. F. F. Loanda, *Panorama da Nova Poesia
Brasileira,* Rio de Janeiro, 1951. Cassiano Ricardo, *22 e a Poesia de Hoje,*
São Paulo, 1962. José Guilherme Merquior, "A Poesia Descobre o Brasil,"
Senhor, Rio de Janeiro, June 1962. *Idem,* "Falência da Poesia," *Senhor,*
May 1962. *Idem,* "Nota Antifática," *Manuel Bandeira: Poesia do Brasil,*
Editôra do Autor, 1963.

98. Cassiano Ricardo, Interview in *Diário Carioca,* Rio de Janeiro, March
30, 1952.

99. On the "Generation of 1945" see: A. Amoroso Lima, *Quadro Sintético da Literatura Brasileira,* Rio de Janeiro, 1956. M. Bandeira, *Apresentação da Poesia Brasileira,* Rio de Janeiro, 1957. S. Buarque de Holanda,
"Ainda a Labareda," *Diário Carioca,* Rio de Janeiro, September 2, 1951.
Lêdo Ivo, Lecture, *Letras e Artes,* Supl. of *A Manhã,* Rio de Janeiro, September 18, 1949. J. Cabral de Melo Neto, "A Geração de 45," *Diário
Carioca,* Rio de Janeiro, November 23, 30, December 7, 21, 1952. Clube
de Poesia de São Paulo, *Antologia da Poesia Brasileira Moderna,* São Paulo,
1953. F. F. de Loanda, *Panorama da Nova Poesia Brasileira,* Rio de Janeiro,
1951. Sérgio Milliet, *Panorama da Moderna Poesia Brasileira,* Rio de Janeiro,
1952.

100. On the problem of the poetical genres of modernism see: Osvaldino
Marques, "Matrizes Estruturais do Verso Moderno," *Modernismo: Estudos
Críticos,* Saldanha Coelho, editor, Rio de Janeiro, Revista Branca, 1954.
Luís Santa Cruz, "Os Gêneros Poéticos do Modernismo," *Jornal de Letras,*
Rio de Janeiro, November 1951.

Santa Cruz shows how modernism freed Brazilian poetry from treatises
of versification and the rhetorical concept of poetry, which we owed to
an education of the preceptistic and mechanically artesan type: it was

only by following the rules of versification, of rhyme, and the choice of traditional stanzas or a traditional number of lines, of the types of stanza and lines (blank or rhymed), which gave them a greater plasticity and depth of poetical content. In *A Escrava que não é Isaura,* the great *ars poetica* of modernism, Mário de Andrade returns to Aristotle's *Poetics* and prescribes an absolute freedom in the choice and treatment of genres, "polyphonism": he accepted both Greek and Latin forms, and Italian (including the sonnet). He accepted even the "poem," to which modernist poetry delivered itself enthusiastically as the perfect lyric instrument, for modernism also incorporated the traditional line of Brazilian poetry, lyricism, although there were examples of an epic note in some like *Martim Cererê* and *Cobra Norato.* The modernist poets, however, cultivated other lyrical forms too: elegy, ode, ballad, rondeau, madrigal, *canção, romance, estudo,* and pastoral forms, as well as the sonnet.

101. On concretism, in addition to the review *Noigandres,* São Paulo, 1955–1956. Nos. 1, 2, and 3, see the following studies, with further details from the Literary Supplement of the *Jornal do Brasil,* which in 1957 was the main organ for debates and samples of concretism: Manuel Bandeira, "Poesia Concreta," *Jornal do Brasil,* February 6, 10, 13, 1957. *Idem,* "A Chave do Poema," *ibid.,* April 3, 1957. Oliveira Bastos, "Por uma Poesia Concreta," *ibid.,* February 17, 24, March 3, 1957. *Idem,* "Poesia Concreta: Palavras e Idéias Cruzadas," *ibid.,* April 21, 27, 1957. *Idem,* "Poesia Concreta: Metas e Límites," *ibid.,* August 18, 25, 1957. *Idem,* "A Poesia Concreta e o Problema de Comunicação," *ibid.,* September 15, 1957. Augusto de Campos, "Poesia Concreta e Palavras Cruzadas," *ibid.,* April 14, 1957. *Idem,* "A Queda da Bastilha," *ibid.,* June 2, 1957. Haroldo de Campos, "Evolução de Formas: Poesia Concreta," *ibid.,* January 13, 1957. *Idem,* "Aspectos da Poesia Concreta," *ibid.,* October 27, 1957. Mário Faustino, "A Poesia Concreta e o Momento Poético Brasileiro," *ibid.,* February 10, 1957. Antônio Houaiss, "Sôbre Poesia Concreta," *ibid.,* May 19, 1957. Antônio Olinto, "Poesia Concreta," *O Globo,* Rio de Janeiro, February 9, 1957. Décio Pignatari, "Arte Concreta: Objeto e Objetivo," *Jornal do Brasil,* April 21, 1957. "Que é Poesia Concreta?" Interview with Haroldo and Augusto de Campos, *Diário Carioca,* January 20, 1957. Pedro Xisto, "Poesia Concreta," *Fôlha da Manhã,* São Paulo, August 4, 18, September 1, 15, 1957.

The question of concretism had a very interesting development from 1961 on, expressed in the papers by Décio Pignatari and Cassiano Ricardo at the Second Brazilian Congress of Literary History and Criticism held at Assis, São Paulo, and in the dialogue between the concretist group of São Paulo and the group of the review *Tendência* in Belo Horizonte. Later on, a new direction arose, with the division of the São Paulo group, giving rise to the "literature-praxis" movement led by Mário Chamie.

The principal bibliography since then is the following: *Invenção* (review), I, Nos. 1 and 2, São Paulo, 1962. *Tendência* (review), No. 4, Belo Horizonte, August 1962. *Revista de Cultura Brasileña* (review), II, No. 5,

Madrid, January 1963. *Praxis* (review), Nos. 1, 2, 3, São Paulo, 1962–1963. Haroldo de Campos, "Maiakovski em Português," *Revista do Livro*, Nos. 23–24, Rio de Janeiro, July–December, 1962. *Idem*, "A Crítica em Situação," *Correio da Manhã*, Rio de Janeiro, December 2, 1961. *Idem*, "Phantasus: a Revolução da Lírica," *O Estado de São Paulo* (Lit Supl.), March 10, 1962. *Idem*, "Phantasus: A Elefantíasis do Projeto," *ibid.*, May 12, 1962. *Idem*, "No Horizonte do Provável," *ibid.*, October 19, 26, 1963. Mário Chamie, *Lavra Lavra*, São Paulo, 1962. *Idem*, "Manifesto Praxis e Ideologia," *O Estado de São Paulo* (Lit Supl.), June 16, 1962. *Idem*, "Crítica e Influências," *ibid.*, July 21, 1962. *Idem*, "Poesia-Praxis e Poesia Fonética," *ibid.*, December 8, 1962. *Idem*, "Ação e Vã Guarda," *Diário de Notícias*, Rio de Janeiro, April 14, 1963. Ferreira Gular, *Teoria do Não-Objeto*, Rio de Janeiro, 1960. Cassiano Ricardo, *22 e a Poesia de Hoje*, São Paulo, 1961. *Idem*, *Algumas Reflexões sôbre Poética de Vanguarda*, Rio de Janeiro, J. Olympio, 1964. *Idem*, "Autonomismo," *O Estado de São Paulo* (Lit Supl.), June 13, 20, 27, 1964. Fábio Lucas, "Inteligência Criadora," *Correio da Manhã*, January 27, 1962. *Idem*, "Perder sem Parceria . . .," *ibid.*, May 5, 1962. Pedro Xisto, *Poesia em Situação*, Fortaleza, 1960. *Idem*, "À Busca da Poesia," *Revista do Livro*, Nos. 21–22, Rio de Janeiro, March–June 1961. *Binômio* (newspaper), Belo Horizonte, August 21, 1961 (Statements by Rui Mourão and Fábio Lucas on concretism and participation). Antônio Carlos Cabral, "Poema-Praxis e Atitude Central," *O Estado de São Paulo* (Lit. Supl.), June 27, July 4, 1964. José Lino Grunewald, "Vanguarda e Retaguarda," *Correio da Manhã*, March 23, 1963. Emílio Santos, "Praxis ou da Necessidade de Renovar," *ibid.*, May 23, 1964.

102. On Brazilian fiction in general, novel and short story, and the modern period in particular, see: Academia Brasileira de Letras, *Curso de Romance*, Rio de Janeiro, 1952. Moacir de Albuquerque, "À Margem do Romance," *O Jornal*, Rio de Janeiro, August 22, 29, September 5, 1954. *Idem*, *Alguns Romancistas Contemporâneos*, Recife, 1954. Heron Alencar, "Precursores: O Primeiro Romance," *A Literatura no Brasil*, Vol.I, p. 840. Hélio Pólvora de Almeida, "O Romance Neo-Realista . . ." *Para Todos*, No. 37, Rio de Janeiro, November 1957. Mário de Andrade, *Aspectos da Literatura Brasileira*, Rio de Janeiro, Americ, 1943. Teófilo Andrade, "Romance do Café e Romance do Açúcar," *O Jornal*, Rio de Janeiro, November 17, 1957. Tristão de Ataíde, *Estudos*, 5th series, Rio de Janeiro, 1929–1932. Francisco de Assis Barbosa, *Romance, Novela e Conto no Brasil*, *1839-1949*, I, No. 3, May–August. Gustavo Barroso, "O Primeiro Romance Brasileiro," *O Cruzeiro*, Rio de Janeiro, March 3, 1951. Rui Bloem, "Teresa Margarida e o Primeiro Romance Brasileiro," *Fôlha da Noite*, São Paulo, August 26, 27, 28, 29, 1957. J. Braga Montenegro, *Evolução e Natureza do Conto Cearense*, Fortaleza, Clã, 1951. Brito Broca, "Houve um Romance Modernista?" *Letras e Artes*, supl. of *A Manhã*, Rio de Janeiro, June 15, 1952. *Idem*, "O Que Devemos Reler nos Romances Brasileiros," *ibid.*, October 19, 1952. Haroldo Bruno, "Notas sôbre o Romance," *Diário de*

Notícias, Rio de Janeiro, August 24, September 14, 1952. *Idem*, "Romance e Novela, *Jornal do Brasil*, Rio de Janeiro, December 23, 1956. Antônio Cândido, "O Nosso Romance antes de 1930," *O Jornal*, Rio de Janeiro, April 21, 28, May 12, 1946. Pinto do Carmo, *Novela e Novelistas Brasileiros*, Rio de Janeiro, Org. Simões, 1947. Oto Maria Carpeaux, "Tendências do Moderno Romance Brasileiro," *O Jornal*, Rio de Janeiro, October 12, 1948. José Aderaldo Castelo, "Como Nasceu o Romance Brasileiro," *O Jornal*, Rio de Janeiro, June 26, 1949. *Idem*, "O Romance Romântico Histórico," *O Estado de São Paulo*, Lit. Supl., March 30, 1957. *Idem*, "Tendências do Romance Romântico," *ibid.*, June 15, 1957. *Idem*, "O Romance do Realismo ao Modernismo," *ibid.*, August 24, 1957. Edgard Cavalheiro, *Evolução do Conto Brasileiro*, Rio de Janeiro, M.E.C., 1954 (Cadernos de Cultura, No. 74). Lia Correia Dutra, *O Romance Brasileiro e José Lins do Rêgo*, Lisbon, 1938. Jaime Cortesão, "A Autoria das *Aventuras de Diófanes*," *O Estado de São Paulo*, September 20, October 4, 1953. Fausto Cunha, "Sumário do Romance Brasileiro," *Fôlha da Manhã*, São Paulo, November 3, 17, 1957. Pedro Dantas, "O Romance Brasileiro," *Revista Acadêmica*, Nos. 48–51, Rio de Janeiro. Miguel Alfredo D'Elia, *El sentido de la tierra en la narrativa*, Buenos Aires, 1948. F. P. Ellison, *Brazil's New Novel*, Berkeley-Los Angeles, 1954. Bezerra de Freitas, *Forma e Expressão no Romance Brasileiro*, Rio de Janeiro, Pongetti, 1947. V. Gama e Melo, "Uma Literatura Parada," *Jornal do Comércio*, Recife, June 23, 1947. Herman Lima, *Variações sôbre o Conto*, Rio de Janeiro, M.E.C., 1952 (Cadernos de Cultura). Álvaro Lins, *Jornal de Crítica*, 6th series, Rio de Janeiro, J. Olympio, 1941–1951. Wilson Lousada, "Três Paisagens do Romance," *Dom Casmurro*, Rio de Janeiro, November 26, December 19, 31, 1938. *Idem*, "Modernismo, Romance . . . ," *ibid.*, March 25, 1939. Lúcia Miguel-Pereira, *Prosa de Ficção: 1870–1920*, Rio de Janeiro, J. Olympio, 1950. Abelardo Montenegro, *O Romance Cearense*, Fortaleza, 1953. Olívio Montenegro, *O Romance Brasileiro*, Rio de Janeiro, 1938. J. Andrade Murici, *A Nova Literatura Brasileira*, Pôrto Alegre, 1936. *Idem*, "A Ficção no Movimento Modernista Carioca," *Jornal do Comércio*, Rio de Janeiro, November 10, 1957. Cassiano Nunes, "Análise e Problemática do Romance Nordestino," *Revista Brasiliense*, São Paulo, December, 1957. Antônio Olinto, "Ficção no Brasil," *O Globo*, Rio de Janeiro, December 14, 21, 1957. José Osório de Oliveira, *Aspectos do Romance Brasileiro*, Lisbon, 1943. Xavier Placer, "Panorama do Moderno Romance Brasileiro," *Revista da Academia Fluminense de Letras*, VIII, Niterói, 1953. Gregory Rabassa, *O Negro na Ficção Brasileira*, Rio de Janeiro, Tempo Brasileiro, 1965. Jorge Rizzini, "A Renovação do Romance Brasileiro," *A Gazeta*, São Paulo, July 19, 1957. Rodrigues Alves Filho, *O Sociologismo e a Imaginação no Romance Brasileiro*, Rio de Janeiro, 1938. *Idem*, *O Romance Brasileiro: de 1752 a 1930*, Rio de Janeiro, O Cruzeiro, 1952. João Gaspar Simões, "Introdução ao Estudo de Literatura de Ficção dos Novos Escritores Brasileiros," *Letras e Artes*, Supl. to *A*

Manhã, Rio de Janeiro, January 21, 1951. Ademar Vidal, "O Romance Brasileiro," *O Jornal*, Rio de Janeiro, January 8, 1939. Nestor Vítor, *Três Romancistas do Norte*, Rio de Janeiro, 1915. Adonias Filho, *Modernos Ficcionistas Brasileiros*, Rio de Janeiro, 1958. Haroldo Bruno, *Estudos de Literatura Brasileira*, Rio de Janeiro, 1957. Assis Brasil, "Ficção: Últimos Livros," *Jornal do Brasil*, December 24, 31, 1960, January 7, 14, 21, 1961. *Idem*, "O Romance Brasileiro de Hoje" *Cadernos Brasileiros*, II, No. 4. October-December 1960. Tristão de Ataíde, "Romance Brasileiro Moderno," *Diário de Notícias*, Rio de Janeiro, October 30, November 13, 27, December 4, 11, 18, 1960, January 15, 22, 29, 1961. Walmir Ayala, "Romance Brasileiro," *Cadernos Brasileiros*, V, No. 2, March-April 1962. Antônio Cândido, *Tese e Antítese*, São Paulo, Cia. Ed. Nacional, 1964. José Aderaldo Castelo, *Aspectos do Romance Brasileiro*, Rio de Janeiro, M.E.C., 1961. Eugênio Gomes, *Aspectos do Romance Brasileiro*, Bahia, Publ. da Universidade, 1958. Temístocles Linhares, *Interrogações*, II, Rio de Janeiro, Liv. São José, 1962. Fábio Lucas, *Temas Literários e Juízos Críticos*, Belo Horizonte, Ed. Tendência, 1963. Antônio Olinto, *Cadernos de Crítica*, Rio de Janeiro, J. Olympio, 1959. Franklin de Oliveira, *A Fantasia Exata*, Rio de Janeiro, Zahar, 1959. Joel Pontes, *O Aprendiz da Crítica*, Rio de Janeiro, I.N.C., 1960. Eduardo Portella, *Dimensões*, I-II, Rio de Janeiro, Agir, 1959, 1960. José Lins do Rêgo, *Conferências no Prata*, Rio de Janeiro, C.E.B., 1946. Wilson Martins, "Velhos e Novos," *O Estado de São Paulo*, November 4, 11, 18, 25, and December 2, 12, 1954. *Idem*, "Romances e Novelas," *ibid.*, July 14, 21, 28, 1955. *Idem*, "Os Romances Imperfeitos," *ibid.*, December 1, 1959. *Idem*, "Ponto Morto," *ibid.*, February 25 and March 4, 1961. *Idem*, "Estilo e Assunto," *ibid.*, November 11, 18, 1961. *Idem*, "Estiagem," *ibid.*, June 23, 1962. *Idem*, "Romance em Crise," *ibid.*, October 13, 1962. *Idem*, "Caminhos da Ficção," *ibid.* January 19, 26, 1963. *Idem*, "Uma Década do Romance," *ibid.*, May 11, 18, 25, 1963. *Idem*, "A Ficção," *ibid.*, June 10, 17, 24 and July 1, 1964. *Idem*, "Tendências," *ibid.*, February 1, 1964.

103. On the chronicle see: Paulo Mendes de Almeida, "A Crônica," *O Estado de São Paulo*, October 13, 1956. Tristão de Ataíde, "Contos e Crônicas" *Estudos*, 5th series, Rio de Janeiro, 1933. Afrânio Coutinho, *Da Crítica e da Nova Crítica*, Rio de Janeiro, 1957. *Idem*, "Personalidade da Crônica," *Diário de Notícias*, Rio de Janeiro, December 8, 1957. Bernardo Gersen, "Grandeza e Miséria da Crônica," *Diário de Notícias*, Rio de Janeiro, July 14, 1957. Temístocles Linhares, "Cronistas e Escritores," *Diário de Notícias*, Rio de Janeiro, October 6, 1957. Eduardo Portella, "A Cidade e a Letra," *Jornal do Comércio*, Rio de Janeiro, December 15, 1957; reprinted in *Dimensões*, I, Rio de Janeiro, 1958.

104. Eduardo Portella, "A Cidade e a Letra," *Jornal do Comércio*, Rio de Janeiro, December 15, 1957; reprinted in *Dimensões*, I, Rio de Janeiro, J. Olympio, 1958.

105. See the chapter "A Evolução da Literatura Dramática," in Vol. II

of *A Literatura no Brasil*. See also: Osmar Rodrigues Cruz, "Origem da Renovação no Teatro Brasileiro," *Revista Brasiliense*, São Paulo, November-December 1956.

106. In the preface to his book *Afonso Arinos* (1922), and taken up again on diverse occasions.

107. On this matter see: Afrânio Coutinho, *Correntes Cruzadas* (1953); *Por uma Crítica Estética* (1953); *Da Crítica e da Nova Crítica* (1957); "A Crítica Literária no Brasil," in *Revista Interamericana de Bibliografia*, XIV, No. 2, Washington, 1964; *Decimália*, Rio de Janeiro, Biblioteca Nacional, 1958.

108. It is true that not everything went marvelously, and there were misrepresentations that arose in the name of the new esthetics, as Murilo Araújo showed very well, "dry, cold expressions, without plasticity and without feeling, hermetic, incommunicable, empty and therefore incapable of surviving." Murilo Araújo analyzes some of these aberrations or exaggerations of artistic reform:

"Thus, the *simplicity* that was proper to it degenerated at times into *deficiency, spontaneity* into *improvisation;* the *dynamism* that gave an esthetic to the machine, changed into *automatism,* which, on the contrary, gives man the cold and unfeeling gestures of the machine; the opulent *synthesis* becomes confused with empty *dryness;* esthetic *surprise* with eccentric *artifice;* freedom of *construction* is interpreted as freedom for *destruction;* the *fight against forms;* architectural *functionalism* is exaggerated into a genuine architectural *mechanicism;* the *liberation* of rhythm became an *abolition* of rhythm; the appeal to the *subconscious* gave rise to an imitation of *incoherence;* the preponderance of the *personality* ended up being the predominance of *arbitrariness;* the *surpassing* of the past changed into a *denial* of the past; and lastly, the *control* of emotion turned into a cerebral *sterilization* of emotion." Murilo Araújo, "Evolução e Revolução Modernista," *Jornal do Comércio*, Rio de Janeiro, May 10, 1953; reprinted in *Quadrantes do Modernismo Brasileiro*, Rio de Janeiro, 1958.

109. The idea of the heroic phase of the movement according to which Brazilian literature began with modernism, has been left behind. The revolutionary modernists broke their links with the Brazilian literary past, drawing a curtain of injustices and systematic negations across it.

Wilson Martins has this to say: "Modernism was not only a break with the past, a brutal breaking off in the esthetic 'direction,' but also an interruption of literary history: its twelve apostles began to count from 1922, the year I of Brazilian literature. Hence the impressive list of their necessary injustices, which we are now revising little by little. As always happens in revolutions, modernism recognized a few distant masters who were not the 'masters of the past' of whom Mário de Andrade spoke, and for the very simple reason that this *past* was the immediate past, against which precisely the modernists were rebelling. But the choice of masters, in life as in revolutions, never obeys very rigorous or very rational reasons. Therefore, some true prophets of modernism fell ignored in the night of the ages, and others less worthy were called to the votive feasts. But, alongside the real and false masters, one could count many writers who had conquered their places, great or small, in literary life. There were movements and schools, then as today, that were poorly studied. There was, in a word, a 'variety,' which the modernists, masters of a truth, repudiated in the name of 'unity.' It is explained in this way, that for twenty years and perhaps more, literary activity in Brazil has been exclusively contemporary, has ignored almost completely what went before it, and has, by a deep spiritual attitude, lost interest in what went before; and what we have had, of the past as well as of literary history, as is natural, and for that very reason, is a conventional and false idea." "Poesia de Ontem e de Hoje," *O Estado de São Paulo,* April 19, 1958).

Bibliography

❦❧

PART I

Introduction

LITERARY HISTORY, ITS CONCEPT AND METHODS, THE
PRESENT STATE OF THE QUESTION, RELATIONS WITH
CRITICISM, AND CORRELATIVE PROBLEMS OF THE TEACH-
ING OF LITERATURE AND BIOGRAPHY

Barreto Filho, J. "O Valor da História Literária," *Diário de Notícias,* Rio de Janeiro, July 4, 1943.

Braga, T. *Introdução e Teoria da História da Literatura Portuguêsa,* 1896 (1st edition 1870).

Carpeaux, O. M. "A Querela da História Literária," *O Jornal,* Rio de Janeiro, July 18, 1943.

———. "Crítica e História das Letras Americanas," *O Jornal,* June 19, 1949.

Coutinho, A. *Correntes Cruzadas,* Rio de Janeiro, A Noite, 1953.

Figueiredo, F. de. *Aristarcos,* Rio de Janeiro, Antunes, 1941.

———. *A Crítica Literária como Ciência,* Lisbon, Livraria Clássica, 1920.

———. *A Luta pela Expressão,* Coimbra, Nobel, 1944.

———. *Ultimas Aventuras,* Rio de Janeiro, A Noite, n.d.

———. *Estudos de Literatura,* 5th series, São Paulo, 1951 (Boletim da Faculdade de Filosofia, No. 7).

Hankiss, J. *La Littérature et la vie,* São Paulo, 1951 (Boletim da Faculdade de Filosofia, No. 8).

Kayser, W. *Fundamentos da Interpretação e da Análise Literária,* 2 volumes, Coimbra, A. Amado, 1948.

Martins, W. "Duas Histórias Literárias," *O Estado de São Paulo,* July 7, 1955.

Monteiro, Mozart. Series of articles on theory of literature, theory and methodology of criticism, theory and methodology of literary history in *Diário de Notícias,* Rio de Janeiro, October 30, November 13, 20, 27, December 11, 1949; *O Jornal,* Rio de Janeiro, March 15, 22, April 5, 12,

19, 26, May 3, 17, 24, June 14, 21, 28, July 5, 12, 19, 26, August 2, 9, 16, 23, 30, September 6, 13, October 11, November 1, 1953.

Prado Coelho, J. "História da Cultura e História da Literatura," *Revista Filosófica*, II, No. 5, Coimbra, 1952.

ON THE PROBLEM OF BIOGRAPHY IN LITERARY CRITICISM AND HISTORY

Figueiredo, F. de. "Do Gôsto da Biografia," *O Jornal*, Rio de Janeiro, March 19, 1939.

Lins, A. *Jornal de Crítica*, 4th and 6th series, Rio de Janeiro, J. Olympio, 1946, 1951.

Melo Franco, A. A. "Homens e Símbolos," *O Jornal*, Rio da Janeiro, March 18, 1944.

THE CONCEPT OF GENERATIONS

Carpeaux, O. M., "As Gerações e suas Literaturas," *Correio da Manhã*, October 12, 1941.

Cretela Sobrinho, P., and I. Strenger. *Sociologia das Gerações*, São Paulo, Martins, 1952.

THE PROBLEM OF INDIVIDUAL AND PERIOD STYLE— THEIR CLASSIFICATION AND TYPOLOGY

Da Cal, E. G. *Lengua y estilo de Eça de Queiroz*, Coimbra, 1954.

Pontes, M. L. Belchior. *Frei António das Chagas. Um Homem e um Estilo do Século XVII*, Lisbon, Centro de Estudos Filológicos, 1953.

MODERN METHODS OF THE ANALYSIS OF A LITERARY WORK

Costa Margues, F. *Problemas de Análise Literária*, Coimbra, Livraria Gonçalves, 1948.

Kayser, W. *Fundamentos da Interpretação e da Análise Literária*, 2 volumes, Coimbra, A. Amado, 1948.

THE CONCEPT OF THE LITERARY GENRE AND ITS CLASSIFICATION

Amora, A. Soares. *Teoria da Literatura*, 2nd edition, São Paulo, Ed. Clássico-Científica, 1951.

Hankiss, J. *La Littérature et la vie*, São Paulo, 1951 (Boletim da Faculdade de Filosofia, No. 8).

Kayser, W. *Fundamentos da Interpretação e da Análise Literária*, 2 volumes, Coimbra, A. Amado, 1948.

Magne, A. S. J. *Princípios Elementares de Literatura*, São Paulo, Cia. Editôra Nacional, 1935.

PROBLEMS OF MYTH AND SYMBOL
IN LITERARY CRITICISM

Paive, Maria Helena de Novias. *Contribuição a uma Estilística da Ironia.* Lisbon, 1961.

PROBLEMS OF THE CHARACTERIZATION
OF LITERATURES

Figueiredo, F. de. *Características da Literatura Portuguêsa,* 3rd edition, Lisbon, Livraria Clássica, 1923; reprinted in *Literatura Portuguêsa,* Rio de Janeiro, A Noite, 1940, 2nd edition, Livraria Acadêmica, 1954.

———. "Características da Literatura Espanhola," *Esphanha,* São Paulo, Cia. Editôra Nacional, 1945.

Menédez Pidal, R. "Caracteres de la literatura española, con referencias a las otras literaturas hispánicas, latina, portuguesa y catalana," *Historia general de las literaturas hispánicas,* G. Díaz Plaja, editor, Vol. I, Barcelona, Ed. Barna, 1949.

The Renaissance Panorama

Bataillon, M. *Etudes sur le Portugal au temps de l'Humanisme,* Coimbra, 1952.

Braga, T. *História da Literatura Portuguêsa,* Oporto, Chardon (16th century, 17th century, and Arcadism: Vols. VI to XXIII; Recapitulation: Vols. XXX–XXXI).

Carvalho, J. de. *Estudos sôbre a Cultura Portuguêsa* (15th and 16th centuries), 2 volumes, Coimbra, 1948–49.

Cerejeira, M. Gonçalves. *Clenardo e a Sociedade Portuguêsa do seu Tempo,* Coimbra, Coimbra Ed., 1949.

Cidade, H. *Lições de Cultura e Literatura Portuguêsa,* 2 volumes, Coimbra, Coimbra Ed., 1943–48.

———. *A Literatura Portuguêsa e a Expansão Ultramarina* (15th and 16th centuries), Lisbon, 1943.

Figueiredo, F. de. *História da Literatura Clássica,* 2nd edition, 3 volumes, Lisbon, Livraria Clássica, 1922, 1931.

———. *A Épica Portuguêsa no Século XVI,* São Paulo, 1950 (Boletim da Faculdade de Filosofia, No. 6).

Forjaz de Sampaio, A. *História da Literatura Portuguêsa Ilustrada,* 4 volumes, Lisbon, Aillaud e Betrand, 1929–42.

História da Colonização Portuguêsa no Brasil, C. Malheiros Dias, editor, 3 volumes, Oporto, Lit. National, 1921–24.

Silva Bastos, J. T. *História da Censura Intelectual em Portugal,* Coimbra, 1926.

Saraiva, A. J. *História da Cultura em Portugal,* Lisbon, 1955.

Silva Dias, J. S. "Portugal e a Cultura Européia," *Biblos*, XXVIII, September 1952, pp. 203–498.

Literary Language

LINGUISTICS AND THEORY OF LANGUAGE

Elia, Sílvio. *Orientações de Linguística Moderna*, Rio de Janeiro, Acadêmica, 1955.
Matoso Câmara Jr., J. *Princípios de Linguística Geral*, Rio de Janeiro, Acadêmica, 1954.
Sapir, Edward. *A Linguagem*, Rio de Janeiro, Inst. Nacional Livro, 1954.

RELATIONS BETWEEN LITERARY LANGUAGE AND GENERAL LANGUAGE

Said Ali, M. *Dificuldades da Língua Portuguêsa*, Rio de Janeiro, 1930.

THE PORTUGUESE LANGUAGE

Chaves de Melo, Gladstone. *Iniciação à Filologia Portuguêsa*, Rio de Janeiro, Org. Simões, 1951.
Lima Coutinho, Ismael. *Gramática Histórica*, Rio de Janeiro, Acadêmica, 1954.
Paiva Boléo, Manuel de. *Introdução ao Estudo da Filologa Portuguêsa*, Lisbon, Rev. de Portugal, 1946.
Rodrigues Lapa, M. *Estilística da Língua Portuguêsa*, Lisbon, Seara Nova, 1945.
Said Ali, M. *Gramática Histórica da Língua Portuguêsa*, São Paulo, Melhoramentos, n.d.
Silva Neto, Serafim. *Manual de Filologia Portuguêsa* (history, problems, methods), Rio de Janeiro, Acadêmica, 1952.
———. *História da Língua Portuguêsa*, Rio de Janeiro, Livros de Portugal, 1952.
———. Introducao ao Estudo da Filologia Portuguêsa, Sao Paulo, Cia. Editôra Nacional, 1956.
Silveira Bueno, Francisco da. *A Formação da Língua Portuguêsa*, Rio de Janeiro, Acadêmica, 1955.

LINGUISTIC DIFFERENTIATION IN AMERICA (CONCEPTION)

Alonso, Amado. *El problema de la lengua en América*, Madrid, Espasa Calpe, 1935.
Elia, Sílvio. *O Problema da Língua Brasileira*, Rio de Janeiro, Pongetti, 1940.

Monteiro, C. *Português da Europa e Português da América*, Rio de Janeiro, 1952.

Paiva Boléo, Manuel de. *Brasileirismos: Problemas de Método*, Coimbra, 1943.

Xavier Marques, *Cultura da Língua Nacional*, Bahia, 1933.

LINGUISTIC DIFFERENTIATION (CAUSES AND ASPECTS)

Buarque de Holanda, Aurélio. Introduction to *Contos Gauchescos e Lendas do Sul*, by J. Simões Lopes Neto, Pôrto Alegre, Globo, n.d.

Chaves de Melo, Gladstone. *A Língua do Brasil*, Rio de Janeiro, Agir, 1946.

Marroquim, Mário. *A Língua do Nordeste*, São Paulo, Cia. Editôra Nacional, 1946 (Brasiliana, 25).

Nascentes, Antenor. *O Linguajar Carioca*, Rio de Janeiro, Org. Simões, 1953.

Silva Neto, Serefim. *Introducao ao Estudo da Língua Portuguêsa no Brasil*, Rio de Janeiro, Inst. Nacional Livro, 1950.

Sousa da Silveira, A. F. *A Língua Nacional e seu Estudo*, Rio de Janeiro, 1921.

LINGUISTIC DIFFERENTIATION (DETAILED BIBLIOGRAPHY)

Manual Bibliográfico de Estudos Brasileiros, Rubens Borba de Morais and William Berrien, editors, Rio de Janeiro, Gráfica Editôra Sousa, 1941.

Brazilian Folklore

Almeida, Renato. *História da Música Brasileira*, Rio de Janeiro, 1942.

Alvarenga, Oneyda. *Música Popular Brasileira*, Pôrto Alegre, Globo, 1950.

Andrade, Mário de. "As Danças Dramáticas do Brasil," *Boletim Latino-Americano de Música*, VI, 1st part, Rio de Janeiro, 1946.

———. *Música do Brasil*, Curitiba, 1941.

Barroso, Gustavo. *Ao Som da Viola*, Rio de Janeiro, 1921.

Carneiro, Édison. *Negros Bantus*, Rio de Janeiro, 1937.

Cascudo, Luís da Câmara. *Antologia do Folclore Brasileiro*, São Paulo, 1944.

———. *Cinco Livros do Povo*, Rio de Janeiro, J. Olympio, 1943.

———. *Contos Tradicionais do Brasil*, Rio de Janeiro, 1946.

———. *Dicionário do Folclore Brasileiro*, Rio de Janeiro, Instituto Nacional do Livro, 1954.

———. *Geografia dos Mitos Brasileiros*, Rio de Janeiro, J. Olympio, 1947.

———. *Literatura Oral*, Rio de Janeiro, J. Olympio, 1952.

———. *Vaqueiros e Cantadores*, Pôrto Alegre, Globo, 1939.

César, Getúlio. *Crendices do Nordeste*, Rio de Janeiro, 1941.

Freyre, Gilberto. *Açúcar*, Rio de Janeiro, 1939.

Gomes, Lindolfo. *Contos Populares Brasileiros*, 2nd edition, Sao Paulo, 1948.
Gonçalves, Fernandes. *O Folclore Mágico do Nordeste*, Rio de Janeiro, 1938.
Magalhães, Basílio de. *O Folclore no Brasil*, Rio de Janeiro, 1939.
Mata Machado Filho, Aires da. *Curso de Folclore*, Rio de Janeiro, 1951.
Meyer, Augusto. *Guia do Folclore Gaúcho*, Rio de Janeiro, 1951.
Melo Morais Filho. *Festas e Tradiçoes Populares do Brasil*, Rio de Janeiro, 1946.
Mota, Leonardo. *Cantadores*, Rio de Janeiro, 1921.
Pereira da Costa. *Folclore Pernambucano*, Rio de Janeiro, 1908.
Querino, Manuel. *Costumes Africanos so Brasil*, Rio de Janeiro, 1935.
Ramos, Artur. *O Folclore Negro do Brasil*, Rio de Janeiro, 1935.
Ribeiro, João. *O Folclore*, Rio de Janeiro, 1919.
Ribeiro, Joaquim. *Folclore Brasileiro*, Rio de Janeiro, 1944.
Romero, Sílvio. *Cantos Populares do Brasil e Contos Populares do Brasil*, 3 volumes, Rio de Janeiro, 1955.

PART II

History of Brazilian Culture & Literature

GENERAL

Academia Brasileira de Letras, *Curso de Crítica*, Rio de Janeiro, 1956.
Abreu, J. *História da Literatura Nacional*, Rio de Janeiro, Tip. Mundo Médico, 1930.
Aderaldo, M. S. *Esbôço de História de Literatura Brasileira*, Fortaleza, Clã, 1948.
Almansur Haddad, J. *O Romantismo Brasileiro e as Sociedades Secretas do Tempo*, São Paulo, Gráfica Siqueira, 1945.
Almeida Nogueira, J. L. de. *A Academia de São Paulo; Tradicoes e Reminiscências*, 9 volumes, São Paulo, Tip. Venordem, 1907.
Amora, A. Soares. *História da Literatura Brasileira*, São Paulo, Edição Saraiva, 1955.
Amoroso Lima, Alceu. *Intrudução a Literatura Brasileira*, Rio de Janeiro, Agir, 1956.
——. *Quadro Sintético da Literatura Brasileira*, Rio de Janeiro, Agir.
Anais do I Congresso Brasileiro de Crítica e História Literária (Recife), Rio de Janeiro, Tempo Brasileiro, 1964
Anais do Segundo Congresso Brasileiro de Crítica e História Literária (1961), São Paulo, Fac. Filosofia, Ciências e Letras de Assis, 1963.
Andrade, J. Oswald. *A Arcádia e a Inconfidência Mineira*, São Paulo, 1945.
Andrade Murici, José Cândido. *A Nova Literatura Brasileira*, Pôrto Alegre, Globo, 1936.
Araripe Júnior, T. A. *Literatura Brasileira, Movimento de 1893*, Rio de Janeiro, Democrática Ed., 1896.

Azevedo, F. de. *A Cultura Brasileira*, 2nd edition, São Paulo, Comp. Editôra Nacional, 1944.

Bandeira, M. *Noções de História das Literaturas*, São Paulo, Cia. Editôra Nacional, 1942 (2nd edition 1953).

Barbuda, P. J. *Literatura Brasileira*, Bahia, Dois Mundos, 1916.

Beviláqua, C. *História da Faculdade de Direito do Recife (1827-1927)*, 2 volumes, Rio de Janeiro, F. Alves, 1927.

Bezerra de Freitas, *História da Literatura Brasileira*, Pôrto Alegre, Globo, 1939.

Bitencourt, Liberato. *Academia Brasileira de Letras, Estudo Crítico dos Patronos e Ocupantes*, 2 volumes, Rio de Janeiro, Of. Gráfica do Ginásio, September 28, 1941.

———. *Nova História da Literatura Brasileira*, 6 volumes Rio de Janeiro, Of. Gráfica do Colégio, September 28, 1945.

Broca, Brito. *A Vida Literária no Brasil 1900*, Rio de Janeiro, 1956.

Cândido, Antônio, and others. *Barroco Literário*, São Paulo, Fundação Armando A. Penteado, 1962.

———. *Formação da Literatura Brasileira*, São Paulo, Martins, 1959.

Capistrano de Abreu, J. *Capítulos de História Colonial*, Rio de Janeiro, Briguiet, 1928.

———. *Ensaios e Estudos*, 3 volumes, Rio de Janeiro, Briguiet, 1931-1938.

Carneiro Leão, A., and others. *À Margem da História da República*, Rio de Janeiro, Anuário do Brasil, 1924.

Carvalho, Aderbal de. *O Naturalismo no Brasil*, São Luís do Maranhão, J. Ramos, 1894.

Carvalho, R. de. *Pequena História da Literatura Brasileira*, 9th edition, Rio de Janeiro, Briguiet, 1953.

Castelo, José Aderaldo, *A Era Colonial*, Volume I of "A Literatura Brasileira," São Paulo, Editôra Cultrix, 1962.

———, editor. *Textos que Interessam à História do Romantismo*, 2 volumes, São Paulo, Comissao Estadual de Literatura, 1961, 1963.

Chichorro da Gama, A. C. *Românticos Brasileiros*, Rio de Janeiro, Briguiet, 1927.

Costa, J. Cruz, *Contribuição à História das Idéias no Brasil*, Rio de Janeiro, J. Olympio, 1956.

Coutinho, Afrânio. *Conceito de Literatura Brasileira*, Rio de Janeiro, Acadêmica, 1960.

———, editor, *A Literatura no Brasil*, 4 volumes, Rio de Janeiro, Livraria São José, 1955-1959.

Denis, F. *Résumés de l'histoire littéraire du Portugal et du Brésil*, Paris, Lecointe et Durey, 1926.

Fernandes Pinheiro, J. C. *Literatura Nacional*, Rio de Janeiro, Garnier, 1883.

Figueiredo, F. de. *História da Literatura Clássica*, Volume III, 3rd edition, São Paulo, Anchieta, 1946.

————. *História da Crítica Literária em Portugal,* 2nd edition, Lisbon, Teixeira, 1916.

————. *Literatura Portuguêsa,* Rio de Janeiro, A. Noite, 1941 (2nd edition, Rio de Janeiro, Acadêmica, 1954).

Forjaz de Sampaio, A. *História da Literatura Portuguêsa Ilustrada,* 3 volumes, Lisbon, Bertrand, n.d. (1930–1932); Volume IV, Oporto, F. Machado, n.d. (1942).

Gomes, A. "História Literária," *Dic. Histórico, Geografico, e Et. do Brasil,* Volume I, Rio de Janeiro, Imprensa Nacional, 1922, pp. 1297–1526.

Grieco, A. *Evolução da Poesia Brasileira,* Rio de Janeiro, J. Olympio, 1947 (1st edition, 1932).

————. *Evolução da Prosa Brasileira,* Rio de Janeiro, J. Olympio, 1947 (1st edition, 1933).

Henríquez, Ureña Pedro. *Literary Currents in Latin America,* Harvard University Press, 1945.

Jucá Filho, C. *Curso de Português,* 3rd series, São Paulo, Cia. Editôra Nacional, 1955.

Lacerda, V. C. *Unidades Literárias,* 3rd series, Rio de Janeiro, Simões, 1952.

Lima, Ébion de. *Lições de Literatura Brasileira,* São Paulo, Livraria Editôra Salesiana, 1963.

Lincoln, J. N. *Charts of Brazilian Literature,* Michigan, 1947.

Macedo, S. *A Literatura no Brasil Colonial,* Rio de Janeiro, Brasília, n.d.

Magalhães, Valentim. *A Literatura Brasileira (1870–1895),* Lisbon, A.M. Pereira, 1896.

Martins, M. R. *A Evolucao da Literatura Brasileira,* 2 volumes, Rio de Janeiro, 1945.

Melo Franco, A. A. *Mar de Sargaços,* São Paulo, Martins, 1944.

————. *O Indio Brasileiro e a Revolução Francesa,* Rio de Janeiro, J. Olympio, 1937.

Meneses, D. *Evolução do Pensamento Literário no Brasil,* Rio de Janeiro, Org. Simões, 1954.

Miguel Pereira, Lúcia. *Cinquenta Anos de Literatura,* Rio de Janeiro, M.E.S., 1952 (Cadernos de Cultura, No. 28).

Neves, Fernão. *A Academia Brasileira de Letras (1896–1940),* Rio de Janeiro, Academia Brasileira de Letras, 1940.

Monteiro, Clóvis. *Esboços de História Literária,* Rio de Janeiro, Colégio Pedro II, 1961.

————. *Traços do Romantismo no Poesia Brasileira,* Rio de Janeiro, 1929.

Mota, A. *História da Literatura Brasileira,* 2 volumes, São Paulo, Editôra Nacional, 1930.

————. *Vultos e Livros,* São Paulo, 1921.

Mota Filho, C. *Introdução ao Estudo do Pensamento Nacional,* Rio de Janeiro, Hélios, 1926.

Oliveira, J. Osório de. *História Breve da Literatura Brasileira,* Lisbon, Inquérito, 1939.

Oliveira Lima, M. *Aspectos da Literatura Colonial Brasileira*, Leipzig, Brochaus, 1896.

———. *D. Joao VI no Brasil (1808–1821)*, 3 volumes, 3rd edition, Rio de Janeiro, J. Olympio, 1945.

Pacheco, Joao, *O Realismo*, Volume III of "A Literatura Brasileira," São Paulo, Cultrix, 1963.

Paranhos, H. *História do Romantismo no Brasil*, 2 volumes, São Paulo, Cultura, 1937–1938.

Peixoto, A. *Noções de História da Literatura Brasileira*, Rio de Janeiro, F. Alves, 1931.

———. *Panorama da Literatura Brasileira*, 2nd edition, São Paulo, Cia. Editôra Nacional, 1947.

Perié, E. *A Literatura Brasileira nos Tempos Coloniais*, Buenos Aires, 1885.

Piccarolo, A. *O Romantismo no Brasil*, São Paulo, Conferências Soc. Cult. Art., 1914–1915; São Paulo, Levi, 1916.

Pinto Ferreira. *Interpretacao da Literatura Brasileira*, Rio de Janeiro, 1957.

Pires de Almeida. "A Escola Byroniana no Brasil," *J. Comércio*, Rio de Janeiro, February 5, 26, March 22, June 8, July 13, November 20, 1905.

Portella, Eduardo. *Literatura e Realidade Nacional*, Rio de Janeiro, Tempo Brasileiro, 1963.

Prado, P. *Retrato do Brasil*, São Paulo, 1928.

Prado Coelho, J. *Dicionário das Literaturas Portuguêsa, Galega e Brasileira*, Oporto, 1960.

Putnam, S. *Marvelous Journey; A Survey of Four Centuries of Brazilian Literature*, New York, A. Knopf, 1948.

Rizzini, C. *O Livro, O Jornal e a Tipografia no Brasil, 1500–1822*, Rio de Janeiro, Kosmos, 1946.

Rizzini Rio, João de. *O Momento Literário*, Rio de Janeiro, Garnier, n.d.

Rodrigues, J. Honório. *Teoria da História do Brasil*, São Paulo, Ipê, 1949.

———. *A Pesquisa Histórica no Brasil*, Rio de Janeiro, I.N.L., 1952.

Rodrigues Lapa, M. *Licoes de Literatura Brasileira*, 2nd edition, Coimbra, 1943.

Romero, Sílvio. *História da Literatura Brasileira*, 5 volumes, 5th edition, Rio de Janeiro, J. Olympio, 1953.

———. "A Literatura 1500–1900," *Livro do Centenário*, Rio de Janeiro, 1900.

Romero, S. and F. Ribeiro. *Compêndio de História da Literatura Brasileira*, 2nd edition, Rio de Janeiro, F. Alves, 1909.

Silva Brito, M. *História do Modernismo Brasileiro*, São Paulo, 1958.

Sodré, N. Wernecke. *História da Literatura Brasileira, seus Fundamentos Economicas*, Rio de Janeiro, J. Olympio, 1940.

———. *O que se Deve Ler para Conhecer o Brasil*, Rio de Janeiro, Leitura, 1945.

———. *Síntese do Desenvolvimento Literário no Brasil*, São Paulo, Martins, 1943.

Sotero dos Reis, J. *Curso de Literatura*, 5 volumes, São Luís do Maranhao, Tip. País, 1866–1873.

Sousa, Galante de and Brito Broca. *Introducao ao Estudo da Literatura Brasileira*, Rio de Janeiro, Inst. Nacional Livro, 1963.

Tôres, João Camilo de Oliveiro. *O Positivismo no Brasil*, Petrópolis, Ed. Vozes, 1943.

Vampré, Spencer. *Memórias para a História da Academia de São Paulo*, São Paulo, Liv. Acadêmica, 1924.

Veríssimo, Érico. *Brazilian Literature*, Toronto, Macmillan, 1945.

Veríssimo, José. *História da Literatura Brasileira*, Rio de Janeiro, F. Alves, 1916; 2nd edition, J. Olympio, 1954.

Viana, H. *Contribuição à História da Imprensa Brasileira (1812–1869)*, Rio de Janeiro, Imp. Nacional, 1945.

Wolf, F. *Le Brésil littéraire*, Berlin, Asher, 1863; *O Brasil Literário*, translation, with preface and notes, by J.A. Haddad, São Paulo, Cia. Editôra Nacional, 1955.

REGIONAL

Azevedo, Eustáquio. *Literatura Paraense*, Belém, 1922.

Barreira, D. *História da Literatura Cearense*, Fortaleza, Ed., Instituto do Ceará Ltda., 1951–1954, (Coleção Instituto do Ceará. Monografia 18, Volumes I, II, and III).

Braga Montenegro, J. *Evolução e Natureza do Conto Cearense*, Fortaleza, Clã, 1951.

Calmon, P. *História da Literatura Baiana*, Rio de Janeiro, J. Olympio, 1949.

Carvalho, A. dos Reis. "A Literatura Maranhense," *Biblioteca Internacional de Obras Celebres*, Vol. XX, Rio de Janeiro, Jackson, 1912.

César, Guillermino. *História da Literatura do Rio Grande do Sul*, Pôrto Alegre, Globo, 1956.

Dutra, Waltensir and Fausto Cunha, *Biografia Crítica das Letras Mineiras*, Rio de Janeiro, 1954 unpublished.

Frieiro, E. *Letras Mineiras*, Belo Horizonte, Os Amigos do Livro, 1937.

Lima, M. de. *Esbôço de uma História Literária de Minas*, Belo Horizonte, Imp. Oficial, 1920.

Linhares, M. *História Literária do Ceará*, Rio de Janeiro Jornal do Comércio, 1948.

Meireles, Mário M. *Panorama da Literatura Maranhense*, São Luís, Academia do Maranhão, 1956.

Melo, O. Ferreira de. *Introdução a História da Literatura Catarinense*, Florianópolis, 1958.

Montenegro, Abelardo. *O Romance Cearense*, Fortaleza, 1953.

Oliveira, Martins de. *História da Literatura Mineira*, Belo Horizonte, 1958.

Paixão, Múcio da. *Movimento Literário em Campos*, Rio de Janeiro 1924.

Pinheiro, João. *Literatura Piauiense*, Teresina, 1937.

Pinto da Silva, J. *História Literária do Rio Grande do Sul.* 2nd edition, Pôrto Alegre, Globo, 1930.

Sampaio, L. Prado. *A Literatura Sergipana*, Matoim, Imp. Econômica, 1908.

Thiago, A. S. *História da Literatura Catarinense*, Rio de Janeiro, 1957.

GENRES: NOVEL AND SHORT STORY

Academia Brasileira de Letras, Rio de Janeiro, *Curso de Romance*, Rio de Janeiro, Cia. Bras. de Artes Gráficas, 1952.

Bandeira, M. *Apresentação da Poesia Brasileira*, Rio de Janeiro, 1946.

Bezerra de Freitas. *Forma e Expressão no Romance Brasileiro*, Rio de Janeiro, Pongetti, 1947.

Braga Montenegro, J. *Evolução e Natureza do Conto Cearense*, Fortaleza, Clã, 1951.

Cavalheiro, Edgar. *Evolução do Conto Brasileiro*, Rio de Janeiro, M. E. C., 1954 (Cadernos de cultura, No. 74).

Lima, Herman. *Variações sôbre o Conto*, Rio de Janeiro, M.E.S., 1952 (Cadernos de Cultura, No. 37).

Linhares Temistócles. *Introdução ao Mundo do Romance*, Rio de Janeiro, J. Olympio, 1953.

Miguel Pereira, Lucia, *Prosa de Ficção* (de 1870 a 1920), Rio de Janeiro, J. Olympio, 1950 (*História da Literatura Brasileira*, Álvaro Lins, editor V. XII).

Montenegro, O. *O Romance Brasileiro*, 2nd edition, Rio de Janeiro, J. Olympio, 1953.

Morais Neto, Prudente de. *O Romance Brasileiro*, Rio de Janeiro, J. Olympio, 1939. (Rep. in *Revista Acadêmica*, Nos. 48, 49, 50, 51.)

Rêgo, José Lins do. *Conferência no Prata*, Rio de Janeiro, Casa do Estudante do Brasil, 1946.

Rodrigues Alves Filho, F. M. *O Sociologismo e a Imaginação no Romance Brasileiro*, Rio de Janeiro, J. Olympio, 1938.

O Romance Brasileiro (de 1752 a 1930), Rio de Janeiro. O Cruzeiro, 1902. (1st ed. in *Revista do Brasil*, May, 1941).

GENRES: POETRY

Academia Brasileira de Letras, Rio de Janeiro. *Curso de Poesia*, Rio de Janeiro, Companhia Bras. de Artes Gráficas, 1954.

Bandeira, M. *Apresentação da Poesia Brasileira, com Antologia*, Rio de Janeiro, 1946.

Barros, J. de. *Poetas do Brasil*, Rio de Janeiro, J. Olympio, 1944.

Bilac, O. *Ultimas Conferências e Discursos*, Rio de Janeiro, F. Alves, 1924.
——— and Sebastião Guimarães Passos. *Tratado de Versificação.* 8th edition, Rio de Janeiro, F. Alves, 1944.

Cidade, H. *O Conceito de Poesia como Expressão de Cultura.* São Paulo, Saraiva, 1946.

———. *Lições de Cultura e Literatura Portuguêsa*, Coimbra, Coimbra Ed., 1948.

Júlio, Sílvio. *Fundamentos da Poesia Brasileira*, Rio de Janeiro, Coelho Branco, 1930.

Le Gentil, P. *La Poésia lyrique espagnole et portugaise à la fin de Moyen Age*, 2 volumes, Rennes, 1953.

Lins, É. *História e Crítica da Poesia Brasileira*, Rio de Janeiro, Ariel, 1937.

Montealegre, Duarte de. *Ensáio sôbre o Parnasianismo Brasileiro*, Coimbra, 1945.

Rio Branco, M. *Etapas da Poesia Brasileira*, Lisbon, Livros do Brasil, 1955.

GENRES: THEATER

Academia Brasileira de Letras, Rio de Janeiro. *Curso de Teatro*, Rio de Janeiro, Artes Gráficas, 1954.

Chichorro da Gama, A. C. *Através do Teatro Brasileiro*, Rio de Janeiro, Liv. Luso-Brasileira, 1907.

———. *Os Fundamentos do Teatro Brasileiro*, São Paulo, Nova Era, 1924.

Fleiuss, Max. "O Teatro no Brasil e sua Evolução," *Dic. Hist., Geog. e Etn. do Brasil*, II, Rio de Janeiro, Imp. Nac., 1922, pp.1532–1550.

Magaldi, Sábato. *Panorama do Teatro Brasileiro*, São Paulo, Difusao Européia do Livro, 1962.

Morinho, Henrique. *O Teatro Brasileiro*, Rio de Janeiro, Garnier, 1904.

Melo Morais Filho. *João Caetano*, Rio de Janeiro, Laemmert, 1903.

———. *Artistas do meu Tempo*, Rio de Janeiro, Garnier, 1905.

Mendonça, C. Sussekind de. *História do Teatro Brasileiro*, Rio de Janeiro, Mendonça Machado, 1926.

Paixão, M. da. *O Teatro no Brasil*, Rio de Janeiro, Brasília, 1936.

Prado, Décio de Almeida. *Apresentacao do Teatro Brasileiro*, São Paulo, Martins, 1956.

Silva, L. *Figuras do Teatro*, Rio de Janeiro, Leite Ribeiro, 1928.

———. *História do Teatro Brasileiro*, Rio de Janeiro, M.E.S., 1938.

Sousa, C. *O Teatro no Brasil*, Rio de Janeiro, J. Leite, n.d.

Sousa, J. Galante de. *O Teatro no Brasil*, 2 volumes, Rio de Janeiro, Inst. Nacional Livro, 1960.

GENRES: ANTHOLOGIES

Almeida Garrett, J. B. da S. L. de. *Parnaso Lusitano das Poesias Completas dos Autores Portuguêses Antigos e Modernos*, Paris, Aillaud, 1826.

Bandeira, M. *Antologia dos Poetas Brasileiros da Fase Romântica*, 2nd edition, Rio de Janeiro, M. E. S., 1940.

———. *Antologia dos Poetas Brasileiros da Fase Parnasiana*, Rio de Janeiro, M.E.C., 1940.

——— and E. Cavalheiro. *Obras-Primas da Lírica Brasileira*, São Paulo, Martins, 1943.

Barbosa, A. R. and E. Cavalheiro. *As Obras-Primas do Conto Brasileiro*, São Paulo, Martins, 1943.

Barbosa Machado, D. *Biblioteca Lusitana Escolhida*. Lisbon, 1786; *Sumário da Biblioteca Lusitana*. Lisboa, 1786-7.

Buarque de Holanda, S. *Antologia dos Poetas Brasileiros da Fase Colonial*, 2 volumes, Rio de Janeiro, I.N.L., 1953.

Carvalho Filho, A. de. *Coletânea de Poetas Baianos*, Rio de Janeiro, Minerva, 1951.

Câmara Cascudo, L. da. *Cinco Livros do Povo*, Rio de Janeiro, J. Olympio, 1953.

Costa e Silva, J. M. *Ensaio Biográfico-Crítico sôbre os Melhores Poetas Portuguêses*, 10 volumes, Lisbon, 1850-1885.

Cabral do Nascimento, J. *Poetas Narrativos Portuguêses*, Lisbon, Minerva, 1949.

Duque Estrada, O. *Tesouro Poético Brasileiro*, Rio de Janeiro, F. Alves, 1913.

Estnate Clássica da Revista de Língua Portuguêsa, 13 volumes, Rio de Janeiro, 1924.

Freire, L. *Sonetos Brasileiros*, Rio de Janeiro, Briguiet, 1904.

Gomes, L. *Contos Populares*, 2 volumes, São Paulo, Melhoramentos, n. d.

Grandes Poetas Românticos do Brasil. Soares Amora e F. J. Silva Ramos, editors, São Paulo, LEP, 1949.

Grieco, D. *Antologia do Conto Brasileiro*, Rio de Janeiro. A. Noite, n.d.

Lima, M. de. *Coletânea de Autores Mineiros*, I: Escola Mineira. Pré-românticos, Belo Horizonte, Imp. of., 1922.

Lins, Álvaro, and Aurélio Buarque de Holanda. *Roteiro Literário do Brasil e de Portugal* (Antologia da Língua Portuguêsa), 2 volumes, Rio de Janeiro, J. Olympio, 1955.

Machado, A. C. *Coletânea de Poetas Sul-Riograndenses*, Rio de Janerio, Minerva, 1952.

Melo Morais Filho, A. *Parnaso Brasileiro*, Rio de Janeiro, Garnier, 1885.

Moura, Enéas de. *Coletânea de Poetas Paulistas*, Rio de Janeiro, Minerva, 1951.

Murici, J. Andrade. *Panorama do Movimento Simbolista Brasileiro*, 3 volumes, Rio de Janeiro, 1952.

Oliveira, A. de. *Páginas de Ouro da Poesia Brasileira*, Rio de Janeiro, Garnier, 1911.

—— and Jorge Jobim. *Poetas Brasileiros*, 2 volumes, Rio de Janeiro, Garnier, 1921-22.

——. *Contos Brasileiros*, Rio de Janeiro, Garnier, 1922.

Oliveira e Silva. *Coletânea de Poetas Pernambucanos*, Rio de Janeiro, Minerva, 1951.

Panorama da Poesia Brasileira, 6 volumes, Rio de Janeiro, Civ. Brasileira, 1959.

Panorama do Conto Brasileiro, 11 volumes, Rio de Janeiro, Civ. Brasileira, 1959.

Pereira da Silva, J. M. *Parnaso Brasileiro ou Seleção de Poesias*, Rio de Janeiro, Laemmert, 1841.

Pereira da Silva, M. *A Fênix Renascida*, 5 volumes, Lisbon, 1716–1718.

Pinto, L. *Antologia da Paraíba*, Rio de Janeiro, Minerva, 1951.

Primeiras Letras, Rio de Janeiro, Acad. Brasil. Letras, 1923.

Resende, Garcia de. *Cancioneiro Geral*, 5 volumes, Coimbra, Imp. Univ., 1910–1917.

Romero, Sílvio. *Folclore Brasileiro*, 3 volumes (Contos e cantos populares do Brasil), Rio de Janeiro, J. Olympio, 1954.

Siqueira e Sá, M. T. *Júbilos da América* (coletânea da Academia dos Seletos), Lisbon, 1745.

Varnhagen, F. A. de *Florilégio da Poesia Brasileira*, 3 volumes, Rio de Janeiro, Acad. Bras. Letras, 1946.

GENRES: NATIONAL BIBLIOGRAPHIES

Academia Brasileira de Letras. Rio de Janeiro. *Anuário.* 10 volumes, Rio de Janeiro, Civ. Bras., 1935–1953.

———. *Discursos Acadêmicos* (1897–1948), 12 volumes, Rio de Janeiro, Civ. Bras., 1934–1948.

———. *Bibliografia*, 13 volumes (Coleção Afrânio Peixoto, III), Rio de Janeiro, Academia Brasileira de Letras, 1931–1943.

Anuário Brasileiro de Literatura, 1937–1944, 8 volumes, Rio de Janeiro, Pongetti, 1937–1944.

Anuário da Literatura Brasileira, 3 volumes, Rio de Janeiro, 1960, 1961, 1963.

Autores e Livros (suplemento literário de *A Manhã*), Múcio Leão, editor, 11 volumes, Rio de Janeiro, A Manhã, 1941–1950.

Barbosa, F. de Assis. "Romance, Novela e Conto no Brasil (1893–1949)," *Cultura*, I, No. 3, Rio de Janeiro, Servico de Documentação do M.E.S., May-August 1949, pp. 193–242.

Bittencourt, A. *Mulheres e Livros*, Rio de Janeiro, Gráf. Neugart, 1948.

Boletim Bibliográfico Brasileiro, I, No. 1, November-December 1952, Rio de Janeiro, A Estante Pub. Itda., 1952.

Brasil. Instituto Nacional do Livro. *Bibliografia Brasileira 1938*, 5 volumes, Rio de Janeiro, I.N.L., 1938.

Carpeaux, O. M. *Pequena Bibliografia Crítica da Literatura Brasileira*, 2nd edition, Rio de Janeiro, M.E.C., 1955.

Coutinho, Afrânio, editor. *Brasil e Brasileiros de Hoje*, Rio de Janeiro, Foto Service, 1961.

Ford, J. D. M. and others. *A Tentative Bibliography of Brazilian Belles-Lettres*, Cambridge, Harvard University Press, 1931.

Grandes Vultos das Letras. 15 volumes, São Paulo, Melhoramentos, n.d.

Morais, Rubens Borba de, and William Berrien. *Manual Bibliográfico de Estudos Brasileiros*, Rio de Janeiro, Gráf. Editôra Sousa, 1949.

Perdigão, H. *Dicionário Universal da Literatura*, 2nd edition, Oporto, Edições Lopes da Silva, 1940.

Perez, Renard. *Escritores Brasileiros Contemporâneos*, Rio de Janeiro, Civ. Brasileira, 1960.

Rio de Janeiro, Biblioteca Nacional. *Boletim Bibliográfico*, Rio de Janeiro, B.N., 1st series 1886–1888; 2nd series 1918–1921; 3rd series 1945; 4th series 1951–1955.

Sacramento Blake, A. V. A. do. *Dicionário Bibliográfico Brasileiro*, 7 volumes, Rio de Janeiro, Tip. Nacional, 1883–1902.

Silva, Inocêncio Francisco da. *Dicionário Bibliográfico Português*, 22 volumes, Lisbon, Imp. Nacional, 1858–1923.

Simões dos Reis, A. *Bibliografia da "História da Literatura Brasileira" de Sílvio Romero*, Rio de Janeiro, Z. Valverde, 1944.

———. *Bibliografia Nacional, 1942*, 8 volumes, Rio de Janeiro, Z. Valverde, 1942.

———. *Bibliografia Brasileira, I, Poetas do Brasil*, Rio de Janeiro, Org. Simões, 1949.

Velho Sobrinho, J. F. *Dicionário Biobibliográfico Brasileiro*, 2 volumes Rio de Janeiro, Pongetti, 1937–1940.

GENRES: REGIONAL BIOBIBLIOGRAPHIES

Costa, A. *Baianos de Antanho*, Rio de Janeiro, Pongetti, 1955.

Guaraná, A. *Dicionário Biobibliográfico Sergipano*, Rio de Janeiro, Pongetti, 1925.

Leal, A. H. *Panteon Maranhense*, 4 volumes, Lisbon, Imp. Nacional, 1873–1875.

Lery Santos, P. *Panteon Fluminense*, Rio de Janeiro, Tip. G. Leuzinger, 1880.

Melo, L. C. de. *Dicionário de Autores Paulistas*, Sao Paulo, Com. Quarto Centenário, 1954.

Pereira da Costa, F. A. *Dicionário Biográfico de Pernambucanos Célebres*, Recife, Tip. Universal, 1882.

Pereira da Silva, J. M. *Os Varões Ilustres do Brasil durante os Tempos Coloniais*, 2 volumes, Paris, H. Plon, 1858.

Rio Branco, J. M. Da S. Paranhos, Barão do. *Efemérides Brasileiras*, 2nd edition, Rio de Janeiro, Imp. Nacional, 1938.

Studart, Guilherme, Barão de. *Dicionário Biobibliográfico Cearense*, Fortaleza, Tip. Minerva, 1910–1915.

Xaxier da Veiga, J. P. *Efemérides Mineiras* (*1664–1897*), 4 volumes Ouro Preto, Imp. Oficial de M.G., 1897.

BIBLIOGRAPHY OF BIBLIOGRAPHIES

Simões dos Reis, A. *Bibliografia das Bibliografias Brasileiras*, Rio de Janeiro, Imp. Nacional, 1942.

Baroque

GENERAL AND CULTURAL HISTORY

França, E. O. *Portugal na Época da Restauração*, São Paulo, 1951.
Miler, R. F. *Os Jesuítas e Segrêdo de seu Poder*, Pôrto Alegre, Globo, 1935.

HISTORY OF ART

Kelemen, P. *Baroque and Rococo in Latin America*, New York, Macmillan, 1951.

LITERARY HISTORY

Henríquez Ureña, P. *Literary Currents in Hispanic America*, Cambridge, Harvard University Press, 1955.

THE LITERARY BAROQUE

César, Guilhermino. "O Barroco e a Crítica Literária no Brasil," *Tempo Brasileiro*, Rio de Janeiro, II, No. 6, December 1963.
Carpeaux, O. M. "Estudos sôbre o Barroco," *Correio da Manhã*, Rio de Janeiro, January 7, 1945.
Correia de Oliveira, A. *As Segundas Três Musas de D. Francisco Manuel de Melo*, Preface and notes, Lisbon, Clássica, 1945.
Jucá Filho, C. A. "Projeção do Camões na Literatura Barroca," *Revista Filológica* No. 2, 1955.
Montes, J. Alves. *Góngora y la poesía portuguesa del siglo XVII*, Madrid, Gredos, 1956.
Sérgio, A. *Ensaios*, V, Lisbon, Seara Nova, 1936.
———. Preface to *Sôbre as Verdadeiras e Falsas Riquezas* of Antônio Vieira, Lisbon, 1939.

STUDIES OF THE BAROQUE STYLE:

Ferreira, F. L. *Nova Arte de Conceitos*, 2 volumes, Lisbon, 1718.

Neoclassicism and Arcadianism

Braga, T. *História da Literatura Portuguêsa: A Arcádia Lusitana; Filinto Elísio e os Dissidentes da Arcádia; A Arcádia Brasileira*, Oporto, Chardron, 1899–1901.
———. *Recapitulação da História da Literatura Portuguêsa: Os Árcades*, Oporto, Chardron, 1918.
Freyre, F. J. (Cândido Lusitano). *Arte Poética*, Lisbon, Ameno, 1748–1758.

Romanticism

Bell, A. F. G. *Studies in Portuguese Literature*, London, n.d.
Braga, T. *História do Romantismo em Portugal*, Lisbon, 1880.

————. *Garrett e os Dramas Românticos*, Oporto, 1905.

Figueiredo, F. de. *História da Literatura Romântica Portuguêsa*, Lisbon, Clássica, 1913.

————. *História da Crítica Literária em Portugual*, Lisbon, Clássica, 1917.

Michaelis, C. A. *Saudade Portuguêsa*, Oporto, 1914.

Monteiro, C. *Traços do Romantismo na Poesia Brasileira*, Rio de Janeiro, 1929.

Nemésio, V. *Relações Francesas do Romantismo Português*, Coimbra, 1937.

Realism, Naturalism, Parnassianism

Figueiredo, F. de. *História da Literatura Realista*, Lisbon, Clássica, 1914.

Forjaz de Sampaio, A. *História da Literatura Portuguêsa Ilustrada*, IV Oporto, F. Machado. n.d

Romero, S. *O Naturalismo em Literatura*, São Paulo, Tipografia da Província, 1882.

Symbolism

Murici, J. Andrade. *Panorama do Movimento Simbolista Brasileiro*, 3 volumes, Rio de Janeiro, 1952.

Name Index

⋙⋘

Note: Standard Brazilian practice has been followed in alphabetizing Brazilian and Portuguese entries. The name has been entered according to its last element, e.g., Assis, Joaquim Maria Machado de. Other entries follow the standard practice of nomenclature in their various languages.